THEOLOGICAL
INVESTIGATIONS

Volume XI

Also in this series

THEOLOGICAL INVESTIGATIONS

THEOLOGICAL
INVESTIGATIONS

VOLUME XI
CONFRONTATIONS 1

by
KARL RAHNER

Translated by
DAVID BOURKE

LONDON
DARTON, LONGMAN & TODD
NEW YORK
THE SEABURY PRESS

DARTON, LONGMAN & TODD LTD
85 Gloucester Road, London, S.W.7 4SU

ISBN 0 232 51248 5

A Crossroad Book
THE SEABURY PRESS
815 Second Avenue, New York, N.Y. 10017
Library of Congress Catalog Card No. 61–8189

A Translation of the first part of
SCHRIFTEN ZUR THEOLOGIE, IX
published by Verlagsanstalt Benziger & Co. A.G., Einsiedeln

Printed in Great Britain by Western Printing Services Ltd. Bristol.
Nihil Obstat B. C. Butler, *Censor*
Imprimatur + Christopher Butler, V.G.
Westminster, 31st January 1974

The Nihil obstat *and* Imprimatur *are a declaration that a book or pamphlet is considered to be free from doctrinal or moral error. It is not implied that those who have granted the* Nihil obstat *and* Imprimatur *agree with the contents, opinions or statements expressed.*

CONTENTS

PART THREE *Anthropology*

FOREWORD

In the foreword to the ninth (eleventh and twelfth in this English edition) volume of my collected writings it only remains for me to repeat what I have already said in the forewords to the earlier volumes. For this reason I may confine myself to referring primarily to the foreword to the eighth volume. The ninth volume contains the lectures and articles which have been composed over the last two-and-a-half years. I have to acknowledge my heartfelt indebtedness to all my colleagues in the faculty of Catholic theology of the Wilhelms University of Munster, Westphalia, for their help in the work of collecting these articles and preparing them for publication in this volume. My thanks are due, therefore, to Dr Elmar Klinger, Dr Leo Karrer, Herr Heribert Woestmann, Herr Kuno Füssel and Fräulein Annerose Köster. Without their help it would have been impossible to publish this volume so quickly. For the provenance of the individual articles I may once more refer to the List of Sources at the end of the volume.

Munich, March 1970   Karl Rahner

PART ONE

*Tasks and Problems for
Contemporary Theology*

I

PLURALISM IN THEOLOGY AND THE UNITY OF THE CREED IN THE CHURCH

THE theme enunciated in the title to this essay is certainly extremely relevant to the present. For pluralism in theology is making a deep impact in the life of the Church right down to its concrete details, and especially when this pluralism is conceived of in the broadest sense, and without exaggeratedly scholastic restrictions. Now this pluralism confronts the authorities of the Church and her believers alike with the question of how it can be maintained side by side with a true unity of creed, the question of what this unity can mean at all in more precise terms on this showing, and how it can be set apart and preserved from a pluralistic interpretation of the creed itself, while allowing for a legitimate pluralism in theology.

The problem is new. It is a genuine 'quaestio disputata'. We are still far from having obtained a clear enough view of the question to give any clear answer to it, or even an answer which is unambiguous enough and universally accepted enough to provide an immediate solution at least to the practical difficulties to which the problem has given rise in the life of the Church.

This being the situation, it cannot really be expected that in so brief a study as this all aspects, even of the problem in itself, can be brought to view. The author is aware of this impossibility. He knows that he himself is immersed in the midst of these problems without really having mastered them, and that this means that he can only set forth the problem itself in fragmentary form, and that his suggestions as to the lines along which an answer can be found are questionable in the extreme. Indeed on a closer inspection they may even appear false.

One of the consequences arising immediately and precisely from theological pluralism today is that we cannot allow a well-considered answer to mature in the silence and privacy of our own individual minds. Rather we must have the courage to think aloud and in public in order to have

3

any unequivocal results to offer. On this basis the reader may also understand why this study should strike a more personal note than is usual in scholarly essays of this sort.

I

First it is of the utmost importance to recognize that the problem of pluralism in theology really does exist, and that it is new. Even among specialist theologians there is all too often a failure to recognize both of these facts clearly and unequivocally. For it is precisely the specialist theologian who is aware that all along in the history of theology there have been different schools; that there has been a lack of unity among the theologians upon many questions, and that the Church has tolerated, or even made necessary, the differences between the schools, actually taking disputed positions in theology under her protection and guarding them against the accusation of heterodoxy on the part of their opponents.

This and much more besides gives rise again and again to the impression that what we are dealing with in this pluralism among the theologies is an old phenomenon, one which has been with us all along, so that the Church and her *magisterium* have already long since worked out the right principles and the sound practice for dealing with it in such a way that she has easily been able to reconcile her attitudes on the one hand of tolerance of, and even actually requiring, the existence of the many theological schools, and on the other of upholding unequivocally the common creed.

But on this point appearances are deceptive. Until we recognize this and admit it, until we realize that to a certain extent the earlier quantitative proliferation which this pluralism has entailed has led to a qualitative shift, and given birth to a pluralism of a totally different kind – until all this is recognized we are failing to see the real problem and the fresh difficulty which has emerged for the Church and for maintaining the unity of her creed.

What then was the situation (always viewing it as a whole) in earlier times? Certainly in those earlier times there were different schools and orientations in theology. But the divisions between these were in part (e.g. as between the patristics of the east and the west) geographical and due to a sort of intellectual no-man's land dividing the different schools from each other. In some cases, even, the differences between them were not reflected upon in any really effective sense. Or, when they really were recognized and adverted to in the minds of the individual theologians, the opposing theses were set against one another as 'yes' and 'no', and the controversy over them took place within a common intellectual ambience constituted by principles, ideas, and ways of approaching questions which were common to all the parties involved. And in those cases in which later historians have come to recognize that this was not the case, or was only partially so, still the differences these have discovered have been such as those earlier schoolmen, actually engaged in the living and historical controversies, were themselves totally unconscious of.

Formerly it was possible to proceed from the basic principle that one could know the position of one's opponent. One could understand it and could oneself explain to him why one could not share it. The fact that despite having this common ground of understanding, whether real or supposed, with one's opponent, one still could not achieve unison with him was a sheer unanalysable state of affairs, something at which one could only shrug one's shoulders without any further attempt at analysis, recognizing it as a brute fact. At best one could explain it simply in terms of the difficulty of the subject-matter involved, very often in terms of the stupidity of the other theologian or the obstinacy of the heretic. In any case one was convinced either that one knew what one's theological opponent was saying, that one had understood him, or else one was not even aware of his existence and did not recognize him at all. Terminology, philosophical presuppositions, fields of discourse, unanalyzed attitudes and feelings, were either held in common or such differences as did exist in these areas remained unreflected upon.

Today all this is in a real sense essentially different. Very many factors have contributed to this quantitative change, which, to a certain extent, has led to a qualitative transformation. But it is quite impossible to analyze these factors with any precision at this point. The accumulation of historical material which the theological disciplines have to work upon has become so great that it is no longer possible for any one theologian to cope with it. Furthermore the individual theologian (differing in this from his forbears) is actually aware of this. The methods of the individual disciplines have become so complicated that no one theologian can still avail himself of them all. Philosophy itself, as the instrument which the theologian employs of necessity in pursuing his discipline, has itself become so pluralistic that no theologian has any longer any overall mastery of philosophy *as a whole*. Instead he works with one specific philosophy, and perhaps too with a very eclectic one.

Today philosophy is no longer, as it formerly was, the sole and sufficient meeting-place where those theologically relevant findings which man gleans from his everyday experience, from his intellectual life as a whole and from his scientific pursuits can be handed on to theology. The modern sciences (the historical and intellectual disciplines, natural sciences and social sciences) have emancipated themselves from philosophy (rightly or wrongly, it makes no difference here), and although ideally speaking with all of these, in the concrete this is to a very large extent impossible for him, and hence he is in no position to say that something of which he himself is ignorant is theologically irrelevant.

Today the relationship in which a Catholic theology stands vis-à-vis other Christian theologies, whether exegetical, historical or systematic, is quite different in kind from what it formerly was. The Christian theologies today are not diametrically opposed as affirmations and denials of the same simple propositions. Today the real theological frontiers cut across, at least in part, the confessional divisions. This in itself entails a theological pluralism, and one which cannot be overcome merely by teamwork, however necessary such teamwork may be today, and however intensively it may have to be organized. For in fact no team can embrace all the theologians in the world, and even the most broadly conceived team possible in terms of numbers cannot be adequate to cope with the pluralism indicated above.

An additional point is that intellectual disciplines, and so theology too, differ from the natural sciences in that the 'conclusions' cannot really be taken over and understood simply as they stand. Rather it is a necessary condition for any true understanding of the actual conclusions that have been achieved that those who take them over should themselves go through the reasoning process by which they were arrived at. For this reason in theology even teamwork does not help in the last analysis against that pluralism which exists precisely in theology. Today this difficulty is insuperable because there is this difference between the present and former times, that even the substance of the theology and the theologies which are possible and actual today can no longer be contained even approximately by the mind of any one individual theologian, or assimilated in the time available to him. Now this state of affairs is not merely an objective fact, but is something of which the theologian himself is aware and, as a consequence of his own ignorance with regard to a knowledge which he knows exists and yet which he himself has not grasped, it sets the theology of the individual in a strange situation of insecurity and unease.

From what has been said up this point it will be clear that when we speak of a pluralism in theology the decisive factor in this is not that the theologians involved contradict one another, so that according to the simple principle of non-contradiction they cannot both be right at the same time since their respective theses are opposed as the affirmative and negative poles in a contradiction. Such a situation would not constitute any genuine pluralism in theology – at any rate not that pluralism which causes such disquiet today, and which is being referred to here. For when a man is aware of being confronted by two theses which are contradictory alternatives, and when he can recognize them as such, he can, at least in principle, decide between them, and thus both in virtue of the fact that they are alternatives, as also, and still more, by the decision he makes upon the question he finds himself confronted with in this way, he is in a position to overcome the pluralism.

The pluralism of which we are speaking here, rather, consists precisely in the fact that it is quite impossible to reduce the theologies and their representative theses to a simple logical alternative in this manner, in the fact that they exist side by side with one another as disparate and mutually incommensurable. Hence that position of transcendence from which, as being one and common to both a judgement might be arrived at, is totally unattainable to the individual theologian. In other cases there can be some common intellectual ground or ambience of ideas, one which can be accepted as held in common by the rival theorists and recognized, albeit unconsciously and tacitly, right from the first by both of them, so that on the basis of this common ground individual propositions can be discussed. In this case, however, there is nowhere near sufficient common ground of this kind, and this means that the representatives of the different schools cannot achieve, even indirectly, a position in which they can explain to one another consciously and unambiguously in what precisely the difference between their respective intellectual outlooks consists. This difference is only sensed as something vague in virtue of the experience of a mutual state of alienation and disparity through the experience that one's partner in the dialogue constantly proceeds in the dialogue from starting-points which are alien to oneself, or which seem less important to one, and that he presents the subject-matter under discussion, in other words speaks of points which he regards as established, which likewise seem alien or less important to oneself. The result is that the discussion very often, or even in the majority of cases, fails to arrive at any conclusion arising from the subject under discussion itself, but is rather broken off because either the time or the physical resources made available for it make it impossible for it to proceed any further.

In order to clarify what has been said up to this point I must ask to be allowed to strike a somewhat more 'personal' note. In what follows I am speaking of what I know from my own experience. A more senior theologian, one who grew up while the old scholastic tradition was still in force, that tradition which reigned more or less unassailably right up to the time of the Second Vatican Council, cannot easily understand what has been said so far. What approach, then, used we older theologians to adopt, brought up as we were in the orthodox tradition of scholasticism?

If we were obtuse, or somewhat over-convinced of the absolute value of our scholastic theology, we rejected whatever was alien or alienating which we came across from any other theology as false or at least as unimportant, and without really having felt the material weight or the living relevance of an opposed position we found reasons enough and distinctions enough to cope with any such position which struck us as alien, though obviously without really having achieved any clear awareness of the questionable element in our reaction.

If we were cleverer, or more open and alive to new ideas, then we revised our previously held positions, expanded our intellectual horizons, enriched our terminology, and introduced fresh nuances into our points of view and outlooks. We learned to use modern exegesis and a more modern, or a really modern philosophy as the basis for our thought. We arrived at clearer and less prejudiced evaluations of the changing history of dogma and theology (without losing sight of a certain ultimate continuity and consistency in it) etc., and thus we succeeded, to an extent which was certainly significant, in assimilating that which was alien and ran counter to our established ideas, and in making a genuine element in our own theology that which we came across from a different theology (especially a non-Catholic one) or from the theology implicit in the modern understanding of human living. This latter approach, surely a legitimate one, has its due need of success and certainly must not be abandoned. But I cannot escape the impression that today we are experiencing the limitations even of an approach of this kind. The alien is close to us. It is making us aware of itself as such, and yet can neither be assimilated within our own existing framework of thought nor legitimately be rejected as that which is false (or as one-sided, something which we have already advanced beyond in the broader vision and finer distinctions of our own system).

Today it very often happens that we no longer simply succeed in arriving at any fixed or immovable attitude towards the basic theological positions of other theologians when these are specifically different from our own, especially (but not only!) when these belong to other Christian confessions.

In those cases in which another theologian of this sort explicitly and directly denies a proposition of our own Church which has the force of an official ecclesiastical dogma, we still find the position relatively easy. In that case we can, initially at least, counter such a denial with an equally decisive rejection. But then the tormenting question begins to impose itself upon us once more of whether our opponent has really understood the official dogma which he has contested, and therefore whether it was the proposition itself which he rejected and not merely the wrong interpretation of it. The tormenting question begins to impinge upon us of whether we orthodox theologians, taking the proposition which we adhere to, and in the sense in which we understand it, have transposed it explicitly enough into a broader ambience of ideas in such a way that we are reasonably justified in expecting that we have communicated an understanding of this kind of the proposition concerned to the 'opponent' who has rejected it. Have we done this in such a way that we can really expect him to accept it?

But this case is by no means the real one which provokes disquiet with regard to the difficulty in assimilating alien and disparate elements from a different theology. In these alien theologies we encounter basic positions which are far from being in contradictory opposition to our own theology in this sense, but which have been developed within a basic intellectual ambience which their representatives held in common with ourselves. Yet even in such cases as this we have still been unable to achieve any clear or unambiguous analysis of the original disparity which exists between us and them. Now in such cases as this we are no longer in the least capable of arriving at a position in which we can give an unambiguous 'yes' or 'no' to such basic positions.

For instance who among us today can say with sufficient sureness whether the basic conception of the doctrine of justification put forward by Karl Barth is Catholic or heterodox? Anyone among us who believes that he has the precise answer to this is to be congratulated indeed. But what are we to do if we fail to arrive at this position? Who can say precisely that the basic positions held by Rudolph Bultmann are, in the last analysis, really un-Catholic, or whether it is merely that the propositions themselves have not been understood or developed with sufficient precision, and that this is why conclusions have been derived from them by Bultmann or his followers which seem to run counter to the ultimate basic principles of Catholicism and so can no longer be acceptable to Catholics?

What course should we adopt when, for want of time, through the limitations of our physical resources, or because of the other tasks in theology to which we are committed, we are no longer in a position to form any clear or responsible opinion upon this point?

Both in terms of thought and action it would be to evade the real problem involved here if we were simply to say that we could, after all, set these questions aside with untroubled consciences in order to pursue our own theology, and in order to express for ourselves, and in terms of our own theology what we hold theologically with regard to our own Christian and Catholic faith, and to have analyzed this sufficiently to make it understandable for ourselves and to some extent for others also. For a fact that precisely cannot and must not be overlooked is that side by side with our own theology there are other theologies which remain alien to ourselves, and which, nevertheless, claim to be theologically analyzing the same creed. Certainly if this creed were simply presented to one in total independence of these disparate theologies everything would be quite simple. But since it is quite impossible for this to be the case (seeing that faith and theological understanding of the faith cannot simply and unequivocally be separated from one another) how then can one man ascertain whether his faith is the same as that of another when that other's theology is alien to him and existing side by side with his own, unexplored and uncomprehended?

Another example: the discussions between Dutch and Roman theologians with regard to the doctrine of the Eucharist and the interpretation of transubstantiation are well known. Any idea that the Roman theologians are more stupid or uneducated than their Dutch 'opponents' is totally foreign to my thoughts. But nevertheless I do have a suspicion that even with the best will in the world they are simply incapable of mastering the philosophical presuppositions, the ontological categories of thought as they actually exist, which lie behind any serious exposition of the doctrine of trans-signification etc., and that for this reason these discussions remain barren. Of course such an understanding is 'in itself' attainable, and of course if it were in fact to be attained to one would have to use this position to test in turn whether in the concrete case supposed the dogma, even when subjected to the critical judgement of a tribunal, does not give rise to these ontological assumptions, and whether in turn these assumptions cannot be accounted simply as manifestly possible interpretations of the dogma. But what is to be done when we presuppose positions which are not in fact held on the 'Roman' side and which perhaps, while they are indeed maintained on the 'Dutch' side in a real and effective sense, have even there not found any clear or articulate expression? Some such position is possible, and it implies no reproach for any lack of intelligence or will to achieve mutual understanding (how long, for instance, have we had to wait until philosophy in the ecclesiastical sphere has been able, to some extent, to cope with modern philosophy from Descartes onwards?). What are we to do in order that both sides may achieve the initial mastery of the basic assumptions which disparate doctrines of the Eucharist of this kind presuppose?

Nor can it be objected that to establish an incommensurability of this kind as present, at least provisionally, between such doctrines in itself implies that a bridge has been built between these two alien and opposed positions on the grounds that a third and detached standpoint has been arrived at, one from which the presence of this incommensurability has been established, and from which an 'understanding' of both sides has been achieved. For even supposing that someone from this third and detached standpoint can justifiably hold the opinion that he has an equal understanding of both positions, and so has overcome the disparity between them, still the one holding this third position must then presumably anxiously question himself as to whether in other cases he too is not exposed to a similar impossibility of really being able to cope with opposed positions, an impossibility such as, in the case supposed, he actually believes that he has been able to recognize from his own standpoint even though each of the two opponents involved is convinced that he has in all good will tested and really understood the position of the other party.

A third example: How do we manage today when we enter into discussion with contemporary Catholic intellectuals who, though they have no formation in scholastic theology, are nevertheless interested in theology and well read? Very soon we come across a whole complex of theological views which is, in certain cases, extremely rich and profoundly thought out. This complex has a quite different structure and different perspectives from those to which we scholastic theologians are accustomed. For the most part, in the statements deriving from this complex, propositions are enunciated which sound to us, and perhaps actually are, heresies of the grossest kind. In this complex we may perhaps discover lacunae which are astonishing even to us, omissions which, judged by our outlook, are indefensible and, on the other hand, an over-emphasis upon factors to which great weight is attached yet which seem to us utterly secondary. We discover that in such a 'theology' as formulated by an intellectual of this kind the system of ideas involved assumes a quite different form from that which we tacitly presuppose to be present in the minds of an intellectual who wills to be and is a 'practising' Catholic. We always assume that the orthodox answers of the catechism are present in his mind. We expect that from this catechism, which after all is nothing else than the full and valid emanation of our standardized scholastic theology, while there may be some omissions for which the 'fides implicita' of the subject may have to compensate, still on the whole even in this intellectual our own theology will have maintained more or less its own form from the religious instruction which he has had at an earlier stage.

In reality it is quite otherwise. Even in his case we find ourselves confronted with a 'theology' which seems alien and disparate to us. Very soon we recognize that it is impossible, within the space of time available and with the 'technical' equipment available to bring our own theology into harmony with the alien one. The alien theology of the sort of intellectual we have in mind, to a far greater extent than our own, is influenced by his personal lot in life, his distinctive psychological make-up, the intellectual and social milieu in which he lives, in other words by factors which are different and take effect in different ways in the case of the professional theologian, and which are quite impossible to overcome in his encounter with the intellectual through the fragmentary dialogue and instruction which is all that is possible for them in the limited time available. Thus when we encounter a 'theology' which is alien to us and which remains alien we must, as specialist theologians, actually ask ourselves whether among us too, in the form which our theology assumes, the same theological 'proportions' are present which strike us as so alien in the case of an intellectual of this kind: lacunae, deficiencies, oddness of emphasis and perspectives which are anything but obvious etc. We have to ask ourselves whether the only reason why we orthodox scholastic theologians do not notice this clearly is that we discuss these matters too exclusively among ourselves alone, taking it for granted that we should confine ourselves to the terminology and horizons of thought which we hold in common.

II

What then is to be done in this situation in which we are confronted with an insurmountable theological pluralism? This is the real and difficult question, which can put to ourselves only insofar as we really have learned to regard this pluralism genuinely without prejudice or anxiety of any kind. It is only with great difficulty, if at all, that we can supply any answer to this question that is to some extent adequate. It cannot really be expected that any such answer will be wholly satisfying either at the theoretical or at the practical level. For in fact an answer that was completely satisfying could only be given in the form of a solution which itself in turn transcended this pluralism and so in principle overcame it. As has already been emphasized at the outset of this study, it is only quite modest statements that we can attempt here, and even these with all due provisos to the effect that it may later become necessary to revise them.

To begin with, however, two points have to be laid down. *First:* Obviously, however true it may be that pluralism in theology is, and will continue to be an inescapable fact, it nevertheless does not signify a mere static state of affairs which we simply have to accept. Obviously we have to strive again and again and in every possible way to overcome it, to conduct a dialogue between all theological schools and outlooks, to subject our own thought-world to critical examination and to expand it, to learn from others etc. The theological pluralism of today is, if we may actually express it in this way, the self-realization of the individual Christian and theologian as well as of the theological awareness of the Church of the situation in which they stand in terms of epistemology and 'concupiscence'. Once we understand this then properly speaking it must be clear to us theologians that pluralism in theology can neither be eliminated nor simply accepted, but that it belongs to that category of human realities which are entailed by the historical dimension and the abiding contingency of the human state. These can never be overcome in such a way that they no longer exist, and yet at the same time we are compelled to strive again and again to overcome them in the future.

Second: Obviously while recognizing the abiding factor of pluralism in theology, we are not denying to the Church, whether to her awareness of her faith or to her teaching authority, the right to draw new and unequivocal boundaries, under certain circumstances to reject the teachings of a given theology as heretical or (for reasons and in a manner which have still to be described) as not to be tolerated in the Church. The function of the teaching authority as, under certain circumstances actually pronouncing anathemas, is not abolished by the factor of pluralism in theology. This pluralism does not give licence for any kind of weak tolerance of everything and anything, because otherwise in dealing with the mutual interrelationship of creed and theology, and in recognizing the distinction which exists between the two entities – a distinction which can never adequately be analyzed or defined – we could no longer maintain, in the concrete individual case, that unity of the creed in the Church which is constitutive for her. For even the most enlightened understanding in terms of the psychological, historical and sociological factors involved of how and why an individual arrives at an 'insuperably' heterodox view is still very far from requiring that such a view should be upheld within the Church. This latter position is not required for the very reason that the Church by her rejection neither denies the 'bona fides' of the upholder of a heterodox view of this kind, nor denies him any chance of salvation any more than she denies that such heterodox views have a positive function for the further development of the Church's awareness of her own faith when she maintains her separation from other Christian creeds. Now while we must uphold the right and duty of the Church's teaching authority in this matter quite uncompromisingly, still it must be recognized on the other hand that this is not to deny, but rather positively to maintain, that the manner in which this right and this duty are exercised must, at least in many respects, acquire a quite new form in the concrete, seeing that the contemporary pluralism of which we speak is not merely a present factor, but one which in its intractability has arrived at the stage of being consciously reflected upon. The question is, therefore, how in, and in spite of, a situation of theological pluralism which is consciously being reflected upon and recognized as insuperable we can still maintain the unity of the creed in a form which is at least partially new. And this brings us to the real question which concerns us here. The manner in which the unity of the creed must be maintained is new because this pluralism is itself new, and yet at the same time has manifest consequences for the attitude of the Church and her teaching authority in preserving the unity of the creed. Such observations as we can make upon this question are extremely fragmentary, and will be expressed in a few individual statements without any intention of uniting these within a single 'system'.

III

We are wholly failing to grasp the nature of this theological pluralism so long as we fail to recognize that the formulae in which the teaching authority of the Church expresses her creed always include amongst other things an implicit element of linguistics. These formulae have been subjected to rules of language which might have been different. But the formulae have not simply and solely been dictated by the reality itself which they express. Rather they are conditioned by sociological and historical factors in the development of human thinking. These factors, therefore, provide the setting in which the formulae come to be articulated, and the formulae themselves justly demand to be respected in their own right even though the respect we accord to them is not simply identical with our assent of faith to the truth itself which is expressed with dogmatically binding force. Up to this time there has hardly been any conscious reflection upon this element of linguistic conditioning in the formal statements of the Church's *magisterium*, which are designed to preserve the unity of the creed (even though an inkling of this conscious reflection does appear here and there, cf. DS 1515, 1642, 1652). Formerly it was not possible to recognize this by any process of conscious reflection because we held more or less the same field of linguistic discourse in common with our heretical opponents (even when this field of discourse itself was changing gradually and in a way which was hardly adverted to). Because of this the different doctrines were formulated in the same terms as so many affirmations and denials. Today, however, we have only to reflect for a moment on the terms 'person' and 'nature' in the doctrine of the Trinity and christology, and concepts such as 'original sin', 'transubstantiation' etc. (though we cannot do this in any explicit sense in the present context) in order to see that in such dogmatic teachings certain specific rules of language are actually being applied which in other circumstances could have been different, and that the formulations are not simply determined by the truth which they express as such and exclusively. Indeed dogmatic teachings of this kind actually become problematical and provoke great misunderstandings when the secular field of discourse in which such concepts are applied, and on the basis of which they have been understood, is changed without the Church having the power autonomously to guide and control the linguistic development of the concepts themselves which are involved. Viewed from this aspect the unity of the creed and the pluralism of the theologies, together with the mutual interdependence of these two entities can manifestly no longer be conceived of or applied in practice today as it was formerly. Formerly on the one hand it was not only the truly basic statements of the creed *alone*, but those of theology as well which were encountered within this system of linguistic rules, while on the other hand the 'explanations' of such concepts of the Church's teaching authority, though of course always necessary and also actually given in earlier times, appeared and were felt to be merely secondary, and were clearly distinguished from the concepts themselves, as commentaries appended to the theological statements properly so called. What earlier appeared to be, and was thought in theology and by theologians to be, mere subsequent and secondary commentary upon such concepts and statements of the official teaching (for it was these that constituted the true corpus of theological statements as such) can today actually acquire a different status and significance in the theologies as such. It can be included as an intrinsic element in the true corpus of the statements of such a theology.

To put the matter simply and once and for all: whereas earlier the really important theses in a theology were themselves statements of the Church's *magisterium*, this will no longer necessarily be the case in the future for theology itself. Indeed it is probably impossible that it shall be so if a theology of today is effectively to come to grips with its true past. The linguistic rules governing the expressions of the Church's teaching authority have this status primarily and in principle so far as the creed is concerned, and they do not have it in the same basic and binding manner for the actual theologies themselves. These theologies do of course remain attached to the official doctrine of the Church, and thereby to the linguistic rules which are maintained with this. But these linguistic rules must be viewed more clearly than in earlier times as having their force so far as the Church's creed is concerned and as not having the same basic force so far as theology is concerned. So far we have been aware that behind these linguistic rules lies a history stretching into the past, a history in which they themselves first came into being so that they were not always in force. Today in the same way it becomes clear that these too, at least so far as theology as such is concerned, have a further history extending into the future. The attempts which are discernible in 'Humani Generis' and 'Mysterium Fidei' to represent such theological concepts and the linguistic rules which they involve, despite their past history, as indispensable for the future also are ill-conceived and fail to carry conviction. Even if some such approach were right so far as the creed is concerned (and on this point we shall have something to say at a later stage), still this certainly does not also apply in every case to theology and the theologies. The theologies have a basic and intrinsic right from the outset to express even the pith and essence of the realities they are enunciating as theological, and ultimately as official, in a different way from the manner in which they are expressed in the formulations of the Church's *magisterium*. This does not of course mean that they may also simply as such tacitly neglect these formulations of official teaching with the linguistic rules they entail, or that they are not bound by that which is expressed in these formulations in a truly binding manner.

Presumably in a contemporary presentation of the theology of the Trinity one could express that which is dogmatically binding in the Church's faith in the Trinity, one could make it intelligible, one could set it within a framework of thought which has become necessary today, in such a way that in doing so the statement about the 'Three Persons' and 'One Nature' would not occupy the central place with everything else merely converging upon it as so much commentary. What is meant by original sin could presumably be expressed in a theology of the 'sin of the world' in a manner which was orthodox and did justice to the Church's creed without thereby having to speak of original *sin* in the terms of the theological statements as such (for all the binding force of the classic Tridentine doctrine of original sin), and without thereby having to obscure the actual content of the specifically credal element, at any rate any more than in the classic formulation, which in fact also 'obscures' because it fails to bring out the merely analogous relationship between personal and inherited habitual sin. The factor of linguistic conditioning present in the expression of the Church's doctrine and now able consciously to be reflected upon makes it clear that it is both possible and justified for there to be a pluralism among the theologies, and for these to exhibit great differences in their formulations from the formulations of the Church's official teaching.

IV

This in turn, however, serves to bring out still more clearly the real problem with which we are here concerned: How can we ensure that the unity of the creed is maintained, while allowing for a pluralism of this kind in the forms of language used by the theologies?

On the one hand, however, it is impossible to get beyond any one specific theological language in formulating the creed, for even the formulations of the official teaching themselves are inevitably (to some extent at least) *ipso facto* theology and so draw upon one specific theology. Moreover the degree to which the different theologies are commensurable, the degree to which they converge in the unity of the creed, is something that, as has already been said, cannot adequately be established in the concrete by the individual.

In view of this situation, and of course with the provisos already mentioned above, there can be no escaping the conclusion that today the Church and her teaching authority are forced, to a notably greater extent than formerly, to leave to the individual theologies the responsibility for seeing that they genuinely do maintain themselves in agreement with the Church's creed; that their interpretation of this creed is not such as to interpret away the creed itself while paying it mere lip-service, not such as to empty it of its content, but such as really to maintain its truth. Today it must surely be recognized that even the Church's teaching authority is confronted with this situation and the consequences arising from it. For either it is the case that it is upheld by the representatives of one specific individual theology, or else, if its upholders are appointed as far as possible so as to be representative and to include a fair cross-section of the adherents of the different theologies, then the council thus formed simply reproduces the pluralism of theologies which exists in the Church herself, and which cannot be transcended in any adequate sense. The Church of today must, to a far greater extent than formerly, leave to the individual theologies the responsibility of ensuring that they genuinely do preserve the common creed.

Despite the proviso stated above, it is of course still possible that in specific cases the teaching authority of the Church will pronounce specific statements put forward by a particular theology as irreconcilable with the creed itself. But in this it is surely impossible to lay down *a priori* norms which make it clear by the purely formal directives which they provide what the cases are in which a given theology has to bring its own self-responsibility (that is always as limited by the *magisterium* itself) to bear, and what the cases are in which even today the *magisterium* itself has to intervene to draw a possible line of division between orthodox and heterodox theology.

But even in this second case, a point which we must fully and un-reservedly take into account is that to a notable extent, and perhaps even in its real heart and centre, certain rules of theological language are implied. We have to reckon with the fact that when such a line of division is drawn it is a fact, whether consciously adverted to or not, that it is not primarily and immediately a question of truth that the distinction bears upon, but a phenomenon of epistemology and sociology that is involved. In other words when such a line of demarcation is drawn what is really happening is that the Church is making the following pronouncement (albeit in the form of a doctrine bearing upon the truth content itself): 'Such-and-such an assertion cannot be made in the Church without the one making the assertion bringing himself or at least others with whom he has to live in the unity of the faith into the danger of mistaking the reality signified in the creed.' And then the Church once more leaves it to the theology concerned to interpret the common creed for itself and on its own responsibility while paying due respect to this ruling in the matter of language.

Presumably the old credal formulae and doctrinal decisions of the

Church achieve in this contemporary situation a new status and a different significance from that which they formerly had. They are of course (and this applies even to those already contained in the New Testament) conceived of in the language of a specific theology (though this is not to deny that already even in them a certain theological pluralism is objectively present. Only it is such that the reality of it has not yet plainly been reflected upon or adverted to). But these ancient statements of doctrine were after all precisely the common and sole expressions in which the common creed was expressed. And this means that these ancient statements of doctrine, in virtue of the uniqueness of the realities signified in the creed, of the unity of the creed itself, and of the continuity that had to be preserved in the Church's awareness of her faith, the abiding and binding points of departure and the norm (albeit *norma normata*) for the manifold theologies which are only now really emanating from them, and which can no longer adequately be contained within an overall unity. The teaching authority of the Church cannot in principle arrive at its expressions of doctrine except by availing itself of a theology, even though what it refers to is the actual creed itself, and even though, varying, naturally, according to the particular case being treated of, the difference between the creed in what it really signifies and the theology which expresses and interprets it is very great. Moreover the pluralism among the theologies of today can no longer adequately be subsumed under any overall unity. Now because of this we presumably have to reckon with the fact that in the future the *magisterium* will hardly be in a position to arrive at any fresh positive expressions of doctrine. The unity of theology which such expressions would presuppose is no longer present. Presumably it must be expected that in the future the teaching authority will intervene in particular cases as these arise in defence of doctrine, and undertake to define the boundaries in the manner already described. Meanwhile she will protect and encourage the individual theologies which, each in its own way, are striving to make the creed which all hold in common comprehensible and relevant in a manner corresponding to the needs of the particular epoch. In the future, then, the *magisterium* will regard this pluralism among the theologies as an enrichment of the Church and as something which is necessary today. And under certain circumstances, by a certain expansion of the function it has exercised hitherto, it will be inspired by the abiding gospel to permit pastoral movements, prophetic impulses to arise in the Church, which will guide the Church's actions in a particular concrete historical situation.

But presumably the dream which not a few theologians have been indulging in in the very recent past, namely that by a process of ever more refined development of dogma the Church herself will develop her teaching ever further and ever more swiftly in a series of individual pronouncements, has now proved devoid of reality.

For pressed to its logical conclusion such a procedure would only still be possible if some one single theology were at her disposal and were to be accepted by all as the immediately obvious presupposition for such a development in this explicative sense.

The relinquishment of a 'development of dogma' as understood above need not entail any impoverishment of the life of faith in the Church, or any ossification of her awareness of her own faith. This life of faith is simply concentrated all the more clearly upon the ultimately decisive points contained in the Christian faith, and in the contemporary intellectual situation in the world there is every occasion for this concentration. And these most central and most radical points in the content of the Christian faith will be considered, interpreted, and applied to the present by theologies which are, and which will continue to be, very different in character. Both these factors taken together, however, signify an enrichment of the Church's awareness of her faith in terms of content and application which is at least as great as that which would accrue if the 'development of dogma' were taking place in the manner which probably not a few theologians in the last hundred years have thought of it as taking place when they strove to achieve a 'new dogma' as the goal and crown of such a development. Probably too we can understand from this that the earlier and positive doctrinal statements of the Church now acquire a somewhat different function from that which they formerly had. They no longer constitute so much the *terminus a quo* for a further development leading to fresh dogmas through and within a single unique theology, but rather constitute the initial expression of a common creed to which many theologies, while retaining their pluralism, refer, and which they are intended to serve.

v

Presumably, however, we should approach the problem of how the unity of the creed is to be reconciled with the pluralism among the theologies from yet another point. This is necessary if we are really to make it plain how difficult it is to convince ourselves of the uniqueness of the common creed, seeing that on the one hand this conviction is not *ipso facto* achieved by the verbal equivalences between the formulae of the creed as applied in the individual theologies and as recognized and respected by them, while on the other hand the pluralism among the theologies (in which nevertheless it is an understanding of the one creed that is being maintained), cannot adequately be overcome or transcended.

In order to achieve any further advance at this stage the following point must be reflected upon: As understood in the Church faith and creed can certainly not be present apart from words or in a state of emancipation from words. This means that the unity and uniqueness of the faith and the creed can certainly not be realized and adhered to by many simply and exclusively at a level which is beyond words, for instance that of common sympathy, common action, or a common cult etc., quite apart from the fact that even such human realities are in any case never simply beyond words. But precisely this word has at the same time a further character as of its very nature pointing us on to realities, achievements and experiences which are not present to us simply through this word alone. Faith and creed do not constitute a 'verbal event' in such a way that this word is, in a certain sense, simply sufficient to itself. Men communicate with one another and form a unity with one another. But although certainly they never do this apart from the word-event, still this as such never constitutes in itself alone the whole reality of this unity. Rather it points on to a further unity which it indeed initiates but never constitutes of itself alone. The word itself in its comprehensibility points on to the mystery of God, to the historical reality from which man derives, to the common way and the common activity of humanity, and thereby to realities which are indeed never present without any word at all, but which are not simply identical with this word, and which are communicated by this word not as absent but as matters of present experience. To this extent, then, even in the word the assurance of a unity of the word is possible which is not simply or solely achieved by the word itself alone. Now the Christian faith presupposes such a possibility as already given quite independently of the question which is raised by the pluralism among theologies which exists today. For how otherwise could any one individual school of thought assure itself sufficiently of agreement with any other, seeing that this assurance with regard to the attitude and conviction of the other school of thought is, after all, invariably possible only through the medium of one's own awareness? This assurance is never achieved in the processes of human thought merely by establishing a correspondence between the content of conceptual awareness between the two parties. Life in common at the physical level, the same statement (as distinct merely from the same ideas), concrete action in common – these are necessary elements in the process of assuring ourselves of identity of conviction among many parties.

The fact that in Christianity the same baptism exists as a concrete mode of action, that a form of worship is celebrated in common at the physical level, that all words point on beyond themselves to a single historical reality, and in this precisely to that which can no longer be expressed conceptually, that is treated of in community within the concrete dimension of a world that is subject to space and time – these and much else besides are not merely the consequences of a conviction held in common which one has previously assured oneself of as common prior to any action by the process of theoretical discussion. Rather they too are just as much so many elements through which this common conviction can be realized and conceived of as present. In the last analysis there can be no breaking out of the circle. Concrete action (in the broadest sense) is, as common, not merely the consequence of a conviction previously arrived at and already held in common, but the mode in which such a common conviction is brought to its fulness and achieves its realization and its certainty. This means that the maintenance of the unity of the creed within the pluralism of the theologies and the assurance of this are also (though not only!) dependent upon the fact that the community and the unity which are being achieved do not exist simply or exclusively in the dimension of the word as such and at the conceptual level. If we want to bring the unity of the creed to its fulness and to assure ourselves of this unity (of course always with an assurance which remains at the human level, which is never attained to in the absolute, which must be worked out in hope, and which is not even communicated at the theoretical level), then we must *express* this one creed in common, celebrate the Death of the Lord in common in the physicality belonging to this, celebrate the sacraments in their physicality, serve the world in common in action, and then through all this process community of creed is achieved in the midst of all the pluralism of the theologies.

VI

In conclusion the question can be posed – still without any real answer – of what all that has so far been said signifies for an ecumenical theology and for the ecumenical strivings that are made to achieve unity between the Churches. Proceeding from what we have said so far, surely the question is this: Can it perhaps be the case that the theologians of the separated Churches have already, without our really noticing it, entered into that pluralism among the theologies which certainly has its place in the one Church? Has this taken place (and this is a point which is, for the most part considered in isolation) not because these theologies have themselves undergone further development since the Reformation, but, on a deeper and more exact view, because in the awareness of faith of the individual Churches of today they are accorded a different status, i.e. the difference between them and the creed proper is seen and recognized as greater than was formerly thought because in each of the Churches concerned, even in those in which these theologies are maintained, they are from the outset expressed and interpreted in a broader context, i.e. precisely *as* such as can have other theologies existing side by side with them in an abiding pluralism of such theologies? A situation has been arrived at, at least in part, in which these theologies of the different Churches are, in this new context, not in the least incompatible with one another. Perhaps we can be tolerant enough to accord to them, at least in part, that self-responsibility of which we have spoken above without requiring from them, over and above the ancient formulae of faith, or, it may be quite new and original statements of the Christian faith, a common theological mode of expression as the condition for these theologies existing together in common in the one Church. Perhaps there is a genuine theological possibility not only of achieving the unity of the Church on the basis of the unity of the creed as theologically formulated, but also a further possibility of arriving at unity of creed on the basis of unity of life and action in the Church or of acquiring sufficient assurance of the fact of this unity. Our intention is merely to pose these questions, not to answer them. We have no intention of offering a potent recipe for producing a mere seeming solution to all the differences between the creeds. Let us simply put the following question: What significance does it have for the strivings of the ecumenical movement for a workable unity among the Churches, if within the Catholic Church an effective pluralism of theologies exists and has a positive right to exist?

2

ON THE THEOLOGY OF THE
ECUMENICAL DISCUSSION

THE subject of this article[1] is the theology of ecumenism. This has the unusual advantage that in a certain sense the subject under consideration and the considerations themselves coincide: an ecumenical dialogue which treats of ecumenical dialogue. Given a subject of this kind it would be perfectly conceivable to fasten upon one specific question in terms of theological content from the whole group of associated subjects, and thereby to demonstrate by means of one specific example what we mean when we speak of ecumenical theology.[2] But surely

---

[1] The Considerations which follow originally served as a double lecture delivered in the course of a lecture tour in the Scandinavian countries lasting from 21st March to the 4th April 1968, and which was held at the invitation of the deans of the theological faculties of Copenhagen, Lund, Oslo, Uppsala, Helsinki and Abo/Turku. The text was subsequently revised and some additional notes were added to it.

[2] The author must here refer to the different studies which he has published in another context on particular questions in ecumenism. In these it would be possible to see in greater detail what possibilities there are, in the opinion of the author, for ecumenical discussion, even in difficult areas of detail, and how a theology really committed to the realities of the situation can bring life and movement to positions which have become petrified. On this cf. K. Rahner, 'Protestantismus', *LTK* VIII (2nd ed. 1963), 827–831; *idem*, 'On Conversions to the Church', *Theological Investigations* III (London and Baltimore, 1967), pp. 373–384; *idem*, 'The Presence of the Lord in the Sacrament of the Lord's Supper', *Theological Investigations* IV (London and Baltimore, 1966), pp. 291–311; *idem*, 'Questions of Controversial Theology on Justification', *ibid.*, pp. 189–218; *idem*, 'Some Remarks on the Question of Conversions', *Theological Investigations* V (London and Baltimore, 1966) pp. 315–335; *idem*, 'Justified and Sinner at the Same Time', *Theological Investigations* VI (London and Baltimore, 1969), pp. 218–230; *idem*, 'Zur "Situationsethik" aus ökumenischer Sicht', *Schriften zur Theologie* VI (Einsiedeln, 2nd ed., 1968), pp. 537–544; *idem*, 'Katholische Besinnung zum Reformationsjubiläum', *Gnade als Freiheit* (Freiburg, 1968), pp. 177–186; cf. also the further studies on indulgence, *Theological Investigations* II (London and Baltimore, 1963), pp. 175–201, and X (London and New York), pp. 125–199. To achieve a general survey of the literature reference will be made to

24

it is still possible, albeit in an abstract and formal manner, to consider the actual nature of this. It may be that in adopting this method we shall never advance beyond the level of very general principles, and perhaps we shall lay ourselves open to the objection that the difficulties lie in the details. But I cannot escape the impression that even so abstract an approach to the essence of the matter as this has tasks and problems enough to offer, at any rate to attempt it. Since it is not easy to provide a preliminary plan such as would be enlightening in itself of the considerations which will be attempted here, I may be permitted simply to embark upon my subject.

I

Let us measure ecumenical theology against a background in space and time of the divisions which exist within western Christendom, in other words that constituted by the period of the last 450 years. Against this background, then, is the task of ecumenical theology old or new? Are we to say that ecumenical theology has been in existence since the Enlightenment and the awakening of historical awareness in the nineteenth century – in other words, so far as we Catholics are concerned, since Möhler and Newman? Or does ecumenical theology only begin to exist since the modern ecumenical movement in the strict sense of the term, since there has been a World Council of Churches and, so far as we Catholics are concerned, since the Second Vatican Council has been in existence with its Decree on Ecumenism? Or should we perhaps even go so far as to say that ecumenical theology is still more or less something to be desired, a hope rather than a reality? It will be best not to opt for any one of the alternatives presented, or to give any wholly decisive and unambiguous answer to this question. Here rather we must let it remain an open question. Every living reality has a history, and often too a pre-history, and for the most part it is not possible to draw any unambiguous boundaries between history and pre-history, especially since in the case we are considering the mentality of the individual theologians, even in earlier ages, was not the same, but rather exhibits profound differences, so that perhaps in any distinction we might draw between controversial theology and ecumenical theology it might be said that from the Reformation to the

Internationale Ökumenische Bibliographie ed. by L. Gerken, H. Weissgerber *et al.*, I–II (1967), as also to *Oecumenia 1969. Jahrbuch für ökumenische Forschung* (Gütersloh, 1969).

present day there have been ecumenical theologians and controversial theologians.[3]

E. Stakemeier defines controversial theology as the theological treatment of doctrines considered as the official proclamations previously put forward by confessional groups and as reduced to their underlying principles – doctrines, that is to say, which form the basis of the differences which divide the Churches and which exist between the confessional bodies conceived of as Christian and ecclesiastical.[4] This definition of his points the question of whether in any such description of the nature of controversial theology we could not work out a still less ambiguous and more vital difference between this and ecumenical theology, or whether 'ecumenical' as distinct from 'controversial' serves merely to describe the greater hope and a more ironic and understanding approach by which to describe one and the same discipline, a discipline which we call 'controversial theology' or precisely today prefer to call 'ecumenical theology.'[5] We intend actually to abstract from the question of how far ecumenical theology in a given Christian Church is of its nature and inevitably distinct from that of another Christian Church even in respect of its formal essence through the different understanding which is involved of revelation, faith, and thereby too of theology itself in its general nature. But even abstracting from this it can certainly be said that a 'controversial theology', or probably better 'ecumenical theology' in every Church has *first and foremost* the task of providing a presentation of that Church's own teaching in all its breadth and depth. In this connection the theolo-

---

[3] At this point it is impossible to enter in any detail into the history of ecumenical theology. On this cf. in greater detail R. Rouse/S. Neill edd., *Geschichte der ökumenischen Bewegung* (Göttingen, 1957); G. Thils, *Histoire doctrinal du mouvement oecuménique* (Paris, 2nd ed., 1963); G. Tavard, *Geschichte der Ökumenischen Bewegung* (Mainz, 1964).

[4] E. Stakemeier, 'Kontroverstheologie', *LTK* VI (2nd ed., 1961), 511–515, esp. 514; cf. also R. Kösters, 'Zur Theorie der Kontroverstheologie', *ZKTh* 88 (1966), pp. 121–162.

[5] For a definition of the concept 'Ecumenical' cf. W. A. Visser't Hooft, *Der Sinn des Wortes "ökumenisch"* (Stuttgart, 1954); Y. Congar, 'Ökumenische Bewegung', *LTK* VII (2nd ed. 1963), 1128–1137; W. Beinert, *Um das dritte Kirchenattribut*, 2 Vols (Essen, 1964), esp. II, pp. 532–572; W. Seibel, 'Ökumenische Theologie', *Gott in Welt* II (*Festschrift für K. Rahner*), ed. by J. B. Metz, W. Kern *et al.* (Freiburg, 1964), pp. 472–498; P. Wacker, *Theologie als ökumenische Dialog* (Munich, 1965); H. Volk, 'Katholische ökumenismus', *Gesammelte Schriften* II (Mainz, 1966), pp. 161–178; P. Bläser, 'Ökumenische Theologie', *Was ist Theologie?* ed. by E. Neuhäusler and E. Gössmann (Munich, 1966), pp. 358–415; J. Brosseder, *Ökumenische Theologie* (Munich, 1967).

gians of the other Christian Churches must be borne in mind and included in the considerations to the extent that the ultimate self-understanding of the particular Church's own theology allows for this. The *second* task would be the attempt at a thorough presentation of the doctrinal views of the other Churches in respect of their origins, their historical development, and their current positions, and in this deep consideration would have to be given especially to the connection between the individual doctrines, to the roots and sustaining principles and prior assumptions of these, and, in particular cases, to the different concept of truth which lies at the basis of this other theology right from the outset. *Third* the theologians concerned must submit themselves with an unreserved will for truthfulness and unreserved obedience to the revealed will of God, and this implies that they have a duty, and must have the courage, should the need arise, to qualify the particular point of doctrine of the other Church as running counter to the revelation of God in Christ and so, without any false irenics, as an error.

That such a theology – whatever name we may give to it – must be concerned with serving the unity of Christians in the one Church of Jesus Christ, that above all in western ecumenical theology the way that must be trodden is above all (if, indeed not exclusively) that of exegetical and biblical theology and also the theology of the Fathers which these Churches recognize in common as such – all this seems to be obvious. Nevertheless we must not disguise from ourselves the fact that in agreeing in this way to recognize the formal principles and methods to be used the ecumenical theologies in the individual Churches will appear very different from one another, especially since they are precisely theologies, and should not be official confessional pronouncements considered as part of the general or religious phenomenology of the individual Churches taken as a whole. Today, perhaps, there is in fact no longer any agreement as to the premiss which this involves, that in all the Churches which have been separated from one another there either should be or can be any such thing as a unifying doctrine binding upon each of the individual Churches. We have only to consider the radical differences which in fact exist between the individual Churches, at least in part, in their understanding of what theology can be or should be at all,[6] to realize that ecumenical

---

[6] The actual plurality of the Churches themselves is reflected in this different interpretation of the meaning of theology, and in this way this in turn becomes a subject for ecumenical discussion.

On the problem of pluralism in theology on the basis of the numerous philosophical approaches of the parties to the discussion cf. K. Rahner, passim in *Theological*

theology considered as a discussion between the theologies of different Churches constitutes an immensely difficult problem. It could in fact be the case that these theologies, regarded from their ultimate understanding of themselves, are so disparate that they no longer speak with one another, confront one another, or can be measured by one another at all, and, at least in theory, an ecumenical theology would almost be something like a '*contradictio in adiecto*'. And in that case the only insight that could help us to overcome this state of doubt and questioning would be to remember that we are men, that we do recognize one another mutually as Christians, and that for both these reasons we must bend ourselves again and again to the task of speaking with one another, because there is no other way whatever for us to conduct our human lives. We must do this even if we are still far from knowing in what the ultimate prior assumptions and contexts of ideas consist which we hold in common, and even though without this knowledge any discussion seems to be quite inconceivable.[7] It might be said that our *fe dacto* existence as men and Christians has from the first decided the question for us and told us that there can be discussion between us. In an ecumenical theology, therefore, we must consider the question of *how* this is possible, because *prior* to all conscious insight on our part this possibility does *de facto* already exist as a present reality.

II

When we turn back to what the Second Vatican Council has to say with regard to ecumenical theology in the Decree on Ecumenism we come across the key word 'dialogue' again and again.[8] Certainly it can be said that controversial theology and ecumenical theology, even if both have ultimately speaking a common nature, differ from one another in virtue of the fact that the old controversial theology consisted of a controversy, whereas the current ecumenical theology is intended to be a dialogue and is recognized by all Christians of today as having this purpose.[9] However

---

Investigations IX and X (London and New York). What has been said there may analogously be applied here also in our present context.

[7] On this cf. also K. Rahner, 'A Small Fragment on the Collective Finding of Truth', *Theological Investigations* VI (London and Baltimore, 1969), pp. 82–88.

[8] cf. the Decree on Ecumenism, 'Unitatis Redintegratio', Nos. 4, 9, 11, 13, 14, 18, 19, 21, 22, 23, and further the Decree on the Apostolate of the Laity, 'Apostolicam Actuositatem', Nos. 17, 31.

[9] On current ecumenical theology's interpretation of itself cf. G. Thils, *La Théologie oecuménique* (Louvain, 1960). cf. also n. 5.

old the word 'dialogue', and even the element of dialogue in human life may be, still it is, after all, only in very recent times that this word has come to be a key word standing for the manner in which discussion between Christians belonging to separate Churches is meant to be conducted. What this word means is made plain in No. 9 of the Decree on Ecumenism, where it is stated that an attitude of 'par cum pari agere' is required of all in ecumenical discussion. Ecumenical theology is intended to be a theology of open dialogue between those who have equal rights. But can theology really want this to be the case above all among Catholic Christians? Can it be this? The attitude of anxiety and mistrust with which non-Catholic Christians often encounter their Catholic partner in ecumenical meetings must not be straightway condemned as unjustified. It is not to be eliminated even when the Catholic Church declares that according to her understanding too the ecumenical movement and work, and thereby (as we may add) ecumenical theology as such (among Catholics) should not be accompanied by the intention of winning over individual converts to the Catholic Church.[10] The real and ultimate ground of this mistrust lies far deeper, and must clearly be recognized if the nature of ecumenical theology as a 'dialogue theology' is rightly to be understood.

If by dialogue we understand nothing else than the imparting of our own respective opinions to one another, as a mere interchange of information, then naturally no problem exists. Even in that case it may still remain obscure whether in such an interchange of information *theological* opinions really are made comprehensible, since the task of understanding them is certainly more difficult than in an interchange of information, e.g. on economic views and enterprises. Surely it is not absurd from the outset to hazard the thesis that in the sphere of faith and theology the opinion of the other party will be understood only when it too is accepted as having been fully assimilated as one's own and accepted as one's own faith. For there are certainly truths the meaning of which is really borne in upon us only in the very act of giving our practical assent to them, and in positively acting upon them so that to understand their meaning and to give our practical and living assent to them are acts that cannot be separated one from another.

But if for the moment we abstract from this question, and presuppose, at least provisionally, that we can to some extent abstract from it, then ecumenical theology, understood as an interchange of information with regard to the opinions of the partners to the dialogue, raises no initial difficulty. One supplies information, as far as possible exhaustively, with

[10] cf. the Decree on Ecumenism, 'Unitatis Redintegratio', No. 4.

regard to one's theological ideas. Each party apprehends the meaning of this information as supplied by the other just as in other contexts too we experience and understand the opinion of another without thereby being brought to share it. But manifestly ecumenical theology cannot be confined to this interchange of information however much this may constitute the initial stage in it, and however important it may be for it not to be aimed at gaining individual converts for one's own Church. Theology has to do with truth. It is not intended merely to inform but rather to communicate truth – truth which makes valid claims upon the other party and therefore can and should be communicated by the informant only in such a way that he identifies himself with this claim to truth. One may think as one will about the nature of truth, the nature of theoretical reasoning, the nature of truth in the context of faith, truth as universal and as particular. Evidently theological dialogue too is not intended merely to communicate information to the other party of what one thinks oneself, but rather to speak to him that truth which is intended to lay claims upon him. If we were unwilling to attribute this purpose to ecumenical dialogue, then it would be degraded into a mere sociological phenomenon in which mutual information was supplied with regard to attitudes and opinions on either side because this is necessary in order to live peaceably together, and in this every kind of opinion and attitude would at basis be simply a psychological fact on the same level and of the same importance as all the rest, independently of any question of truth. Even if someone feels compelled to hold the view that he cannot regard ecumenical dialogue as consisting in what has just been described, and even if, in view of the account given of themselves by specific theologies, he might legitimately raise the question whether these can attribute the purpose we have mentioned to ecumenical dialogue, we would still have to make two points in reply to his question. First, the mutual presuppositions of ecumenical dialogue are such that they could only have a social significance. For how could the opinion of another be of interest to me if it were not from the outset claiming to be or to become my truth quite apart from the fact that it is also a social reality which plays its part in determining my sphere of existence. Further, the Catholic Christian at least, so far as his theology is concerned, cannot surrender this claim to truth in ecumenical dialogue according to his understanding of his faith. The Protestant partner to the dialogue, therefore, will take this attitude and this purpose into account and ask himself whether he believes that he is open to conduct a dialogue with a partner of this kind to the discussion.

There is yet another way of throwing light upon the problems which

ecumenical dialogue entails. Dialogue presupposes a pluralism of attitudes, convictions and aims in the partners to the discussion. Where there
is complete identity of opinion dialogue, at least in the dimension of
theoretical reasoning, is superfluous to scientific investigations, and therefore to speculative theology too even at the purely informative level. Now
in this pluralism there are on the one hand opinions which are *de facto*
particular and, moreover, are not intended to be anything more than this.
On the other hand, however, there are opinions, the outcome of theoretical
reasoning, which, while they certainly cannot be shared by all, are still put
forward with the theoretical claim and the practical aim of winning over
all as their adherents. That opinion which is in principle and of its very
nature particular implies at most the theoretical problem of whether such
a particularist attitude, the holding of an 'opinion only for myself' is,
in specific cases, reasonable in the very nature of opinion, i.e. whether this
'modesty' does not constitute a gradual death of the opinion of all. For
properly speaking, as emanating wholly from the personal inclinations
of the individuals concerned it is no longer really relevant even to those
to whom it is communicated. And in practice the only problem which is
recognized in this particularism is that of how to achieve a 'technical'
harmonization and mutual co-operation between the parties involved,
in order that such basically particularist opinions can be given concrete
application at the social level and within the activities of one and the same
social group. The real problem of pluralism of opinions only arises at that
point at which *de facto* particular convictions have in principle and of their
very nature to lay claim to a universal validity. They must do this unless
they are willing to surrender their own nature. For example: a society of
entomologists and a society of aquarium enthusiasts uphold a particular
opinion with regard to the significance of what they are doing. But they
do not claim that all must share their opinion. In contrast to this Christianity, a Christian confession (at least if it understands its own significance
in the classic sense), and the ideology of a militant dialectical materialism
are conscious of being (provided they do not deny their own nature)
endowed with gifts and with a vocation which gives them a special claim
to truth and a mission which is directed to all. For what they represent
is a radically universal conviction, a comprehensive view of the meaning
of the cosmos or (if we wish to phrase it so) a faith. To teach that it is in
principle impossible for there to be any system of beliefs having such a
universal claim, and that these are from the outset always, and in every
case false, would itself in turn constitute such a universal opinion with
practical consequences for all.

Let us take then as our starting-point the fact that Christianity too, as it exists in the specifically confessional form which it has acquired, and as the outcome of a process of ecclesiastical institutionalization, is indeed *de facto* a particularist phenomenon, yet in terms of its radical understanding of itself and the claim it makes, a universal conviction with a claim to truth directed to all. Now if this is the case, then the problem arises of whether it is still possible at all to conduct an ecumenical dialogue with this as our premiss, even when it is only one of the partners to the dialogue (in other words the Catholic one at least) who conducts the dialogue with such a claim that his convictions have this universal validity.[11] The principle that an ecumenical dialogue must be conducted without force is clear, and is not in question here even though this renunciation of every form of force has not always been so self-evident, as a glance at the history of western Christianity reveals. But this still does not provide any solution to the question of whether a real possibility of dialogue exists between those who hold convictions of which at least one (if not both) claims to be absolute, i.e., in our case, demands to be affirmed with an absolute assent of faith such that it involves salvation – something which we must not lose at any cost. The basic reason why the earlier controversial theology was so sharp is that it involved this assertion of the absolute value of one's own convictions. And while we can no longer in the least enter into the mentality which made the earlier controversial theology so hard and bitter, still we must begin by asking ourselves whether this lack of understanding on the part of us of today is not conditioned by a relativism deriving from our liberalism, an attitude in which we are quite incapable of understanding what an absolute assent of faith, acquiring a life-and-death importance for us, can signify for the individual's own personal creed as that which alone brings salvation. But can one whose faith is of this kind really enter into any open dialogue, or with such an attitude can he merely be willing to instruct, to bear witness, and to convince, insofar as he is capable at all of advancing beyond the stage of merely supplying information? This is a serious question. At this point we leave it open because probably we shall be in a better position to answer it when we have considered that which constitutes the ultimate theological basis of ecumenical theology.

[11] On this cf. also K. Rahner, 'Reflections on Dialogue within a Pluralistic Society', *Theological Investigations* VI (London and Baltimore, 1969), pp. 31–42; *idem*, 'Dialogue in the Church', Theological Investigations VIII (London and New York), pp. 103–125.

The question I have posed is what constitutes the ultimate basis of ecumenical theology. My answer to this question will initially take the form of a brief thesis which I shall then attempt to explain more precisely. The thesis runs as follows: the ultimate basis of ecumenical theology is that unity, apprehended in hope, which consists in a belief in justifying grace, a belief which, even though in its theological formulation and its explicitation in credal form it is still in process of being arrived at, is nevertheless already in existence as one and the same belief in both of the parties involved in ecumenical theology.

Now what is meant by this thesis in *more precise* terms? First it must be unreservedly conceded that for ecumenical dialogue and ecumenical theology in the form in which it appears today a liberal humanism, with its defence of freedom of opinion and faith within a pluralistic society, has been, and still is, the occasion and the context without which the pursuit of ecumenical theology as it *de facto* exists today is inconceivable. This historical necessity for this liberalism, for the relationship which the separated Christians of today have achieved with one another, does not need to be denied, and must not be glossed over. Certain further observations must be made on this point. This liberalism, however, is hardly the true ground, the ultimate *fons et origo*, of the ability which the separated parties have of conducting a dialogue today. So we must not confuse the essential basis for a given phenomenon with the historical situation in which such an essential basis becomes effective. Now what is the true and effective basis for ecumenical dialogue such that it is constitutive of its essential nature? It is to this question that the thesis formulated above is attempting to supply an answer. When we conduct an ecumenical dialogue, or pursue ecumenical theology with one another despite the fact of our being divided among many Churches, then the ultimate necessary condition which we presuppose for this is that each of us recognizes the others as Christians. But what does this mean in precise and genuinely theological terms? Certainly it does not merely mean that we accept and acknowledge the fact that the other partner to the dialogue regards himself as a Christian. Nor does it merely mean that we mutually credit one another with the fact of all having validly been baptized – provided we are thinking of baptism here first and foremost in its empirical reality as an external fact of cult. Nor does it merely mean that in spite of all the differences between us with regard to the creed we can establish as a matter of empirical fact that there is agreement between us on certain of our tenets, in the sense, for instance, that is implied in the basic formula of the World Council of Churches. What it means, rather, is that we are convinced as a matter of hope, if not of knowledge at the explicit and theoretical level, that the partners to the dialogue on either side live in the grace of God, that they are truly justified by the Holy Pneuma of God and are sharers in the divine nature.

Now there have been ages in which this conviction, in which we mutually recognize in hope the real and triumphant presence of God's grace in one another, has not been felt with the force of a self-evident truth. When for instance Augustine upholds the validity of baptism among 'heretics' against Cyprian and the Donatists, and even outside the 'Catholic' sphere, he is certainly not including in this doctrine of his the conviction that this baptism actually communicates to the baptized individual an effective forgiveness of his sins and the sanctifying Spirit of God. Probably, indeed, right down to the age of the Enlightenment, the prevailing opinion on both sides has been that in the case of the heretic (and both parties have mutually regarded each other as such) it is to be presumed that his heresy must be accounted as guilt, and therefore in controversial discussions each side must presume that the other has not lived in God's grace. It may be that it was not until the eighteenth century that this question was the subject of any close thought. Distinctions may have been drawn between the educated and uneducated, and there may have been a tendency to attribute 'bona fides' to the latter more than to the former. It may be that the interpretation of one's opponent from the other confession as depicted above may not always and everywhere have been raised to the level of an explicit thesis. Nevertheless men lived and acted upon the basic feeling that their opponents could not be living in God's grace as justified and sanctified when nevertheless with regard to the faith that is saving, and without which (according to the Epistle to the Hebrews) man cannot be pleasing to God, they deviated in certain vital points from one's own convictions of faith, points which one regarded either as at least belonging absolutely to one's own faith or even (as in the case of the 'sola fide' doctrine) as the heart and centre of that faith.

Today, no doubt, the situation is different. This is a point which I do not really need to substantiate where Protestant Christians are concerned, especially since if I were to do so I should have to raise the question of whether this attribution of a state of justification to my partner in the dialogue who is confessionally separated from me derived from a liberal and relativist interpretation of my own creed, or whether it exists side by side with, and is to be regarded as reconcilable with, the conviction of the absolute truth and universal claims of my own creed. But for all this I believe that the Protestant partner to the dialogue will not only credit the Catholic one in some sense with 'bona fides' and a genuine conviction at the human level, but also accept that the grace of Christ permeates the innermost roots of his being. And conversely the Catholic will do the same. The Second Vatican Council explicitly teaches that the Protestant Christian too is one who has received grace and justification provided he has not in any way sinfully denied God. The Council recognizes just as unequivocally that such an interior state of grace on the part of the Evangelical Christian can obviously be present even in those cases in which he decisively rejects specific elements in the teaching of the Roman Catholic Church, following in this the claim of his own conscience with regard to truth, since according to his belief they are irreconcilable with true Christianity. This conviction may be utterly obvious from the standpoint of a mere tolerant humanism. But in those cases in which the individual concerned is at the same time convinced of the salvific meaning of his own specific creed, a creed that differs decisively from that of another (and this applies at least to the manner in which Roman Catholic believers think of their faith) this conviction is anything but self-evident, and it is only very gradually, and with great efforts, that it has been brought to maturity in this Church's understanding of her own faith, to the point where it has been given clear expression in the Second Vatican Council. Nevertheless this conviction does now exist on the Catholic side as well.

At this stage we do not need to discuss in any direct sense the question of how the significance of the Catholic creed, salvific and necessary to salvation as it is according to the Catholic understanding of faith, can be reconciled with the simultaneous conviction that one who does not share this faith still does have salvation. The question that we have to ask here is simply what this conviction implies on both sides with regard to the possibility of ecumenical dialogue and ecumenical theology, and to this question the thesis formulated above does supply an answer. This dialogue is possible because, despite the differences in our respective creeds in terms of objective formulation and verbal expression (in other words despite the differences of faith which exist between us in this sense) there is, nevertheless, a unity of faith such that we not only seek it but actually mutually concede it as already present and given in one another, because each of us is aware of the other as believing, hoping, and loving in the power of the Spirit of God possessing us, without whom there can be no belief and with whom there can be no unbelief. This statement naturally forces us to a decision as to what true faith really means. In this we must neither overlook nor neglect the importance of the differences between the forms of words in which our respective creeds are expressed. At the same time, however, each side must credit the other with the presence of the divine Spirit of unity, together with the truth of God, enlightenment and faith. Each of us must recognize in the other the interior witness of the Holy Spirit. And if we do this, then a distinction of the kind we are suggesting here becomes inevitable if we are not simply to allow two contradictory positions to exist side by side. That which we Catholics call sanctifying grace, and that which Protestant theology calls justification and sanctification may still have as many different interpretations placed upon it as there are different theologies. Nevertheless it still remains in any case an act of God wrought upon us in his grace which truly alters us, transforming us from sinners to justified men, regardless of how we may interpret this sanctifying event of justification in more precise terms, whatever concepts we may use to express it, and however different the provenance of these concepts may be. Now precisely upon the Protestant understanding of grace, and at the same time on any truly rational Catholic ontology of grace, the reality involved here cannot be conceived of as though it had nothing to do with 'faith', or as though it could co-exist with a mere state of unbelief. Thus if each of us credits the other with justifying grace, then we also credit one another with a real and true faith, and one which we may certainly not regard as merely empty in terms of the formative impact which it has upon our lives in the concrete, in other words as mere credulousness. Now if we credit one another mutually with true faith in this way, and if at the same time we take due cognizance of the very radical differences between the interpretations of faith put forward by the various Churches to the extent that this faith is objectified in conceptual and verbal terms, then there must be a faith with which we mutually credit one another as true, and yet which is different from this faith that is given objective expression in concepts and words.

This conclusion cannot be evaded merely by saying that even at the level of conceptual and verbal objectification of the content of faith there are, after all, certain fundamental points which all hold in common, which thereby ensure that there shall be one and the same faith common to all despite other secondary points of faith on which these Christians differ. For in the first place it is in fact questionable whether such common principles really are to be found held in common by all Christians. It is questionable whether if there are such, there is sufficient common understanding of what they mean – over and above the mere verbal formulations which are common to all – and whether they have not been so much altered by the further theological statements which have been made and which are opposed to one another that it is no longer possible to speak of any real or effective unity of mind with regard to these more fundamental principles. And finally it may be questioned whether even in those cases in which – as with the Catholics – other points of faith are adhered to with the absolute assent of faith even though they are disputed by other confessions, these do not so intrinsically influence and modify those other points too which seem to be held in common (at least supposing that they are held with this absolute assent of faith) that we can no longer speak of any real fundamentally common mind with regard to the Christian creed. The questionableness of all these points is such that one is certainly forced to conclude that the oneness of mind that is postulated with regard to one and same true faith cannot consist – or at least cannot consist exclusively – in agreeing upon certain fundamental Christian principles (as for instance after the pattern of the basic formula of the World Council of Churches).

The postulate arrived at in this way of one and the same true faith held in common by all (despite the fact that the Christians involved differ from one another in the verbal expressions of their faith in their creed) is not an entity of which man is incapable of forming any idea merely on the grounds that manifestly it must be something that exists beneath and beyond any dogmatic principles which can be formulated in conceptual terms. When we Christians, projecting our ideas beyond the confessional boundaries, credit one another with the presence of the Holy Spirit of grace, then manifestly what we are saying is, after all, that the ultimate and most interior 'testimonium spiritus' is present in all, or at least must be presumed to be so present, that all of us are endowed with the 'illustratio et inspiratio' of the Spirit (concepts with which tradition throws light upon the movements of grace), with the wordless groanings and utterances of 'Abba' of the Spirit within the depths of our hearts, with the anointing of the Spirit spoken of by John which instructs us – all this is present even though this innermost reality of the Spirit and faith is objectified and interpreted differently in terms of words and ideas between the individual confessions. Thus we still accept that in any anthropology of man as spiritual and free which is capable of looking rather deeper into him a difference always prevails (and one which can never adequately be overcome or transcended) between two factors in man's consciousness of himself: on the one hand an ultimate self-possession of the subject as free, i.e. a presence to himself which is never consciously explicated, a self-understanding on man's part which is never fully reflected upon; on the other man's objectified awareness of himself, his subjectivity and his capacity for free decision as objectified to himself.[12] Now if this is true then the postulate we have put forward on theological grounds of a true faith held in common between separated Christians through and beyond that faith which can be objectified in concepts and words does not signify something of which man himself is totally incapable of forming any idea. All of us 'know' in the Spirit of God something more simple, more true, and more real than that which we are capable of knowing and expressing in the dimension of our theological concepts.[13]

At this point we must, of course, pass over the question of why faith in the form in which it is objectified in conceptual terms is not rendered meaningless by a true faith of this kind present in the midst of our lives in the power of the Spirit of God himself, yet pre-conceptual in form.[14] This faith which we hold in common at the heart and centre of our lives through the grace of God is the same true faith in all and incapable of deceiving. And it constitutes the true basis and the ultimate prior condition for ecumenical dialogue and an ecumenical theology. Once we recognize it as the basis and prior condition for such dialogue and theology in this sense then, even when one or both parties to the ecumenical dialogue have given their absolute assent of faith to the particular propositions of faith which they uphold, the ecumenical dialogue can never be the sort of discussion in which one or both sides seeks to communicate purely *ab*

[12] On this distinction cf. J. B. Metz, 'Befindlichkeit', *LTK* II (2nd ed. 1958), 102–104.

[13] On the distinction between the reality of faith and faith as consciously reflected upon cf. K. Rahner, 'Reflections on the Experience of Grace', *Theological Investigations* III (London and Baltimore, 1967), pp. 86–90; *idem*, 'Theology in the New Testament', *Theological Investigations* V (London and Baltimore, 1966), pp. 23–41; *idem*, 'What is a Dogmatic Statement ?', *ibid.*, pp. 42–66; *idem*, 'Universal Salvific Will of God: General', *Sacramentum Mundi* V (New York/London, 1969) pp. 405–409 *idem*, 'Heresies in the Church Today?', *Theological Investigations* XII.

[14] This question is also to be met with in a different form. It recurs once more in the distinction which is drawn between 'personal' and sacramental devotion, private and liturgical prayer, personal sacrifices and the sacrifice of the Mass, existential and essential morality, sacramental and extra-sacramental justification, charism and institution, the act of faith and dogma, particular and universal revelation, personal and universal saving history, Church and world, *and* also in a theological context it is once more a particular form of the general problems involved in the relationship between transcendentality and the 'this worldly' categories of being in human life in general. Again it plays a central part with regard to the possibility of ecumenical discussion. On the positive function of the institutional factor cf. amongst others K. Rahner, 'Dialogue in the Church', *Theological Investigations* X (London and New York, 1973), pp. 103–121 *idem*, 'Die neue Kirchlichkeit der Theologie', *Gnade als Freiheit* (Freiburg, 1968), pp. 131–143.

externo to the other parties to the discussion at any given time some doctrinal point which those other parties have so far simply failed to recognize or which is rejected as an erroneous belief. Ecumenical discussion consists rather in the attempt through dialogue to render intelligible to the other parties the fact that what is being expressed to them in conceptual terms is simply a more correct, a fuller and a more precise expression of something which they have already apprehended as their own faith through the Spirit in the ultimate depths of their lives as already justified, and which they have laid hold of as their own truth.[15]

On this basis an answer can also be given to the question which we have posed but left unanswered so far in section II, the question namely of why an ecumenical dialogue is still possible even without any liberalizing prior assumptions, i.e. even when an absolute assent of faith has been given to a controversial proposition of faith on the part of one or both parties. Even under these conditions ecumenical dialogue can be carried on as open to further decisions and results. For even an absolute assent of faith on the part of one party to an article of belief that is controversial can and must presuppose the difference we have indicated between faith that is absolutely basic on the one hand and faith as objectified in words and concepts on the other. Such an absolute assent of faith, therefore, is perfectly compatible with the recognition that even a true objectification of the faith that is absolute and basic never adequately or fully expresses this, so that it is always open to further and fuller expression. For this reason precisely this growing understanding of ourselves and of our own faith as objectified

---

[15] On this cf. also the discussion of anonymous or unacknowledged Christians as a whole. In this connection cf. especially 'Anonymous Christianity and the Missionary Task of the Church', *Theological Investigations* XII. The critical evaluations of my interpretation [cf. H. U. von Balthasar, *Cordula oder der Ernstfall* (Einsiedeln, 1966), pp. 85–97 or (2nd ed. 1967), pp. 84–96; L. Elders, 'Die Taufe der Weltreligionen', *ThGl* 65 (1965), pp. 124–131; H. van Straelen, *The Catholic Encounter with World Religions* (London, 1966): H. Kruse, 'Die "anonymen Christen" exegetisch gesehen', *MThZ* 18 (1967), pp. 2–29; E. Biser, 'Ausgegrenzt und eingewiesen', *MThZ* 19 (1968), pp. 1–16, esp. 7 f.]. simply overlook the fact that this 'Christianhood' of man, which is already present as a concomitant of grace, is precisely the condition for any proclamation of truth on the part of the Church, while conversely this grace itself only achieves its full consummation and becomes fully apprehensible as a historical phenomenon when it achieves and sustains an explicitly Christian creed, and a state in which it is embodied in the social life of the Church. Furthermore such an authority as Balthasar himself puts forward the very same doctrine as that which he disputes in my interpretation. cf. *idem, Cordula* (2nd ed. 1967), p. 95; *idem, Wer ist ein Christ?* (Einsiedeln, 1966), p. 100; *idem*, 'Spiritus Creator', *Skizzen zur Theologie* III (Einsiedeln, 1967), pp. 160 ff., 318 ff.

in concepts (even when these concepts are correct) can be promoted in an open dialogue by our partner in the discussion even though heterodox. Even when an absolute assent of faith has been given, this need not mean that the party to the dialogue must either be able to indoctrinate his partner through the propositions which he firmly upholds without any alteration, or else, if he cannot succeed in this, the dialogue must again and again be broken off without result, or be degraded to the level of a mere mutual interchange of information between the two sides with regard to their respective beliefs. Even one entering into dialogue when he has already given his absolute assent of faith to controversial articles of this kind can in a true sense learn from his partner in the discussion and thus conduct a dialogue that is open and that can yield fresh insights and results.

IV

We may permit ourselves to draw yet another conclusion from what has been said above with regard to ecumenical theology, one which is for the most part overlooked in ecumenical dialogue. We have seen that a necessary prior condition for this dialogue is the distinction that must be drawn between that basic and ultimate faith which is present in the midst of our lives through the Spirit of God on the one hand and that faith of the Church on other which is expressed in objective concepts. At the same time we must recognize that what is being treated of here is an ecumenical dialogue between Churches whose faith must necessarily be formulated in concepts for sociological reasons. Now if we recognize this then those participating in the ecumenical dialogue must take into account the fact that at least on the Catholic side it is circumscribed by certain official definitions the terms of which are laid down by the Church's *magisterium*.[16] For Catholics these are indeed binding, but nevertheless different in quality from the absolute truths to which an absolute assent of faith has to be given.

The parties to the discussion need to bear in mind that in an official and conscious sense at least on the Catholic side and, it may be, in an unconscious sense, and one that is merely conditioned by the facts of history on all sides, there are certain theological definitions which on the one hand are present and on the other are nothing more than (however

[16] On this cf. J. Feiner and M. Löhrer, edd., *Mysterium Salutis* I (Einsiedeln, 1965), pp. 693–696 and in the present volume the chapter entitled 'Pluralism in Theology and the Unity of the Creed in the Church', pp. 3–23.

reasonable and perhaps necessary they may be in terms of religious sociology) definitions which are to some extent conventional in character.
Now if we were to recognize this then, it may be presumed, ecumenical
dialogue could often be conducted more freely and with a greater hope
of being fruitful. Words such as 'person' and 'nature' in christology,
'*original* sin' in the theology of sin, 'transubstantiation' in the doctrine
of the Eucharist, 'infusion', 'habitus', 'increase of merit' etc. in the doctrine
of justification certainly do point to a reality of faith and of binding conviction. But they also always imply the influence of certain linguistic
conventions and language in the forming of definitions within a given
confession which are not necessary and could in principle be altered without any surrender of what is really being expressed in such definitions.
If, for instance, someone put forward the proposition (as Emil Brunner
has) that there is no such thing as original sin then this need not necessarily imply for a Catholic understanding of faith that something heretical
in the true sense is being expressed. Certainly all that would initially be
taking place in such a case is that a particular ecclesiastical definition, in
some sense binding for Catholics, would be being rejected. For the question would in fact still remain completely open as to whether the rejection
of the term 'original sin' really entailed a rejection of the reality signified
by and under the term original sin in a Tridentine formulation of a proposition of faith.

Let us pay due heed, therefore, to the difference which has been explained above between the two levels of faith. And let us further consider
that the formulations of Catholic dogma on the part of the authorities of
the Catholic Church always involve a concealed element of a definition in
linguistic terms addressed to that particular community even when there
has been no real conscious reflection upon this fact. Finally let us not lose
sight of the fact that every theological expression, however acute and
profound it may be, is, nevertheless, measured by the reality to which it
points, inadequate (which is not the same thing as false) to express this.
Now if we recognize all these factors then we must take into account
the possibility that in ecumenical dialogue what we are disagreeing about
is not the truths and realities signified but simply the words in which they
are expressed. We should consider that it is only rarely that the true subject of a dialogue of this kind is the question of whether the parties
involved can advance beyond that unity which is already in principle
achieved with regard to the actual matter concerned so as to arrive at a
common definition. This question, therefore, is not so devoid of hope,
because Catholic theology too is aware that concepts of this kind which

have been officially laid down in the Catholic Church and the definitions thereby produced are in need of explanation and interpretation, and that obviously this can be achieved only through the use of different words and concepts. This means that even ideas and definitions of this kind which have been produced by the official Church are not thereby exempted (by the fact of having an official status of this kind) from the process of historical development.

v

I believe that those involved in working out a theology in the form of an ecumenical dialogue should all in common have the courage and, moreover, today actually do have the common task of pronouncing a common 'No', under certain circumstances, to real heresies, for probably such heresies are emerging today in all the Christian Churches, albeit with varying degrees of clarity, and are threatening the gospel of Christ.

Certainly in the individual Churches there can be a pluralism of theologies without prejudice to the particular creed held by each.[17] Certainly this pluralism of theologies has also grown up in the Catholic Church – especially in connection with the Second Vatican Council. Certainly as a result of fresh questions, such as the Reformation period alone was not of itself sufficient to bring to the surface, the leading currents in theology today not infrequently cut across the confessional boundaries and the theologies that correspond to these. Certainly, without prejudice to an abiding question of truth, many of the old questions which were matters of controversy between the confessions have ceased to have that weight attached to them which is always subject to historical conditions and particular concrete situations, and have lost their significance in the theology of today. But in the midst of, and in spite of all this the theologians of the different Christian Churches who are conscious of their responsibility to uphold the gospel and the Christian faith whole and untruncated can help and encourage one another in certain circumstances to pronounce an unambiguous 'No', a 'damnamus' (as for instance the Confessing Church in Germany did with regard to the teaching of the German Christians within the Evangelical Church) against heresies which also threaten the stock of basic doctrines of the Christian faith which all hold in common.

Of course these different theologies, as upheld in the individual

[17] On this cf. also 'Perspectives for the Future of the Church', *Theological Investigations* XII.

Churches, all have to begin by helping one another mutually within the framework of an ecumenical theology to distinguish in such new questions and doctrines between that which on the one hand constitutes a justified and perhaps necessary expression of Christian faith, and so genuine progress in the history of dogma or theology, and on the other that which for any genuine Christian and theologian, and for any genuinely Christian Church, must uncompromisingly be accounted as heresy. Certainly such a distinction will require consideration, prudence, restraint, patience, and finally time. Obviously in an ecumenical discussion the theologians of the Christian Churches can be of assistance to one another in this discerning of the spirits, and under certain circumstances too can exhort one another to prudence and tolerance in the face of such new currents in theology. In this connection it is in fact interesting that, for instance, such a theologian as Karl Barth believes that he has discovered in not a few representatives of contemporary Catholic theology in Germany an excessively favourable attitude and leaning towards the school of Bultmann, that in fact even Bultmann himself confirms that there is such an understanding among these Catholic theologians, and considers that it is greater among them than on the right wing of German Protestant theology. But what I am speaking of here is rather that over and above all this, however necessary and urgent it may be, the theologians of the different Churches should work together in ecumenical collaboration to the point where they can define unambiguous boundaries upheld by all towards attitudes and doctrines which are simply no longer Christian at all, although their practitioners still claim a right to exist within the Churches and are unwilling of their own volition to leave the Churches. So long as the Churches are in a state of pilgrimage in this world they can only pronounce their assent to the gospel and no less to the Deutero-Pauline Epistles and the First Epistle of John if they also have the courage to pronounce their dissent. An ecumenical theology could make it easier for the theologies in the different Churches to achieve that clarity of insight and that courage to arrive at a decision at the appropriate point and in the appropriate manner, and with sufficient practical down-to-earth effectiveness within the Churches, actually to pronounce a 'No' to false interpretations or invalidations of the Christian message. Certainly in doing this they would not be depriving the leaders of the various Churches of their proper task and function. Rather they would be lightening this task and function and giving it a practical effectiveness within the communities. An act of dissent of this kind, made in common by all, even if it entailed a loss of some or of many who would thereupon leave the Churches, could also promote the aims of the ecumenical movement, the unity of the Churches, because in this way the least that would be achieved (this is a point to which we shall be returning at a later stage) would be that the unity between the Churches in the fundamentals of the Christian creed would already be made clearer here and now.

This demand should not be taken as an incitement for ecumenical theology to become a sort of heresy hunt and persecution on the part of the united Christian community. But the Churches must not be degraded to mere umbrella organizations, supplying, by the historical conditions under which they have grown up, a specious appearance of Christianity within which the upholders of absolutely any opinion, however arbitrary, can be gathered. It must not be thought that that principle which has its basis in Christianity, namely of absolute freedom of conscience and tolerance, should actually be pressed so far as to include absolute freedom for any kind of opinion within the Church so long as its upholder does not wish to leave that Church of his own volition. If we were to fall into this error then an ecumenical theology likewise would be degraded into a mere conversation between the upholders of any kind of opinions, and the Churches would only survive as separate entities from one another at the organizational level, no longer at the level of theology and creed. And ecumenical theology would have lost its purpose, because in fact that purpose would, at basis, long since have been achieved. Or, to put it better, it would have vanished. The ecumenical movement would no longer have any content in terms of faith and theology, it would only still continue to survive in the discussions of the official functionaries of the various Churches as to what better arrangements might be made between the Churches in terms of religious organization, or even how they might amalgamate. And the only function which the ecumenical movement could have beyond this would consist in a mutual acclimatization process in which the points of dissimilarity due to psychological and historical conditions, but ultimately speaking theologically irrelevant between the Christians of different confessions, would be smoothed out.

Now if ecumenical theology and the ecumenical movement is to be something more than this, then the Churches must have, and must maintain, a substantial nucelus of beliefs as the necessary prior condition for this 'something more' regardless of whether this substantial nucleus is interpreted more in terms of the nature of Christianity, its doctrines, its application in human life, its concrete realization, or in some other way. This substantial nucleus of Christian faith, however it is conceived of, is certainly not identical with that which is present in every upright and human individual in the dimension of his conscious thought and sense of social responsibility. Otherwise the opinion might be upheld that the Christian Churches as such have long since absolutely outlived their usefulness and should be transformed as quickly as possible into a humanist and democratic society purely secular and a-religious in character, and only having the function of providing a field of intercommunication between individuals. If, on the other hand, there is a genuine substantial nucleus of Christian faith of the kind we have referred to, then certainly it will, in the end, be the task of an ecumenical theology to support the different theologies and Churches even as separate from one another in upholding this substantial nucleus.

VI

In what follows a confrontation will be attempted between ecumenical theology and the situation in terms of religious sociology[18] in which all Churches find themselves today.

The question of truth as between the separated Christian creeds is certainly the concern of ecumenical theology as such. We can say this even while not overlooking the fact that the separated theologies are disunited not only on the question of whether the statements made by any given theology are true or false, but also on the question of what truth and error mean at all in this context. This latter point is in fact strikingly illustrated by the very fact that in the last few decades the focus of interest has been transferred (at least in Protestant theology) to the question of hermeneutics. At the same time, however, this does nothing in the last analysis to alter the fact that ecumenical theology consists of a dialogue with regard to the truth or erroneousness of propositions which are expressed in the separate Christian confessions.

But however seriously ecumenical theology may be taking what is certainly its legitimate task in this sense, it is still insufficiently aware of the situation in which it is pursuing its activities in terms of religious sociology. What then was the position of the earlier controversial theology with regard to the situation in the sociology of religion in which it was pursued? It consisted of a discussion, more or less irenic or controversial,

---

[18] On this situation cf. K. Rahner and N. Greinacher, 'Die Gegenwart der Kirche. Theologische Analyse der Gegenwart als Situation des Selbstovllzugs der Kirche', *Handbuch der Pastoraltheologie* II/1 (Freiburg, 1966), pp. 178–276. Further, N. Greinacher, *Die Kirche in der städtischen Gesellschaft* (Mainz, 1956) esp. pp. 293–369; A. Jansen, *Kirche in der Grossstadt* (Freiburg, 1969).

between theologians and churchmen of the separated Churches who, so far as their theological convictions were concerned, justifiably felt themselves to be the legitimate spokesmen and representatives of their Churches. Now the reason why they were able to feel themselves to be the representatives and spokesmen of the Church community standing behind them in this way was on the one hand that this Church community, to the extent that it had any theological opinion at all, by and large neither could have, nor did have, sociologically speaking, any other opinion whatsoever than that of these representatives and spokesmen who were authorized as such even as a matter of civic and state appointment, and because, moreover, it was the prerogative of these spokesmen and representatives to an extent which was certainly not inconsiderable, to impart this distinctive confessional creed of theirs to this Church community, and so also *de facto* to inculcate a single homogeneous confessional awareness with a specific stamp of its own in the Church concerned. In this sense the Evangelical Churches too were themselves, right down to the end of the nineteenth century, clerically dominated Churches. And they were this despite their avowed belief in the universal priesthood, despite the sectarian and revivalist movements which arose again and again from within the rank and file, and despite notable differences of opinion between the Evangelical Churches and between their theological representatives themselves. In other words a distinct formal group, separated sociologically and institutionally from the rest, was in respect both of its claims and its effective influence, the channel for the particular Church community concerned in every detail of its life, and, moreover, was in a position really to be this. This group could speak with the other Churches as representative of the people belonging to its Church in discussions either in controversial theology or in the more irenical ecumenical theology. Today, however, this situation manifestly no longer exists, a point which we shall shortly have to develop in somewhat greater detail. Yet it is still tacitly and unreflectingly assumed to exist because in fact even today this ecumenical theology is *de facto* still engaged in almost exclusively by such churchmen and theologians although these have a quite different relationship towards the confessional creed which has been handed down to them. In fact they still act as the representatives of their Churches in ecumenical theology even in those cases in which they adopt an extremely critical attitude towards the creed of their Church, while still acknowledging it and taking it seriously and still remaining constantly under its influence, and so still constantly feeling themselves at variance with the creed of any other Church.

But what is the real situation today in which ecumenical theology is engaged in by these theologians and churchmen? If we want to express it in terms of popular sociology, and without any claims to religious sociology in the specialist sense,[19] then we might perhaps state it somewhat as follows: For historical reasons a series of human groups is living, each under the umbrella of a specific religious organization, as a so-called Church community. Each of these organizations, religiously separated as it is from the rest, has a 'unifying constitution' recognized as more or less binding and called its creed. This 'unifying constitution' in its specifically distinct character, and its differences from other Christian and religious organizations, is, however, in practice known only to the functionaries and specialist theologians of the organization concerned, while the actual people belonging to that Church remain, to a very large extent, ignorant of it. But if and to the extent that the actual people of that Church recognize and assert that their religious organization is separated from the rest in this way, and feel that it is different from, and must reject the other religious organizations as alien to it, this is in very large measure due to historical, cultural, psychological and institutional factors which, precisely according to the agreed judgement of the functionaries and theologians, are not such as to justify a division of the Churches at all. An example of this is the external differences in forms of worship, in religious usages, differences of a cultural kind etc. What a Church community of this kind *de facto* derives from its particular Church is to a large extent common to all Christians: belief in God as providing the assurance and goal of the moral order, hope in the forgiveness of sins, acknowledgment of Jesus Christ as the mediator of salvation in which it is recognized (though perhaps only vaguely) that he has this function in some sense, prayer for, and hope in eternal life. If we may permit ourselves a general estimate in terms of religious sociology which is of course to some extent rough and ready, we may say that the different Church communities are not aware, or are hardly aware of the official and institutional reasons for the separation between the Churches, and that the real and *de facto* reasons at the level of the sociology of religions for the separation between the Churches are to a very large extent theologically and institutionally irrelevant. It is in fact only in this way that we can explain, for instance, the fact that in Holland, in very recent times, Eucharistic

---

[19] For an initial orientation in this field reference may be made to J. Matthes, *Religion und Gesellschaft* (Reinbek bei Hamburg, 1967); *idem, Kirche und Gessellschaft* (Reinbek bei Hamburg, 1969) (Bibliog).

intercommunion has been taking place in many areas between communities which are institutionally separated, and even between Catholics and Protestants. This is because the Christians involved, though officially separated from one another, experience themselves as not separated at all in the creed as they *de facto* realize it to themselves. Again this is the only possible explanation of the fact that the question is already seriously being canvassed in the communities of Catholic and Protestant students in Germany of whether these communities should not be amalgamated. This situation in terms of the sociology of religions does not, of course, imply that ecumenical theology as understood by churchmen and theologians has been false in its approach, or that the real question of truth with regard to the traditional points of theological controversy have simply disappeared. But nevertheless the question must be raised of what the situation as depicted above implies for ecumenical theology. We can perhaps divide this question into two: (1) What are the implications of this situation in religious sociology as it exists today and as presumably it will become still more acute in the future in its immediate bearing upon ecumenical theology? (2) What does this situation also imply for the question of truth as such?

With regard to the *first* question we are surely compelled to assert the following principle: In the future the difference between the institutional status of the individual Churches on the one hand (which in fact also defines the attitude they ought to have and the creed which their members ought to uphold) and the *de facto* attitude, the *de facto* content of faith on the part of their members on the other, will become very much wider. This is to be expected among the Protestant Churches or, on a Catholic view, has actually already come about. Because on this view it is actually possible openly to express theological opinions such that they retain nothing or almost nothing of the traditional credal position of the particular confession concerned, and to do this quite openly in the Church without any contradiction on the part of that Church's authorities. But a widening of the difference of which we have been speaking in this way is also to be foreseen as coming in the future concrete life of the Catholic Church too as a phenomenon of religious sociology, even though, measured by this Church's understanding of herself, and in view of the greater exercise of her teaching authority it raises great theological difficulties, and even though the authorities of this Church have probably more means at their disposal than the Protestant Churches of excluding heterodox opinions from the Church, or at least of preventing them from being disseminated among the Church's members. In the Catholic Church too there are today, and presumably will be still more in the future, not a few of those to whom the doctrine of the seven sacraments, the infallibility of the pope, the veneration of the saints and of Mary, the doctrine of indulgences etc., are matters which play no part in their real religious practice and, moreover, these are to be found not only among the adherents of the new heresy of indifferentism or among those who are merely baptized and pay the Church's dues and nothing more, but also among those who actually practise Christianity in its basic elements within the Church. There are those who doubt, deny, or simply ignore in practice all these things, without thereby feeling any cause for leaving the Catholic Church; and they remain within the Church (at least so long as these differences are not unequivocally proclaimed in public in the Church) without the official authorities of the Catholic Church excluding such people 'from the official body', even though they do have the practical powers necessary for this ready to hand.

Now if, by reason of the pluralism at the intellectual and political levels which exists today and will exist in the future, by reason of the constant mutual interprenetration of Church and world, this difference remains as a constant factor for the future and is, indeed, increased and made more acute – what then? Several possibilities are conceivable. First it must presumably be expected that a not inconsiderable number of these peripheral groups within the individual Churches will, after all, separate themselves officially and in terms of civic and religious organization from the Churches to which they have traditionally belonged. The manner in which such separations will be effected will of course vary from country to country according to the particular relationship which a given Church bears in a specific country to the civic society and the state. For our present purposes, however, the manner in which such separations will take place have no further interest for us. Such a separation from the Churches at the level of religious organization need not *ipso facto* imply that the separated totally remove themselves from the sphere of spiritual influence of their Churches and of the Churches in general, or that they will become committed enemies of the Churches and of Christianity. They can perhaps very well remain as 'sympathizers' with the Churches, and indeed may in some cases find it easier to maintain a positively favourable attitude to the Churches 'from a distance', and pass in and out of the Churches through the 'open doors'. A situation may arise similar to that which prevails in missionary countries today with highly developed cultures, as for instance in Japan or India. A relatively large group of individuals may perhaps be formed in this way which, without any fixed connection with any specific Church, no longer maintains any very exclusive adherence to a specific Christian confession but takes its stand round the Christian Churches as a whole as a kind of 'Christian orientated' group; and in such a case this group may regard itself from its own standpoint more or less as a unity with differences which, so far as it is concerned are unimportant.

A further course is conceivable for events to take in the future. In the course of being transformed from national Churches to Churches of individual believers the Churches may more easily discover and apply resources of their own: the courage and also the institutionalized means, to draw clearer dividing lines between those who really believe in them, acknowledge them, and fully adhere to them in the life of the Churches themselves on the one hand, and on the other those who only still continue to regard themselves as Christians and members of a specific Church in virtue of having belonged to them as a matter of social tradition. If the individual Churches were to find within themselves the courage and resolution to draw such distinctions (we have already spoken of the contribution which ecumenical theology could make towards stimulating so bold a course), then surely the difference which we have taken as our starting-point in this consideration would once more be diminished (though admittedly only on condition that one section of those traditionally belonging to an ecclesiastical community would be separated from the Churches concerned).

What we are envisaging for the future, therefore, is a twofold process (active and passive) by which the Churches would be concentrated each upon themselves, a concentration which in fact already seems to be in process of being arrived at even now. For this seems to be the significance of what we see in the swiftly advancing process of secularization in society at the civic level in the so-called Christian countries. Now if this is true we must once more ask the question what the outcome of this should be for ecumenical theology. If this took place would we once more arrive at a situation in which the distinctive confessional form of the individual Churches would once more be asserted in terms of religious sociology, and not merely in the official theory of the churchmen, with the result that the possibility of the unification of Christianity as realized in the Churches would once more be relegated to an indefinite and remote future, and still more than at present? I believe not. This twofold process of concentration of the Churches (in German it would be possible to express this somewhat ironically as a 'Gesundschrumpfen' or 'contraction for the sake of health') could, if it was carried through successfully and not made the occasion on the part of the individual Church of each becoming an encapsulated sect closed in upon itself, have a positive significance for ecumenical theology and, on the basis of this, for the unification of the Churches, and this for two reasons. First, as a result of their greater interior unification and the greater homogeneity they thereby achieved in the awareness of their respective faiths such Churches, each in its own right, would be able to commit themselves to a binding assent to the effective findings of an ecumenical theology to a greater extent than at present, because then they would be subjects conducting an ecumenical discussion on behalf of their own real selves, and not merely through individual theologians representing them. It is important to perceive the ecumenical significance of such a process in terms of religious sociology, and ultimately of theology too, of each of the individual Churches of today concentrating upon a clear and decisive creed. And in order to do this we have in fact only to ask ourselves the simple question of from where, on this showing, the Churches, and above all the non-episcopal ones, derive their official authority, by and large, that authority in virtue of which they can commit themselves with real effectiveness to such an assent to any possible positive findings arising from ecumenical theology. Finally it is, after all, only Churches which in some sense know what beliefs are and should be held and acknowledged within their folds that can conduct on behalf of their members, and with a certain binding force, an ecumenical discussion leading to the unification of the Churches which will not be endlessly prolonged and never achieve such binding force.

What we are envisaging, then, is a concentration, at once theological and democratic, on the part of the individual Churches, a process of radicalization and a serious commitment to a binding creed, as well as the effectiveness in terms of religious sociology of such an attitude upon those members still remaining within the Churches. Now this process of concentration will not be focussed upon the traditional doctrines which divide the individual Churches because in the world as it actually exists today those who are *de facto* the members of these Churches, or who will be so in the future, have, after all, too little interest in these, and also because many such controversial doctrines from former times no longer constitute real points of conflict at all, or at least the interpretation of such controversial doctrines from former times within the individual Churches is not compelling in such a sense that they must perforce constitute in some sense an official ground for separation between them. The process of radicalization, and the serious commitment to a binding creed as developed within these individual Churches will in the future be concentrated upon far more central factors within the 'hierarchy of truths'.[20] Even if, for instance, an individual is a dedicated Catholic, one for whom the whole dogmatic teaching of his Church is felt in its totality to be binding upon his personal faith as an individual, and even when such an individual has the fullest possible interior understanding with regard to the claims which every dogma of this Church has to be truth, and with regard to the value and significance of truth in itself, without any undervaluing of the question of truth as such on existentialist, dogmatic, or utilitarian grounds, still such a one can commit himself unreservedly to the position that not every truth has in itself always, and in every age, in relation to others, the same significance and concrete effective force in the realities of human life. Let us take a small example, in itself unimportant, yet significant as illustrating the fact that even in the Catholic Church of today it can be recognized more clearly than formerly that an individual dogma can vary in the significance it has in particular sets of circumstances in human living. For this we may point to the fact that Pope Paul VI has reiterated what is more or less traditional Catholic teaching on indulgence, yet at the same time has added that every Catholic Christian enjoys the freedom of the children of God as to whether he avails himself of such indulgences or not.[21] In spite of particular examples which might be adduced, and which either seem to point in the opposite direction or really do so in fact, we can, without embarrassment, assert the following: The *de facto* situation as it exists today is such that it is not on the basis of the really classical points of controversy between the Churches that an individual Christian (apart from certain specialist theologians whose theological conscience is precisely differently constituted from that of the rest of men) either enters or leaves a specific Church. At a later stage we shall have to consider further the theological relevance of this fact. But to express it in different terms: With regard to the really effective forces which constitute membership of a Church as distinct from their theological claim to truth, which exists merely 'in itself' and in the absolute, the basic truths of Christianity which will really be constitutive of Church membership in the future (within the mass of genuine 'sympathizers') will be first and foremost belief in the living God and in Jesus Christ as Lord and as absolute mediator of salvation, in other words basic truths upon which, in spite of the pluralism in the interpretations of them which will pre-

---

[20] cf. at this point 'The Teaching Office of the Church in the Present Day Crisis of Authority', *Theological Investigations*, XII.

[21] cf. Paul VI, 'Indulgentiarum Doctrina', *AAS* 59 (1967), pp. 5–24; No. 11, p. 20.

sumably remain, there are no longer any serious differences between the Churches.

Whereas formerly these basic truths were simply presupposed on all sides as given and self-evident, in the future it is precisely *these* which will be the sole body of truth constituting in all the Churches the power to form a Church. The doctrines which have been matters of controversy hitherto are, in the process of history, being removed from the body of those principles which are socially effective forces in constituting the Church. But this precisely gives rise to a quite new situation for ecumenical theology and the ecumenical movement. For once the questions and ideas which have hitherto been matters of theological controversy have lost their force in this sense as at once constituting the Church and also separating the Churches (even though their claim to truth has not thereby been eliminated) then, surely, it will after all be easier to arrive at the possibility of setting aside these questions for theological, and above all for practical purposes, even though in theory they still continue to be matters of controversy. The very fact that the situation has been altered means that they are rendered less acute, because in the case of no one party to the discussion do they any longer have any real effective force as constituting the Church, although they do of course retain their significance in theory as constituting the Church and as dividing the Churches. We are dealing with a truth such that it no longer enters, or at least does not enter so directly, into our hearts, and is no longer capable of so entering, because the situation for this does not exist, or does not impinge so much, and in view of this it is possible to conduct our discussions quietly, '*sine ira et studio*' and to achieve unity more easily. This is all the more true in view of the fact that in such a fresh situation too the precise interpretation and the practical concretization of a point of controversy of this kind (as for instance that of the primacy of the Pope) will differ to a not inconsiderable extent from the interpretation and concretization formerly attached to it.

There is a further point. The Churches, and above all the Roman Catholic Church, for all the necessary unity of creed and the courage to maintain this, are accustoming themselves to a greater pluralism in the theologies and modes of life which take place within them. Thus in the case of us Catholics, for instance, the element of Roman legalism and the scholastic element are no longer the sole form in which the dogmatic nature of this Church has to be presented in the concrete for those outside it, and which make it notably more difficult for him to arrive at the possibility of disinguishing between the nature of this Church as presented dogmatically and the form in which he encounters her in the concrete. In this new situation too it will be easier both for the authorities of the Catholic Church and for Catholic theology itself effectively to 'realize' in spirit what the Decree on Ecumenism of the Second Vatican Council calls the 'hierarchy of the truths of faith', a hierarchy which is both an objective and abiding entity, and at the same time conditioned by the epoch in which the Church is living at any given time. Once this distinction between the objective significance and the epochal significance even of effectively true and dogmatically binding statements within the Catholic Church is clearly realized, it will presumably be easier to make the meaning and force of Catholic dogmas which are still matters of controversy in interconfessional discussion more understandable and more accessible for non-Catholic Christians. When we think of the process, so largely achieved, of the 'enfranchisement' (*sit venia verbo*) on the Catholic side of the threefold 'sola' of the Reformation during the centuries which have elapsed since Trent, and especially today, we no longer need to regard such ideas and hopes for the future as utopian. With the altered situation of the Churches in terms of religious sociology it may perhaps be easier in the future to achieve agreement on some points of theory as the outcome of this new situation, and from these it may be that practical consequences too will develop. And this may be the case in the future even though theological progress in ecumenical theology towards a consensus has not produced any alteration in the 'immobility 'of the Churches as they exist in the concrete, and has not advanced beyond irenical words and friendly gestures. In brief: The situation of the Churches in the future in terms of religious sociology can, if it is rightly interpreted and exploited, in itself signify a positive opportunity for ecumenical theology.

At this point, however, we must pass on to a *second* stage in which we consider the real theological relevance of this situation in terms of religious sociology gradually advancing upon us to the question of truth as such. This situation as it *de facto* exists induces in a large section of the membership of the Churches a sort of confessional relativism. A great number of the members of the Churches are ignorant of the classical points of controversy separating the Churches, or regard them, insofar as they do recognize them at all, as so much wrangling between the theologians, and as such quite uninteresting. In itself this is not very surprising. For it is not astonishing to find that the average Christian does not succeed in so reflecting upon and articulating that faith of his of which we have spoken earlier present at the depths of his existence but *ex supposito* still quite unreflected upon, that anything arises from this so far as he is concerned with regard to these classic points of controversy. Thus it is almost impossible for him to take any other course than to regard these as unimportant and so to become confessionally speaking a relativist, one who feels able to choose any particular confession he likes, or to change from one to another at will as though they were so many businesses of different proprietors, where one could purchase the same goods or refuse any longer to accept goods which had fallen out of fashion.

Now certainly the theologian or (may I say?) at least the Catholic theologian cannot identify himself with any such *a priori* confessional relativism, even though he may concede that much in his Church does *de facto* lend support to such a relativism in historical terms, even so far as the perspectives and formulations of that dogma are concerned which he recognizes as inseparable from the Church and as binding upon himself. Surely there is no need to treat of this point at any greater length here. At least so far as the Catholic theologian is concerned he is once and for all bound beyond all shadow of doubt to reject any such confessional relativism when he acknowledges that according to the faith to which he is committed the Church of Christ 'subsists' in the Roman Catholic Church, and this Church considers herself as constituted, among other factors, by the totality of her dogmatic teaching taken as beyond dispute.[22]

But when we reject any such confessional relativism as an illegitimate consequence arising from the situation in religious sociology described above, has this no significance whatever for the question of the actual truth of those propositions which are matters of theological controversy, and which divide the Churches, and therefore no significance either for ecumenical theology as such apart from that indirect one which we have already attempted to formulate? This is the question which we must now consider in still greater detail. Obviously this more detailed consideration leads us into an almost incalculable series of problems, such as we cannot survey here. Thus surely the problem of the relationship between truth and institution would have to be discussed, for in fact we with our western individualism are presumably being over-hasty if we take it for granted that the bearer of knowledge and therefore truth is in fact the particular individual in each case. Obviously any knowledge can exist only in the real physical individual. But this still leaves the problem open as to whether particular truths are not so orientated to human societies, and in fact even expressed in an institutional form, that they can only be expressed in them, and in the individual to the extent that he belongs to this

[22] cf. the Dogmatic Constitution on the Church, 'Lumen Gentium', No. 8.

community and, moreover, in an institutional manner. Let us presuppose for the moment – more is not possible here – that we can give a positive answer to this question. In that case the further problem emerges of how the individual in his individual awareness shares in knowledge, the true bearer of which is the community to which he belongs. Manifestly this sharing does not necessarily have to consist in the fact that the individual awareness completely and adequately reproduces the collective awareness of this community. Surely on the principle we are invoking here it is perfectly legitimate to distinguish between individual and collective awareness in general, and therefore a distinction of the same kind is also conceivable in our particular case.[23] This distinction could certainly not legitimately or *de jure* consist in the fact that the individual awareness of faith simply contradicted the collective awareness of faith of the Church. Yet the former does not necessarily have to be the total and adequate repetition of the latter. It could legitimately be narrower in extent, it could be compatible with some subjective choice, it could justifiably be in part only *fides implicita*, and not merely *de facto* remain distinguished in this sense from the total faith of the Church, but actually recognize such a distinction, be aware of it and accept it freely as such, provided only that it remained open in principle to the greater and collective awareness of faith of the Church.

In this connection we should then also have to consider, at least as a question, whether in that case every disparity which exists between the individual and the collective awarenesses of faith really is of the same kind, and therefore illegitimate at least in principle. The scholasticism of former times already drew a distinction between a 'judicium' properly so called, i.e. a proposition taken over and adhered to by an act of radical assent and decision on the one hand, and an 'opinio', i.e. a mere opinion on the other, this latter being conceived of in an experimental sense, with an awareness of its provisional character and vulnerability, and with a certain readiness to abandon it should the need arise. Now if we were to apply a distinction of this kind in the present context, the legitimate difference which we have described above between the individual and collective awarenesses of faith might perhaps be rendered still more precise. Perhaps we would only be transgressing the limits of a justifiable distinction and reaching the stage of an individual state of error and heresy if at that point at which some personal conviction which we held in our individual awareness of faith, and which ran counter to the collective

---

[23] cf. 'Heresies in the Church Today?' *Theological Investigations*, XII.

awareness of faith, was put forward as 'judicium' and not merely as 'opinio'.

On the basis of these and similar considerations, which we have only been able to indicate here, the situation in terms of the sociology of religion which we have depicted at an earlier stage could be subjected to a theological interpretation in terms of which it would no longer appear as a mere state of affairs, but could be justified in positive terms at least in part. On this basis it would perhaps be possible to imagine, at least in many instances, that an ecumenical dialogue and an ecumenical theology might in all patience admit of many differences of doctrine between the various parties. In such a case a dialogue and theology of the kind we are thinking of would not have to be excluded totally by theoretical theology to a point where it was no longer possible to arrive at even a form of words expressing agreement. Nor, on the other hand, would the differences of doctrine involved have to be regarded as still making it necessary for the Churches to remain separate. After all in pastoral practice at the individual level these presuppositions are acted upon, albeit quite unreflectingly. In other words the pastor concerned, when faced with 'difficulties of faith' on the part of an individual, rightly refrains from trying to overcome these in any direct or total manner, and merely says to him: 'For the time being just quietly leave the question open and do not close yourself rigidly to the Church's explicitations of faith. Rather live without straining in the hope that your individual experience of faith and that of the Church will be able to grow towards one another. In this sense you can in all honesty retain your own subjective position and still be a member of the Church.' One cannot, it is true, transfer an approach of this kind at the individual level, designed indirectly to meet the difficulties of faith which may be felt by an individual in relation to his Church, to the relationship between the Churches themselves. But conversely it still does not seem certain that many differences of doctrine between the Churches in ecumenical theology might not be overcome in an analogous manner at least for the time being.

The situation in religious sociology which we have taken as our starting-point surely entails, in its bearing upon the question of truth, not merely the problem of the relationship between truth and membership of an institutional community, but also the problem of the relationship between the objective status and the concrete existential application of theological propositions which are true, but at the same time always importing salvation. Propositions of faith are always and in all cases propositions of salvation too. It is perfectly true that we can never nelgect

the 'objective' truth in our quest for salvation because man precisely as
spiritiual asks himself, and must ask himself, in a 'selfless' manner what
the nature of reality is 'in itself'. But while recognizing this to the full,
it still remains equally true that the truth which is pointed to in theological
propositions cannot really be apprehended unless it is understood as
salvation. There is, therefore, both a difference and a radical interpenetra-
tion of two elements here, the element of 'objective' truth and subjective
salvific significance in theological propositions. But while recognizing
this we must also say that these propositions have a subjective significance
which has nothing to do with any subjectivism. All theological propositions remain in their truth (as recognized) orientated towards concrete
individuals who as individuals and as belonging to particular epochs and
particular human groups are situated in history.

The situation in religious sociology of which we have been speaking
should be thought out anew in theological terms from this basic standpoint. The question should be formulated in the concrete and faced up to
as to what significance is to be found for ecumenical theology and the
dialogue that goes with this (and that too precisely with regard to the
question of truth) in the fact that theological propositions, both as com-
pared with one another and also in the developing process of history, do
not always have the same bearing, whether remote or proximate, to the
subject in his subjectivity and so to his salvation. This question has, after
all, in a genuine sense been envisaged in the Decree on Ecumenism of the
Second Vatican Council when an explicit exhortation is included in that
document to pay heed in ecumenical dialogue to the 'hierarchy' of truths,
and to their different bearings upon the fundamentals of faith. After all
such an exhortation only has any real meaning if, in striving for the
unification of the separated Churches on questions of faith, the purely
formal equality of status in the definitions of dogma by the Catholic
Church, for instance, and the formal equality of authority of the Catholic
Church which is prior to all these dogmas is not taken to mean that any
possibility of distinguishing between them is ruled out from the outset
in the manner in which agreement upon them is arrived at. Now if this
is the case then even on a Catholic interpretation of faith and of the
Church the question should perhaps be asked whether from the Catholic
point of view particular Churches, hitherto separated, should not be
allowed to retain their existing forms while achieving union, since,
despite the fact that they do not accept all propositions defined
by Rome, provided only that they do not positively deny these
as irreconcilable with the substantial nucleus of Christian teaching held

in common by all. I believe (to give a still more precise example) that even a Roman theologian can concede the following position: a member of his Church certainly cannot decisively contradict a papal definition without thereby ceasing to be a Catholic. But still this does not mean that he is bound to give any positive agreement to the material content of the definition involved. Rather this content can be left to his 'fides implicita'. Now if this is correct, what are the consequences of it for an ecumenical discussion? Surely that is a question which has not yet received sufficient detailed consideration in Catholic ecumenical theology. Yet even abstracting from the subject of ecumenical dialogue it is a question with which the Catholic really finds himself confronted the moment he considers the situation in terms of religious sociology for his own Church as it is in itself. For after all in this Church there already is a very notable difference, which is at least in part legitimate, between that which belongs to the collective awareness of faith of this Church as such and is explicitly stated to do so in the definitions of her teaching authority, and that which *de facto* is explicitly believed by the individuals belonging to this Church. If we were not content merely to accept this situation as already *de facto* existing, and if instead of this we really thought out its theological relevance, surely this would have the effect of opening up many insights and possibilities for an ecumenical theology which, at least so far as we Catholics are concerned, have hardly been considered at all as yet, yet which could open up more fruitful prospects for ecumenical theology.

VII

Perhaps I may be so bold as to put forward the following proposition: Ecumenical theology is for the most part the theology of the future,[24] which has to be worked out by all the Churches, each from its own starting-point as previously determined by its past history.

When I speak of 'the theology of the future' what I mean by this in the present context is not a theology of the futurology of mankind, the element of the 'apocalyptic' which is hoped for in the Christian faith and the question of how this should be realized, or the element of political involvement etc. What I mean by the theology of the future is something far more simple: that theology which is necessary as a prior condition for any proclamation of the gospel in order that the gospel may appear credible in a future conditioned by science, technology, cybernetics, the

[24] cf. the study entitled 'The Future of Theology' in the present volume, pp. 137–146, as also 'Perspectives for the Future of the Church', *Theological Investigations*, XII.

social unification of mankind on a global scale, a future which has already begun.

When one has participated for many years in ecumenical discussions between specialist theologians belonging to the various separated Churches it is not very easy to achieve a mood of hopefulness with regard to the outcome of such ecumenical theology. Whereas ecumenical discussion between everyday Christians all too easily goes astray and leads to a confessional relativism, and the doctrines which divide the confessions are all too cheaply and too hastily by-passed, ecumenical discussions between specialist theologians on the other hand are for the most part still concerned with the traditional and classic doctrines which divide the Churches as these have come down to us from the past. The result is that these discussions do not advance any further in the problems involved even when the theological premises conditioning the formulation of these divisive doctrines today are those supplied by modern exegesis, the historical sciences, and the differences in modes of expression at the philosophical and conceptual level of today, differences which have become almost too complex for the human mind to cope with them. Certainly in the last few decades we have, to a greater extent than formerly, been able to speak with one another. The theologians of the separated Churches have achieved a new interest in one another's views. A greater exchange of subjects, viewpoints, methods etc. has been achieved and still is being achieved. But if we ask what results have been achieved from this ecumenical dialogue with regard to the unification of the Churches we are forced to reply with sober realism: these results are very slight. The reason for this is certainly not that we have not come much closer to agreement with regard to the traditionally controversial doctrines.[25] The main reason for the paucity of results is perhaps to be sought in the following fact: on the one hand the scholastic theology of the Roman Church is still as a whole very far from having arrived at a position in which it can make the dogmas of this Church sufficiently clearly comprehensible to the average Protestant Christian. On the other hand, within the Protestant Churches such differences exist with regard to the most fundamental interpretation of Christianity, differences which the leaders of those Churches cannot overcome or which, perhaps they are simply willing to accept (because it may perhaps be that to attempt to overcome them would itself be regarded as running counter to the principle of

---

[25] On this cf. also the whole discussion about H. Küng's book *Rechtfertigung* (Einsiedeln, 4th ed. 1964). After an initial agreement attitudes have changed and very many considerations have been put forward against the position outlined here.

Protestant freedom of faith) that for this very reason any collective union between these Churches as they now exist and the Roman Church is impossible. For from the standpoint of her own faith the Roman Church is forced to reject many of these interpretations of Christianity as heretical, even though they are tolerated in the Protestant Churches and in fact, to a certain extent, recognized as legitimate.

In this situation, setting aside that hope against all hope which is enjoined upon the Christian, there is only *one* real chance. Only if the theologians of the separated Churches devote themselves intensively to the task of shaping the theology of the future, does any hope or prospect exist of these theologies arriving in the future at one and the same meeting-point. This is not to say that the direct and immediate discussion of questions of controversial theology should be broken off. This is necessary, and in fact does achieve certain partial results in the 'public opinion' of the theologians, even though it has achieved as good as nothing to alter the immobility of the Church leaders beyond producing irenical words and friendly gestures. But in the last analysis it seems to me that the greatest chance for ecumenical theology will consist in working for the Christian theology of the future, when the adherents of all theologies and Churches, each in his own way, have learned to bear witness in a credible and comprehensible manner to the gospel of Jesus Christ as addressed to the man of that future age which has already commenced, no longer demanding of him as a condition for being a believer that he shall grapple with unnecessary difficulties in addition to that attitude of metanoia involving the whole man which he must embrace; and when furthermore the adherents of these theologies of the future avoid betraying the true gospel by accommodating it to the fashions of the moment, then, as I hope, these theologies of the future as upheld in the separated Churches will increasingly approximate to one another and draw closer to one another than the traditional theologies which are immediately conditioned by the controversial questions of the past. Thus I like to feel that the most important work for ecumenical theology consists not in the least in a theology which is to be developed as an explicit dialogue side by side with the rest of the theologies of the separated Churches, but rather one which is pursued in them as a whole, and in all the disciplines pertaining to them. For in the last analysis and taken as a whole this theology has, after all, no other task than to think out to the full the question of how the gospel can be preached in a way that arouses and demands the response of faith – and that too not merely for a traditionally minded remnant of mankind who, on historical grounds, have still remained believers, but for those men who have to become Christians in the future and from their own special situation in the future. From this point of view ecumenical theology absolutely coincides with theology as such. If therefore ecumenical theology is understood in this sense as the theology of the future, and if it actually becomes the theology of the future because wherever it is practised it has this one and the same task, and because it is pursued in the closest possible collaboration between the theologians of all the confessions, then it will of itself become ecumenical theology.

In conclusion a few further considerations may be put forward with regard to the limits which must be recognized in determining the meaning and the possibility of ecumenical theology. In this we shall take as our starting-point the recognition of the fact that that which constitutes concrete history and that which constitutes a concrete decision both at the individual level and also at the level of social groups can never be brought about solely by rational speculation as such, and that the nature of history as concrete and the attitudes freely adopted within it cannot be comprehended in any adequate sense either by any process of subsequent reflection. Certainly it is true that an element of reflection and speculation always belongs to concrete history as this is imposed upon us by the past. The explicitation of objectively real motives and the assigning of theoretical reasons constitute in themselves an intrinsic element in this history. But the history itself is always something more than that which is brought to light in its scientific awareness of itself. This is not merely because the whole of reality at the material and biological level belongs, in all its dimensions to history also, or because in this there is something more than man is conscious of in it, so that the computer which sought to record and store the whole of this reality as so much data of human knowledge would have to be richer in content than the structure of the material world in itself. It is also because that element of self-command which is intrinsic to the act of personal freedom (setting aside the intrinsic prior orientation of this) is, of its very nature and as such, incapable of objectifying in any adequate sense its own intrinsic significance. Human knowledge, therefore, considered as the science of nature and of the human spirit, is in principle always that which is incomplete, that which can never adequately objectify the intrinsic self-possession of reality. For this reason historical decisions are never merely the outcome of scientific speculation, which in fact is not only incapable of stating unambiguously and in an ultimately concrete formula what will be, or should be the case, but is even incapable of stating what unequivocally and really is the case. This applies to the context with which we are concerned also.

The Church, the separated Churches, and the unity which ought to exist between them can never adequately be comprehended in the science of theology by a process of human speculation. This science is not the mistress of history. She cannot even legitimately claim any such dominion within the history of the Churches themselves. On the contrary in this history of the Church and of the Churches she is simply one element among many, one which remains dependent upon the whole of this history which can never adequately be analysed by her, for only he who stands outside history altogether can be said not to be subject to it. Now certainly the science of theology and ecumenical theology in particular cannot be said to stand outside history in this way. However important and necessary this may be in the life of the Church, it can never produce any such theoretical project of an ideal unity and unification of the Churches of this kind such that the real unity and unification would be nothing more than the mere transposition of these theories into reality. It is here that we come to the ultimate limits of ecumenical theology. It always derives from those concrete historical conditions belonging to the individual Churches which can never adequately be analysed or reflected upon, and it remains confined within these limits as imposed by its own origins, so much wider in scope than it is itself. It still remains restricted in this way even in those cases in which, and even at that stage at which, a theologian might bring about in his theology some kind of revolutionary break with his own past and contradiction of it. This theology takes as the starting-point for its speculations an existing situation in the intellectual life of the Churches and their theologies as these exist here and now, a situation which always contains something more than that which can be reflexively apprehended and reflexively criticized by it. This theology puts forward ideas for the future with regard to the relationships of the Churches to one another which, so long and to the extent that it is only the exponents of theoretical theology who pursue them and make themselves responsible for them, can never remove that difference which prevails between the real and the conceivable, nor yet the difference between the conceivable and the reality that lies in the future. Ecumenical theology as a science, therefore, is ultimately addressed, incapable as it is of ever achieving a total analysis of its own subject, to the element of the incalculable in history, which is also the sphere in which the Spirit of God moves and exercises his freedom, a freedom which cannot be subjected to man's control. Ecumenical theology at the theoretical level, therefore, while never pronouncing its own nature to be meaningless or superfluous, is constantly reaching out anew beyond itself into that wider sphere which is constituted by the concrete history of the Church. To the extent that the Church has humanity as its subject at all, it will in fact never properly speaking be represented by the theologians, the 'doctores', but rather by the prophets and bishops in the Church. And although the unity between these is likewise something that can never be calculated, still they do together constitute first and last the upholders of the history and the decisions of the Church. This is, of course, not to deny that in the concrete instance a 'doctor' of theology, in a certain sense in a personal union of roles, can also be a prophet or bishop in the Church.

What we have stated in abstract terms with regard to the limits of ecumenical theology will also constantly be confirmed by the experience of our work in ecumenism. In fact it is a strange phenomenon: all speak of unity, declare their will to achieve unity between the Churches and their conviction that it is a duty to work for this unity. Nor have we any right, at least in principle, to doubt the honesty of this attitude and this will to work for the unification of the Churches. And yet in historical fact nothing, or almost nothing, actually takes place. For the umbrella organization of the World Council of Churches is not itself a Church and is not intended to be such, and all friendly contacts and discussions between the World Council of Churches and the Roman Catholic Church have still not yet achieved any effective unification. This in itself would in fact be understandable, but more than this they have not even discernibly drawn any closer to one another. In spite of all the ecumenical good will, the real frontiers are still very rigidly and immovably maintained. And yet given such good will and the ecumenical courage to call our own convictions in question, it might properly have been expected that however the Churches themselves might maintain themselves in their traditional positions, still at least among those engaged in ecumenical work in theology, and not merely among other Christians, some real and not inconsiderable degree of interchange would necessarily take place to and fro across the confessional boundaries. Yet in fact the cases of such 'individual conversions' between the individual Churches among the practitioners of ecumenical theology are so rare as to be almost non-existent. And surely this phenomenon cannot wholly be explained by the fact that it cannot be the task of ecumenical theology as such to achieve individual conversions from one confession to another, or that many of these theologians hold from the outset that the time for individual conversions of this kind between the Churches is past because of the real and serious hope of a collective unification of the Churches, or because each theologian can and must work best for this collective unification by remaining within the Church in which he has grown up. For firstly this opinion too could and should in fact also be subjected to the judgement of an ecumenical theology as practised by the individual confessions, and examined as to its validity. And furthermore it would have to be considered that any ecumenical theology is itself confronted with two alternatives: either it takes tacitly and ultimately as its starting-point the position that objectively speaking all the individual Confessions are equally justified as they stand before the judgement-seat of the gospel (in which case it itself stands revealed as unnecessary or at least it reduces its aims once more to something that is entirely secondary) or else – the second alternative – it still remains a recognized truth that in the very last analysis the real unity of the Churches, which is after all the goal of this theology, cannot be brought about except through individual conversions taking place. And in this, so far as the purely *abstract* nature of ecumenical theology is concerned, it makes no difference in which direction they do take place,[26] and these individual conversions must be such as to bring what is validly and abidingly Christian in one confession into the other.

Now if we abstract from the higher providence of God at work in the history of his Church we must surely recognize that ultimately speaking we cannot explain the fact that such conversions do not take place merely by the fact of the weight of the past and the *de facto* present situation of the individual Churches, factors which have not been, and cannot be consciously analyzed or reflected upon. We cannot simply point to the fact that the individual ecumenical theologians have in fact been born in these Churches and have experienced the living power and grace of Christianity within them. At this point the limits of ecumenical theology at the theoretical level become palpably clear. This witness may appear alarming. But without either underestimating or denying the alarming element in this, it can still once more serve to console us too. For if the 'doctrinal structures' set up in the individual confessions were nothing more than so many elaborations of theological reasoning at the purely speculative level, they would certainly be just as unstable, just as much in

---

[26] Ecumenical dialogue *precisely as dialogue* signifies, in its formal essence, a readiness to allow oneself to be 'converted' by the other party to the dialogue to his own opinion. How this character of dialogue can be reconciled with the absolute conviction of faith of the Catholic party to the dialogue with regard to the truth of his own confessional beliefs is a question which has been treated of by K. Rahner, 'Reflections on Dialogue Within a Pluralistic Society', *Theological Investigations* VI (London and Baltimore, 1969), pp. 31–42.

a constant state of flux in the mode in which they have been realized in history, just as subject to change under one another's influence, as the systems of the philosophers. The fact that this is not the case is only intelligible, and can only be explained on the basis that despite the contradictions between them they all live in some degree from that original and true faith brought about by the Spirit of grace in the heart and centre of their lives, and at the same time also that all of them contribute to this original state of being in the truth as that in which God communicates himself in his justifying grace in all the confessions. This positively salvific function of the original faith common to Christians and already present from God and for God can also be recognized as present in the various confessions even by one who rejects any kind of confessional relativism and is convinced of the fact that the real, legitimate, historical and social objectification of the Church of Christ is present (in a manner not to be defined any more precisely here and now) in his Church in contrast to other confessions and Christian Churches. It is true that the Roman Catholic Church is the one who, as a result of her own understanding of herself, finds it most difficult to ascribe any such positive significance in terms of salvation and faith to the other Christian confessions. Nevertheless she has struggled through to a position where she can clearly achieve such a recognition in the Second Vatican Council. And if this is the case, then surely the other Christian Confessions must find it still more easy, again without any danger of falling into a confessional relativism, to arrive at such a judgement and such a recognition, which is an important presupposition for ecumenical discussion as such. Even when, for the sake of conscience and for the sake of the Gospel, they do not acknowledge the 'popish Church' as such, and cannot recognize it, from this point of view, as a legitimate objectification of the nature of Christianity and of the Church of Christ, still today they will no longer find it necessary to view the Roman Church as the synagogue of the Antichrist in which man cannot find his salvation, and from which he cannot receive that which is most true and most ultimate, namely the absolute fundamentals of the Christian faith of which we have been speaking, as present in the heart and centre of his human life.

Thus our consideration of ecumenical theology returns for its answer to the question of what truly and ultimately constitutes its prior theological assumption. This is that faith which transcends all theological speculation, all objectification at the theoretical and social level, in virtue of which justifying grace is already present in all Christians of good will. On this basis ecumenical theology can and must say: We must arrive at the unity of faith in the dimension of conscious thought and social living too, because we already possess this unity at the level of the justifying grace of God. The unity of faith already present at this level, points both to the possibility and also to the necessity of ecumenical theology. For obviously we cannot say: Because we already possess the unity of faith, being basically constituted in grace as Christians, we no longer need the unity of faith at the level of theological objectification and social living. Rather we must say: Because we have the former unity we must also strive for this latter one, which is the incarnational consummation of that more fundamental unity. On this basis the Catholic will think of the Lutheran as already being, at the heart and centre of his life, an anonymous Catholic, while the Lutheran will regard the Catholic as being at the heart and centre of his life an anonymous Lutheran. Which of us two is right is a point on which we are not at one, and this is the point which ecumenical theology has to consider in any genuine dialogue between Christians. But the fact that we can think of ourselves in this way, that what we are seeking is not to attain to unity from a position of absolute and total division, but rather to achieve it from a unity already existing in grace and in the truth of God as already apprehended by us, means that we can and must strive for that unity of truth in the one Church which constitutes the value and the hope of ecumenical theology.

3

REFLECTIONS ON METHODOLOGY IN THEOLOGY

I

THE task I have been given of providing some exposition of my theological methods at first threw me into considerable confusion.[1] My initial reaction to this request was to ask, 'Have I, in fact, any theological method which is in some sense peculiar to *my* theology, or is my theological method simply that which any Catholic theologian conditioned by tradition applies, and that too without any further or more far-reaching reflection upon it? Certainly it might be said that I too have put forward some views in writing with regard to theological method and with regard to theological hermeneutics. But in comparison with the multiplicity of theological topics which I have considered and written about over the last thirty years, any reflections I have put forward with regard to theological method in general, and still more with regard to my own personal methods, represent only a very small and modest part of this work. Perhaps I can add to this the further point that in the first years of my appointment as professor of dogmatics I did explicitly concern myself to some extent with the history of dogma, i.e. my written works were chiefly concerned with penitential theology as found in the Fathers, and besides this I did write an outline (unprinted as yet) of the history of the theology of penance. But it is now about fifteen years since I was

---

[1] This study was originally prepared for a theological symposium which was held in Montreal in the summer of 1969. On what follows cf. also in general the following articles of the author's: 'The Concept of Mystery in Catholic Theology', *Theological Investigations* IV (London and Baltimore, 1966), pp. 36–73; 'Theological Principles Governing the Hermeneutics of Eschatological Statements', *ibid.*, pp. 323–346; 'Theology and Anthropology' *ibid.* IX (London and New York), pp. 3–101 (with bibliog.); 'Dogmatik', *LTK* III (2nd ed. 1959), 446–454; 'Formale und fundamentale Theologie', *ibid.* IV (2nd ed. 1960), 205–206; 'Dogmatics', *Sacramentum Mundi* (London and New York); 'Theology', *ibid.*

either able or willing to concern myself any further in a strictly scientific manner with the history of dogma and theology (unless we include in this a sketch, likewise still unprinted, of the history of the dogma and theology of the doctrine of the Assumption of the Blessed Virgin into heaven – in other words of the dogma defined by Pius XII in 1950). My constant and overridng preoccupation, especially in the last twenty years, has been with systematic theology. Yet this has been characterized by the fact that I have had to treat almost exclusively of *individual* schemes in an unsystematic manner and as dictated by the needs of the moment. Actually this state of affairs is reflected in the ten volumes of my *Theological Investigations*, in which my particular studies have been collected. The only book which I have published with a systematic overall plan is that entitled *Hörer des Wortes*, and consists of a small outline of a philosophy of religion written more than thirty years ago. The same lack of systematic planning in my theological work is likewise reflected in my work of editing the theological lexicons, *Lexicon für Theologie und Kirche* and *Sacramentum Mundi*, and likewise in the work of editing the *Quaestiones Disputatae*. Such individual questions as I have treated of in the volumes in this series of which I personally have been the author do not alter in any essential respect the picture of my theological work as outlined above. I have also striven to achieve a development and deepening of Pastoral Theology and of Practical Theology within Catholic theology in general. But these surely must be left out of the present consideration from the outset. All this may perhaps serve to explain the fact that it has not been possible to allow questions of methodology to play any major part in my theological interests, at least in any attempt to define those interests as a whole, or measuring them by what has been achieved and worked out on the Protestant side in theological hermeneutics. On this basis it appears reasonable and justifiable to adopt an approach in these three lectures in which I do not so much reflect upon my own theological methods, which I have either put into practice or already reflected upon elsewhere, but simply to attempt to put forward a few observations with regard to theological method such as seem to me to be demanded by the direction which Catholic theology is taking today quite independently of the question of how far I myself have sufficiently mastered this method or consciously reflected upon it up to now. In view of the brevity of these three small lectures it is necessary and justifiable that these reflections on theological methods as practised today should not attach any particular value to a strictly systematic approach, but should seize upon one point or another from a far wider range of subject-matter which might have been investigated and to allow myself a certain arbitrariness in doing this.

The first particular area of the general subject-matter to which some thought must be devoted here might be entitled *The Situation Which Provides Current Theology with its Starting-Point*. In this first lecture we shall properly speaking have only two points to make about this:

1. In contrast to earlier ages this situation has, for the individual theologian, a special and peculiar element which renders it less capable of analysis and calculation. This point will be clarified to some extent in what follows.

2. This situation is, however improbable it may at first appear, precisely determined by the ecclesiastical context in which the theology of today must, more than ever before, be practised.

The situation in which a systematic theologian has to pursue his theological investigations today is in certain respects markedly different from earlier ages which, so far as Catholic theology is concerned, extends perhaps as far back as the first decades of the twentieth century. This new situation, then, is characterized by the fact that it has become in the highest degree incapable of analysis and, so far as the individual is concerned, incapable of being grasped and apprehended as a whole. Such was the situation in earlier times. I can still remember those who taught me theology then, and so can still perceive how they felt about themselves and their theology, and how they understood their situation. In this connection it is no idle question to ask whether their personal understanding of their role as theologians was 'objectively speaking' altogether justified, or whether, on the other hand, it failed wholly to correspond to the real factors with which they were confronted and which they did not altogether succeed in realizing. These theologians of the generation before our own went about their work in a theological territory which was already defined for them, one with which they were familiar. They spoke a common language. They had almost a fixed repertoire of 'quaestiones disputatae', and if they disagreed about these they did so in a manner such that each of them knew why and in what respect they did disagree, and that in these respects they actually could disagree without the teaching authority of the Church being invoked against them. At the same time they were likewise aware of those areas in which they were and had to be in agreement, namely on a number of particular theses traditionally defined, and which could be expressed in precise theological terms. They developed their scholastic theology along lines which were already determined by tradition. It was a sort of 'Denzinger theology', and they were convinced that they had at their disposal in the practice of this a sufficiency of clear, exegetically unassailable 'dicta probantia', and at the same time a sufficiency of assured knowledge from the history of dogma and theology to confirm their own propositions as the outcome of a permanently valid tradition. Certainly they were more or less adequately aware of modern and scholastic philosophy since the time of Descartes down to the present day, and also of Protestant theology from the Reformation down to the present, although for the most part their knowledge of this was over-simplified and they availed themselves of it only to the extent that it helped them to justify their own personal standpoint in terms of scholastic theology and apologetics. But nevertheless both these areas of thought were, after all, simply that which was alien, that which had to be contested. In no sense did they constitute that which, in the very doubts and questionings which it raised, in its questionability (in the original sense of the term), was something which was itself present and intrinsic to their own proper 'system' itself as the seeds of a greater future that involved both threats and promises. One could put it in this way: as little as thirty years ago the state of Catholic theology was that of a system closed in upon itself in such a way that any further developments that took place within it took place according to laws which were both already given within it and also already known to the upholders of the system, namely the theologians. In the light of this we can also understand that it was taken for granted that any further developments in dogma and theology would constitute so many further logical explicitations and articulations of propositions already given. So much was this the case that it was only really possible to conceive of these further explicitations as taking place on the periphery of the system of ideas, as for instance in the sphere of Mariology. It was hardly possible to imagine that the substantial nucleus of the faith itself (which was, of course thought of as the object of devout mediation) could once more be thrown afresh into the area of theological questioning. Certainly there was an awareness that this central nucleus was also contested, but it was so contested precisely by enemies from without. And against them the only duty the Catholic theologians had was to defend this central nucleus of the faith.

Today all this is quite different. And if we are to speak of any theological method which is to conform to the current situation, then it is worthwhile to reflect upon this *new* situation. The matter might be expressed somewhat as follows: Unless we undertake some systematic arrangement of the material involved in this situation by enumerating the elements which characterize it, then there can no longer be any common philosophical or theological language which can serve as a straightforward basis for theological work and a theological dialogue. Obviously so far as Catholic theology is concerned there are certain definitions by the teaching authority of the Church which are binding, and to which every theology must continue to adhere. But today precisely these doctrinal formulations of the official Church seem to a large extent to be no longer simply the sort of statements which are already formulated in a truly theological language. Rather they give the impression of being statements which, for all their binding force, need to be interpreted, translated, transposed into a different theological language, in order to be assimilable at all in any effective sense in their application to the world of ideas characteristic of the present day. In any case the theological language used within the framework of Catholic theology is no longer one and the same. Considered as a philosophical instrument of theological thought, and as one and the same entity understood by all in the same sense and ready to hand to each, to be used in the same sense, neo-scholasticism has ceased to exist. It has undergone so many transformations and new interpretations under the influence of the most varied systems of modern philosophy that it itself has come to be dissolved and lost in the whole complexity of philosophies which have grown up, for these no longer constitute a unity in virtue of the very fact that they are all still aware of the heritage which has come down to them from the scholastic philosophy of the Middle Ages. Now this situation of philosophical pluralism is not, as philosophical, transformed into a unity in virtue of the fact that the practitioners of these various philosophies all adhere to a single common credo in a single Church. For the articles of the creeds as such are not, in any true sense, philosophical. And the ultimate question still constantly remains open as to whether they themselves are interpreted in the individual philosophies in such a way that the unity of faith they express can still assure a sufficient unity of philosophical thought. This is not, of course, to maintain that these different philosophies (considered as instruments of different theologies) cannot stand in any relationship to one another in terms of dialogue, or that simply of their very natures they must, once they are clearly apprehended, contradict one another. But to say this is not remove that pluralism of philosophies which exists today even within the Church herself, and it remains in practice too much for the individual to gain a comprehensive view of all this, because the prior factors in terms of the history of philosophy and of human thought, culture, and much else besides entailed in this pluralism are so great and complex that they can no longer be mastered by any one individual. Only those remaining at an intellectually primitive stage, or the victims of their own fancy, can deceive themselves with regard to this situation, which in itself alone and of its very nature produces the conditions of an uncontrollable pluralism of theologies. This philosophical and theological pluralism, this situation of gnoseological concupiscence, constitutes a situation in which the individual theologian has to perform his task. This situation is rendered still more acute in the pluralism it entails, and which cannot be controlled or mastered, by numerous further elements. Here it is only possible briefly to draw attention to a few of these.

When we consider the position of the systematic theologian we recognize on the one hand that even as such he cannot avoid being a biblical theologian. He cannot simply leave the work of biblical theology to the exegete alone. On the other hand, however, present-day exegesis and biblical theology, in the problems they have raised, in the complexity of their methods and their presuppositions, have become so complex and difficult that the present-day practitioner of systematic theology finds himself in a totally different situation from that in which his predecessors were placed a few decades ago. Where today can he still find those 'dicta probantia' from scripture which he could avail himself of in earlier times to prove his own theses? Today it has become evident as a result of historical and critical exegesis that it is no longer so clear what the genuinely binding message of scripture to us really is, as distinct from the conceptual models and modes of expression belonging to it which are conditioned by history, and what does not constitute this binding message. And precisely because of this the situation in which the systematic theologian stands in relation to exegesis is quite different from that of a few decades ago, when for instance, he could, with a few simple and briefly stated arguments, establish a firm bridge extending from Mt. 16 to the dogma of the First Vatican Council.

Even the material and the methods of work in the field of the history of dogma have come to involve so many fine distinctions and have become so complex that the assertion of what is dogmatically binding, and the process of distinguishing this from mere theologumena as conditioned by the history of particular epochs in tradition, have become different in kind and essentially more difficult than in earlier ages; for then on the one hand we always had ready to hand a few sentences from the Fathers to prove the positions of current theology and of the official pronouncements of the Church, while on the other we could always overlook in a calm and broadminded way other opinions in the Fathers which were less suitable to our purpose. Today the position is to a large extent such that theology must engage consistently in a direct dialogue with the modern natural and social sciences, and that this dialogue, in the very nature of the subject-matter involved and the manner in which the modern sciences are presented, can no longer be communicated through what was earlier called philosophy, the nature and function of which in the light of current unphilosophical sciences, is more obscure and more threatened than is commonly admitted among us. Finally it is also a special problem in its own right, whether modern man's understanding of himself (a factor which is always involved in theology, and which in fact enters into theology as such, as distinct from revelation, as an intrinsic element in it) is communicated to the theologian at all through mere words, as he still always tacitly presupposes, or whether this self-understanding even for theologians has original sources of knowledge of its own such that they cannot be replaced by words, and which consist on the one hand in images and on the other in the concrete exercise of the practical reason, something which can never adequately be communicated or expressed merely through the insights offered by the speculative reason.

This situation in which the individual theologian stands and has to work, then, is conditioned by an uncontrollable pluralism of theologies, and by a state of affairs in the development of human thought which is likewise incalculable, and it is something that must be recognized soberly and without any inhibitions, and from which the due consequences have to be drawn. The individual theologian in his work today is the theologian who is alien, alone, and isolated. Today it is no longer so easy for him as it formerly was to think of himself as a worker on a common building site on which a single building is being erected according to a plan which has already been worked out and is known to all. He works on the basis of a world of ideas, from certain premisses, and with certain philosophical preconceptions as his tools, yet is well aware that these are subject to historical conditions and the limitations of particular epochs. Yet for all this formal awareness of his he is incapable of eliminating or overcoming these limitations. For the first time in the history of theological thought theology is not only conditioned by history, but is also aware of being so conditioned, and besides this is aware of being unable to avoid this conditioning. It is only in the second part of this first lecture that we shall be able to consider what all this implies for the ecclesiological element in the theology of today. At this initial stage we must simply concentrate upon the situation itself, the fact that it cannot be overcome and the isolating effect which it has.

The alienating effect of this situation in present-day religious belief is rendered particularly acute because in theology what is being treated of is a discipline which, more than any other, has to uphold the rightness of its propositions with a certain absolute binding force. Certainly this does not simply mean that they can claim the same absolute commitment as faith itself. Yet at the same time, in a manner which is far from being clear, they do participate precisely in the nature of this absolute commitment, for it is quite impossible to arrive at any completely clear dividing line between the propositions of faith and the propositions of theology. In any case in this situation, to the extent that theology should be, and is intended to be, the justification of the intellectual honesty of faith, a theological method is necessary which is itself in turn rationally justified, one which, in contrast to so many which have commonly been practised hitherto, avoids from the outset adopting many of the approaches by which the theologians of earlier times sought to overcome all the problems of philosophy, exegesis, and the history of dogma upon the pretext that all these difficulties could be overcome positively and in a way which the individual could understand by means of a frontal attack upon them. Now it is of course in principle possible to solve all the philosophical and historical problems entailed in theology in a direct and positive manner (at any rate to an extent which is sufficient). But while recognizing this we must also say that this possibility, so far as the individual theologian is concerned, and therefore so far as the individual Christian is concerned also, in practice no longer exists because of the immense variation in all the scientific methods which are employed, and because of the impossibility of acquainting oneself with all the literature that has been produced, within the space of any one finite life. Yet having recognized this we must also say that in all intellectual honesty we must provide the justification for faith both as a whole and in its individual propositions. In view of this, then, it is necessary for theology today, in this contemporary situation in which it stands and which it can no longer control, to develop *indirect* methods of achieving a justification of faith such as will satisfy the demands of the individual conscience on the question of intellectual truth. These methods will be indirect in the sense that they will legitimately by-pass the particular material problems involved, and that they will apply first and foremost in the particular concrete situation of the individual in the development of his thought, and not lay claim to any permanent or universal validity. But what all these methods will assume in the concrete depends on the concrete material which is being treated of at any given moment. Now obviously this indirect form of justification will assume one form when it is applied to some intellectual decision to be taken in a context involving metaphysical problems which have not yet directly been tackled or positively solved, and will assume a different form when it is some specific historical question which is being treated of. For instance I may concern myself with the question of why, in all intellectual honesty, I can assent to the existence of God even though the most recent linguistic philosophy and the systems of modern structuralism remain closed books to me, while at the same time they manifestly do have a bearing on the question of God. But this is a quite different question, and demands a different indirect method of approach, from the question, for instance, of how I can accept the claims of the Catholic Church, including the doctrines of the papal primacy and the apostolic succession of her episcopate, to be founded by Christ even though I cannot perceive how this Church developed from the historical Jesus to the stage of early Catholicism, and even though I know, or at least suspect, that much must have taken place in the social development of the Church during this interval.

All that has been said up to now still has not made it clear what the special quality is of these various indirect methods considered as justifying the Christian faith. Before we go on to invoke at least one example intended to throw light to some extent upon such a method, we must begin by establishing two points: *First:* that a methodology of this kind, worked out by a process of conscious reflection, does not yet exist in Catholic theology, or at least that it exists at the semi-conscious level in the sphere of apologetics. Moreover this apologetics is of such a kind that it undervalues itself, considering itself merely as an 'argumentatio *ad hominem*', and with an exaggerated modesty imagining that its achievements are less than those of the supposedly higher discipline of 'scientific' fundamental theology. In reality, however, such apologetics represents a more direct approach and achieves more than this fundamental theology. The *second* point is this: When we apply indirect methods of the kind of which we have been speaking these can very well serve to yield insights into the actual matter itself which is being treated of in the concrete case, insights which would have remained unrecognized if we had attempted to apply only those methods which seem to be at a higher level, because they involve a more direct and positive approach to the work.

Now let us pass on to a particular example of what we mean, because we have reached a point at which it is no longer possible to treat of these indirect methods of theological investigation and justification with all their manifold complexities at a purely abstract level. How, for instance, can we attempt to make it clear that it is justifiable to belong to the

Catholic Church as distinct from the Churches of the Reformation? If we were to attempt to work out all the points of controversy in exegesis, biblical theology, and the history of dogma positively and in particular, we would, presumably, never come to an end, and never achieve any conclusions. And in fact (this is the decisive point) it is not merely the normal Christian today, but the learned theologian too whose contemporary situation is in fact such that any such line of investigation would manifestly be (to say the least) as difficult for him as for any ordinary Christian. This aspect alone will serve to demonstrate in the concrete that the indirect method, as applied in the present context, does not constitute any merely supplementary or secondary theological approach such as is applied only by way of additional support in those cases in which no further progress can be made when dealing with some concrete individual. Rather it is a method which, whether consciously reflected upon or not, constitutes an intrinsic element in theological methodology as such. For today even the learned have to see and recognize in all honesty how impossible it is for them to work out exhaustively all the aspects of the problems with which they are dealing by a direct and positive approach. They must recognize this because they too (to express the matter in the parlance of the 'analysis fidei') can no longer perceive any essential difference between themselves and the 'rudis'. In other words they have explicitly to allow for, in all their considerations and calculations, the fact that their own recognition of truth is subject to historical conditioning, and they must make this an explicit subject of consideration.

Now to concentrate in greater detail upon our example. The first point that should be made is that every Christian has the right to presume, until the contrary is proved, that his own Christianity and his adherence to the Church in the concrete are valid on the basis of the power of grace and the workings of the Spirit which he feels within him. Why this is so, and why such a presumption does not produce a state of absolute immobility among the Christians of the various denominations so that any passing from one Christian Church to another becomes impossible – this is a point which does, of course, also need to be made clear.

A second stage in the indirect methods which we are envisaging here as applied to our particular question (and abstracting from a point that would also have to be established, namely that of its very nature Christianity is always and necessarily in some sense embodied in a *Church*) would consist in the recognition of a further fact, namely that the nature of any conceivable Church of Christ and of the ultimate eschatological validity to which it lays claim is such that that Church has the best chance of authenticating itself as the Church of Christ which stands more clearly, more fully and, from the historical and sociological point of view, in a manifestly more unbroken line of continuity with the Church of the origins, provided only that the Church in question does not also stand in clear and manifest contradiction to the basic essentials of Christianity at the theoretical level as recognized universally and as applied in practice by every individual in the particular concrete circumstances of his life.

From this point a third step would then have to be embarked upon in which it would have to be established that the threefold 'sola' of the Reformation, as understood rightly, and precisely in the sense, and with the due distinctions of contemporary Protestantism, certainly has its place in the Catholic Church, and that for this reason the Catholic has no grounds for withdrawing from his Church in the name of some pure Christianity, seeing that he is aware of this Church of his as standing in a more unbroken line of historical continuity with the Church of the origins than the other Christian Churches.

These considerations are absolutely basic. But of course a whole series of other supplementary considerations would have to be added to them, which it is necessary here to pass over, as for instance the question of how such a recognition, in which a considerable degree of historical relativity is involved, is adequate as a rational justification for an assent of faith that is absolute, or that other question of how this way in which Catholics justify their Church might be transposed and reapplied in an (ecumenical) enquiry among the Protestant Christians, for whom the whole problem equally exists in a manner corresponding to our first stage, yet in a pre-dominantly different form. But these indirect methods which we are considering here do take into consideration and allow for the situation in terms of concrete human living of the individual right from the outset, and if in our question these methods are taken as our starting-point, then surely it is still clear that in this way a whole range of particular historical questions can be bypassed right from the outset, which today would otherwise, at least in practice, be insoluble. A more detailed working out of such a methodology would surely serve too to show what has already been indicated, namely that in itself it actually carries with it certain implicit insights into the actual matter under consideration which would presumably never have been won in any other way. This indirect metho-dological approach would, for instance, in the case we are considering here, be able to make it clear that there is an element of historical con-tingency in the constitutional law of the Church without this element of historical contingency either on the one hand removing the *jus divinum* of this constitution, and without on the other hand this *jus divinum* as rightly understood necessarily ruling out this genuine element of historical contingency in the constitutional law of the Church. The indirect methods which we are aiming at, and the very structure of the matter itself, could be understood as having a mutual bearing upon one another.

Evidently it is not possible at this point to enter any further into all this. Only one further particular example may be invoked in order to show what is meant in general by this indirect methodological approach in theology, which has been suggested by the contemporary situation in theology in which the theologian himself is placed, and which he can neither master nor control. The only further point which we can still make in passing is that this indirect method precisely as indicated also has a vital bearing upon the methods employed in the 'course of basic theology', the 'cursus introductorius' recommended by the Second Vatican Council as providing the foundations of the study of theology in general.

Clearly although we have actually mentioned only one consequence arising from the contemporary situation in theology, this does not mean that there are not many other consequences also, just as important for the work of theology. Many of these are such that we cannot enter into them any further here. Here we shall attempt to throw light only upon a single further consequence when we shall have occasion to speak in the second part of this first lecture of the ecclesiological element in theology as this is demanded by contemporary circumstances. Eccesiology has always been an essential element in Christian theology. Here we cannot repeat what has been said with regard to the permanence and fundamental significance of this ecclesiology of theology. Hence we shall not be speaking of verbal revelation in general, of scripture and tradition and the bearing which each has upon the other as a result of their interrelationship, of kerygma and faith on the one hand, and theology on the other, and the manner in which these mutually condition one another, of the Church's teaching authority and theology, of the immutable element and the historical element in the truth of revelation within the Church. All this is presupposed here. Here we shall be treating simply of specific aspects of the ecclesiological element in theology as these arise precisely from the contemporary situation in which theology stands.

First it can readily be understood that in a situation in which it has come consciously to be recognized and reflected upon that every kind of knowledge, including theological knowledge, is subject to the vicissitudes and the conditioning process of history, the ecclesiological element in theology is confronted both with greater threats than formerly and at the same time with fresh opportunities. The first point is self-evident. The factors of the Church, the authority of her official teaching, the ecclesiological element in theology, are factors in a more general awareness which has itself become the subject of conscious reflection in its state as in a real sense subject to the conditioning processes and the vicissitudes of history, and which, therefore, has limitations of its own. This means that we feel that even these specific factors have to be enquired into from a quite fresh point of view. The point we are making here does not need to be developed any further. But this contemporary situation implies at the same time a fresh opportunity for the ecclesiological element in theology. Contemporary man, who consciously reflects upon and recognizes the fact that his own knowledge is subject to historical conditioning, and that it is impossible for him to achieve any completely adequate reflection upon the presuppositions of his own knowledge, can achieve a typical standpoint with regard to *his own self* in a way which was quite impossible in earlier times. He can realize more clearly that his views are in danger of being influenced by his own subjective inclinations the very moment they cease to be confronted with the convictions of society as a whole in an open and effectively maintained dialogue at a fundamental level. Today he is in a better position to understand that truth actually has something to do with institutional life and practice; that even in respect of his know-ledge man cannot be an individual subject in isolation; that truth can, to an extent greater than was formerly supposed, be measured by its effectiveness as a social force; that practical reasoning and decision-making are not simply derivatives from the speculative reason, but also entail factors which are autonomous and original to themselves even so far as knowledge is concerned. For in themselves these are only conceivable within the context of social living.

From these and similar considerations, which cannot be developed further at this point, the contemporary situation in which theology finds itself has acquired, precisely in respect of its eccesiological element, a quite new importance in terms of human living in the here and now, a new understanding of itself, and a new opportunity. The statement that theology either constitutes a process of responsible reflection upon the faith of the Church or ceases to be theology at all has, on a fundamental view, acquired a new intrinsic meaning and a new importance for the theologian himself such that today he is, less than ever before, in a position to regard his own personal opinion taken in isolation as important and worthy of consideration because less than ever before is he able to hold that he has, on his own personal responsibility and of his own resources, evolved what he feels to be the correct view of the world in which he lives. For today, less than ever before, has such a view any prospect of being accepted by many others. Theology is only of interest when it constitutes a process of reflection (though obviously of course critical reflection) upon the faith of a Church which is actually using this faith as the basis of its activities. This does not mean that we are canonizing a collective (as opposed to an individual) subjectivism or pragmatism, but simply that we are applying to the nature of theology the insight that that which is subjective in a radical sense (which is necessarily the inter-communicative subjective) is also that which is most objective, and that the highest truth remains in practice only attainable in that love which is most all-embracing and free. From this point of view it is obviously part of any sound theological method to take as its starting-point the average and representative awareness of faith to be found in the Church as it exists in the concrete. This does not mean that we do not have to subject this to a process of critical questioning. It does not mean that it is obvious from the outset what the real and true meaning of this representative awareness of faith actually is. It does not imply any denial of the fact that it is necessary to bring to bear upon it a constant process of critical discrimination between that which is really meant and asserted in the absolute and that which, while connected with this essential nucleus of real meaning, nevertheless belongs to the category of presuppositions, patterns of thought etc. which are subject to the conditions of particular epochs (naturally when we speak of such a process of discrimination we do not mean one that leads to a 'chemically refined' residue of true and proper meaning of the object of belief in itself and for itself alone. Such a process leads rather to this object of faith in itself being presented in a new form which is, no less than formerly, conditioned by the circumstances of history).

But unless a theologian is willing to take as his starting-point this aware-ness of faith of the Church as it exists in the concrete today, autonomous and capable of providing a safeguard against any deviations in the subjective awareness of the individual theologian himself, he will neces-sarily remain pent up in his own personal subjectivity even in those cases in which, for instance, he is in principle ready to submit to the authority of scripture or the material arguments of some intellectual discipline. If this were to be his attitude he would never be able to achieve any standpoint as a starting-point for his active work which would be really independent of his own subjective awareness as an individual theologian.

Now what we are about to describe is precisely such a standpoint. The situation today is that those universal *auctoritates* which were earlier tacitly presupposed are less than ever before present in a form that is clear and beyond all contradiction. And in this situation it has become more necessary than ever before to apprehend and to recognize as a matter of conscious reflection the specifically ecclesiological element in theology. Of course this is not to assert that the authority of this ecclesiological element could ever be present and effective otherwise than in virtue of the fact that it is also recognized and apprehended as such at the subjective level also. What we are saying, rather, is that the most objective form of knowledge is bound up with the most insuperable subjectivity at the same time, so that we cannot escape from the circle in which the processes of our thought move to and fro between both these two elements.

Thus at the level of the question of truth too an ecclesiological element in theology is making itself felt, just as the individualism of the recent past is giving way to a higher form of socialism in the future. But to say this is not to dispute the fact that precisely this eccelsiological element must constitute a fulfilment of that enduring and permanent essence of the ecclesiology inherent in theology in a quite new situation and in a quite new form. First and foremost the critical function with regard to the Church's awareness of faith has become more necessary and come to play a greater part. For this awareness of faith as it exists in the concrete in the present-day Church entails an unconscious interplay of the most varied elements: real faith in all its radical openness to the absolute mystery called 'God' and in its unequivocal attachment in history to Jesus of Nazareth as the eschatologically definitive and historically manifested self-communication of this mystery; the models, thought-patterns and modes of expression in the concrete in which this fundamental faith is objectified and rendered communicable in the social life of the Church; the numerous opinions, theologumena etc. which are concomitant with, but not intrinsic to the faith, yet which are all unreflectingly accepted as part and parcel of the faith. Now the process of discriminating in this way, or of reformulating the elements of one and the same faith and the same creed into various theologies each differing from the others, and either appearing one after the other or existing side by side, inevitably and invariably causes theology to stand apart from the Church and her teaching authority with a certain attitude of criticism. For in this situation two things are possible: in this process of critical discrimination and reformulation of truths and realities which belong inalienably to the Christian faith and the Church's creed, the individual theologian may go astray, and second it is equally possible that the Church in her *magisterium* may seek to resist a process of this kind even when it takes forms which are perfectly legitimate. This situation gives rise to a dialogue between the theologians and the Church which is never finally completed. The reason why this dialogue is never finally completed is that even in the case in which a particular theologian puts forward an interpretation of this awareness which the Church has of her faith to be subjected to the judgement of the Church in this same awareness of faith of hers, and if the Church then, with a greater or lesser degree of authority, herself rejects this interpretation in one or other of the various ways in which this can be done, even then the theologian must still in fact continue to ask himself what such a decision on the part of the Church rejecting his interpretation does or does not mean in precise terms. Because of this the dialogue between the theologian and the Church is never brought to a definitive conclusion even by a definition on the part of the Church's *magisterium*. The only way, therefore, in which the theologian can actively engage in theology is for him to be prepared again and again to incur the risk of involuntarily finding the Church against him in his interpretations. If he is unwilling to incur this risk, and confines himself simply to repeating the formulations of the Christian faith put forward by the Church's teaching authority or in other traditional formulae in order to achieve safety in his work, then he runs the (greater) risk of uttering formulae which he only imagines that he has understood. From this point of view the theologian's conviction that his personal theology does include this necessary ecclesiological element is, in the last analysis, an act of hope which, ultimately speaking, can only prove justified by its own results.

In conclusion two further supplementary points must be made: First it must be explicitly reiterated yet again that the pluralism of theologies in the Church as it exists today is such as can no longer be controlled or mastered, though this is not to assail the unity of the Church or the unity of her creed. For the implications arising from this I must refer to another study in this volume,[2] in which I have attempted to set these forth.

Thus I may be permitted to express my decided and radical mistrust of any attempt to reduce theology in any adequate sense to the methodology employed in it, or to reformulate it in these terms. Theology always is, and always will be, even in the future, something more than its own hermeneutics. Certainly we must constantly reflect also on those methods which at first were not reflected upon, and which we applied when we

[2] 'Pluralism in theology and the unity of the creed in the Church,' pp. 3–23.

were enquiring into the actual subject-matter of faith in itself. And to this
extent the teaching of theological method, hermeneutics, fundamental and
formal theology etc., are themselves necessary themes for theology to
investigate. And certainly it is regrettable that in Catholic theology as it is
de facto practised far too little attention has been paid to these themes. Is it
true that it is impossible to know what 'fides qua' is without defining
'fides quo'. But however true this may be, it is no less true that theology
cannot be reduced merely to theological hermeneutics or a formalized
system of teaching on the subject of speaking about God. Of course the
converse is also true. If we want the knife to cut we must first sharpen it.
But if we confine ourselves to sharpening the knife alone then we have
not yet done any good cutting. It is the same with theology, although in
this case the two processes do enter more closely into one another than
in the case of the knife which we use in everyday life. In the long run
theological methodology will only be convincing when it brings man into
immediate contact with the subject-matter itself, and in the last analysis
this is, once and for all, not faith and the theology that goes with it, but
that which is the object of faith, because faith itself is only itself insofar
as it surrenders itself to that which it itself is not, even while the man of
faith is convinced that this greater entity which he cannot comprehend
can become an event in this faith of his.

II

The second lecture could be entitled 'transcendental theology'. Certainly
transcendental theology is not simply the whole of theology and must not
claim to be anything more than one part or one aspect of it. Certainly
transcendental theology is a theology in which the specific themes of
traditional theology (the doctrine of God, Christology, the doctrine of
grace etc.) are considered under one quite specific aspect. In other words
this discipline is not concerned simply or exclusively with theological
method. Nevertheless it does imply a quite specific line of enquiry and
methodology with which it approaches the material subjects of theology,
and to that extent the term 'transcendental theology' can also unreflectingly be used for one specific theological method. It is in this sense that
we shall be speaking of it here, though at the same time what is meant by
transcendental theology considered as a method must once more be
clarified by examples which we shall at least be able to point to of transcendental theology as a theology with a subject-matter of its own.

It is not easy to say what is really meant by the theology thus designated. The concept is, of course, based upon an analogy with the term 'transcendental philosophy'. But it is not *merely* a verbal analogy that is indicated here. Transcendental philosophy and transcendental theology are interconnected in terms of their subject-matter, and it is quite impossible for them to be separated one from another. From the historical point of view a transcendental philosophy consciously conceived of as such made its appearance prior to the advent of any transcendental theology, likewise as consciously reflected upon. Because of this it is conceptually impossible to begin simply with the following statement: transcendental theology is that theology which uses transcendental philosophy as its method. Philosophy is not merely an instrument for the practice of theology introduced into theology from without. Rather it is an intrinsic element in theology itself. This being the case, we can say that the provisional definition of transcendental theology which we have just put forward in terms of transcendental philosophy does not represent any alienation of theology from its own true nature. This definition does not constitute any merely external specification of theology which has nothing whatever to do with its intrinsic nature. This is not to say that this definition of transcendental theology as the theology which involves transcendental philosophy in itself comprises the total and fundamental nature of transcendental theology. But it is only at a later stage that we shall have to speak of this.

When we define transcendental theology as that theology which involves transcendental philosophy we have admittedly still not come very much nearer to an understanding of transcendental theology, in terms either of history or of systematic thought. For everything now depends on what is to be understood by transcendental philosophy, once more in terms of history and systematic thought. Now in both respects this is a very difficult question. Let us take as our starting-point the principle that *every* philosophy, i.e. every genuine metaphysics worthy of the name must proceed along the lines of transcendental philosophy, or else is not philosophy in this authentic sense at all; then it is of course possible to reply that every theology which really involves conscious reflection and, thought, and is intended to be something more than a mere record of saving history – in other words which is philosophical in character – is *ipso facto* at the same time that theology which involves transcendental philosophy – is, in other words, transcendental theology. And since on any showing there is a certain entirely correct element in this identification of metaphysics with transcendental philosophy in terms both of subject-matter and of historical development, it must not be disputed for one

moment that certain qualities of transcendental theology can be discovered in every genuine theology, for instance that of an Origen, an
Augustine or a Thomas Aquinas. It is not necessary to maintain that
transcendental theology is an absolutely new discovery of an area of
investigation which did not exist in former times.

But if we regard transcendental philosophy as some special and peculiar
form of philosophy which has existed as a matter of explicit and conscious
reflection only from the time of Descartes onwards, subsequently emerging still more clearly in the philosophy of Kant and of the German idealism,
then it is likewise permissible and reasonable to say that a theology
involving transcendental philosophy could only have emerged since
Descartes, and indeed that a transcendental theology in this sense could
exist, insofar as it existed at all, only because modern philosophy has at
last been accepted – admittedly very tardily – within the faith of the
Catholic Church more or less today, and since Catholic thought has
emancipated itself from neo-scholasticism.

But whether we hold this opinion or another, whether we allow both
developments to exist side by side or argue that this is impossible, it
remains true on any showing that the concept of transcendental theology
is still obscure, and we are leaving it in this state simply because no one
universally accepted and unequivocal concept of transcendental philosophy exists, and because even from the historical point of view – i.e. if we
characterize the whole modern and metaphysically orientated developments in philosophy up to and including existentialism as transcendental
philosophy, it is evidently clear that the most contradictory systems can
be brought under the general 'umbrella' concept of a transcendental
philosophy, as is shown by the history of philosophy in the last few
centuries.

Now within the framework of the present theological consideration
there can be no question of developing a concept of transcendental
philosophy (whether from the historical or the systematic points of view
or from both) which fulfils the requirements of a philosophical concept
in all their rigour. It would be too much to demand such a thing of a
theologian who, after all, can only be a philosopher in a very weakened
sense, and furthermore any concept of transcendental philosophy which
he might develop would be one which could not possibly be very useful
since it would be open to dispute with regard both to the understanding
of and to the practical application of a transcendental theology. For this
reason we have the right to take as our starting-point a somewhat less
precise, an almost popular concept of transcendental philosophy, yet one

which for this very reason is also broad enough to cover the very hetero-geneous manifestations of the modern history of philosophy. A further point is that it is possible to develop a concept of transcendental philoso-phy of this sort from the lines of enquiry which are followed immanently within theology as such. This is a point which we shall have to clarify at a later stage. But because of it we do also have the right to take this sort of concept of transcendental philosophy as our starting-point. In other words it is not in the least dependent upon a general consensus of the philosophers as such.

Quite simply, therefore, and in a sense that is almost pre-philosophical, we shall make the following statement: A transcendental line of enquiry, regardless of the particular area of subject-matter in which it is applied, is present when and to the extent that it raises the question of the conditions in which knowledge of a specific subject is possible in the knowing subject himself. The fact that an enquiry of this kind is in principle possible, legitimate, and under certain circumstances even necessary hardly needs to be discussed in general terms or at any length. In any act of cognition it is not only the object known but also the subject knowing that is involved. It is dependent not only upon the distinctive characteristics of the object, but also upon the essential structure of the knowing subject. The mutual interconnection and the mutual interconditioning process between the subject knowing and the object known precisely as known and as know-able are in themselves the object of a transcendental enquiry. The *a priori* transcendental subjectivity of the knower on the one hand and the object of knowledge (and of freedom) on the other are related to one another in such a way that they mutually condition one another, and they do this in such a way that knowledge of the *a priori* conditions which make know-ledge possible in the subject necessarily constitutes also an element in the actual knowledge of the object itself both with regard to the question of what the nature of the object known is as a matter of metaphysical necessity, and also with regard to the question of what the concrete historical conditions of this object are, factors which are precisely not intrinsically necessary. Thus a transcendental enquiry constitutes not merely the posing of a question which is supplementary to the question of the object in its autonomy and as it is presented *a posteriori* and at the empirical level. Rather it is only in this transcendental enquiry that knowledge of the object as it exists in itself achieves the fulness proper to it. Knowledge on the part of the knowing subject in himself is always at the same time a knowledge of the metaphysical (and in an objective sense transcendental) structure of the object in itself.

At this point we cannot devote any further consideration to the metaphysical presuppositions and implications of this statement. But in order to guard from the outset against any fundamental misunderstanding as to the nature of a transcendental enquiry of this kind certain further observations are, nevertheless, necessary.

There is a basic thesis, commonly attributed to the German school of idealism, according to which the subject as such in his act of apprehending himself transcendentally constitutes the event of the absolute spirit in itself at least in those cases in which that subject, in a real and radical sense, apprehends itself in its own transcendental purity and pure subjectivity, and realizes itself at this level. Now it would be wrong to suppose that this basic thesis is implicit in a transcendental enquiry or method of the kind which we are considering here. This basic thesis, therefore, is not as such present in the transcendental enquiry, because the transcendental subject, even in the boundlessness of his own transcendentality, ultimately apprehends himself and must apprehend himself as a *question*. For he always experiences himself in this transcendentality of his as open, as of himself an empty question, as that which refers beyond and outside of himself to that which he himself precisely is not. Now he experiences the act of self-realization of his own transcendentality as communicated to him through the *a posteriori* experience of the object which of itself manifests itself to him or refuses to manifest itself to him. As an object in this sense the subject is not master of it. Nor does the transcendental enquiry in the sense in which we are using the term here signify any devaluation of history or of the experience of that which is factual and irreducible to the transcendental. For when the subject turns in upon himself to recognize the transcendental conditions of the possibility of his own knowledge (and his freedom) this in fact means precisely that he apprehends himself as inescapably anchored in history, and realizes the *a posteriori* nature of his experience, something which precisely cannot be reduced to the transcendental dimension. To the extent that in the transcendental mode of cognition man reflects upon his own historicity as a factor of this kind, and one that is transcendentally necessary, and to the extent that he achieves reflection upon himself at this level, the full rigour and inescapability of his history is borne in upon him. And conversely, anyone who says that man is that being which is inescapably pent up in the concrete experience of his own history has thereby either sought simply to put forward an assertorial proposition (in which case it can be hoped that it will eventually turn out to be invalid), so that he has utterly failed to express the real historicity of man's nature, or alternatively, by saying this he has expressed an apodictic proposition which as such can be attained to only by a transcendental approach and methodology. In other words he has practised transcendental philosophy. Perhaps it is also useful to isolate and to emphasize one further point, namely that transcendental philosophy in the broader and to some extent pre-philosophical sense in which it is conceived of here does not constitute any true object for an anthropology of freedom either, for in this man considers himself as a subject of the hope and promise of a future to be created and made real of his own resources. On this approach, then, he is not the subject which, in its *a priori* aspect, has already all along anticipated its own future. No such opposition exists, therefore, for the precise and simple reason that a futurologist anthropology of this kind, if rightly understood, is rendering itself transcendental to the statements on which it itself is based or is rendering itself blind to the radical nature of the human reality which it is attempting to express. Of course this is not to deny that any transcendental philosophy is in constant danger of interpreting the *a priori* element as that which alone is important, of being intolerant of the historical element and failing to take it into account, and instead seeking to approach it theoretically or aesthetically and so to neutralize its effects. But in that case precisely this transcendental philosophy is entertaining a false understanding of its own nature.

Nor does our interpretation of transcendental philosophy involve any denial of the fact that in the concrete situation of a particular epoch or a particular individual it may be necessary, in coming to a decision of the practical reason, in concrete practice to be 'one-sided' and in a certain sense to forget the prudent balancing of one factor against another in the dialectic of a transcendental philosophy, because otherwise it would deprive the legitimate one-sidedness of the concrete decision of its force.

For our present purposes we must satisfy ourselves with this quite modest pre-philosophical concept of transcendental philosophy. Properly speaking it is sufficient for us to achieve the insight that the question of the knowing subject signifies not one particular department of knowledge which exists on an equal footing with many others, but a reality which is prior to every kind of knowledge which introduces material divisions of the subject-matter into particular departments as the prior condition making this possible. We must also recognize that we have only arrived at the level of real philosophy and metaphysics in the strict sense of the term, and that we can only make apodictic judgements at that stage at which, while according all due recognition to the objectivity of the reality investigated, we also include as an object of conscious reflection as such the subject which is always and in every case also involved in every act of cognition as such, albeit without always being explicitly adverted to as an object of investigation. It is in this sense, then, that philosophy is necessarily transcendental philosophy, even though that stage at which its true nature is explicitated as a theme in its own right is arrived at only later in the history of philosophy. And it is also true that theology is necessarily and of its innermost nature in the truest sense also philosophical theology. For otherwise it would comprise faith and creed indeed, but no longer theology precisely as such. Indeed it would no longer even comprise faith and creed in any real sense unless it also included this philosophical element. Now if this is true then it is in principle evident that theology must be transcendental theology. As has already been said this does not mean that all theology is transcendental theology. For it is clear that theology must restate and reflect upon the propositions of faith with regard to saving history as such. And the account of that history contained in it does not become a scientific discipline only at that stage at which this history is subjected to philosophical reflection as to the transcendental conditions which make it possible. On the contrary there is a science of history as such (although the theology of the Middle Ages was unwilling to concede this). Now if this is true then theology already exists as a science at that stage at which, prior to any explicit transcendental reflection, it records saving history and considers its significance. But conversely this does not exclude the fact that theology, in virtue of the element of philosophy necessarily immanent in and intrinsic to it of its very nature must also necessarily be transcendental theology. In this connection it is ultimately of little importance whether the statement that theology is necessarily transcendental theology and yet is not developed solely and exclusively in this form as such leads to the setting up of distinct theological disciplines divided from one another materially and departmentally (somewhat in the sense of the distinction between positive and speculative theology within one and the same discipline of dogmatics and fundamental theology), or whether the effect of this statement is merely that different aspects and methods are mentioned which must be considered in their mutual interconnection in any one investigation of the material subject-matter of theology.

After all these considerations all that we have achieved by way of beginning still remains a very abstract concept of transcendental theology. We must now deepen this somewhat further and fill it out with content by showing that a transcendental enquiry must constantly be undertaken afresh and, as a matter of concrete history, has been so undertaken, from the very nature of theology itself, though it is far from following from this that any explicit recourse need be had to a transcendental philosophy. The second way in which we shall deepen and fill out our initial concept of transcendental theology is to show, by means of a few small concrete examples from theology itself, how urgent such enquiries in transcendental theology are today if contemporary man is genuinely to be able to assimilate the propositions of faith. In both cases we must not tacitly presuppose (thereby becoming entangled in insoluble problems) that a transcendental enquiry into how some specific reality can be known must as such, either in principle or in fact, come before the *de facto* knowledge of the object in question. Since in an enquiry of this kind it is always the *a priori* conditions which make the knowledge of a specific reality possible that are being enquired into, it is always true that in practice and in the concrete it only becomes possible at that stage at which the object involved has already come to be known. Thus for a transcendental theology it is neither surprising nor scandalous that theology has all along been practised even before its character as transcendental theology has been conceived of in explicit terms and made the object of conscious reflection. It is also evident that, throughout theology and from the first, statements are made and have been made which of their very nature belong to the context of transcendental theology and have come to be recognized as such precisely at *that* moment at which an enquiry in terms of transcendental theology has explicitly been undertaken.

Perhaps the presence of such statements in traditional theology can be established most easily and directly in the case of the teaching on faith. In the 'analysis fidei' it is in fact not merely the question pertaining to fundamental theology) of the connection between the 'preambula fidei' and the absolute assent of faith that has to be treated of. Also and in addition to this an answer has to be given to the question of why revelation as heard should constitute and should remain not merely a human word about God, albeit one brought about by God himself, but actually God's word itself, even though it has still entered into the world of ideas proper to man. After all it has its existence in man's own conscious thought and hence is subject to the *a priori* structure of human knowledge. Now if theology says that any act of hearkening to God's revelation is possible only in the power of the *growth* of faith, and if theology interprets this growth of faith ultimately as 'uncreated grace', in which, therefore, God himself becomes in himself the constitutive principle of the subject of faith, then in principle a theological answer has been given to a question of transcendental theology: the act of hearing divine revelation as the word of God himself, as something more, therefore, than a word uttered about God and caused by God, presupposes, as the condition which makes it possible in the subject, that God himself through his own act of self-communication upholds this act of hearing as an intrinsic principle. And this is precisely what we are accustomed to call the supernatural grace of faith.

Although there may be no conscious reflection on this, such statements are, in the nature of the case, statements of transcendental theology, and they still appear in manifold ways precisely in the context of the teaching on grace and the supernatural theological virtues. In this respect as in the example just given it might be shown again and again that the answer to any such enquiry in terms of transcendental theology is arrived at not simply *ab externo* by some theological datum which is initially foreign to this enquiry itself. Rather it derives from this actual question of transcendental theology. For it is from the limitless *a priori* transcendentality of knowledge and freedom in themselves that we come to know what is really meant when we speak of God as absolute being and absolute good, recognizing that the absolute goal of this transcendentality is not something additional to, or external to itself, but rather something that is present all along and in its very origins, albeit without being recognized as a conscious theme of thought. And the same is also true in the dimension of a transcendentality and freedom to which man is raised by grace. Here too the goal of this transcendentality is not some point of refuge towards which this transcendental movement of knowledge and freedom tends as something that remains for ever asymptotically unattainable to it. Rather it is that which as such freely communicates itself to the finite spirit to the point of being immediately present and proximate to it at its very roots. Let us therefore take as our starting-point the idea of transcendentality as understood here, to which man is raised by grace (in the usual theological parlance this would mean God's universal will to bring men to supernatural salvation). And taking this as our starting-point we can make clear that in which supernatural grace and the theological virtues properly consist. Once they are recognized as having a transcendental derivation and significance of this kind these concepts also acquire a point of contact with the transcendental experience of the human spirit. They can be 'verified', albeit in a manner corresponding to these realities, because what they express is neither more nor less than the absolute radicalization of the transcendentality of the human spirit in knowledge and freedom.

We must now invoke a few more concrete examples in order to throw light upon the question of how such transcendental theology can be made effective in treating of the themes proper to dogmatic theology, however varied these may be. In this connection it is obvious that the concept of a transcendental theological method is modified very considerably according to the particular subject to which this method is applied. Such modifications may indeed be so considerable that it might be disputed whether one or other application of such a method to a specific subject can or cannot be said to belong to transcendental theology at all. However all the examples which we are about to adduce are intended to render intelligible and assimilable that particular object in them which is actually being called in question here by attempting to point out in the knowing subject an *a priori* reference to this object. And because of this they can all be understood in a transcendental-theological sense despite the variations between them.

In this attempt it is not merely obvious (as has already been emphasized) that this transcendental-theological disclosure of an *a priori* reference on the part of the knowing subject to its specific object is *de facto* possible only after this object itself has revealed itself and so communicated to the subject the knowledge of its own reference to that object as a matter for conscious reflection. While explicitly abstracting too, for our present purposes, from the problem of the precise relationship between nature and grace, still we can and must say that this transcendental reference to a reality of supernatural verbal revelation, to a mystery that has been revealed, is thought of throughout as constituted by God's grace itself. Thus the attempt at achieving a disclosure of this kind in terms of transcendental theology of an *a priori* reference on the part of the subject to a reality of supernatural salvation freely posited by God is not to be objected to on the grounds that we are attempting to deduce the mystery of this unmerited reality of salvation *a priori* from the mere nature of man as such. At an earlier stage it has been argued that the acceptance of the saving mystery of God by faith as it is revealed in his word is possible only in virtue of the self-communication of God himself. Now in the very nature of the case it has already thereby been laid down that the acceptance of the realities of salvation through the word of revelation *ab externo* takes place in the power of the saving reality itself as communicated to the *a priori* and transcendental subjectivity of man.

An initial example of such transcendental theological methods can be adduced from the theology of the Trinity. Here this example can, of course, only be presented in the briefest possible terms. We shall take as our starting-point the following principles, which derive partly from a metaphysical anthropology and partly too from an ultimate and utterly irreducible experience of grace which explicates itself in Christian revelation and in the history of revelation itself: 1. In respect of his knowledge and freedom man constitutes absolute and limitless transcendentality. 2. This in itself has a historical process of explicitation of its own which belongs essentially to itself and only communicates an awareness of itself to man in the total history of man considered as a historical being precisely in its transcendentality. 3. In this transcendence man is radically orientated to the absolute mystery which we call 'God', and which, in a free manner (which we call creation), opens up this transcendentality of man and sustains it. 4. In respect precisely of *this* (grace-given) transcendentality the abiding mystery of God is not merely the asymptotic point of refuge which provides it with its goal, and towards which (as the 'unmoved Mover') the transcendental movement of knowledge and freedom in man tend, even while it always remains remote from him; rather this infinite point of orientation of the transcendental movement discloses itself, at least in the mode of that which is offered, as a free miracle of a love that reaches out beyond itself in self-communication to man, to achieve a state of absolute immediacy and proximity to him, and in this act of self-communication itself sustains this transcendental movement on the part of man himself. 5. In accordance with the second statement this self-communication of God to man in the transcendental dimension of his being has a history of its own within the history of man, and as such becomes the history of God's self-communication which we call saving history and revelation history, taking the offering of salvation and revealing of the word as together constituting a unity. Where this history of God's self-communication to the world attains its absolute highest point, its point of irreversibility, and where the offering of God's self-communication to the world as a whole as endowing it with grace at the transcendental level has brought about the definitive acceptance of this offering on the part of the world itself, there is achieved that which is designated as the hypostatic union and also (naming it according to its concrete realization in history) that which we call the absolute bringer of salvation, Jesus as crucified and risen, the Son of the Father.

What we have expressed in these five statements is the mode in which man is constituted in a state of grace-given transcendentality, and the historical process in which this takes place. On the basis of this we can now acquire an understanding of the doctrine of the Trinity in terms of transcendental theology. First on the basis of the principles we have formulated we can recognize a threefold presence of God in the economy of salvation. In the self-communication of the one God this constitutes that incomprehensible mystery which never ceases to be such even in a really radical act of self-communication. To that extent the God who imparts himself in a (forgiving) love is called 'Father'. Now this God imparts himself in such a way as to be in himself in a state of absolute proximity to man, and as a sustaining principle of the transcendentality of man in his act of knowing and loving. To that extent he is called 'Holy Spirit'. Now this self-utterance of the one God to man is manifested in history as the irreversible faithfulness of God in Jesus Christ, and as such is called the incarnate Word of the Father.

Only under all three of these aspects, all three of these modes of God's giving of himself to the world, is the one act of self-communication on the part of the one God fully achieved, though this does not mean that these three aspects can either be thought of as identical or considered independently one of another.

On the basis of a transcendental approach, then, we have acquired an idea of the Trinity on the level of the economy of salvation. From this we must now advance a stage further to the idea of the Trinity as immanent, in the knowledge that unless this Trinity at the level of the economy of salvation were not that of God in and for himself we could not really speak of any true *self*-communication of God. For any distinction in this act of self-communication such that it was not attributed to God in and for himself would appear as merely creaturely. The 'self-communication of God' would be mediated through a creaturely act. We would have God not in himself and for himself, but merely as he is reflected in a creaturely reality. We would have failed to pass beyond the sphere of the merely creaturely so as to attain to God himself as he is in himself in his own divine glory, and as he wills, precisely as being this, to be for us as an act of free grace which is not ultimately a creaturely reality at all, even though it does have creaturely effects and creaturely modes in the manner in which it reaches us. But for all that this free grace is God himself. All these considerations do of course presuppose 'faith' in the self-communication of God. But this faith is not merely indoctrinated into us *ab externo*. Rather it is an experience of a transcendental kind (called the grace of faith) such that the reality of it cannot be denied merely on the grounds that it is only through revelation *ab externo* that it is brought to its full self-realization and certainty at the level of conscious thought.

In a similar manner too we can develop a transcendental christology, and for this too we must take as our starting-point the principles already mentioned above. Such a transcendental christology, which develops the 'idea' of a bringer of salvation in the absolute, a manifestation in history of the irreversibility and the victory of God's self-communication over the denial of the unbelief of the world, can of course never be a substitute for the historical experience of Jesus of Nazareth – in other words of that reality in which this 'idea' has been made real, and only precisely in virtue of this permits the idea as such to become real in history. Nevertheless there is, and necessarily must be, such a thing as a transcendental christology. Without it the traditional christology would today be in the gravest danger of being regarded as a mythology which is no longer capable of being made real to the man of today. Admittedly explicit plans for such a christology at the level of transcendental theology are extremely rare. In addition to certain attempts which I myself have made, I may refer to the article by Bernhard Welte in the third volume of the work entitled 'Chalkedon' (Würzburg, 1954) edited by Heinrich Bacht and Alois Grillmeier. And surely a christology of this kind at the level of transcendental theology would have two tasks to achieve which of course are closely interconnected.

First, therefore, taking as its starting-point the principle of God's will to save all men, in other words a self-communication on God's part which supports the whole of history and supplies it with its goal, and also taking as a starting-point the principle of a historical development in this transcendental self-communication of God to the world which is necessary of its very nature, such a christology in transcendental theology would have to develop the concept of an absolute mediator of salvation. In other words it would have to show that a historical development of the transcendental self-communication of God in this sense (provided that it does not lead to the absolute perdition of the world) must necessarily be developed to a point at which this self-utterance of God appears as addressed to the world irreversibly (as 'effective' and not merely 'sufficient' grace for the world in its power to lay hold of this grace in the dimension of history), and at which it is freely accepted as such. Further a christology of this kind in terms of transcendental theology would of course have to do something more than to enable men to understand that the event of God's self-communication as posited in history and as made irreversible on the one hand, and the definitive acceptance of this on humanity's part on the other, implicitly expresses in the unity of both these aspects precisely what the classic doctrine of the hypostatic union, on any right understanding of this, is intended to convey. Over and above this this transcendental christology would also have to enable men to understand how the endowment of the world as a whole with grace and the hypostatic union constitute the necessary unity of a mutually conditioning relationship, how, in other words a supralapsarian christology and a universal christocentricity are the necessary postulates for any christology to be credible today. Such a christology would also have to enable men to understand, likewise in terms of transcendental theology, why a hypostatic union exists only in a *single* instance, and how this fact does not mean that the universal God-manhood inherent in the spiritual creature as such is not in some sense degraded to a secondary category such that in and for itself it could conceivably be surpassed.

Secondly, the christology of transcendental theology would also have to develop what might be called the 'christology of awareness' (understanding this term in the right sense) such that the hypostatic union of the Logos with the human reality would be described not merely in the ontic categories of the traditional theology of the hypostatic union, but actually with concepts that are onto-logical in the true sense. In other words it would have to be made intelligible why and how the human being in the transcendentality of its constitution as such is the 'potentia obedientialis' for the hypostatic union. Then this would no longer appear merely as a unity between two substances conceived of on the analogy of material things, between the hypostasis of the Logos on the one hand and a creaturely substance on the other, thought of in material terms, for this kind of unity could just as well have been achieved with a sub-spiritual substantial reality as with the Logos as it exists in itself. But in the 'christology of awareness' of which we are thinking here we could then go on to give an account of the interior grace with which the human reality of Jesus is endowed such that this no longer appears as a 'fitting' equipment bestowed upon the human nature hypostatically assumed by the Logos, but rather as something which was already present as a matter of ontological necessity in the hypostatic union itself. Once this 'in itself' was understood onto-logically, in terms of a transcendental christology, this point would become clear. Admittedly what we would be presupposing in all these considerations would be an understanding of the fact that spirit and spiritual quality in their true and original essence are not secondary epiphenomena added onto a substantiality conceived of in material terms, but rather constitute the authentic existence of a being as such (here we are not treating of the negativity of matter as such) and so too the constitution of an existing entity as a being can be expressed in its ultimate and radical reality by means of the concepts of a transcendental ontology. All this is of course merely to indicate in barest outline the task of a christology worked out in terms of transcendental theology.

Probably too (if we may mention one further and final example) something like an eschatology of transcendental theology would have to be developed, and only by means of this would it be possible for the man of today so to transpose the dogmatic statements of eschatology (which right down to the present day still remain stuck fast in the imagery of a vanished world of ideas), and that too at a radical level, and not merely through subsequent re-touching undertaken only with reluctance, that these statements really would be intelligible and credible. An interpretation of these eschatological statements in terms of transcendental theology, therefore, is both conceivable and necessary for the very reason that the eschatological statements of scripture and tradition certainly do not constitute any anticipated descriptions, as though by an inspired journalist, of God and in the light of that which will one day come to pass. Rather they are anticipations of final consummation based upon that which, considered as God's deed of salvation, is already present, or which implies simply and precisely a state of radical openness to an absolute future the nature of which cannot be calculated beforehand. An interpretation of eschatological statements in terms of transcendental theology is also demanded for the very reason that that final and definitive salvation which finds expression in eschatology precisely does not signify any secondary and departmentalized specification of man on the basis of, and within the framework of the human possibilities which he already experiences, but rather the radically transformed reality of man as one and whole who, as subject to time and in process of dying, is utterly incapable of conceiving his salvation as the outcome of this reality of his as he experiences it empirically within the framework of human existence. If therefore eschatological statements about the salvation of man as understood here are still to be possible at all, they can only be formulated in the concepts proper to a transcendental ontology, i.e. as statements about a force inherent in man (remaining at a very abstract level) in his 'body-spirit' nature considered as transcendentally necessary and as the radical and ultimate realization of this achieved through the self-communication of God (this remains true however legitimate it may be to retain the imagery of apocalyptic language which also still has a significance of its own for metaphysical concepts, since these too can be conceived of only in a 'conversio ad phantasma'). Until that end has come in which history is consummated, in which that consummation does not consist simply in its own reality, all eschatological statements are simply propositions which on the one hand express the fact that man, as he who exists in grace through God's self-communication and so precisely as historical, will one day achieve his consummation, and which on the other hand guard against any filling out of this hope and this anticipation in more concrete terms, seeing that the future to which it points is absolute and inconceivable, which is God himself and which can only be laid hold of in an act of freedom which is itself intelligible only if, and when it is actually achieved. The dissatisfaction which is so generally felt with the existing state of traditional eschatology could be removed by an eschatology expressed in terms of transcendental theology, if this eschatology conceived of man as a being destined to an absolute future in a transcendental anthropology which included within its purview the self-communication of God to man.

In concluding this lecture the following further point may be made: it is of the utmost concern to theology to recognize the limitations which transcendental philosophy imposes on itself by the nature of its 'own' proper work. If a transcendental philosophy were to present itself simply in the absolute as the exclusive basis, without any further presuppositions, of human existence in the concrete, if it were to lay claim solely and exclusively to express that which is 'necessary' for this human existence and in this sense salvific, then, any 'positive' revelatory religion based on a saving *history* which as such affects the existence of man as a whole (in other words salvation itself) would be impossible from the outset. This limitation of *itself* on the part of transcendental philosophy (as the outcome of reflecting upon the historicity of human life, something which cannot be thematized systematically, or on the nature of dialogue, language, and hermeneutical experience) is itself an essential element in any true transcendental philosophy. Without this self-restriction philosophy would fall into the error of hybris and the crudity of claiming to solve all things in terms of reflective thought. If this self-restriction were not the work of philosophy itself this would lay claim to be able of its own nature to enquire into everything, and would thereby destroy itself. This self-restriction which man's transcendental understanding of himself imposes upon itself is, however, at the same time (in principle, and above all in the current situation of philosophy and theology) a task of fundamental *theology*. For this must show proof of the positive possibility of a saving history and revelation – that history as such and in the concrete, and not as susceptible of analysis by reflective thought, affects man in his ultimate and essential nature as subject. In other words that it is capable of being either *saving* history or the history of *perdition*. But when fundamental theology exercises this function it *ipso facto* constitutes transcendental theology: the act of consciously reflecting upon the fact that the creaturely subject as such is of its very nature rooted in that history which is precisely that of the subjectivity most proper to its own nature as such. The self-communication of God in grace in virtue of God's universal will to save all men is certainly (initially at least in the form of something offered) a transcendental existential modality of man. But it achieves the fulness of its own nature precisely in the history of salvation and revelation (both at the individual and collective levels), and in this history as that which mediates it comes to its own realization and to us. The metaphysical nature of a reality and the history belonging to it, and therefore grace considered as an existential modality on the one hand, and the history of salvation and revelation on the other, are not merely entities existing concomitantly with one another. Rather they mutually condition one another, and this is something which must be shown precisely in terms of a transcendental theology. This means that transcendental theology neither can nor will constitute theology as *such*, but is rather an element in it, because theology (or better and more precisely faith, the element of reflective thought inherent in this, and the elements which are ultimately incapable of being reflected upon in it which theology has to consider) are always intended to express that which is concrete and historical in its irreducibility, and in this must precisely render intelligible the fact that this concrete element in history can really affect man at the ultimate level of his existence and his subjectivity. The significance in terms of concrete human living (i.e. as affecting the whole of man in his salvation) of historical facts is something which man is quite incapable of rendering intelligible without transcendental theology. This is so for the very reason that the knowledge of the factuality of such saving events cannot be achieved *merely a posteriori*. If they are intended to affect man as such, man himself must achieve contact with himself as a whole. In other words he must discover that he is, of his very nature, orientated to them. Insofar as he recognizes their bearing upon himself he engages in transcendental theology. Reflection upon the transcendental reference of man to these saving events is not rendered impossible by their historicity or the fact that they are freely posited, by their *a posteriori* character, or by their factuality as freely posited by God. For that which is initially and in the truest sense freely posited by God is precisely the enduring and supernatural existential modality of grace considered as the offering of God's self-communication – in other words a transcendental state in which man is constituted. And this free grace, considered as a transcendental determination of man, has a history of its own in that which we call the history of salvation and revelation, which it is quite impossible to conceive of precisely *as* such without this *a priori* possibility on man's part.

Now it is this that is the object of consideration for transcendental theology.

III

A single phrase could be used, a title to sum up the theme of this third lecture: *reductio in mysterium*. Obviously such a theme does also constitute a special area of subject-matter in theology. At the same time, however, and over and above this, it also expresses a methodological pointer for the theologian, serving to warn him against falling into a certain kind of illusion, at least so far as theology is concerned. This is the illusion that the mystery of reality as such is merely that part of it which still remains obscure for the time being even though in principle it is comprehensible, a part, therefore, which is constantly being diminished as the various branches of science advance, and which is destined ultimately to disappear completely at least in the 'visio beatifica'. Now this illusion, this radical misunderstanding of himself on man's part, is *de facto* constantly asserting itself again and again in theology, and for this reason when we come to speak of the *reductio in mysterium* of all theological proposition which takes place in theology, this also constitutes a methodological guide which is of fundamental importance. Precisely today it is of the utmost importance that we shall understand the significance which theology has as *reductio in mysterium*, i.e. we must understand that this *reductio* constitutes not a regrettable imperfection in theology, but rather that which is most proper to it of its very nature. Theology must be bold enough to make it clear to modern man that this *reductio in mysterium* is its positive distinguishing characteristic and at the same time the task most proper to it — something, in fact which arises as a matter of transcendental necessity from the very nature of man himself. If theology fails to do this, then in an age which sets a premium upon scientific knowledge, men will inevitably receive the impression that theology is the mere external facade for an intellectual discipline which increasingly dissolves and frees itself from theology itself. It is all too easy for modern man to receive the impression that theology supplies answers of a mythological kind or otherwise unscientific answers to questions which either have no communicable meaning or which in reality will only be answered by the sciences of the day. It is all too easy for modern man to receive the impression that theology is a mere interweaving of ideas which are, of their nature, incapable of any verification, which remain at the level of poetical concepts and can still be upheld, at most, simply by pointing with a certain arbitrariness to those dark and subconscious levels in man which have not yet been illumined by the anthropological sciences and so, for the time being, are not yet really capable of being used in any constructive system of thought. Now in reply to such an attitude on the part of modern man what can the theology of faith say when it sets itself resolutely to stand and to make a direct counter-attack upon this attitude, i.e. when it manifests its position with the utmost conscious rationality of which it is capable as a transcendental discipline? It can only assert that this reference to the absolute mystery which it involves is in fact the condition which makes all the perceptions available to the human reason possible. It can only point out that 'mystery' is not merely another word for that which for the time being has not yet been comprehended and perceived, that it is both possible and meaningful explicitly to come to terms with mystery as such and in itself, so that we precisely do not have to say with Wittgenstein that we should simply be silent about anything concerning which we cannot speak clearly. Theology then is to be understood as the 'science' of mystery as such (though admittedly it is this as sustained by *that* proximity of this mystery to man which is designated by Christians as grace etc.). Furthermore the only chance which theology has of providing for the future is for it to show itself openly and with the utmost resolution true to its own nature in this sense, and for it to refuse to conceal its true nature for fear of modern man's opinion. And if all this is true, then theology must not forget this nature which it has in the manner in which it is practised from day to day among the theologians themselves either. It must understand itself not as that science which develops itself more and more in a systematic drawing of distinctions down to the last possible detail, but rather as that human activity in which man, even at the level of conscious thought, relates the multiplicity of the realities, experiences, and ideas in his life to that mystery, ineffable and obscure, which we call God. How strange it is in fact! We are accustomed to understand the history of revelation and dogma according to the conceptual model of a logically developing system in which ever finer distinctions are drawn. There may be some element of truth in this, and it may be that those phases in the history of dogma and theology which now lie behind us can to a large extent be rendered comprehensible in terms of a conceptual model of this kind. After all even Thomas Aquinas regarded the true nature of theology as consisting in a progressive exposition in terms of concepts of this kind, and the same idea still dominates the modern interpretation of the history of theology. And yet the question may be asked whether it really does constitute the basic principle of development of the history of dogma and theology as such, or merely that of one specific epoch in it, and one which, even though it has lasted for almost two thousand years, is in our own days drawing to its close. And further, is it not possible to understand even the history of dogma and theology up to the present as a *reductio in mysterium* constantly renewed, constantly made more radical, of all theological statements, so that precisely the believer actively engaged in theology knows better than anyone else that every theological statement is only truly and authentically such at that point at which man willingly suffers it to extend beyond his comprehension into the silent mystery of God?

First an attempt must be made very briefly to say something about mystery as such, before we undertake the further attempt to understand theology itself as *reductio in mysterium* (in all this it is, of course, self-evident that theology as such constitutes such a *reductio in mysterium* only in a *derived* sense, since the original act by which man surrenders himself to the mystery is as such the act of faith). Again in defining what mystery means the declarations of the Church's *magisterium*, and still more the general tendency in theological thinking, take as their basis that which is not mystery at all. Thus mystery is made to appear in a purely negative guise as that which has not been comprehended, that which can only with difficulty avoid giving the impression of being contradictory, and yet at the same time that which is destined to be illumined for man too one day, and as mystery to be dissolved at latest in the '*visio beatifica*', or perhaps only at that stage. Mystery is restricted almost inadvertently to a pilgrim mode of existence here below. Thus mystery is presented under a merely negative aspect. In comparison with that which man can comprehend that which he recognizes as mystery may be in its own objective reality for the most part or even always of greater importance for his salvation. But even so the very fact that he is still aware of it precisely as mystery makes his present knowledge of it negative by comparison with any other knowledge which he has, and still more by comparison with knowledge of this mysterious entity in itself, for he thinks of this as in principle possible and as something that he will later attain to, so that then this knowledge will itself dissolve the element of mystery in his earlier knowledge and in the entity that was mysterious in itself. The measure and ideal of knowledge that is applied to knowledge of mystery is that which comprehends and thoroughly sees into the object known.

In reality, however, this is not the case. The concept of mystery that is commonly accepted is false, or at any rate superficial. This is implied even by the dogmatic teaching of the abiding and essential incomprehensibility of God, which is not eliminated even in the '*visio beatifica*', but on the contrary is borne in upon us in its most radical, most infinite, and most blessed form precisely there. In this statement the word 'blessed' needs special emphasis. For manifestly the incomprehensibility of God as made immediately present to the creature signifies not the limit, the mere borderline showing the finitude of the beatific vision of God. Rather it is a positive element in this vision in itself, because clearly man can achieve the truest fulfilment of his own nature at that point, and only at that point, at which he reaches beyond himself and oversteps the limitations of his own knowledge, being definitely drawn out of himself and ecstatically attaining to the incomprehensibility of God as such, which we only truly grasp in its immediacy when it is accepted by us as that which abidingly blesses us. This in itself is sufficient to reveal every kind of comprehensive knowledge for what it really is: the knowledge appropriate to a finite reality considered as that which is provisional, part of our pilgrim mode of existence, not bestowing any blessing upon us. The dogma of the incomprehensibility of God is in itself enough to show that comprehensive knowledge is a deficient mode of knowing when measured by that knowledge which is beyond all doubt the highest, the most intensive, and that which bestows the deepest blessing upon us, that which takes place in the immediate vision of the incomprehensibility of God.

Now the same conclusion which we have been able to demonstrate on the basis of a direct dogmatic datum can also be arrived at by approaching the question rather from the standpoint of the philosophy of transcendentality. Man is the subject of a transcendentality that is limitless. As such he apprehends each of the objects of his knowledge and freedom in a prior awareness, itself not contained within any finite limits, of the original and infinite unity of all possible objects. Yet at the same time man as subject in this sense of a transcendence that is limitless must not, even as such, be understood as the absolute subject, for this would be God. Now if this is true then the condition which makes any individual act of cognition possible is this prior awareness of that horizon of all knowledge and freedom which is absolute. In other words it is that which, while not simply identical with the knowing subject, is the condition which makes any act of cognition on his part possible. It can never be known in the same way as the individual objects of cognition which are rendered intelligible and comprehensible precisely in virtue of the fact that they fall within the ambience of this horizon of all knowledge. This horizon, then, which makes knowledge possible within its ambience, this ultimate point of reference towards which all knowledge tends, is itself radically beyond all comprehension, and its incomprehensibility is such that it is not removed even when, in accordance with the Christian doctrine of the 'finitum' considered as 'capax infiniti', the absolutely original cause and the ultimate goal of this transcendental awareness, prior to all knowledge, actually imparts itself directly to man. Indeed it is precisely at this moment that this first cause and ultimate goal really manifests itself as incomprehensible in the most radical sense. Thus the *mysterium* reveals itself as the condition which makes it possible for us to know that which is not mysterious. The relationship in which man stands to the *mysterium* is a primary and an ultimate datum of his own nature and his mode of existence, one of which, in his transcendence, he is constantly aware, though not as the object of his conscious thought, and one which cannot be deduced from any other datum as a secondary phenomenon. The *mysterium*, therefore, is that which alone is genuinely self-evident, and for that very reason that too which can always be overlooked and misinterpreted as a negative phenomenon belonging to the periphery of human living.

Taking the concept of the *mysterium* in the sense in which we have presented it here (though admittedly we have only given a brief indication of what we mean by it) we can now begin to understand the nature of theology as *reductio in mysterium*. The fact that Christian theology has to do with mysteries (in the plural) is something that this theology itself regards as immediately obvious. Moreover this point has been formulated still more explicitly and precisely in the official teaching of the Church by Pius IX and the First Vatican Council in answer to a kind of rationalism which had come to regard every theology of revelation involving faith as constituting merely the prelude to a philosophical vision. In this official teaching of the Church, however, these mysteries as such continued to be viewed in their relationship to the situation of man as pilgrim, and hardly any attempt was made to bring this teaching about the mystery explicitly into connection with the eternal and abiding incomprehensibility of God. And even abstracting from this point, no consideration was ever given to the strangeness of the fact that the mysteries of faith as such should be manifold. The question of whether in fact there could be many real mysteries in the strictest sense of the term such that they were really distinct from one another was hardly touched upon, if indeed it was adverted to at all. It seemed more or less obvious that this question would have to be answered in the affirmative in view of the many mysteries with which theology *de facto* has to deal. And yet it is perfectly possible to lay down the following thesis: there is, and there can be, only one single absolute mystery in the strictest sense of the term, namely God himself and in relation to him all those aspects under which man with his finite knowledge has to conceive of God to himself are specified in the same manner by this character of the *mysterium*. The thesis can also be formulated negatively: a finite being as such can never be a *mysterium* in the strict sense of the term, but is, of its very essence, merely that which has not yet been fully understood. On any correct ontology of the relationship between being and knowledge, which ultimately speaking consists in the confrontation of a being with itself, it belongs to every finite being necessarily and of its very nature that it should be endowed with a kind of cognition appropriate to itself such that for its own cognitive powers this being cannot be a mystery to itself (apart from its radical orientation to the one mystery which is God). The reason for this is that this mode of cognition is either simply identical with the being concerned or, in virtue of its unlimited transcendentality, it offers every finite being sufficient scope for it itself to be understood within this. Every finite being, therefore, as such, and in its very nature as positive is (abstracting from its intrinsic reference to God) non-mysterious. For this reason it also constitutes as such a mere object for the sciences to investigate to the extent that these are different from theology. Just as all worldly realities are withdrawn from the sphere of the numinous through recognition of the fact that they have been created and are different from God, so too they must in themselves also be removed from the sphere of any ideologizing, i.e. they must be radically submitted to the control of the sciences in the knowledge that no being accessible to the categories of human cognition can be mysterious, unfathomable or obscure. It cannot be this except of course through and in its reference to the incomprehensible horizon of all apprehension in terms of human categories, namely God. Now this reference of which we have just been speaking (and it is this alone that renders the particular being mysterious and at the same time *non*-mysterious in that special 'quiddity' which is proper to *it* in itself) can be a twofold one: the reference to God as remote and the reference to God as making himself near by an act of self-bestowal. It is the first of these two aspects that constitutes the element of mystery inherent in the world and in worldly knowledge. The second ultimately speaking constitutes (a point which we still have to develop) the whole content of the Christian mysteries.

In the light of this it is in a true sense clear that theology cannot contain as many mysteries as one wishes to ascribe to it. Basically speaking there can only be *one* mystery: God as he is in himself. This means that theology has the task of reducing the mysteries which manifest themselves, or appear to manifest themselves in it to this single mystery, in order thereby to avoid the danger of invoking mysteries in those areas in which all that is really needed is a more penetrating consideration, or perhaps even the 'de-mystification' in some respect of a given proposition of theology. Now this process of reducing the many mysteries in theology to the single mystery which is God is not particularly difficult. The fact that God in and for himself constitutes mystery in the strictest sense of the term and eternally – even, therefore in the '*visio beatifica*' – this is a point that needs no further explanation here. Insofar as there are propositions in theology over and above this which do constitute mystery in the strict sense, this can only mean two things: on the one hand, in accordance with what we have said, they must refer to God himself, while on the other, in order for them not simply to be identical with the mystery thus mentioned, even formally speaking so far as we are concerned, they must signify God himself in his reference *to us*. This reference cannot simply be that which is constituted by the relationship in which God stands to the world and the individual elements in this as their creator. For abstracting from the scholastic principle that as creator God has no real relationship to the world, and that it is only the world that has the relationship to him, the content of this relationship, over and above the element of mystery in it deriving from its single point of reference, God, would be identical with the reality of the creature itself, and therefore in principle no true mystery at all. The relationship of God to the world in which God is mystery, therefore, can only consist in the fact that it is constituted by God himself and not by any created reality distinct from himself. In other words this means that over and above his 'intrinsic' status as mystery, God can be mystery only in virtue of a quasi-*formal* causality in which he makes not some entity different from himself, but rather *himself* (in his freedom and abiding sovereignty) the specification of the creature. Let us put the same point in a different way: over and above the mystery intrinsic to his own nature God can only be a mystery in virtue of his self-bestowal, in which that which is bestowed is formally speaking God himself as mystery. Probably there is no need to spend any further time in demonstrating the point that here we have arrived at the key mysteries which are pointed to in traditional theology. For in the very meaning of this concept of God's self-bestowal both that which is designated as the hypostatic union is signified and at the same time that which is referred to as super-natural grace and '*visio beatifica*'. The reason is that in both of these what takes place is truly one and the same act of self-bestowal on God's part, an act which cannot be subsumed with other acts under the concept of the power of God's efficient causality as creator. This means that we are in a position to make the following assertion: That mystery which Christian faith acknowledges consists in the sheer fact that the absolute reality of God himself (of course understanding this as personal, loving, and grace-giving) cannot only achieve a creative confrontation with that which is other to itself, but actually wills to commit itself to, and bestow itself upon this. Then, from the point of view of the creature we can go on to say: the mystery here consists in the fact that it truly is, in the radical sense already referred to, '*capax infiniti*'.

In order to clarify still further this unity which belongs to the one mystery, we would have to go on from this point to work out in detail the unity and the mutually conditioning relationship between the Incarnation and the process by which the world is assimilated to God by grace, a development which we cannot undertake at this point. We may say here, however, that both of these factors constitute the free act of God, yet that at basis they constitute only one single object of the exercise of his freedom as such. Here then we have a theology of the one mystery of God's self-bestowal upon the world with its two mutually conditioning aspects of Incarnation and grace. Now if it is clear what is meant by this theology then the mystery of the Trinity is *ipso facto* given in such a theology and rendered intelligible as mystery. All that has to be done – and that too precisely on the basis of the concept of God's *self*-bestowal is to show that the Trinity as present in the economy of salvation through the two '*missiones*' (of grace and the Incarnation) necessarily embodies also the Trinity as immanent.

Once the two central mysteries of Christianity are recognized as constituting the single mystery of God's self-bestowal upon the world, then we might go on to ask in more precise terms whether other mysteries apart from these do not arise in dogmatic theology such that on the one hand they cannot be subsumed under the one mystery of the self-bestowal of the absolute mystery which is God, while on the other they can justifiably be claimed to be absolute mysteries in the true sense. In my opinion we can unhesitatingly answer this question in the negative. This opinion is based not only on *a priori* considerations put forward above, but also on certain *a posteriori* considerations in which the assertions of dogmatic theology are put to the test to see whether they can justifiably be claimed to be mysteries in the true sense without constituting an element in the mystery of God's self-bestowal and coming to be recognized as such. At most the question might be raised whether the character of mystery is not so unambiguously ascribed by tradition to transubstantiation that in this particular case we have to recognize a mystery in the strictest sense, and one that is supplementary to and distinct from the mystery of God's self-bestowal. But surely we can at least leave this question open, for it can at least be asked whether on the one hand tradition does not cling to an exaggeratedly 'physical' understanding of this mystery, and on the other whether we do not have to regard the real presence of Christ as so closely bound up with the mystery of the Incarnation that from the outset it is only possible to conceive of any transubstantiation at all insofar as it is related to the reality of Christ in general. Here we have only been able to indicate the considerations which we feel to be relevant, yet precisely on the basis of these transubstantiation does nevertheless seem not to tell against our general thesis, namely that there is only *one single* mystery in the strict sense, that of God's self-bestowal by which he extends himself into the dimension of that which is most interior to existence (Spirit) and into the dimension of the history of man (Incarnation).

Now to reduce the actual statements of revelation in this way to the one single mystery has a further significance beyond that which it has for the development of a distinctive theological system as such. The true significance of this *reductio in unum mysterium* is to be found elsewhere. We are taking as our starting-point the intrinsic unity and the mutually conditioning relationship between Incarnation and the grace by which the world is assimilated to God, and we are not overlooking the fact that of his very nature as a historical being man necessarily seeks for the concrete historical manifestation of that which he is as a transcendental being in his own history. This is because history is precisely that process in which the fulness of his own transcendental being is progressively made over to him. On the basis of all this, then, we can here concentrate upon the process by which man is endowed with grace and so assimilated to God without thereby losing sight of the single mystery of salvation in its totality. But on this basis we are compelled to state the matter as follows: that supernatural grace which has supernaturally orientated the transcendentality of man to the immediacy of God must not be conceived of merely as a material addition or supplement such that the only kind of knowledge which can be had of it is that which comes through indoctrination from without. Rather it is something of which man himself must necessarily be aware, even though he does not consciously objectify it to himself. Now if and to the extent that this is true it follows that the totality of the message of the Christian faith is in a real sense already given in a transcendental experience. This does not of course make the history of revelation or the act of bearing witness to the faith, which comes from hearing, superfluous. It is precisely this history of revelation and history of faith at the social level that constitutes the historical process by which this grace-given transcendental experience, constituted and upheld as it is by the self-bestowal of God, is brought to the stage of self-realization. It is precisely in order to arrive at the most ultimate and transcendental dimension of his own nature that man is orientated towards his own history at both the individual and collective levels. But precisely as such this is the history of his own transcendental nature itself. Hence it is that revelation as the transcendental experience of grace and revelation as history do not mutually contradict one another but rather are the mutually conditioning elements in one and the same event. In this sense, then, theology constitutes the *reductio in mysterium* and in fact *in unum mysterium*. But this still does not mean that what we are treating of here is merely a process of unifying and systematizing at the conceptual level the various dogmatic statements in which revelation is expressed. Equally, and in a more basic sense, we are concerned with the attempt to interpret all these various statements as a summons to that ultimate and transcendental experience of grace which is implicit in all these statements and which signifies the ultimate verification of them all.

What is meant by this is already to be perceived in scripture itself. For theologians scripture is indeed the absolute norm. But it is this not because the revelation imparted by God takes place originally and for the first time in these human statements as such, but rather because in them the original experience of the Spirit and of its eschatological address to man in Jesus Christ has been objectified in a form which has abiding validity and with a purely normative force. Measured by this original experience scripture is in itself theology, albeit at the normative level, and even though obviously an original and basic experience of this kind never takes place without some kind of conceptual objectivation in terms of human categories. Thus the task of theology must precisely be to appeal in all the various conceptual forms in which it is objectified, to this basic experience of grace, to bring man again and again to a fresh recognition of the fact that all this immense sum of distinct statements of the Christian faith basically speaking expresses nothing else than an immense truth, even though one that has been explicitated throughout all the levels of man's being; the truth namely that the absolute mystery that is, that permeates all things, upholds all things, and endures eternally, has bestowed itself as itself in an act of forgiving love upon man, and is experienced in faith in that ineffable experience of grace as the ultimate freedom of man. So long as theology remains stuck fast at the merely conceptual level – however necessary this may be in itself – it has failed in its true mission. And if we seek to take refuge in the consoling thought that after all the statements of theology still speak constantly of God, and therefore of mystery, then it must be rejoined that this alone is not enough to avoid the danger of sticking fast in this sense. It is not only the 'fides quae' that must come to terms with God as mystery, but also the 'fides qua'. The act of faith as such in itself, and not merely its conceptual objectifications, must in some sense come to terms with the mystery as such. For this too theology (considered as a whole) should offer guidance and direction. It should constitute a 'mystagogia' leading men to the experience of grace, and should not merely speak of grace as of a material subject which is present in man's life solely through the conceptions which he formulates of it. Theology as science must certainly not be confused with kerygma, with parenesis, with the immediate utterance of the Spirit. But at the same time it must not forget either, as it all too often does, that it dervies from the utterance of the Spirit and has to serve it. For unless this utterance of the Spirit and the theology deriving from it are related to the ultimate experience of the Spirit in the life of man they lose their distinctive subject-matter altogether.

This task of theology, then, can be defined as a *reductio in unum mysterium*, and that too in terms of its own subject-matter and in the concrete circumstances in which it is currently formulated. From this very many consequences can be drawn for the practice of theology today. Here we can mention only very few of these, which we have selected at random. The propositions of theology must constantly be referred back to the single indefinable mystery and the ultimate and grace-given experience of this. In fact all of them express, ultimately speaking, nothing else than the fact that this mystery has imparted itself so as to achieve a state of absolute proximity to man, in which it becomes his authentic consummation and the future that lies before him. The process by which the connection between these propositions and the mystery itself is firmly established belongs to the true nature of theology as such, and this ultimately speaking constitutes the true difference between these propositions and those pertaining to the secular sphere. For these latter too do indeed express realities related to God, but in what they express the actual mystery remains unaffected and still more fails to reveal the reference latent in them to the *im*mediacy of God. This, however, is not to deny, but on the contrary once more to reiterate, that the statements of theology are different from that which they point to, even though the difference here is not self-evident, as it is in the case of statements belonging to the secular sphere. This means that theological statements have a special and peculiar theological relativity of their own, i.e. their radical reference to that which infinitely transcends them, such that without this reference they become meaningless. Now this distinctive relativity in theological statements is something constantly to be enquired into anew in a peculiar and special form of dialectic. It is one that cannot be replaced by an attitude of silent adoration, by a '*theologia meditativa*' which effectively reduces itself to silence. Nor can we express these statements in a form which suggests that the actual formulation of them in human words is the ultimate goal at which we are aiming. Rather it is the attitude of trembling and silent adoration which is intended to beget these statements, and this belongs to that deathly silence in which man's lips are sealed with Christ's in death. It is, therefore, a very difficult task with which theology has to cope in these statements. They must be expressed in words in order that we can arrive at the authentic silence which we need. They must be borne with in patience and hope in respect both of their necessity and of their incommensurability, in which they attempt to utter the ineffable. I believe that theology today has still very much to learn before it speaks in such a manner that men can achieve a direct, effective, and clear recognition of the special quality of this language.

It always remains true, then, that theological statements only authentically become such in a process in which they reach out to a point radically beyond themselves. And if this is true, then, so it seems to me, we in the Church could often show ourselves far more favourable and tolerant with regard to those statements which we may be tempted to qualify as 'heresies' on the grounds that they seem so inappropriate to the reality they express. This applies both to ourselves and to a *magisterium* in the Church which may be excessively self-confident in the manner in which it does its work. Of course the Church has a right and a duty to reject certain theological statements as irreconcilable with her own conviction of her faith. And indeed properly speaking anyone who is suspected of 'heresy' in this way should not be so very resentful that his statement has been rejected provided that in this statement of his he too really has arrived at the *reductio in mysterium* without which his statement certainly would be a heresy. This *reductio* is certainly neither prohibited nor rendered impossible by the fact that his statement has been subjected to censure. The situation today is that every statement of the Church's *magisterium* includes an element of regulating the actual language of theology, something which, fundamentally speaking, has nothing to do with the actual reality in itself. Moreover our position today is quite different from that of earlier times. Today we have to take into account a situation in which on the one hand loyal believers and adherents of the Church, with the best will in the world, cannot come to terms with specific statements of the official teaching of the Church, while on the other they have not *de facto* simply arrived at an interpretation of such statements of their own such as could find acceptance on the part of the teaching authority of the Church. Now in this situation it is surely justifiable and necessary for the Church's *magisterium* to show more patience and prudence than it probably brought to bear in practice in earlier times in many cases in which its authority was exercised. We must really and effectively practise theology on the basis of a *reductio in mysterium* in terms of its material content and of the actual concrete circumstances in which we practise it. We must genuinely, effectively, and radically realize the incommensurability of our own theological formulations, a point which in itself is self-evident. And if we do this, then, so I believe, we will very often find it possible to be more modest in presenting our own theology and more indulgent in considering that of others which we are tempted to qualify as heretical. Certainly we cannot hasten at will the gradual advance of history. But did not individuals on both sides already find it possible, even at the time of the Reformation, to perceive that the really fundamental positions of both sides with regard to justification, scripture, faith, etc. certainly did not positively contradict one another, a fact which today is, after all, conceded by both sides? I believe that in a theology which genuinely and effectively, and not merely verbally, realized its own nature as *reductio in mysterium* we of today could in many cases be more patient with so-called 'heresies', of course always with the proviso that the theology suspected by anyone of being heresy is intended in itself to be a *reductio in mysterium*. In fact in the theology put forward by many individuals this actually has been achieved with a notable degree of effectiveness. The theology in question must not merely be a superficial rationalism intended to preserve the individual from having to commit himself to the unfathomable depths of the mystery. And of course a further proviso must be that a theology which is 'under suspicion' in this sense must itself not represent any *schismatic* tendency, any attitude of arrogance in which it refuses to pay heed to the formulations of traditional theology. Rather it must in a right manner and in the right place pay due heed to the prescriptions with regard to language put forward and maintained for theology by the Church's *magisterium* in order to preserve the unity of the Church's own creed. With these provisos, however, we of today both can and should show ourselves generous, patient, and tolerant with regard to theological statements which do not immediately strike us as being 'orthodox'. We should adopt this attitude in view of the fact that the pluralism among the theologies of today is too great for us to control or comprehend. Moreover we ourselves should have a little trust in the power of the reality itself which is being referred to, i.e. in the one single mystery of the proximity of the incomprehensible God who sets all things free to come to himself and to be drawn into his infinitude.

4

THE NEW CLAIMS WHICH PASTORAL THEOLOGY MAKES UPON THEOLOGY AS A WHOLE

THERE can no longer be any doubt that pastoral theology, at least on the radical view taken of it at the Second Vatican Council,[1] and especially in the formation of future priests, has achieved a far higher status among the theological disciplines and a greater importance than it

[1] The pastoral task laid upon the Council from the outset was repeatedly given expression, and also formulated in programmatic terms by John XXIII; 'Neque opus nostrum, quasi ad finem primarium, eo spectat, ut de quibusdam capitibus praecipuis doctrinae ecclesiasticae disceptetur, adque fusius repetantur ea, quae Patres ac theologi veteres et recentiores tradiderunt . . . Etenim ad huius modi tantum disputationes habendas non opus erat, ut concilium oecumenicum indiceretur . . . oportet ut haec doctrina certa et immutabilis cui fidele obsequium est praestandum, *ea ratione* pervestigetur et exponatur, quam tempora postulant nostra . . . scilicet eae induendae erunt rationes res exponendi, quae cum magisterio, cuius indoles praesertim pastoralis est, magis congruant', *AAS* 54 (1962), 791–793.

However obvious this exhortation may seem – for nothing is more obvious than to preach the faith according to the particular needs of the day – there are certain problems of scientific theory which underlie it and which must now be coped with, and certainly these were not presented to the Council in their full difficulty. Yet they did find expression with all the clarity that could be desired even within the Council and, as it appears, with unprecedented acuteness in the official sphere. This was in the Pastoral Constitution on the Church in the Modern World. The sustained conflict which took place over the various forms of the text between the rival claims of dogmatic content and understanding of the contemporary situation must here be regarded as particularly symptomatic. On this cf. Ch. Möller, 'Die Geschichte der Pastoralkonstitution', *LTK* Suppl. Vol. III (revised and expanded, Freiburg, 1968), pp. 242 ff.

On the problems referred to here cf. J. B. Metz (ed.), *Weltverständnis in Glauben* (Mainz, 1965); K. Rahner, 'On the Theological Problems Entailed in a "Pastoral Constitution" ', *Theological Investigations* X (London and New York), pp. 293–318; *idem*, 'The Church and The World', *Sacramentum Mundi* I (1968), pp. 325–327; E. Schillebeeckx, 'Kirche, Lehramt und Politik', *Gott – die Zukunft des Menschen* (Mainz, 1969), pp. 119–141.

These unsolved problems appeared in a still more acute, and apparently still more

formerly possessed.[2] Pastoral theology is a relatively young discipline.[3] It derives from the age of the Second Empire, and for this reason has, up to very recent times, really been able to exercise any effective influence only in the central European sphere.[4] According to the document 'Optatam totius' of the Second Vatican Council, however, it should not only be one distinct discipline among other special branches of theology, but should be accorded a role in the shaping of theological studies as a whole and should permeate them throughout their whole extent.[5] So far not much progress has been made in the fulfilment of this task in the Church, however, and it is rendered particularly difficult by the fact that among the theologians and those responsible for arranging the programmes of theological studies there is, and has been, a total lack of unanimity as to what the essence of pastoral theology actually consists in. This appears from the history of pastoral theology and the considerations of the specialist theologians as to its true nature. It is true that Anton Graf, the theologian of Tübingen (1811–1867) developed an idea of pastoral theology which has only been taken up once more in very recent times.[6] But apart from this the average idea which prevailed in the nineteenth and in the first half of the twentieth centuries amounted to saying that pastoral theology (insofar as it was accorded the status of an intellectual discipline at all) consisted of a collection of practical instructions for the cure of souls such as chaplains and parish priests (and apart from these

---

intractable form in the post-conciliar situation. But the true task of pastoral theology, to which it is urgently summoned at the present moment, is for the Church both at the universal and the individual levels, to develop a strategy which gives a precise theological formulation to, and at the same time advances further, the contemporary situation.

On the efforts which have been made in recent times to recognize these problems and (at least incipiently) to find a way of overcoming them, cf. n. 7.

[2] cf. 'Optatam totius', No. 16–21. Here too it is emphasized that formation in pastoral theology must equally include practical exercises within its scope. We shall not be entering any further into this question in the present study, because it is concerned with formation in pastoral theology as such and not directly with the 'demands' which pastoral theology makes upon theology as a whole.

[3] On the history of pastoral theology cf. especially H. Schuster, *Handbuch der Pastoraltheologie* I (Freiburg, 1964), pp. 40–92.

[4] What we mean is a scientific pastoral theology as a theological discipline in the true sense, and not as a practical introduction to catechesis, preaching, and practical work in the confessional ('casus conscientiae') etc.

[5] cf. No. 19.

[6] cf. A. Graf, *Kritische Darstellung des gegenwärtigen Zustandes der praktischen Theologie* (Tübingen, 1841), and on this H. Schuster, *op. cit.*, pp. 56 ff.

at most only the 'spiritual directors' in the confessional) have to exercise. It is not surprising, then, that a widespread opinion was that these pieces of practical advice for the concrete cure of souls at the level of the parish could already be imparted by the practitioners of other disciplines (chiefly moral theology and spiritual theology) as part of their courses without constituting any distinct discipline in its own right. It was felt, therefore, that the special functions which, after all, pastoral theology still really does have to achieve could in practice be achieved in several other branches of the more practical kind more or less independently of one another, as for instance in homiletics, catechetics, pastoral liturgy, so that it would be superfluous to have any special pastoral theology existing side by side with these more readily understood branches of instruction or practical work.

Against this view an essentially different and deeper concept of pastoral theology was developed in the *Handbuch der Pastoraltheologie*[7] which appeared in four volumes between 1963 and 1969, and also in the preliminary studies leading up to this. At the same time it still remains to be seen whether the new and deeper concept will achieve general acceptance at the levels of theory and above all of practice in the Church. In this conception

----

[7] F. X. Arnold (Vol. III: F. Klostermann, K. Rahner, V. Schurr, L. M. Weber edd., *Handbuch der Pastoraltheologie. Praktische Theologie der Kirche in ihrer Gegenwart*, Vol. I (Freiburg, 1964), Vol. II/1–2 (Freiburg, 1966), Vol. III (Freiburg, 1968), Vol. IV (Freiburg, 1969). Several translations are being prepared.

Apart from the studies by H. Schuster and K. Rahner in this manual (cf. especially I, pp. 93–114, 117–215, 323–332, 333–343; II/1, pp. 181 ff., 233 ff., 256; II/2, pp. 19 ff., 46 ff.) cf. also, especially on the whole range of problems treated of here, H. Schuster, 'Pastoral Theology: Nature and Function', *Concilium* I 3 (1965), pp. 4–9; *idem*, 'Pastoral Theology', *Sacramentum Mundi* 4 (New York and London, 1969), pp. 365–368: K. Rahner, 'Zur gegenwartigen Situation des Christen, Theologische Deutung der Position des modernen Christen in der modernen Welt', *Sendung und Gnade* (Innsbruck, 4th ed. 1966), pp. 13–47; *idem*, *Theological Investigations* X (London and New York, 1973), pp. 293–371; 'On the Theological Problems Entailed in a "Pastoral Constitution" ', *ibid.*, 'Practical Theology and Social Work in the Church', *ibid.*; cf. also F. Klostermann, 'Pastoraltheologie heute', *Dienst an der Lehre*, ed. by the Faculty of Catholic Theology of the University of Vienna = *Wiener Beiträge zur Theologie* X (Vienna, 1965), pp. 51–108; F. X. Arnold, 'Was ist Pastoraltheologie?', *Wort des Heils als Wort in die Zeit* (Treves, 1961), pp. 296–300; K. Delahaye, 'Überlegungen zur Neuorientierung der Pastoraltheologie heute', *Gott in Welt* II (*Festschrift für K. Rahner*), edited by J. B. Metz, W. Kern, A. Darlap, H. Vorgrimler (Freiburg, 1964), pp. 206–218. In addition cf. the general summary in the article by K. Rahner entitled 'Pastoraltheologie', *Was ist Theologie?* edited by E. Neuhäusler and E. Gössmann (Munich, 1966), pp. 285–309.

pastoral theology or 'practical theology',[8] as it should more rightly be
called, consists in scientific and theological research into the task laid upon
the Church in the present of achieving the fulness of her own nature as
Church. Two main features distinguish this concept of pastoral theology
from the earlier conceptions which prevailed: first, it is not confined
exclusively to the work of the clergy (and especially the 'lower ranks'of
them) or to the 'cure of souls' exercised by these in the narrower sense of
the term. Rather it extends to everything with which the *Church* as such
has to do, beginning from the worldwide Church and extending right
down to the local churches and the individual communities of believers.[9]
Thus (to select a few examples at random) among the questions pertaining
to a pastoral theology of this kind would be, e.g. a scientifically conducted
investigation into the form which a Roman congregation should assume
today, where as a matter of concrete practice a balance can be struck
between centralization and decentralization in the Church of today, how
large a diocese ought to be today having regard to the particular circumstances in particular societies in which it exists in any given case, what
ecclesiastical institutions ought to exist at the supra-parochial level apart
from the curia attached to the bishop of a diocese, what the constitution
of a national conference of bishops ought to be.[10] Such questions as this

[8] Protestant theology has long since given preference to this term (particular
reference should be made at this point to as early a writer as Schleiermacher). It is
also better because the term 'pastoral theology' always suggests the idea that it is
only the clergy (the 'pastors') who are the upholders of the Church's active work
which 'pastoral theology' is designed to study scientifically. But it is precisely this
point that is contested by the new and more comprehensive conception of 'pastoral
theology', and for this reason it ought to be called 'practical theology' as being less
liable to misapprehension.

In accordance with the fundamental ontological difference between the theoretical
and the practical reason, we might go on at this point to conceive of the two basic
branches of theological investigation each according to its own distinctive nature:
on the one hand those theological disciplines which are pursued at the level of the
theoretical reason (in other words systematic and historical theology), and on the
other hand precisely 'practical theology', which properly speaking once more transposes the whole of theology from the level of the theoretical reason to that of the
practical reason.

[9] On what follows cf. the author's study, 'Die Grundlegung der Pastoraltheologie
als praktische Theologie', *Handbuch der Pastoraltheologie* I (Freiburg, 1964), pp. 117 ff.

[10] In addition to the study in the *Handbuch* just mentioned cf. also on these particular specific questions K. Rahner, 'The Episcopal Office', *Theological Investigations*
VI (London and Baltimore, 1969), pp. 313–360; *idem*, 'Pastoral-Theological Observations on Episcopacy in the Teaching of the Vatican II', *Theological Investigations*
VI, pp. 361–368; *idem*, 'On Bishops' Conferences', *ibid.*, pp. 369–389.

and others almost beyond number belong (of course in addition to those already customarily regarded as belonging to it) to a pastoral theology of this kind[11] because today these questions can no longer be left solely to the prudent estimation of the higher authorities of the Church or to mere practical experience to decide.[12]

The second characteristic of a pastoral theology as understood here consists in the fact that an exact scientific investigation must be made into the concrete situation of the Church both interior and exterior, since in practice the achievement of her own fulness depends upon this. Moreover this investigation must be conducted in a theological manner since while the analysis of the contemporary situation does indeed presuppose the findings of the secular sciences, still for the purposes of pastoral theology it must be conducted in a specifically theological way.[13] If pastoral theology today is to take into consideration something more than the activities of the parish priest, having rather to work out in a process of scientific speculation the 'higher strategy'[14] of the Church in the fulfilment of her salvific task, then the findings of the secular sciences must be brought into theology and subjected once more to examination from the theological point of view in a way which certainly has not been achieved

[11] In making this point here we do not forget that the actual practice of the Church in all such questions always remains in itself one element in the decision in which a choice is implied. It is an element which cannot be replaced by any process of speculation, even as this is applied in practical theology. Nevertheless there still remains an essential difference between the two kinds of speculation: that of the theoretical reason, which is concerned with that which is and always must be the case (or alternatively speculation on the historical past insofar as this is presupposed in 'systematic theology', as for instance in the history of dogma or theology), and speculation upon the contemporary situation and on the question of what the appropriate action of the Church is to be in the *present* and future arising from this situation. Moreover while this kind of speculation does not lead unequivocally and of itself to a concrete imperative, still it does open up the field and define the limits within which a decision becomes possible and reasonable.

[12] In other contexts too in the sphere of secular politics etc. we notice an inevitable tendency to reduce everything to 'scientific method' through the 'social sciences', which are intended not merely to yield 'factual findings' but also to use the elements of creative imagination and critical speculation in order to provide patterns for social decision.

[13] On this cf. likewise the contribution of K. Rahner and N. Greinacher entitled 'Die Gegenwart der Kirche. Theologische Analyse der Gegenwart als Situation des Selbstvollzugs der Kirche', *Handbuch der Pastoraltheologie* II/1 (Freiburg, 1966), pp. 178–266.

[14] On this concept, and the problems it involves cf. K. Rahner, 'Das Verhältnis der Kirche zur Gegenwartssituation im allgemeinen, *ibid.* II/2, pp. 19 ff.

in any traditional pastoral theology so far. It is this theological analysis
of the contemporary situation which radically distinguishes pastoral
theology in this sense for instance from ecclesiology, which investigates
the nature of the Church, or even from canon law, to the extent that this
has as its proper field merely that law which is actually in force and the
history of this but not the 'jus condendum'.[15] At this point, however, we
cannot go any further in developing and justifying this new conception
of what pastoral theology must mean. For this we may refer to the
Handbuch already mentioned, though this is not to assert that this manual
has already achieved anything more than a fairly modest progress in
working out its own basic conception.

Before we can go on to consider the old and new conceptions of pastoral
theology in their relationship to theology and the study of theology in
general we must refer to yet 'another' theology which is new, and which
can by no means be passed over in the question of the relationship of
pastoral theology to theology in general. We are referring here to
'political theology'. It is not possible at this point to provide an account
of the nature of this 'political theology', still less to give an account of the
various interpretations of it which have been put forward by Catholic
and Protestant theologians.[16] Here we must content ourselves merely
with characterizing this theology in completely general terms by saying
that it is intended to overcome the tendency to restrict theology as a whole
exclusively to the private sphere of the salvation of the individual taken in
isolation, and to consider the relevance of all theological statements to the
politics of society and to sociology in general. Political theology is not,
however, intended itself to practise 'politics'. For precisely on its own
terms this must be left to a world which has 'become worldly' and autonomous. All that interests us here in view of the special subject with which
we are concerned is the relationship which political theology bears to
pastoral theology on our own understanding of what pastoral theology
means. Now any theological statement can have its points of relevance to,
and its implications for social politics and sociology in general – including,
therefore, those statements which pertain to the essential theological
disciplines which are distinct from pastoral theology itself. To this extent,

[15] If canonists were to consider their work as also and primarily concerned with
scientific speculation on the 'jus condendum' as this is required on the basis of a
theological speculation on the present and future of the Church, then this kind of
canon law (or this part of it) would constitute an element in pastoral theology.

[16] For a summary of this cf. J. B. Metz, 'Political Theology', Sacramentum Mundi
5, (1969), pp. 34–38.

therefore, and despite the fact that it is the activities of society as such that constitute the special concern of political theology, it does belong to the essential theological disciplines precisely because it is not in fact intended to be a special discipline with a particular 'area' of its own, but is rather conceived of as an essential element in all 'systematic' disciplines. To this extent, then, political theology constitutes no difficulty for pastoral theology, since the latter is in fact conceived of as a special theological discipline distinct from the others. An additional point is that political theology is orientated towards the task of the Church in the 'world' and secular society in the sphere of social politics and sociology. In other words it itself, even if it is not intended to be thought of as purely investi-gating an aspect of the actual 'nature' of the Church, is still concerned with a specific area in which the Church achieves the fulness of her own nature in the concrete. Nor would it make any difference to the points which we have made if it were to be pointed out that everything which the Church does also has a social significance and must be subjected to theological investigation from this aspect also.

Now if we accept the existence and special nature of pastoral theology, what are the consequences of this for the study of theology as a whole? What claims[17] does pastoral theology make on theology in general? Two points are obvious from the outset, and they are also points which are brought out in the documents of the Church with regard to the reform of theological studies.

First, in our own times pastoral theology must certainly constitute an important and significant branch of study among the other branches which are included in the theological formation of future priests.[18] This at least must be granted if the division of theology into its various branches which has been customary up to the present is by and large taken as given. Let us consider the normal formation of a young theologian on his way to becoming a priest, one who is destined to work at the cure of souls in the ordinary sense. Obviously the emphasis here will firmly have to be laid upon those sub-disciplines within this general subject entitled 'pastoral

---

[17] On this cf. E. Jüngel, 'Das Verhältnis der theologischen Disziplinen unterein-ander' = *Studien zur praktischen Theologie* edited by R. Bohren, K. Frör, M. Seitz (Munich, 1968), pp. 11 ff.; M. Seitz, 'Die Aufgabe der praktischen Theologie', *ibid.*, pp. 65 ff., and on this W. Herrmann and G. Lautner, *Theologiestudium. Entwurf einer Reform* (Munich, 1965).

[18] On the need to include pastoral theology already in the first semesters cf. the memorandum on the formation of students of theology in pastoral theology in *Diaconia* 3 (1968), pp. 372–375.

theology' which are particularly important for the practical activities of
a priest of this kind, that is e.g. on catechetics, homiletics, pastoral liturgy,
the scientific application of caritas, and (so far as priests working in the
missions are concerned) missiology. At the same time, however, it would
be regrettable if even in the formation of priests of this kind pastoral
theology were, in practice, to be reduced from the outset to the specific
department of 'practical' work which we have mentioned, and others of
the same kind, and if the future priest were not made familiar with the
other problems which belong to pastoral theology on a modern and more
comprehensive view of what this means. Attempts are constantly being
made to educate the members of a society to a point where they can
become active supporters of the life of the society equipped with a critical
awareness of the problems involved, and moreover, they must become
this (with the due and necessary reservations) by scientifically thinking
out the problems involved. On this view, then, every priest too ought to
have the sort of formation which does not merely equip him to fulfil the
immediate pastoral task to which he will be committed, but also, and more
than this, to take an active share in the responsibility of the Church as a
whole in the process of achieving the fulness of her own nature. He should
have a social and political awareness sharpened by scientific training with
regard to the life of the Church *as a whole*. He should be able to contribute
actively in his own way to the great decisions of the Church etc. Now the
necessary equipment to do this could be imparted to him through pastoral
theology, provided that the true nature of this is understood and realized
to the full, and provided that pastoral theology is not reduced simply to
the level of mere useful ideas and relegated to those sub-disciplines which
alone, so it is alleged, are interesting and important for the normal pastor.

The *second* point which is immediately obvious is the need for all
theological disciplines to be given a certain pastoral orientation. All of
them must, each in its own way, be ready to contribute to the man, the
Christian, and the future priest and the task which he will subsequently
have to fulfil. In the formation of the theologians our attitude towards the
theological disciplines in which we are engaged should not be research
for research's sake, or any kind of lofty 'l'art pour l'art'. Rather those
engaged in these disciplines must have an awareness of the fact that in this
formation of future priests the function they have to fulfil is one of contributing to that pastoral work. This does not imply any cheap populariza-
tion of the intellectual disciplines involved, nor, properly speaking, any
'haute vulgarization', any 'adult education courses' in the sphere of
theology. For the first consideration must be that the priest must be

educated in a conscious critical awareness of what his task involves, and this implies that he must be shown how to think out theological questions in a critical and scientific way, and the second consideration is that theology itself and the problems which constantly arise in it must be 'translated' in a manner that really is appropriate to the subject-matter involved and to the particular epoch. Now to express these matters in a way that is suitable to the times, and which makes it possible to preach them, is itself in turn a task to be scientifically worked out, and one which often demands more in terms of living awareness and strength on the part of the specialist theologian than if he confines himself merely to contributing to his own special branch of theology at the scientific level. Yet in the way in which these particular subjects are studied this process of orientating all theological disciplines towards the practical work of the future priest still remains to a large extent an unfulfilled need. We cannot enlarge any further at this point on the question of what is implied in particular detail by this need for all theological subjects to be orientated, in this way, towards the practical pastoral activities of the priest.[19]

All that we have said so far, however, is totally inadequate as an explanation of the claims which pastoral theology makes upon theology in general. In order to achieve any further progress in this direction we must present certain preliminary considerations with regard to specific aspects of the reform of theological studies in general which has been recognized as due in our own times.

Let us consider first the theory of the nature of a university. In this a justifiable distinction is drawn with regard to the tasks of a university or university faculty and a teacher of academic subjects between teaching and research. The teacher of academic subjects has not merely to teach, not merely to hand on a certain amount of scientific knowledge which he has already gained, or to transmit this to his students with didactic skill He should also undertake 'research', i.e. he should make a critical and positive further contribution to the problems which arise in his particular science. These two tasks are of course intrinsically connected, and ultimately speaking mutually condition one another. But the teachers at the academic level need not merely to strive to fulfil them and to achieve them by their own personal work. Most tasks also need the institutional conditions necessary for their fulfilment as also does research itself. Now among these institutional conditions we have today to include, and that too

---

[19] On this cf. also the idea of a basic course in theology which I have developed extensively in connection with 'Optatam totius': K. Rahner, *Zur Reform des Theologiestudiums* = Quaestiones Disputatae 41 (Freiburg, 1969), pp. 51 ff.

in a higher degree than formerly, the factor of 'teamwork'. This need not necessarily consist solely in the collaboration of researchers at the same level of formation, but can be conceived of in the form of a collaboration of those who are still at the formative stages in their scientific work ('doctorandi', 'habilitandi') working with an experienced researcher. Here too this collaboration can in its turn assume the most varied forms. At this point a special kind of contact is achieved between teaching and research such that they can actually constitute a practical unity. Nevertheless teaching and research are ultimately speaking *not* simply identical with one another. For even instruction at the academic level in the universities is, in the vast majority of cases, aimed at the formation of individuals who themselves are not in turn destined to become scientific researchers as their own vocation for life. Rather they are intended to apply what they have learned in some 'practical calling' outside the university itself. It is of course a question in itself whether in view of the immense mass of scientific material which has been accumulated, the increasing complexities in scientific method in research etc., we should not introduce a new kind of school intermediary between the high school (secondary schools designed to mature the students to the point where they are ready to enter university) on the one hand, and the universities themselves on the other (considered as institutions for research and for the introduction of the new generation into research as such). These intermediary schools, then, would be 'schools for advanced specialist studies', and in them the material findings of science aimed at by research properly so called would be communicated to those who were intended to apply it in the sphere of a practical calling not designed to make any practical contribution to research itself. In other words it is certainly an open question today whether research and teaching can still remain united institutionally in a single university or university faculty without one or other of the two tasks having to suffer by this. But even if we hold firm to the idea of the university as a single institution sustaining both tasks at once, research and teaching together, and even if we do not regard this idea of the university as utopian in the conditions prevailing today, it must still remain clear that research and teaching do constitute two tasks which, both at the personal and institutional levels, are very different.

Everything which has been said precisely with regard to the university or university faculty in general applies also to a theological faculty and the tasks with which it is confronted. In earlier times in the majority of countries in the Catholic world the theological institutions were more or less identical with the seminaries, and very often these served only to teach, to impart material scientific knowledge, to the next generation of priests, so that in them the teacher of theology was not a researcher in the real sense. By contrast with this the recent pronouncements of the Church with regard to the study of theology do show a certain tendency (to express it prudently) towards the position that all theological study should take place at an 'academic level' after the manner of the theological faculty in a university.[20] Of course this has a positive importance of its own which is very great. But at the same time it also raises, of its very nature, all those problems which are today connected with the ideal of a university as combining research and teaching and pursuing them as a unity. It is of course obvious that in instructing future priests a teacher of theology must not simply provide a higher level of catechetical instruction – in other words that he can only impart the kind of knowledge required for this if he himself is also in some sense a researcher in the sphere of theology. But however true this may be, it still does appear today that in the sphere of theology too research and teaching (considered as the formation of future priests who are not destined to be specialist theologians) can be practised in combination only with great difficulty.

This difficulty is not *merely* that difficulty which threatens the unity of research and teaching at the university in general. There are special reasons, over and above this, that apply to the study of theology in particular. The chief of these consists in the multiplicity of disciplines which have accumulated in the course of the last hundred years as special subjects of instruction within the single discipline of theology, all of which are of obligation. These special subjects are there. They have almost universally been taken as given in the considerations and dispositions which have been put forward for a reform of the studies. And on this

---

[20] By way of example we might adduce the following: *Sacra Congregatio pro Institutione Catholica, Normae quaedam ad constitutionem apostolicam 'Deus Scientiarum Dominus' de studiis academicis ecclesiasticis recognoscendam* (Rome, 1968). While the term 'Theologia pastoralis' does occur in this programme of studies, nevertheless the reality signified by this does not constitute a principle by which the whole of theology is structurally organized (p. 69). Moreover it can hardly be accepted that the pastoral theology signified in these *normae* is in itself aimed at 'practical theology' as briefly outlined above. With regard to these *normae*, therefore, the question has to be raised whether a central theological discipline is not needed in order that there may be an overall orientation of the Church in modern society, and whether this theological discipline should not be developed in terms of scientific theology precisely in the sense intended by the Council with a view to the organization of the Church and her overall strategy (e.g. with regard to the 'political' effectiveness of the central organs of the Church) for the world of tomorrow.

view, and with these presuppositions the only question which can still be raised and solved with regard to a reform of the studies is where the individual disciplines should come in the course of the years of study, and how many semesters and lecture periods should be devoted to each particular discipline. Now it must not be contested here that all these disciplines have their own justification as branches of theological *research*. The question is, however, whether it is equally necessary for all these numerous branches, autonomous as they are and therefore inevitably coming into rivalry with one another, to constitute particular subjects in the teaching and formation of future priests. I may suggest that this is in fact *not* the case, even though at this point I shall not be putting forward any more detailed arguments in support of this view.[21]

Provided a clear distinction is drawn between research and teaching there is at any rate no need to maintain the view that every area of research must also constitute a special branch of teaching different from the other branches, and which, without much regard to the other branches, is accorded a position governed by laws of its own within the general formation of young theologians. A different approach must be adopted, particularly today, because otherwise the proliferation of such special subjects, the material content of which has increased beyond all bounds, is brought to a point at which in studying all of them the theological student knows nothing of any. The organization and presentation of the subject-matter pertaining to the formation of the theology student for his future pastoral activities, and which has to be suitable for this end, must not be determined according to the branches into which theology is divided for the purposes of research. Insofar as it is meaningful at all to regulate the study of theology in terms of the various branches of research, it has at most a certain significance in the formation of future researchers. Though there has been a certain awareness of this in earlier attempts at working out the curriculum of studies, it has not been explicitly reflected upon. For in these earlier attempts there has been an intense concentration upon dogmatic and moral theology, and the other special subjects have been much neglected in favour of these – insofar as they have been accorded any place at all in the official timetable of study. Alternatively

[21] On this cf. the 'Quaestio Disputata' by K. Rahner already cited, *Zur Reform des Theologiestudiums* = Quaestiones Disputatae 41 (Freiburg, 1969), pp. 19 ff. and the positive counter-proposal on pp. 48–50.

'*Optatam totius*', No. 17 does indeed warn us against any 'nimia disciplinarum multiplicatio', but seems at least to accept the usual subjects as a fact which is inevitably given and which raises no problems.

a so-called 'seminarists' course' has been provided side by side with the academic one, in order thereby to orientate the subject-matter and mode of presentation of theological instruction to the real goal of this formation, at least to some extent.[22]

We may speak of the unity of theology and its pastoral orientation, but in reality the unexpected pluralism of the theological disciplines as they have developed in history has been left unaffected by this in the anxiety to achieve a course of studies which is as far as possible 'academic'. And so long as this is true any reform of theological studies is foredoomed to failure. For the purposes of teaching theology, as distinct from researching into theology, the traditional theological disciplines must be broken up, and the subject-matter which has to be taught must be organized on quite different principles. In demanding that the subject-matter of theology shall be presented according to a single unifying principle of organization[23] we are not, of course, implying that henceforward anything and

[22] An attempt is actually made to justify this in terms of 'scientific theory' by drawing a distinction between an 'academic' and a 'kerygmatic' theology. On this cf. J. A. Jungmann, *Die Frohbotschaft und unsere Glaubensverkündigung* (Regensburg, 1936); F. Lakner, 'Theorie einer Verkündigungstheologie', *Theologie der Zeit* 3 (Vienna, 1949), pp. 1–63; J. B. Lotz, 'Wissenschaft und Verkündigung', *ZKT* 62 (1938), pp. 465–501; H. Rahner, *Eine Theologie der Verkündigung* (Freiburg, 2nd ed. 1939) and against this E. Kappler, *Die Verkündigungstheologie* (Freiburg, 1949). While this distinction is not actually justified, since every theology must be scientific in its approach, and at the same time every theology as *'intellectus fidei'* must also be orientated towards preaching, still the whole range of problems raised in the thirties of the present century [on this cf. also K. Rahner, 'Kerygmatische Theologie', *LTK* VI (Freiburg, 2nd ed. 1961), 126; *idem*, 'Über die Verkündigungstheologie. Eine kritisch-systematische Literaturübersicht', *Paṛmanita Tudósító* (Dunaszerdahely, Hungary) 16 (1941–42), pp. 3–10] does show that even today a considerable part of theology as *de facto* practised is still not making a clear enough contribution to a form of preaching that is really relevant to the times, one which reaches modern man and touches his need for faith, and educates the young pastoral cleric in *his particular* tasks. One expression and cause of this deficiency, however, is also the excessive pluralism of the subjects included in the course of theological instruction. Unless this excessive pluralism is eliminated all reform of the curriculum of theological study remains at the level of mere theory. One might regard the determination to overcome this excessive pluralism, which is dictated by the subjects chosen as areas of research, as a touchstone for determining whether the will to undertake a far-reaching reform is real and sincere.

[23] The old and famous question of the 'formal object' of theology (in its unity and presupposed as constituting that unity) would provide a starting-point for investigating the question of a principle of structural organization for the whole course of theological instruction. But presumably it could never be anything more than such a starting-point.

everything which a young theologian has to hear and learn in the course of his studies must positively be integrated into this intrinsically structured corpus of his theological formation. Not only is this impossible from the technical point of view, but also it would lead to the forcing of a 'system' upon him, or at least the setting up of a 'system' which existed merely formally and on paper. Moreover to demand this would be to do violence to the very nature of human knowledge as such, and to the 'gnoseological and concupiscent' conditions to which the individual is subject and in which he is from the outset constantly exposed to a pluralism in the various branches of knowledge such that these do not mutually throw light upon one another.

When we say, therefore, that the special subjects in theology which have become traditional must be broken down in order that an intrinsically articulated structure may be imparted to the corpus of theological teaching, and in order that this teaching may be effectively imparted, this demand is not invalidated when the corpus properly so called comes to be surrounded by a whole circle of 'ancillary' subjects, 'special lectures', 'special courses', or even by particular courses of lectures in which at least a certain idea of the 'pursuit' of theological research and the methods and problems it entails is imparted to the student of theology. Hence we can leave open at this point the question of *which precise* special subjects in theology as taught up to now will have to be transformed so as to be included in this corpus of theology properly so called, and which other subjects as taught up to now can continue to exist as formerly, but now more or less as autonomous disciplines in their own right, i.e. as 'ancillary subjects' attached to the corpus of theology.[24] It is of course likewise impossible to enter here into the question of whether any consequences arise from the considerations we have put forward so far with regard to the relations between philosophy and theology on such a view of theology as this, and what those consequences are.[25] A further question of which

[24] There will be no attempt artificially to force such subjects, for instance, as Church history or history of philosophy, introduction to textual criticism of the New Testament etc. into this course. Rather they will firmly be allowed to remain as special courses in their own right. Otherwise there will in fact be no place for a corpus of teaching in which everything which the student of this body of doctrine needs to know can be integrated within a single dicipline.

[25] In the 'Latin' scheme of studies, which was different from the 'German' one, it was taken for granted that some years of the course of studies should be devoted to philosophy purely as such before the theologian began his theology. The justification for this Latin scheme is anything but obvious. It proceeds from a fundamental idea of the relationship between nature and grace, philosophy and theology, which was

we shall not be speaking here is concerned with exegesis, and that too not merely from the point of view of its very nature as theoretically conceived of, but also in view of the fact that it is not only the specialist, but every priest who must be a reader and interpreter of scripture as such. In exegesis, then, we cannot avoid the responsibility of ensuring that it shall not consist of an artificial and *a priori* interpretation of prescribed texts in answer to questions set for it by systematic theology. But the question concerning exegesis of which we shall not be speaking here is whether it can be incorporated into this newly structured corpus of theological teaching, and if so how, or alternatively whether it should exist autonomously side by side with this corpus as an independent discipline equal in importance to the corpus itself.[26] Thus a question which now arises is what, in more precise terms, the structure of this corpus of theological teaching should be, given that the process of working out this structure must not be prejudiced from the outset by the traditional disciplines of theology. Here we must mention two principles for working out a structure of this kind. They are not simply two principles among many other conceivable ones which we might perhaps have selected. Rather they have to be understood as arising fundamentally from the very nature of the question as the only two possible ones. A priest has to be trained for his future priestly tasks. But that which he has to impart to others as an official priest of the Church is precisely that which also constitutes his own personal existence as a man and a Christian. If both of these aspects are borne in mind then we can perhaps say that two and only two basic conceptions and principles of organization are possible for a

---

tacitly assumed, but which can surely no longer be accounted as self-evident, at any rate today. This is not in any way to deny the possibility of an independent, relatively autonomous philosophy, or the necessity for distinguishing in principle a '*duplex ordo cognitionis*' (*DS* 3105). But surely we must object to the procedure of a superficial departmentalization of philosophy and theology in which one is made to follow upon the other in the formation of a theologian. For today it is quite impossible for him any longer to be a 'philosopher' in the sense in which this was formerly conceived of. On this cf. K. Rahner, *Theological Investigations* IX, (London and New York, 1973) passim; and the author's article, 'Philosophy and Theology', *Theological Investigations* VI (London and Baltimore, 1969), pp. 71–81, and most recently 'Philosophy and Theology' in *Sacramentum Mundi* (New York and London, 1969) (bibliog.).

[26] On this cf. the discussion between N. Lohfink, 'Text und Thema', *Stimmung der Zeit* 181 (1968), pp. 120–126 and K. Rahner, 'Die Exegese im Theologiestudium', *ibid.*, 181 (1968), pp. 196–201 and in general my study, *Zur Reform des Theologiestudiums* = Quaestiones Disputatae 41 (Freiburg, 1969).

course of studies of this kind. For want of a better terminology we shall call the first of these the '*existentielle*' concept of theology, and the other the 'vocational' concept of theology. The first concept seeks to organize the corpus of theology on the basis of a 'Christian anthropocentricity'[27] (which does not imply any opposition to a theological theocentricity) in that it seeks to awaken the student and to cause him constantly to reflect upon the question constituted by man himself (from the philosophical point of view and drawing upon the other anthropological sciences of the present day), and to answer this question in terms of the message of Christianity. Of course it might be said that this too has been, and continues to be, the task and the achievement of the theological disciplines as practised up to now. But what we mean here is that by presenting the question in this way a structured development can be achieved of the subject-matter which has to be taught in theology without referring back to the theological disciplines as formulated in earlier times. To this structured development of the subject-matter which has to be taught in theology the specialists in the particular branches of theological research have to make their contribution precisely at *that* point at which it is demanded by this 'system' as a whole. They do not make this contribution on the basis of each particular theological discipline as such taken autonomously and in isolation from the rest. This 'existentielle' concept of theology cannot be considered any further at this point; for this reference may be made to considerations which the author has put forward elsewhere.[28]

As a result of this long and apparently devious development we have now arrived at a point at which we are in a better position to clarify the demands which pastoral theology makes upon theology as a whole. The 'vocational' concept of theology as a whole means, in material terms, nothing else than that the structural organization of the whole corpus of theology must be provided by pastoral theology.

The fact that a project of this kind need not remain at the level of pure theory is demonstrated by the new theological faculty at Heerlen (Hoogeschool voor Theologie en Pastoraat) which was founded a few years ago in the diocese of Roermond in collaboration with certain members of religious orders and societies.[29] In this faculty the scientific and theoretical

[27] cf. K. Rahner, 'Theology and Anthropology', *Theological Investigations* X (London and Freiburg, 1973), pp. 28–46, and also the literature cited in n. 25.

[28] cf. K. Rahner, *Zur Reform des Theologiestudiums* = Quaestiones Disputatae 41 (Freiburg, 1969).

[29] cf. e.g. *Over de nieuwe opleiding tot priester en pastoraal werker aan de Hoogeschool voor Theologie en Pastoraat te Heerlen* (Heerlen, 1969).

formation is provided in a 'basic course' lasting five years, followed by two years of directly practical pastoral formation. To give only one example of how such a 'vocational' concept of pastoral theology can supply the principle of organization for the whole of theology considered as teaching a brief outline may be given of the 'basic course' provided by the Heerlen faculty.[30] In the *first* year of this 'basic course' (the 'propaedeutic year') the organization of the subject-matter is aimed primarily at an exposition of the student's understanding of himself (to the extent that he is aiming precisely at making a pastoral contribution to the Church's mission). This is achieved by giving a description of society and of the Church of today, together with a special philosophical and theological evaluation of this. In addition an introduction is given to the methodology of scientific thought. The subject-matter in the *second* year is the wellbeing of society: problems such as work, technology, welfare, leisure-time, catering for the welfare of the individual in the contemporary developments of industry, the progressive unification of the world, salvation and perdition, politics, communism, the consummation of the world and eschatology. All these questions are treated of in an inter-disciplinary manner by a team of lecturers (sociologists, psychologists, exegetes, dogmatic and moral theologians). In the *third* year the development of the person in society is treated of. Light is thrown upon the various aspects of man as sinful, as free, and as redeemed, by the various specialists. The subject-matter of the *fourth* year falls under the heading of 'Man in the Christian and Religious Aspects of his Life'. Here

[30] We should not, of course, overlook the great difficulties which such a conception entails. For certainly we should not fall into the mistake of seeking absolutely to transform all theology into practical work. Such a thing would be quite impossible in view of the difference between the two spheres, which is radical and irremovable. But even abstracting from this, it is also necessary to accord 'pure' theory its own due place in the concrete development of the course of studies. Nevertheless we cannot overlook the fact that in the discussion of the reform of studies which has taken place in the central European sphere there has been pressure to give a greater place to practical work. In this respect we should have to regard the Dutch scheme described above and the Roman scheme which has prevailed hitherto as at opposite extremes to one another in the Catholic sphere. For my own conception, which bears more on the concrete existing circumstances, cf. the *Quaestio Disputata* already referred to, *Zur Reform des Theologiestudiums* = Quaestiones Disputatae 41 (Freiburg, 1969), p. 48; in addition reference may be made to my study in *Handbuch der Pastoraltheologie* IV (Freiburg, 1969), pp. 497–515; for other attempts of this kind we should mention the survey of studies in the article entitled 'The Renewal of Training for the Priesthood', *Concilium* 3/5 1969, pp. 91–98, especially note 1 and note 14, and also H. E. Hess and H. E. Tödt, *Reform der theologischen Ausbildung*, I–II (Stuttgart, 1968–69).

such questions are raised as the existence of God, the nature of God, and religion, and all of these are treated of in an interdisciplinary manner. In the *fifth* and final year of the 'basic course' the subject treated of is the Christian and religious community. In this year an extensive treatment is given to such subjects as the Church, the sacraments, liturgy, preaching, and other means of communication, and a treatment of these questions is given on the basis of the various disciplines. In this connection too it is obvious that, as has already been laid down as a matter of principle at an earlier stage, the corpus of these courses of lectures is supplemented and surrounded by special lectures, the subject-matter of which, so far as the Heerlen faculty is concerned, has an explicitly missionary character.

Here we have given only a fragmentary account of the programme followed in this theological faculty. But even so, when we view this programme, the first point that immediately becomes clear is that the classic theological disciplines are no longer provided as special subjects for instruction, but are rather accorded an 'interdisciplinary' status in which they assist and make a contribution towards a single unified subject-matter to which all of them are subordinated. In practice, perhaps, this 'vocational' concept of theological formation is, after all, not so far removed from the 'existentielle' concept of theology as indicated above, so that perhaps the two conceptions do not necessarily have to be presented as mutually exclusive alternatives so far as the concrete development of the studies is concerned. The conception of the course of theological studies at Heerlen as set forth in the small programme published in April 1969 still remains at a very general stage, although it is clear that the process of using the subject-matter of pastoral theology to determine the structure of theology as a whole has been carried through uncompromisingly and without any false concessions. A possible criticism might be, however, that it does not yet appear from this programme whether the traditional subject-matter of dogmatic and moral theology has been included.[31] Other special subjects, such as the history of philosophy and

[31] There is no need to deny that in a 'vocational' concept of this kind the *danger* does exist of orientating the work of teaching theology in *too* pragmatic and utilitarian a manner towards something which – all other problems apart – already no longer exists or will no longer be the case if the priest is constantly engaged in pastoral work. For those problems which are most immediate and urgent today may soon perhaps no longer be so. Thus we would certainly be doing no service to the future priest if in dogmatic and moral theology we were to treat merely of what is the subject of discussion in all 'public circles' precisely today and is of 'burning' interest to young theologians. But while recognizing the truth of this principle it still does not justify the practice of continuing to hand on questions which have become obsolete

Church history can be interpreted even now as permanent 'ancillary subjects' supplementary to the corpus of theology proper, and this procedure does not constitute any special difficulty. But the subjects covered in dogmatic and moral theology as previously understood must certainly also be included in the corpus of this unified theology in itself (though this is certainly not to exclude the possibility of holding individual courses of special lectures in these areas), and here a difficulty does arise which has probably hardly been overcome as yet.

Our reason for referring to this order of studies at Heerlen at this point is simply that we wish to point to a concrete example of how pastoral theology can be something more than merely an important special subject within theology, and one that as such has to be taken into account in all the other special departments of theology too. Pastoral theology, rather, or the subject-matter and function belonging to it, can provide the principle according to which the whole of theology is structurally organized. Certainly the way in which this is done precisely at Heerlen is not the only possible way. In principle other concrete approaches are conceivable in which pastoral theology can be made to provide the structure and unifying principle of theology as a whole. Nor let it be said that all these considerations are so much word-play, serving only to organize into a formal system a multiplicity of subjects or courses which in any case do exist and always have existed from the first, without doing very much to alter the realities of the studies that are undertaken. There is very much that is changed in the practical application of the studies when a principle of structural organization of this kind is really put into force clearly and decisively. It becomes clear how specific subjects must necessarily be included in the curriculum, even though they were hardly treated of at all in the earlier disciplines. Other areas of subject-matter recede into the background which formerly simply took up too much time, attention, and energy, and imposed too great a strain on the memories of the students. A division of the number of periods available can be arrived at which is effective and realistic, being decided by the individual themes themselves, and not according to the already established division of the theological disciplines. As for the fresh themes for theological investigation which arise, we need only recall the whole range of subject-matter in pastoral theology mentioned at the beginning of this study, which

in theological teaching. In view of the fact that the Second Vatican Council itself warns us against this ('Optatam totius' No. 17) the suspicion of this cannot be based on mere fancy.

extends far beyond the themes which have already become traditional in this particular discipline, and extends to all those questions which fall under the heading of 'political theology'. By introducing a clear and unambiguous structural organization into the corpus of theology in this way we could also avoid the burden and waste of time entailed by the fact that certain themes tend to reappear again and again in different disciplines (for instance in the case of the sacraments, they are treated of very extensively in dogmatic theology, but also in moral theology, canon law, pastoral theology and liturgy).

Of course we might consider the demands which a pastoral theology of this kind makes upon theology as a whole from certain quite different points of view.[32] For instance it would have to be shown in the concrete how practical theology can and must be the critical conscience of the other theological disciplines (taking these also in their role as branches of research). What we mean by this is that practical theology should provide the particular disciplines with an awareness of the element of practical theology inherent in themselves, and which must be taken into account by themselves (something which in practice is often neglected). If, for instance, homiletics is to be something more than mere rhetoric as applied to preaching, it must in principle also be a *material* homiletics, i.e. it must make actual and relevant to the present, by means of a 'hermeneutics appropriate to the existing situation of the world' the message of the gospel in the teaching of the Church with a view to proclaiming it in a manner appropriate to the needs of the present day. A major part of this material homiletics, however, will in principle and for practical reasons (to avoid repetition etc.) have to be included in the study of dogmatic theology itself. And practical theology must again and again draw the attention of the dogmatic theologians to this point. It must raise the relevant questions in a more acute form and promote active consideration of them – those questions with which dogmatic theology is confronted as a result of practical experience. A similar point could also be shown to apply to Church history, exegesis, and biblical theology, canon law, and the study of the liturgy (considered primarily as instruction in the *liturgia condenda*).[33] This is not to say that it is only in a formal sense that practical theology constitutes the conscience of the other theological disciplines, rousing them to activity in a critical and creative way. But there is in fact much which must be considered necessary precisely in

[32] On this cf. also my study in *Theological Investigations* X (London and Freiburg, 1973), pp. 293–317.
[33] cf. *ibid.*, passim.

THE NEW CLAIMS

135

order that the Church may achieve the fulness of her own nature in the
concrete (in other words for her 'practical life' in the specific situation
prevailing 'today'), and yet which cannot be achieved in pastoral theology
taken as an individual discipline in isolation. In other words it must be
achieved in the other theological disciplines. But it is precisely practical
theology itself that must ensure that this is in fact done.

A further question might be raised, this time from the standpoint of
the history of human thought in general. It concerns the fact that today
the theoretical reason has lost a certain primacy which it once enjoyed,
and pride of place has come to be accorded to the practical reason.
The reason is that the world itself, even so far as the mind of man is
concerned, has become dynamic, with the result that man and his environment are no longer merely the object of contemplation, but constitute
rather the object and the material of human activity itself. What, then, it
may be asked, are the implications of this for the theology of today and
tomorrow and for practical theology in particular. The moment we consider this question from the point of view which we have only been able to
indicate here we can conjecture that theology will inevitably be transformed to a far greater extent than we of today can yet perceive. A further
general perspective within which our question must be considered is
provided by the growing recognition that today, for all the unity of the
creed in the one Church, a pluralism of theologies[34] has inevitably come
to prevail within the one Church, which is far deeper, more far-reaching
and more uncontrollable than formerly. This is something which in
principle must by all means be considered a positive enrichment of the
Church herself. From this point of view a further distinction would have
to be drawn within the questions we have raised, so that it would lead to
the further question of whether perhaps there must be, and will be,
another theology besides those already existing (the theologies of the
theoretical reason, of contemplation, of an 'aesthetic' interpretation of the
world, of a transcendental metaphysic etc.). This other theology would
be the theology of the practical reason, of human activity, of the decisions
which have to be taken in the Church and in the world at the social level.
The effect of all this would be that while these theologies would certainly
have a unifying point of reference among themselves in the common
creed and in the unity of the Church's hope and love, still it would no
longer be possible in any adequate sense to produce a single overall

[34] On this subject cf. also *Theological Investigations* IX and X, as also *idem*,
'Pluralism in Theology and the Unity of the Creed in the Church', in this volume
pp. 3–23.

concept of theology to cover them all and relate them all to one another. When we view the question in this perspective surely we can no longer doubt that two consequences follow: on the one hand, even if we produce a single universal theology structurally organized in terms of the practical reason and of practical theology, it will still not be the only theology in the Church. On the other hand, however, it is surely true that it will be this theology that will most clearly make the nature of our own times subject to conscious reflection. And it is this reflection on the special nature of our own times that will constitute the signature of the Church of tomorrow, and therefore of her theology as well.

5

THE FUTURE OF THEOLOGY

THE man who seeks to look into the future of theology is in the same position as anyone else attempting to say in other contexts how the future will turn out. All he can do is to throw onto the screen of the future a broader and vaguer projection of certain special features of the present. But whether these features he projects really will be included among the distinguishing characteristics of the future is something that ultimately speaking no-one knows.

So it is too with regard to the future of theology. Everything which we are about to say is subject to this proviso. Let us attempt, without systematizing, and in the knowledge that the selection we make must necessarily be extremely arbitrary, to depict certain traits of that future of theology which has already begun.

The Catholic theology of the future will be a theology of the one abiding creed of this Church. We do not know how large this Church will be in terms of numbers, or what influence it will have upon society in the future. But in any case it will endure, and it will aways be constituted by its proclaimed belief in the living God who, by his act of gracious self-bestowal, has penetrated into the world to become the ultimate strength underlying the unfolding process of its history and to be the absolute future towards which it tends. This is achieved through acknowledged belief in Jesus Christ in whom this absolute proximity of God to the world has achieved its climax in history and the manifestation of its eschatological victory. It is achieved through that creed which leads to unconditional love of neighbour and hope for eternal life.

This ancient creed of the Church is of course itself something that has constantly to be thought out afresh, to be made actual, and to be expressed in a manner appropriate to the times. Yet it endures. It can endure because what it proclaims as creed is precisely belief in an infinite future; belief in the immediacy of man's confrontation with God considered as the absolute point of reference by which every ideology bound up with history and subject to its conditions is to be judged.[1] And it is to this creed of the Church abiding, yet ever new, that the theology of the future in the Catholic Church also remains ceaselessly attached. It will continue to be the task of that theology to reflect upon this creed with all the energy of the spirit and all the power of the heart in the light of each new situation as it arises in the life of believing and thinking man.

The Church's creed is the creed of a Church which constantly adheres to the basic structures with which she was founded, a Church which retains a living historical continuity with her own origins, a Church which has her officially constituted authorities, and therefore a teaching authority also. And to the extent that all this is true the theology of the future also retains a permanent connection with the teaching authority or *magisterium* of this Church, the upholders of which are the pope and the whole body of bishops considered as the unity.

The critical function which theology as a science obviously has can only be exercised by it precisely insofar as it acknowledges this necessity of adhering to the creed of the Church and to her teaching authority. This abiding connection which theology has does not exclude, but rather includes the fact that the concrete forms which it assumes are themselves subject to a process of historical change, so that theologians must constantly show themselves anew bold enough to commit themselves to a future that is still unknown.

The theology of the future, for all the unity of the abiding creed, will include a very high degree of pluralism in theology,[2] and one which can no longer be mastered by any one mind. It may be true that as a result of modern rationalization, technical skill, and the intermingling of all those spheres of human living which were previously kept distinct, a single world civilization has emerged. But however true this may be, still, by reason of the interior differences which still exist within this single world civilization a far more manifest pluralism of theologies will develop such that, however firmly they may remain attached to the one creed of the Church, still they will remain quite different from one another in

[1] On this cf. K. Rahner, 'Das Christentum und der "neue Mensch" ', *Schriften zur Theologie* III (Einsiedeln, 7th ed., 1967) , pp. 159–179; *idem*, 'Marxist Utopia and the Christian Future of Man', *Theological Investigations* VI (London and Baltimore, 1969), pp. 59–68; 'Ideology and Christianity', *ibid.*, pp. 59–76; also the chapters entitled 'The Function of the Church as Critic of Society' and 'The Question of the Future' in *Theological Investigations* XII.

[2] cf. the chapter entitled 'Pluralism in Theology and the Unity of the Creed in the Church' in this volume, pp. 3–23.

respect of their methods, their structural developments, their outlooks, their terminologies, and the practical trends to which they give rise. These differences will be so great that as theologies it will be quite impossible for them to be covered by, or subsumed under any one single homogeneous theology. It must be recognized that in terms of sheer time and energy it is quite beyond the resources of any one individual Christian and theologian to achieve a comprehensive grasp of all the material with which each theology has to work at the scientific, social, and cultural levels, and so to incorporate it in his own theology. And this fact alone makes it impossible for the pluralism of theologies which will exist to be subsumed within a single homogeneous theology in this way.

It is of course necessary for these theologies to maintain a constant dialogue among themselves. But however actively this may be pursued, still there will no longer be any one theology of the Church. Rather there will be theologies of the Church in the plural, each of them having a different bearing upon, and approach to the one creed, though this does not of course mean that they will be in contradiction to it. All this will be borne in upon us more clearly and more forcefully than formerly, so that it will become clear that we can no longer achieve a comprehensive view of all the differences involved. This also has implications for the teaching authority of the Church. The function of this in preserving the unity of the creed must be maintained to the full. But for all this it will have to accord to all these various theologies a greater degree of self-responsibility in the particular bearing which each has upon the single abiding creed of the Church. Presumably this pluralism among the theologies of the future will also open up quite new possibilities, for then there will be no attempt at falsely smoothing out the differences between them and so reducing them to a single uniform theology in order to cope with the danger of a confessional pluralism among the theologies leading to illegitimate divisions within the Church.[3]

Nor will the theology of the future be able to dispense with a certain boldness in which all the powers and resources at man's disposal are brought to bear in seeking out the problems involved – a boldness, therefore, in applying philosophical thought to these problems in the broadest sense of the term. Yet the theology of the future will no longer be able, as in former times, simply to presuppose a single philosophical system common to all which is already more or less worked out and ready

[3] cf. esp. the article entitled 'On the Theology of Ecumenical Discussion', in this volume, pp. 24–67.

to hand when theology enters upon its own specific province.[4] These theologies will, to a certain extent, have to manage for themselves in working out the particular philosophies with which they will have to work. Obviously they will not be able to presuppose or to develop on their own account a philosophy which is consciously opposed to or contradicts some other philosophy which has been presupposed or developed in another theology within the Church. But the theologies of the Church in the future can freely commit themselves to different philosophies existing side by side and allow for the fact that they may, to a certain extent, be disparate and alien to one another. And in this situation it may be quite impossible in the concrete to achieve any higher level of integration at which all these various philosophies are subsumed within a single system of philosophy which is regarded as absolute. This insuperable pluralism of the philosophies which are in turn pursued within the theologies is in itself a cause and a factor in the pluralism of the theologies in the Church.

The theology of the future considered precisely as theology, and so not primarily in its bearing upon the future but in its enduring validity as such, will concentrate very decisively upon the heart and centre, the ultimate and basic questions of the Christian message. Certainly this does not mean that we shall have to abolish, or interpret in a quite different sense than formerly, certain expressions of the Church's awareness of her faith which were formulated at some point in the past as claiming an absolute commitment of faith on the part of the Church, and so considered as having the force of official dogma. But this concentration of the theology of the future on the most radical questions and the most ultimate content of revelation surely does imply that the future developments in theology itself, and so too in that understanding of the faith which it helps to condition in history, will consist less than formerly in drawing further distinctions at the conceptual level within the existing statements of the faith; that the aim of the theology of the future will be not so much to produce 'new dogmas' as to achieve a radical understanding of what it means most ultimately and most fundamentally to speak of divine revelation and grace, of the one mediator, of the Church's responsibility for the world, and of eschatological hope.

However regrettable this may appear at first sight, the theology of the future will be one that speaks at what is, comparatively speaking, a very abstract level. This statement is not intended to decide the question of

<hr>

[4] cf. K. Rahner, *Theological Investigations* X (London and Freiburg, 1973), pp. 235–242.

whether and how the man of the future can regain a new and unconstrained attitude towards images, symbols, and therefore too towards myth in the true sense of the term, and so too in his theology, despite his critical rationalism. But even if this were to be successfully achieved the language of the theology of the future would still necessarily be a very abstract one. It must be remembered that in the secular sciences concerned with man, and even in those concerned with the world as subject to sense perception, the treatment of these subjects is always and necessarily an abstract one.[5] This fact alone makes it not so very surprising that theology too has to be treated of at a very abstract level.

Right from the first there has always been, in the treatment of theology, a certain awareness of the fact that all theology can only speak of its subject in analogous terms; in all its statements a difference has to be recognized between the idea and its expression, the image and that reality which it properly signifies. Theologians have had to be aware of this even though they can never overcome the situation in which vision and expression are simultaneously one and distinct. But this distinction is recognized more clearly today than it was formerly. It constitutes the basis, materially speaking justified, for a programme of demythologizing which is for the most part misunderstood or falsely applied. Once this distinction is more clearly grasped at the conscious level it will have the effect of making the language of the theology of the future more abstract. It is true that we have consciously to be aware in theological language of a figurative element which is not simply a quality inherent in the reality signified in itself. It is true that ultimately speaking this figurative element can be expressed only in statements which themselves in turn have to work with a figurative approach of this kind. Moreover this criticism must precisely be applied to every statement of this kind, since it points to a factor inherent in theological expression in itself. It involves a constant movement to and fro between various conceptual patterns. It means that in seeking to understand such statements we must constantly subject our hermeneutic methods to fresh questioning. Now it is precisely this that forces upon us what at first sight appears as the pallid abstraction of theological language. We will have to accustom ourselves to this just as we have accustomed ourselves to the formal abstractions involved in modern physics. We will have to learn freely to allow the vivid imagery of the ancient formulations of the creed to retain their force as being still

[5] We might for instance adduce the example of the Quantum Theory in Physics, the subjects of which can only be referred to by means of complicated comparisons.

significant for us in the future also. But we will have to stand back from them, so to speak, at a greater distance than was formerly the case, in order to express in relatively abstract theological terms what is truly meant by such credal formulae, yet at the same time we must not imagine that that single reality which is signified in both modes of expression can be attained to and lived by solely by a process of mere theological abstraction.

The theology of the future will bear an ecumenical stamp. In the future ecumenical theology will be not so much a special discipline existing side by side with others, but rather an intrinsic element imposing its stamp upon all theological thought and work. The very fact that every theological discipline has a duty to contribute to the life of the Church, and that it belongs to the life of the Church to maintain always and everywhere the ecumenical will to achieve the unity of the Churches and at the same time a living multiplicity within the one Church[6] – this fact in itself is enough to make it necessary for all theology to bear this ecumenical stamp.

One factor will make it more and more possible to impart an ecumenical character of this kind to each specific discipline within the future theology. It is that the methods of work adopted in the theologies of the particular confessions are coming increasingly to approximate to one another. This is because biblical theology is coming to be recognized in all of them as the starting-point and the norm for theological work, and also because nowadays the real theological frontiers to a large extent cut across the confessional boundaries. Again the theologies of the particular confessional groups the ultimately basic positions and basic attitudes (as distinct of course from the further consequences which are drawn from such basic positions, these being still matters of genuine controversy between the confessions) have perhaps already everywhere overcome the limitations inherent in maintaining schools of theology proper to particular confessional groups. Hence with regard to these basic attitudes and basic positions the various Churches no longer differ so very much among themselves. The differences still outstanding between them are concerned rather with some real factor in the life of another Church which makes it different from one's own. In saying this however we do not deny that precisely this difference of attitude towards the realities which divide the confessions from one another has in its turn a certain theological relevance. The theology of the future will have an ecumenical quality. The theologies of the various Churches will be conscious of their responsibility to maintain a constant dialogue with one another, and will be ready mutually to learn from one another.

Again with regard to the choice of subject-matter, the emphases in the theology of the future will be very different from those of the theology of the last century. The greater pluralism among the theologies of which we have already spoken will in itself be enough to ensure this. Of course it is difficult, or even impossible, to say what the central subject-matter of these individual theologies will be. In theology too it is justifiable to allow for something like a fashion. For this means nothing else than the attitude of according due importance to a specific historical situation which is not always the same, which implies fresh tasks for man at any given time, and therefore too which justifiably imparts to theology itself a form appropriate to the particular epoch. But how this will take place is something which we can hardly guess at in advance. For the present itself is always ambivalent and susceptible of more than one interpretation, and hence in itself lays special claims upon theology. Yet we have to recognize an inescapable circle here such that theology in its turn has itself to interpret this claim which the present makes upon it. Moreover however justified futurology may be in itself, the real future, and that too precisely as the situation in which theology has to develop, remains obscure.[7] Thus with regard to the choice of subject-matter, and the preference given to special subjects in the future theologies, we can perhaps only raise questions, even though we know that these future theologies, even in respect of their content, will have a different structural organization from the theology of the past.

Will the theology of the future be intrinsically anthropocentric in character? This would not imply any contradiction of the fact that theology in itself is radically theocentric, provided only it is borne in mind that man only realizes the theological dimension in his nature in the act of totally committing his own existence to the ineffable mystery which we call God. But concentration upon the anthropocentric element of this kind could mean that in all theological statements the fact that their contents refer to man as subject, as the embodiment of freedom, and as the formative agent of his own world, constantly remains clear.

What will be the principle of structural organization in the theology of the future, and the preference given to specific theological themes which this will quite inevitably entail? Will the principle here be a theology of the practical reason, of action, a political theology of the social responsibility

[7] cf. esp. the chapter entitled 'The Question of the Future', *Theological Investigations*, XII.

of the Christians and of the Churches towards the secular world?[8] Will the structural organization of the theology of the future be determined by its task of maintaining a constant ideological critique of the secular ideologies and false social utopias, and also of any attitude of ideological mistrust towards the message of the gospel and of the Church herself? Will the theology of the future maintain a far more direct and explicit dialogue with the modern sciences, in which the subject-matter will be arranged by the parties involved instead of being imposed from without, seeing that today and in the future these sciences will have to be understood as existing autonomously in relation to a philosophy which stands apart from the individual sciences? As a result of this these sciences no longer allow philosophy to be the sole sphere in which ideas are exchanged bearing upon man's understanding of himself at the secular level, or upon revelation and theology. Will the theology of the future be organized on different lines in terms of its subject-matter too, in view of the fact that like the other sciences it will have to work out in far closer detail its own methodology and its own hermeneutics? For in a certain sense it has itself to become the theology of theology, even though here it is threatened by the mortal danger of sticking fast in barren reflection upon its own nature, and never coming to terms with the actual reality to be investigated. This is a danger which must at all costs be overcome. Will the theology of the future have to adopt a more transcendental approach in reflecting upon the formal historicity of saving history, towards which of course it remains constantly orientated, or will it rather very quickly find that it has to commit itself with a new freedom to history itself with its openness to the future?

These and similar questions might be raised with regard to the choice of subject-matter in the theology of the future, and many further ones might be added to these. Today, surely, we are hardly yet in a position to answer them, and the multiplicity of such questions, which presumably cannot possibly be decided in terms of any one individual question and answer, points once more to a pluralism of theologies which we must expect for the future.

In its own way this theology of the future must give the Christians and the Churches of the future the courage to take decisions and to engage in concrete action in shaping the future. It can only do this in its own way provided that it ascribes to itself a prophetic function of advising, exhorting, and summoning, while recognizing that the practical sphere has an intelligibility of its own. For it itself is once and for all committed to work

[8] cf. the chapter entitled 'The Function of the Church as Critic of Society', *Theological Investigations*, XII.

in the sphere of speculative reason, and concrete decisions and actions can never be forged solely and exclusively on this anvil. At the same time theology itself is recognizing this more clearly, and conveying it to the Churches. Of itself it justifiably attributes a certain primacy to the practical reason, to freedom, to action, to the future. And at least in virtue of this fact it can make the Christians and the Churches more clearly aware of the truth that Christianity consists in something more than a mere contemplation of essences or an attitude of passively waiting for the advent of the kingdom of God. Rather it consists in bold decisions, in action, in transforming the world, and in these alone is the eschatological hope for the advent of the absolute future made real.[9] Of its very nature as a science theology must constantly be pointing the way on from itself towards a Christianity of action, one which is life and not merely the outcome of theological speculation. In this way theology itself must be that which maintains a living awareness of the fact that Christianity is something more than merely the upholding of a given dogmatic statement as true and something more too than contemplation, cult, and right moral conduct in the world.

The theology of the future will discover in a fresh and more living way that ecclesiological element which is proper to it and which belongs permanently to its very nature. In the future humanity will achieve a higher degree of social organization, and in these conditions the sense of community in the Church's awareness of her own faith, and also in the indissoluble connection which truth itself has with social institutions, will once more become clearer in theology itself. Again in this theology that indispensable element which is the individual's own sense of truth will have to be actively and manifestly engaged. But precisely through this sense of truth which he has the individual will experience more clearly that it is abidingly related to community, to society, and so also to the Church as socially constituted. He will experience that this sense of truth of his will never achieve its due fulness so long as it is allowed to wander alone in the isolated sphere of private opinion. On this basis, I believe, the theology of the future will come to acknowledge with a new freedom, and also with a new firmness of resolve, the ecclesiological element inherent in its own nature.[10]

It is to be hoped that the theology of the future will become more

[9] Also on this cf. the literature mentioned in n. 1.
[10] cf. K. Rahner, 'Die neue Kirchlichkeit der Theologie', *Gnade als Freiheit* (Freiburg, 1968), pp. 131–143; Concerning our 'assent to the Church as She Exists in the Concrete', *Theological Investigations*, XII.

clearly aware that of its very nature it is meant to contribute to Christian living in the concrete and to the self-fulfilment of man in a truly religious sense. It is not a science for its own sake. Having this function, it should perhaps not be a theology of praying and bowing the knee. For it will have to be a critical theology. Yet at the same time it should proceed from prayer more than it has done in the past hundred years. It should not exhaust its resources in mere theological, historical, or speculative learning. As far as possible it should throw light upon the existence of man in the real circumstances of human living, and give him the boldness to commit himself in adoration to the incomprehensibility of existence, at the very roots of which God rules with his grace. It should give him the courage to commit himself to this incomprehensibility with courageous hope and in that love which, in a single act, reaches out to God and man.

PART TWO

Natural Theology and Christology

6

THE EXPERIENCE OF GOD TODAY

IF we are to speak of the experience of God today we must, in the very nature of the theme we have set ourselves to explore, presuppose two points:

1. That there is such a thing as an experience of God, and
2. That it has a special and peculiar quality of its own, which it derives from our contempoary situation.

In this context the phrase 'experience of God' implies two things: first that what we call God is a reality, and a reality with which we have to do, and therefore that three attitudes on this point are false: (a) atheism, (b) a sceptical positivism which restricts man exclusively to the data accessible to him from the natural sciences, (c) the theology of the absolute remoteness of God, the 'Death of God' theology in the popular sense of the phrase. All these positions imply a denial of man himself and his reality. The second thing that is implied in the phrase 'experience of God' is that there is something more, something different, and something more fundamental than that knowledge of God which can be acquired through the so-called proofs of God's existence, though this is not to deny that these are possible and meaningful in their own right. But in terms of human living in the concrete they are possible and meaningful only as the outcome of an *a posteriori* process of reasoning as the conceptual objectification of what we call the experience of God, which provides the basis and origin of this process of reasoning. At the same time, however, these proofs of God's existence should not be conceived of as mere intellectual indoctrination informing man of an objective state of affairs which (as for instance in the case of existence of a subparticle in the physical sphere) lies outside and beyond his basic human experience, and of which, therefore, he cannot possibly become aware otherwise than through an indirect and *a posteriori* knowledge of this kind.

Now let us turn to the second word in our title, the word 'today'. At this preliminary stage we have only two points to make about this: *first* that it is no part of our intention to try either to assert or to prove that there is an experience of God such that it is absolutely new and proper to the present day, and which, therefore, simply did not exist in earlier times. If God exists, if it is rightly understood what is meant by the term 'God', and if man himself, for all the radical changes which have taken place in his history, does still continue throughout to be precisely man, then it is inconceivable from the outset that some experience of God should have arisen today which did not exist in any sense in earlier times. Our *second* point with regard to the term 'today' is this: it is equally obvious that the present-day situation of man, in which he has to achieve the total fulness of his own selfhood (for apart from this there is no experience of God), also in a very essential sense imposes its own distinctive stamp upon this experience, more so even than the subsequent process of rational reflection upon it, whatever name we may give to this process, 'proving the existence of God' or anything else. But surely both together, the initial experience and the subsequent reflection, make it justifiable to speak of the 'experience of God of today' without thereby restricting our considerations exclusively to the mere fact that this experience takes place in the present day.

The difficulty of, and at the same time the necessity for these considerations of ours derive from the fact that we are seeking to reflect upon an experience which is present in every man (whether consciously or unconsciously, whether suppressed or accepted, whether rightly or wrongly interpreted, or whatever the way in which it is present), and which involves the following factors: *on the one hand* it is more basic and more inescapable than any process of rational calculation in which we follow a line of causality leading from the egg to the hen, from the lightning to the thunder, in other words from the world to an originator, but which can also be broken off, leaving the conclusions which might have been arrived at unrecognized. *On the other hand*, however, this experience does not impose itself upon us irresistibly (as does the physical existence of a datum of sense experience or an organic sensation) in such a way that the transition from the experience itself to an explicit recognition of it in which we reflect upon, interpret, and express it, imposes itself upon us irresistibly. There are other basic experiences also, as we shall shortly have to show, in which the transition from the experience itself (even though it is inescapably present) to a recognition of it at the conceptual and reflexive level is more difficult for the actual subject undergoing the experience, so that this subject can actually prevent this transition from taking place. Moreover the interpretation of these basic experiences which is achieved in this transition can be more or less successful and clear, or the subject can even fail to make the transition at all. Such considerations, therefore, can only serve as pointers or appeals inviting the listener to make the attempt to discover this experience, previously perhaps quite unrecognized within himself, to admit it and to accept it instead of suppressing it, and to ask himself whether he can understand that this appeal to his experience is actually to some extent interpreting it correctly. It is possible for someone hearing a word addressed to him by another not to be ready to listen to that other word uttered from within himself, to become aware of the silent word which his own existence addresses to him. It is possible for him to be unwilling to allow himself to be drawn out of a kind of knowledge in which he is in control of himself, which he has at his disposal, and which is therefore called 'clear', into that mystery which reduces us to perplexity, which controls us and is not controlled by us, and in cases in which we meet with a reluctance of this sort all such appeals to this kind of experience are doomed to failure from the outset. But in that case the subsequent reflection upon this experience at the conceptual level, which we call the proof of God's existence, likewise falls into a void.

Such experiences do exist, and the very mode of their existence is such that they are inescapable. They exist in addition to our sensible experiences of objects in the external world and our vital sensations of joy, sorrow, etc., and quite apart from the experience of God, even though this too has a unique quality of its own which prevents us from grouping it under a *single* concept together with the other experiences and ascribing the same meaning to it as they have. What joy is, what anxiety, faithfulness, love, trust, and much else besides are, what constitutes logical thinking and responsible decision – these are things which man has already experienced before he reflects upon them and attempts to say what it is that he has all along been experiencing as an intrinsic part of his life. Indeed the expression of these experiences arising from his reflection upon them can actually be false or inadequate. It is possible for someone to achieve and to experience a love that is genuine and personal, a radical faithfulness and responsibility even though what he says about these experiences of his when he is asked what really takes place in them may be very mistaken. On the other hand a man who has been instructed by indoctrination from without can perhaps give a very clever and correct account of this even though properly speaking he has as yet not really experienced anything, or hardly anything, of them. Experience as such and subsequent reflection upon this experience, in which its content is conceptually objectified are never absolutely separate one from the other.

Experience always involves at least a certain incipient process of reflection. But at the same time the two are never identical. Reflection never totally includes the original experience. Indeed there are experiences which the subject really undergoes as such even though in his reflections upon them they are wrongly interpreted, denied, or suppressed. For instance let us take the case of someone who asserts that there is no logic and no truth such that they are fundamentally different from error, such that they can properly be so called; one who asserts that so-called logic and truth are merely the product of specific mechanical processes of the brain, or due simply to social pressures, all of which could no less justifiably be different from what they actually are. In making an assertion of this kind such a one is by implication declaring the opposite of it to be false. But in the very act of doing this he is achieving and experiencing in his turn, whether he admits it or not, the meaning and the claim of that very truth and logic in the absolute which he denies in his conscious assertion. Of course in the unfolding course of an individual's life an experience of the kind we are speaking of, as for instance that of love and faithfulness, is capable even in itself (and not merely in his reflection upon it) of growing, of becoming more radical, of being accepted more totally in his free decision. Or alternatively it can become atrophied and be frustrated in its proper tendency to become more clearly objectified through the process of reflection. Or it can almost cease altogether.

Even such experiences as these take place in a certain mode proper to the particular age. It is true that such basic experiences are prior to any conceptual objectification or interpretation of them, and are in principle independent of these processes. But however true this may be, still we cannot regard this process of objectifying reflection as superfluous, or say 'If such an experience is inescapably present in itself there is in fact no need for us to expend our efforts in reflecting upon it. Rather we can let such experiences remain as they are.' Such an opinion is just as false as if someone were to say that in the sphere of medicine a theoretical knowledge of the nature of a micro-infarct of the heart is superfluous, seeing that even without this knowledge he may perhaps have undergone this experience and never noticed it at all. The actual *experience* of love is indeed absolutely basic and absolutely indispensable. But despite this fact the experience itself as such can in itself be accepted more profoundly, more purely, and with greater freedom when we achieve a knowledge of its true nature and its implications at the explicitly conscious level.

An experience of this kind can also be related to God, and this experience of God is inescapable. It precisely does *not* depend upon whether we do or do not call the reality to which it refers 'God', whether or not we express the experience to ourselves in conceptual terms in a theoretical statement about God, whether the individual concerned freely identifies himself with his experience or denies it, suppresses it, or leaves it unexplored. The experience of God which we are pointing to here is not some subsequent emotional reaction to doctrinal instruction about the existence and nature of God which we receive from without and at the theoretical level. Rather it is prior to any such teaching, underlies it, and has to be there already for it to be made intelligible at all. This experience of God is not the privilege of the individual 'mystic', but is present in every man even though the process of reflecting upon it varies greatly from one individual to another in terms of force and clarity. Of course it is an experience of a unique kind, and the interpretation of it at the philosophical and theological level is extremely difficult, so that it cannot properly speaking be achieved here. Otherwise we would have to go on to consider in more precise terms the peculiar and unique mode in which the 'object' of this experience is made present, in other words that reality which we call 'God'. On the one hand, therefore, we would have to say that that which we call 'God', considered 'as' the object of this experience is not present in a manner which should be thought of as analogous to that in which we view an object immediately confronting us (the manner, therefore, which so-called 'ontologism' ascribes to this experience). We should say, rather, that God is present as the asymptotic goal, hidden in itself, of the experience of a limitless dynamic force inherent in the spirit endowed with knowledge and freedom. On the other hand, however, we should have to emphasize that this dynamic force which the spiritual subject experiences within itself is experienced not as an autonomous power of this subject, but rather as initiated and sustained by the goal towards which it tends. We should have to emphasize that this dynamic force is experienced as 'grace-given' in virtue of the fact that it also includes within itself the powerful hope of achieving a state of ultimate proximity and immediacy to that goal towards which it is tending, so that this goal does not remain merely the power that draws it yet remains eternally asymptotic and remote from it, but really does constitute a goal that can be reached. In this way it would have to be shown that even in the dimension of human awareness itself 'God' is present in a manner which does not have to be defined in terms of either of the two following alternatives: either that 'God' can be present merely as 'conceived of' (almost 'ideologically') or that he can be present in an immediate vision in the sense implied in ontologism. But, as we have said, it is not possible here to enter into these and similar questions concerning the correct metaphysical and theological interpretations of this experience.

A further point is that it is also meaningless to subject this experience, in a manner which is, theologically speaking too hasty, to the question of whether it belongs to 'nature' or 'grace'. Such a distinction belongs to the subsequent process of reflection, and does not need to be treated of systematically in dealing with the experience itself. In the very nature of the reality we are concerned with we would have to describe this experience in the concrete situation of our human lives as belonging both to 'nature' *and* to 'grace' at the same time, though in saying this the 'grace' aspect of this experience does not signifiy a privilege belonging only to particular individuals, while conversely the question of whether this experience is freely accepted in the concrete circumstances of the individual's life remains completely open. This experience of God must not be conceived of as though it were *one* particular experience *among* others at the same level, as for instance an experience of pain at the physiological level can be regarded as at the same level as the experience of an optical reaction. The experience of God constitutes, rather (though here we should perhaps abstract from certain mystical experiences in the true sense) the ultimate depths and the radical essence of *every* spiritual and personal experience (of love, faithfulness, hope and so on), and thereby precisely constitutes also the ultimate unity and totality of experience, in which the person as spiritual possesses himself and is made over to himself.

But *how* does man undergo this experience? At what point does he begin, if not actually to make this experience for the first time, still to recognize that it has been present all along in his life? Only at this point do we arrive at the true heart and centre of our subject. Once again it must be reiterated: we can only point to this experience, seek to draw another's attention to it in such a way that he discovers within himself that which we only find if, and to the extent that we already possess it. It is however possible to have it and to discover it in oneself even when one has never yet called it the experience of *God*. In pointing to, and attempting to describe this experience we are constantly faced with a dilemma: in pointing to it and appealing to another to discover it within himself we either attempt to touch the spirit and heart of the individual concerned in the most concrete possible way, and in the particular situation which belongs to him personally – and in that case an appeal of this kind gives the impression of expressing something subjective or poetic, a mood which is too vague to be verifiable. And then our appeal is open to the objection that after all it cannot be taken seriously on any realistic view at the 'down-to-

earth' level of everyday life. Alternatively the appeal in which we point
to this experience is formulated in terms of the greatest possible philosophical exactitude and at the strictly conceptual level. In that case we shall be
discussing it in such very abstract terms that they are difficult to understand,
and we are faced with the objection that we are indulging in mere subtle
word-play, so that in the end the discussion is abandoned from sheer
weariness. In order at all costs to avoid being defeated by this dilemma it
will perhaps be best for us to try and express what we mean without
indulging in any separate speculation as to the actual language itself
which would be employed. In appealing to this experience in our fellows
we must ourselves be aware that it is impossible for our words to avoid
meeting with a blank wall of incomprehension in those cases in which
they are not genuinely ready to open their minds to them, and this must
be our consolation. We must remind ourselves that that which we are
appealing to, namely the unrecognized experience of God, is present,
whether accepted or denied, even in those cases in which any discussion
of it meets only with incomprehension. We must remember that what we
have to say necessarily presupposes a certain experience of life on the
part of our hearer. And in view of this we must not be surprised to find
that if he is one who, from a spirit of youth, still feels compelled without
misgiving to conquer the external world, he continues to reject or to dis-
regard what we have to say. He has not yet been able to put the question
to himself of what it means to have met with disappointment and failure
in the effort to conquer the world.

A potent factor in every life is a certain element of the ineffable, namely
mystery. This does not signify that part of reality which still remains to
be explored, which we have not yet thoroughly understood or achieved
or made real to ourselves. Mystery, rather, is the underlying substrate
which is presupposed to and sustains the reality we know. For the condition which makes it possible for man to achieve the fulness of his own
existence, and which gives it its special character, is precisely a certain prior
apprehension which transcends every particular concrete reality which we
conceive of or make real to ourselves, a certain radical limitlessness inherent in every movement of knowledge and freedom even though this
stops short at some finite level of significance and is initiated by some
specific and individual reality. We exist, think and act in freedom only in
virtue of the fact that we have already all along transcended that which is
specific and particular, that which we can comprehend, in a movement
which knows no boundaries. The moment we become aware of ourselves
precisely *as* the limited being which in so many and such radical ways we

are, we have already overstepped these boundaries. Admittedly in doing so we step, as it were, into a void. But nevertheless we have overstepped them. We have experienced ourselves as beings which constantly reach out beyond themselves towards that which cannot be comprehended or circumscribed, that which precisely as having this radical status must be called infinite, that which is sheer mystery, because as the condition which makes every act of apprehending, distinguishing and classifying possible, it itself cannot in turn be experienced in *that* mode which it itself makes possible and of which it is the condition. It is present as the abiding mystery. This ultimate and original reality, therefore, which has no other basis beyond itself, even though the experience of it is mediated through our apprehension of some concrete object, cannot properly speaking be explained in terms of anything else than itself. It is the experience of that mystery which abides, which has been present all along, and precisely as such is both the inconceivable *and* that which alone is self-evident both at the same time. The dynamism of this limitless movement, and in it the ultimate point of reference towards which it tends, are of course experienced in a *single* act, and at the same time are in this experienced as distinct. But the 'ultimate point of reference' of this movement is *per definitionem* precisely *not*, and cannot be, an 'object' in the same sense as the object aimed at in acts of knowledge and freedom at other levels, so that it can be brought under the control of the knower as the preliminary stage in this movement in such a way that he can assign it a specific place in a co-ordinated system. Moreover this ultimate point of reference is experienced *in* the infinite movement of the spirit and *in terms of* it, even though it is also precisely that which in itself initiates and sustains this movement. And for these reasons the question of where this movement culminates is ultimately a secondary one. One man may say that the infinite sphere opened up without bounds or end in this movement is the void which, in order to be able to exist at all, points on to an infinite fulness, because nothingness, if the term is taken seriously, cannot be extended so as to become the sphere within which this movement takes place. Another may say that this ultimate point of reference is the infinite fulness itself which is aimed at. Which of these two alternatives we choose is secondary. Hence too it is also a secondary question whether we decide to speak of an experience of God or of the experience of an orientation towards God. Certainly we must always maintain the distinction between the 'objective' and 'subjective' sides of the experience in this context (if man is to avoid making himself God), but nevertheless these two sides are, in a unique and radical manner, inseparable one from the other.

In accordance with the warnings which we gave at the beginning of this study, what we have just said is extremely abstract, and it must never be forgotten that a statement of this kind does not bring about the experience referred to, but refers to it retrospectively as something that already exists. We do not therefore bring about the experience itself by speaking about it retrospectively and in the abstract. The form in which it impinges upon us is extremely concrete, even though it manifests itself as the element of the ineffable in the concrete experience of our everyday life. While it is present unacknowledged and unexpressed in *every* exercise of our spiritual faculties, it nevertheless manifests itself more clearly and in some sense as an object of enquiry in those episodes in which the individual, normally lost amid the individual affairs and tasks of his everyday life, is to some extent thrown back upon himself and brought to a position in which he can no longer overlook those factors in his life which he customarily evades. Thus it is when man is suddenly reduced to a state of *'aloneness'*, when every individual thing recedes, as it were, into remoteness and silence and disappears in this, when everything is 'called in question', as we are accustomed to say, when the silence resounds more penetratingly than the accustomed din of everyday life. Thus it is when man suddenly experiences that he is inescapably brought face to face with his own freedom and *responsibility*, feeling this as a single and total factor embracing the whole of his life and leaving him no further refuge, no possibility of acquittal from guilt. Thus it is in those cases in which man can no longer find any approval or support, can no longer hope for any recognition or any thanks, in which he finds himself called to account for his actions to that silent and infinite reality which is not ours to shape or control, which exists and is not subject to us, that which is most interior to us and most different from us at the same time. Thus it is when man experiences how this reality silently extends itself, as it were, throughout the whole of existence, permeating everything, unifying everything, while remaining itself incomprehensible; when he experiences the fact that this reality which calls him to account is ultimately speaking not that which is, and which takes effect because we ourselves freely posit it, but is rather that which lays claims upon our freedom, that from which there is no appeal, that which is still present in the form of judgement even when we deny that we are answerable to it and seek to escape from it. Thus it is when man suddenly makes the experience of personal *love* and encounter, suddenly notices, startled and blessed in this both at once, the fact that he has been accepted with a love which is absolute and unconditional even though, when he considers himself alone in all his finitude and frailty, he can assign no reason whatever, find no adequate justification, for this unconditional love that reaches out to him from the other side. Thus it is too when man experiences the fact that he himself likewise loves – loves with an inconceivable audacity that overcomes the questionability of the other even though he is aware of this, when he experiences that this love of his is so absolute that it commits him to finding support in a reality which is no longer subject to his control, which is most interior to the love itself in its inconceivability and yet at the same time is different from it. Thus it is when *death* silently directs its gaze towards a man – that death which causes all to fall into its own nothingness and precisely in doing this, provided only that it is willingly accepted (thus and only thus), does not strike man dead but itself transforms him, liberates him, endows him with that freedom which no longer appeals to or finds support in anything beyond itself, and yet at the same time is unconditional. This is a line of thought which we could and should follow further so as to point out how this single basic experience of man is present in a thousand different forms, and in this experience it is borne in upon him that his existence is open to the inconceivable mystery. In it he remarks that he is the prisoner of his own terryifying finitude (which does exist, and which cruelly torments him) only so long as he turns his eyes away from the infinitude and inconceivable reality which encompasses him on every side, or when he shrinks from it in terror because its power silently and un-controllably pervades all. It is at this level that we should speak of joy, of faithfulness, of the ultimate *angst* to which man is subject, of the yearn-ing which transcends every individual reality, of the fear which we feel at the inexorability of truth – that truth which is still there even when it is denied or mocked at. This is the level at which we should speak of the peace that comes from that detachment which never clings onto any individual reality in the absolute, and so gains all of the experience of the beautiful which is the assured promise of that which still lies in the future, of the experience of that radical and inescapable guilt which is nevertheless suddenly and inconceivably forgiven. This is the level at which we should speak of our experience of the fact that that which seems simply to belong to the past nevertheless in truth. having come to be, *is* and in a true and sacred sense is still in force. This is the level at which we should speak of our experience of the infinite openness of the future which is inex-haustible promise. We might proceed still further along this line of thought, and our vision would have to become far more concrete still – concrete not in the sense that it would cause us to lose ourselves in the particular realities of the external world, but rather in the sheer density of that experience which is ultimate and yet present at the same time everywhere in our everyday lives, for in these man is forever occupied with the grains of sand along the shore where he dwells at the edge of the infinite ocean of mystery.

Admittedly we should now go on to bring out more clearly two further truths: first that all these experiences of the absolute imply an original and ultimate unity among themselves, second that these experiences really do point to that which – or better him whom – we call God. Now this second question should in fact be approached from two different directions. We should not merely confine ourselves to saying that what is experienced in this way signifies God, for in that case we should be presupposing that it is clear from the outset what is meant by God. We should also have to state the converse of this: what is meant by God is to be understood on the basis of this experience, because otherwise we are in constant danger of supposing that the term God stands for something meaningless, and so of rejecting this, and then believing that we are compelled to be atheists. However, since we still have much more to speak of apart from this, yet still in the very nature of the case have to make some reply to both these questions, let us take it as given here that both questions are to be answered in the sense we have indicated.

But before we go on to ask ourselves what that special quality in the experience of God is which is peculiar to the *present day*, two further points must first be noticed: this experience of God should not be discredited as a mere mood carrying no conviction, or as an unverifiable feeling. Nor is it merely a factor in our private interior lives. On the contrary it has a fully social and public significance. This experience is no mere mood, no matter of mere feeling and poetry carrying no conviction. It is of course different from that knowledge which the individual achieves at the conceptual level, and *within* the sphere of knowledge. In fact it bears upon the totality of knowledge and freedom as such. But this is still far from implying that the experience in question consists in a feeling devoid of conviction. For it is present irremovably, however unacknowledged and unreflected upon it may be, in every exercise of the spiritual faculties even at the most rational level in virtue of the fact that every such exercise draws its life from the prior apprehension of the all-transcending whole which is the mystery, one and nameless. It is possible to suppress this experience, but it remains, and at the decisive moments of our lives it breaks in upon our awareness once more with irresistible force. Nor can we say that we should be silent about it on the grounds that we cannot speak 'clearly' about it. For what is clarity? Have we not already spoken about it the moment we say that it is illegitimate to speak about it, that properly we must not speak about it? And if the rationalist philosophers and positivists are unwilling to speak about it, does this mean that the saints, the poets, and other revealers of the fulness of existence as a *whole* must also be forbidden to speak? The term 'God' is there, and it asserts itself even in the struggle which the atheist wages against God. And will this term 'God' not raise the question ever anew of what is meant by it? And even if this term were ever to be forgotten, even then in the decisive moments of our lives we should still constantly, though silently be encompassed by this nameless mystery of our existence, judging us and endowing us with the grace of our ultimate freedom, and we would discover the ancient name for it anew.

Nor let it be said that this experience is of no account for the social and public areas of our lives. Religion, which constantly draws its life from this experience, is a social reality even though the atheist may believe that it would be better if this reality did not exist. This experience of God would not be made irrelevant in its social aspects even supposing that those realities which we call religions, and which consist in a conceptual reflection upon, and a social institutionalization of this experience of God, were totally to disappear. For even in that case the transcendentality inherent in human life is such that man would still reach out towards that mystery which lies outside his control. The experience of God itself would still take effect, however unconsciously, in terms of faithfulness, responsibility, love and hope, extending beyond all those particular realities which justify such attitudes in human life, and it is these attitudes which, even though they seem to be wholly non-political and private in character, and not susceptible of being directed or controlled from without, do in fact sustain the social level of human living.

Finally we must apply ourselves to the question of what the special characteristics of this 'experience of God today' may be which are proper to our own times; the question, therefore, of whether, despite the fact that up to now we have been describing this experience of God in almost 'supra-temporal' terms, it does not, after all, derive certain quite special characteristics from the special situation in which man stands today. Four brief indications must suffice by way of reply to this question to the extent that any such reply is possible at all here.

1. First the following consideration has to be borne in mind with regard to the 'transcendental' character of the experience of God: the man of earlier times assigned a place to God precisely as a factor in his world even though in doing so he did say that this 'factor' was the highest and

most perfect, upon which everything else depended, and even though the philosophers and theologians did teach, in their statements at the theoretical level, that properly speaking it was contrary to the 'nature' of God and of the experience of him to think of God in this way. In spite of this God was thought of in the world as an element of it, and not as that which supported it or as the unfathomable depths beyond it, such that from the outset it could not be accounted as itself belonging to it. God was one particular reality in the world (however much it might be asserted that he had caused all of it to exist), a contributory cause engaged in a constant mutual interchange of activities with the other realities in it. In this way God was rendered 'comprehensible', and the teaching about him was such as every man could readily apply at the practical level. He was the 'good God' who acts as a ruler of the world, acting to ensure the good moral conduct of its inhabitants and at the same time capable of restoring it to his grace. The ultimate content of man's beliefs was indeed valid and true all along. But the actual manner in which he applied those beliefs was less so. This is something that we have only come plainly to recognize today. For now it has become clear even to the average man (who in earlier times still restricted himself to the practical level even in his more lofty speculations) that *this kind of* God does not exist, that he is not to be found within the world, that he has no heaven above the clouds, that he does not work miracles in order to remove any disturbances in the machinery of the world. The average man of today has come clearly to recognize that God is absolutely incommensurable with the world, and that he cannot be included as one item within our calculations – and so on. It is no wonder, then, that the death of a more primitive idea of God has come to be interpreted as the death of the true God himself, or that God has come to be thought of as unspeakably remote. In truth, however, the position is this: the deepening of our rational comprehension of the world, which has the effect of eliminating the divine from it, is wholly legitimate provided only that this elimination of the divine from the world gradually comes to be experienced more and more as supported and upheld by that transcendence of the world and of the finite subject in which the true experience of God takes place. This experience of God, precisely as it exists *today* is, much more clearly and radically than in earlier times, an experience of transcendence, a transcendence which eliminates the divine from the world and is thereby enabled to let God be God.

2. A further peculiarity of the experience of God today consists surely in the distinctive character of the medium in which it is communicated in

the present. Every experience of God has its medium of communication in virtue of the fact that there always has to be some starting-point from which the process of transcending the world and the subject himself can proceed. And that which constitutes the medium in this sense can change at least in respect of the outward stamp which it bears and which is borne in upon us at the public and social levels of human life and thought. The first point that strikes us is that today, in contrast to earlier times, the medium of this experience has shifted from the world to existence. In earlier times it was the external world with its order and harmony that provided the initial start for man's experience of transcendence. Today it is his existence with its unfathomable depths, and it may be conjectured – though perhaps there is some small element of prophecy here – that the mode of existence which is typical precisely of this *present* age, and which is destined gradually to fulfil this role of being the medium in which the experience of God is communicated, is not so much the existence of the saint with his wisdom and contemplation, but rather that of the man whose life does not appeal to our feelings, who bears responsibility for himself in silence and solitude, yet who exists selflessly for the sake of others.

3. A third element serves further to characterize the distinctive nature of the experience of God of today, with the dangers which threaten it and the new function which it has to fulfil. Formerly religion reigned undisputed at the social level, however many different forms it may have assumed. For there were no nations without gods. And so long as religion had some public expression of this kind the individual who admitted and accepted this experience of God at all had no further special problem in finding it possible to communicate with this God at the personal level, to call upon him and to adore him. Now today this is, perhaps, *the* real and central problem for man, even when he clearly undergoes this experience of God. Given that this God is radically different from ourselves, and at the same time that which upholds our own activity – including, therefore, the attempt to speak to him and freely to respond to him – can we then really address him and achieve a personal relationship with him? Certainly we should not say that we are too insignificant for him to be able to 'interest' himself in us, for such a line of thought in fact makes him precisely one element in our world, so that his relationship with a smaller element in it would be more tenuous than his relationship with a greater one, whereas in truth he is able voluntarily to enter upon the most immediate possible relationship with us as we are.

But this in itself is not enough to solve the problem. Here we cannot enlarge upon it at any length. But the first point is that this question must be taken seriously. But in that case it has an extremely positive effect in itself in helping to determine our attitude towards God. It makes this attitude something which, in the traditional terminology, is called adoration, total commitment in which man falls into silence, in which the word he addresses to God is merely the prelude to his silence, in which he veils his countenance before the majesty of the ineffable mystery, and in which he is aware that contrary to all appearances today man cannot contend with God. Further: if man feels that actually to address God in this way is unheard of audacity, if indeed he feels the concrete act of venturing upon such a thing as a pure grace, in which God, by his own free act, empowers man to undertake this venture, this is nothing but good. For in that case he will feel that it is anything but obvious that God should empower him to do this, yet at the same time he must not deny the possibility of God doing so, for otherwise he would once more be thinking of God according to human standards. And finally: it is no matter for regret, if we find the courage to address God in this way only by keeping our eyes fixed upon Jesus, seeing that even in death he still managed to call this Mystery 'Father', and to surrender himself into his hands even as, in slaying him, it withdrew itself from him and threw him into the most inconceivable state of dereliction from God.

4. It seems that we should include one further factor among those marks of our 'experience of God today' which belong particularly to our own times. At first sight it seems as though there were hardly anything specifically Christian in this experience of God, and this seems particularly to be the case in those cases in which it either remains alive or comes to live once more in our conscious awareness, even though all the trends of the time are against it, and even though it receives no significant support from the tradition of Christianity as this survives at the merely social level. We ourselves have in fact treated at length of this experience of God, and in doing so have spoken of it apparently almost without any reference to Christianity or to the Christian message as it has emerged in history. And today there is no lack of religiously motivated individuals – even Christians – who bring their own basic experience of God to the stage of conscious awareness and reflection with the help of witnesses which they are convinced that they perceive everywhere throughout the history of humanity and of the nations and religions of the world, and which they feel to be genuine and inspiring. On this point too we can only make a few brief remarks. We may take two contrasting lines of approach here.

First, the ultimate depths of this experience of God to which we have sought to appeal are precisely the experience of an ineffable nearness of God to us such that for all the adorable inconceivability which abides throughout he bestows himself upon man with an immediacy that brings him forgiveness and a share in his divine life. This experience, therefore, is something more than that of an ultimate point of orientation for all the movement in human life that remains eternally remote from it. Now it is precisely in Christianity that these radical depths of the experience of God are clearly grasped. They are grasped as grace and as something that imposes itself victoriously in Jesus Christ, something that is borne witness to and apprehended in the dimension of history. The experience of God to which we have appealed, therefore, even in the form in which we encounter it in our own times, is not necessarily so a-Christian as appears at first sight. On the contrary, among the religions which *de facto* exist (considered as historical and social phenomena) it is precisely Christianity which makes real this experience of God in its most radical and purest form, and in Jesus Christ achieves a convincing manifestation of it in history.

Now let us approach the same point from the opposite direction and under a different aspect. Today it is becoming clearer, and that too within Christianity at the doctrinal and institutional level, that this experience of God (admittedly as rightly interpreted and in its most radical form) really constitutes the very heart and centre of Christianity itself and also the ever living source of that conscious manifestation which we call 'revelation'. Now if this is true then through this experience of God Christianity itself simply achieves a more radical and clearer understanding of its own authentic nature. For in fact in its true essence it is not one particular religion among others, but rather the sheer objectivation in history of that experience of God which exists *everywhere* in virtue of God's universal will to save all men by bestowing himself upon them as grace. Today, therefore, Christianity recognizes more clearly than formerly, and makes real in the concrete conditions of human living, the fact that it constitutes the historically pure realization of God's self-bestowal upon mankind which takes place everywhere and in every experience of God, even where, without any fault on the part of the individuals involved, this experience is wrongly interpreted. Christianity, then, is this achieved fulness of God's self-bestowal upon mankind as made definitely victorious in Christ. Now if this is true then recognition of it signifies one element by which Christianity itself can realize its own nature more effectively. It is, therefore, a task precisely for Christianity itself to point ever anew to this basic experience of God, to induce man to discover it within himself, to accept it and also to avow his allegiance to it in its verbal and historical objectivation; for, in its pure form and as related to Jesus Christ as its seal of authenticity, it is precisely this that we call Christianity.

7

THEOLOGICAL CONSIDERATIONS ON SECULARIZATION AND ATHEISM

B Y way of introduction I may be permitted a brief remark concerning the functions and methods of the Secretariat for Unbelievers which has recently been instituted.[1] Since in fact there is also a Secretariat for Non-Christian Religions as well as the Secretariat for Ecumenical Questions we can in practice conclude that the unbelievers with whom this secretariat is intended to deal comprise only the atheists. This secretariat, therefore, must concern itself with atheism and atheists, with maintaining a dialogue with these, and with the struggle against atheism as such in the world. But what is it really intended to do in this respect?

In accordance with the exhortation of 'Gaudium et Spes' of the Second Vatican Council we can of course distinguish the most varied forms of atheism. We can study its roots and origins at the theoretical, historical, and social levels, and in the concrete conditions in which it actually exists.[2] We can attempt to learn more about the various forms of atheism too by entering into dialogue with their representatives, and by arriving at an understanding with these atheists on this or that point which may actually be of real and great importance at the social level, for this clears the way for the subsequent decision which has to be taken between theism and atheism, and is something that can be striven for as the goal of a real and workable humanism which we can join with them in aiming for. But in doing all this are we really achieving anything else than what has been done all along in Catholic theology, in Christian philosophy, and fundamental theology, and in the Christian kerygma? Of course it is

---

[1] *AAS* 56 (1964), p. 560. See also F. König, 'Das Zweite Vatikanische Konzil und das Sekretariat für die Nichtglaubenden', *Internationale Dialogzeitschrift* 1 (Vienna, 1968), pp. 79–88.

[2] On this cf. the Pastoral Constitution of the Second Vatican Council 'Gaudium et Spes', Nos. 19–21, with the commentaries in J. Chr. Hampe (ed.), *Die Autorität der Freiheit* III (Munich, 1967), pp. 574–615.

possible to say that all these undertakings must be pursued more intensively today, that in order to achieve a form in which they can be more
vigorously pursued these interests must be co-ordinated within the Church,
that contact with Christian and non-Christian theists must be strengthened
in this struggle, and that in all these tasks the Secretariate for Non-
Believers must lend its assistance. All this is certainly true and important.

Yet the impression is borne in upon me that, abstracting from the
organization and technical aspects of these movements, which must not
be underestimated, we cannot say in any real sense to what extent and in
what way these movements are effectively aimed at something that is new
at the theoretical level,[3] something that has not been recognized or put
into practice hitherto. Finally it does after all seem to be the case that we
are simply putting forward once more the old and certainly important
teaching of a philosophical and theological theism, albeit in a form which
is somewhat deeper and more precise, and that we are hoping thereby,
by bringing to bear the necessary patience and zeal in our preaching,
actually to win over those who were formerly atheists. To this factor of a
certain stagnation, present though unadmitted in the theoretical teaching
in defence of theism and against atheism, a further one must be added,
one to which, after all, we have as yet hardly given any serious consideration. For today we are confronted with the task of bringing about a change
at the level of social psychology and, if we may so put it, inherited psychology, in the awareness of the broad masses of society, a change which has
become necessary in view of the worldwide atheism which has come to
prevail at least at the practical level. The question is, therefore, what form
our attempts to bring about this change should take in order to achieve the
necessary prior conditions for a theism that is really powerful and effective
in men's eyes and at the social and public level. The two questions we
have raised and the two deficiencies we have pointed to are of course
intrinsically connected. And since in respect of both we do not really
have any new idea to offer, we are in no position either to develop any

[3] On the question of God cf. the author's 'Gott', *LTK* IV (2nd ed. 1960), 1080–
1087; 'Gotteslhere', *ibid.*, 1119–1124; 'Meditation über das Wort "Gott" ', *Gnade als
Freiheit* (Freiburg, 1968), pp. 11–18; 'Gott ist keine naturwissenschaftliche Formel',
ibid., pp. 19–23; 'Gott, unser Vater', *ibid.*, pp. 24–29; 'Remarks on the Dogmatic
Treatise "De Trinitate" ', *Theological Investigations* IV (London and Baltimore,
1966), pp. 77–102; 'Observations on the Doctrine of God in Catholic Dogmatics',
Theological Investigations IX, (London and New York, 1972), pp. 127–145 and 'The
Experience of God Today', in this volume, pp. 149–165.

effective strategy for the struggle against atheism.[4] Neither of course is it possible for me, and within the scope of this study, to devise remedies for the two deficiencies I have indicated. Nevertheless we should have an awareness of them, and moreover, for our present purposes this awareness will be presupposed, while we must also hope that the extreme problematical considerations put forward here will meet with sufficient good will and a sufficient readiness to understand the problems involved.

Absolutely speaking it would be my task to discuss that form of atheism which is conditioned by the movement which we of today are accustomed to call the process of secularization. Properly speaking, therefore, in order to describe the characteristics of the atheism to be treated of here, I would have to begin by speaking of this process of secularization in itself, to say what is meant by this, to give an account of its causes and origins in history, to distinguish the various forms which it assumes, to work out the difference between two factors within it: on the one hand a worldliness of the world which has been brought about in a long process of development by Christianity itself, a de-numinization and de-sacralization of the world which is in accordance with the nature of Christianity itself; and on the other hand a secularism which is at basis identical with atheism and is the mortal enemy of Christianity itself.[5]

In all this we would have to draw far more precise distinctions. For instance we would have to raise the question of a justifiable and a false distinction between Christian faith and religion. We would have to investigate what is really involved in the 'Death of God' theology.[6] We would also have to enquire more precisely at the level of empirical sociology into the question of whether this secularization of the world in which we live today is in fact so intense as is often maintained, or whether

[4] On the idea that it is necessary for the Church to have a strategy cf. the author's 'Das Verhältnis der Kirche zur Gegenwartssituation im allgemeinen. Globale kirchliche Strategie', *Handbuch der Pastoraltheologie* II/2 (Freiburg, 1966), pp. 19–24.

[5] cf. K. Rahner, 'Theological Reflections on the problem of Secularization', *Theological Investigations* VIII (London and New York, 1973), pp. 318–349. Here of course we cannot enter any further into the theses of Schillebeeckx, Metz, Schlette *et al* with regard to this problem.

[6] On the whole it is true to say that even in the Church herself the understanding of God is beginning to change. cf. A. Vanneste, 'Le problème de Dieu de Vatican I à Vatican II', *Revue Clergé* 22 (1967), pp. 234–251.

In recent times the discussion of the 'Death of God' theology and the efforts to achieve a fresh understanding of God by changing our understanding of transcendence have resulted in such an increase in the literature on this whole complex of questions that it would exceed the limits of a footnote if we were to give even an introductory list of references.

what is referred to in these terms is often simply a change in the outward form which religion assumes, which we and others are simply confusing with secularization because this religious element no longer falls within our traditional theological and religious categories. But so much has already been written on all this that here we shall not have anything further to say about the process of secularization as such.

Here, therefore, we shall proceed straight away to enquire into that form of atheism as such which corresponds to this state of secularization in the world of today. We shall adopt this procedure even though in doing so we are aware of the fact that our starting-point, namely this state of secularization, is a phenomenon that is very obscure, has many different levels, and many different shades of meaning. We shall say therefore quite crudely: there is today an atheism which exists in virtue of the fact that the world has become worldly, i.e. so far as man's feelings are concerned it is not easy for him to discover anything which he can call God in the sphere of his manifold experience of a world that has become ever more complex, but at the same time too ever more comprehensible and controllable. For contemporary man every element in his world which he can experience seems to point on to some other element of the same kind, so that no element ever seems to stand outside this process of functional interplay. In its individual elements the world seems to be a system closed in upon itself which has no outlet leading to a reality which is real and yet at the same time does not belong to the world. And even if we achieve a metaphysical plane of thought at which, by some kind of supreme effort of mind, we seek to say that precisely this closed system called the world, in which these individual elements are closed in upon themselves, points on to a sustaining and originating cause of an absolute kind, with a unity of its own that transcends the world, and that it is this that we call God, still even then the man of today all too easily receives the impression that so lofty a line of thought, which transcends the whole, is demanding too much of him, no longer has any message for him, is unrealizable in the concrete conditions of his existence, and leads only to a mythological reduplication of his world. Yet, as has been said, this is the kind of secularism we are assuming to be present and we believe that it enables us to understand a specific kind of atheism which exists at least at the practical level, and in particular that atheism which from the outset declares that it is incapable of achieving any understanding of a metaphysical question even considered merely as a question.[7]

[7] The historical, philosophical, psychological and sociological assumptions of atheism are treated of at great length in the symposium volume edited by J. Girardi, *L'Athéisme dans la vie et culture contemporaine*, 2 vols (Paris, 1968/69).

I

The first point which has to be made with regard to this atheism that derives from the secularization process is this: that it does exist as one specific phenomenon of this secularized world, yet that in principle, and even today, it should be regarded as the sole form of atheism.[8]

The positive part of this statement surely does not need any separate treatment in order to explain it in greater detail or to prove it. The only further point which we have to make on this is that in their practical lives men have the impression that they can manage even without God (we shall have to speak further on this at a later stage) and that the sciences by which the men of today live – independent of any philosophy – and which appear to the men of today as providing the standards by which they conduct their lives, are in principle, at least so far as their methods are concerned, a-theistic. In other words every phenomenon which engages their attention is reduced by them to another empirically verifiable element in the world as to its original cause. The second part of our introductory statement is initially and for our present purposes somewhat more important: it would be superficial and false to regard the atheism which proceeds from secularization as the only important form of the atheism of today. There are forms of atheism which are quite different in their nature and origins even though in a world that has become secularized these atheisms manifest themselves more easily at the social level and have become more numerous than formerly, and these different atheisms have of course been able to combine in the mind of the individual in the concrete to form a single atheistic mentality and way of life.

Now if these various atheisms really do differ from one another right at their very roots then it is false from the outset to maintain that they can all be reduced to a single common system of so-called atheism in the singular, for since the various systems grouped under this heading spring from quite different roots, any one of them has little more in common with the rest than the name 'atheism'. From this it clearly follows that the struggle against the different atheisms must be conducted in quite different ways. The atheism that springs from secularization, therefore, requires a quite different treatment from that which we accord, for instance, to an atheism springing from an attitude of despairing pessimism which declares that after Auschwitz it is no longer possible to believe in God, or to an atheism which consists merely in an aversion from any

[8] On this cf. K. Rahner, 'Atheism', *Sacramentum Mundi* I (New York and London, 1968), pp. 116–122.

thematic treatment of the transcendental reference which man bears to the absolute mystery in and over his own existence, which is merely afraid of adoring an idol once he begins to speak of God and to allow him to enter into his calculations or to have a place in his life. Such an atheism as this seeks to be Godless out of respect for God, and to remain Godless honestly and courageously in the desert of an existence within which no such reality as God is to be found or may even be sought for at all if God is to remain God. Of course between these different atheisms, only a few aspects of which have been indicated here, there is a constant mutual interplay and inter-influence both at the theoretical level and in their application to human living in the concrete. Nevertheless it must still clearly be recognized that they differ from one another in their roots, and so too in their essence, and hence too in the struggle we wage against them our approaches to them must be different. So great are these differences indeed that it would almost be true to say that it is only the label 'atheism' that they have in common. Anyone who is not prepared to recognize this truth must allow the question to be put to him of what precise and really credible idea of God he has. He must allow us to ask him whether what the term 'God' represents for him cannot, in some sense, really and validly be denied or called in question, and whether on this account the atheism which he rejects is not an extremely obscure and dubious entity.[9]

The seriousness and effectiveness of the considerations, proofs, means and methods put forward at the theoretical level and proposed to be used in the struggle against the various forms of atheism, which differ so much from one another, must therefore be measured by this standard: whether on the one hand they really do relate specifically to one particular form of atheism, and whether on the other they do not express mere self-evident truisms which have been and are valid always and everywhere, whereas the specific form of atheism concerned has origins and a background of its own in the history of human thought which have by no means been present always and everywhere, but which are present today, and therefore cannot be overcome in their atheistic developments solely by *those* considerations, means, and methods which have been put forward and applied always and everywhere. Considerations of this kind at the

[9] For a more extensive treatment of this point cf. K. Lehmann, 'Some Ideas from Pastoral Theology on the Proclamation of the Christian Message to Non-Believers of Today', *Concilium* 3/3 (Pastoral Theology) 1967, pp. 43–52, and the revised and expanded version of this study in *Handbuch der Pastoraltheologie* III (Freiburg, 1968), pp. 638–677.

theoretical level, therefore, and means and methods of this kind at the practical level, must surely be worked out from the first. They are not simply weapons which have all along been there ready to hand in the arsenal of the *Ecclesia militans*, so that all that we have to do now is at most to polish them somewhat more brightly and to give them a somewhat sharper edge. But if such considerations means and methods need to be worked out afresh, then it is inevitable that any suggestions in this direction must give due and serious consideration to the fact that some of them may be problematical and liable to be contested, that they will have to stand up to discussion or possibly to practical testing insofar as such a thing is possible, and even to a determined attack upon them. All that we shall have to say in what follows is to be understood in this sense and with this proviso. What we are treating of is mere material for discussion and nothing more, though admittedly we shall be treating of this at a very serious level.

II

Against the atheism that derives from secularization, with its pragmatic and positivist mentality which we have already pointed out, there is little sense and little prospect of success in conducting our defence of theism and our struggle against this atheism either explicitly or implicitly merely from the general standpoint 'we cannot manage without God'.

Even on the basis of a true understanding of God it is extremely questionable whether we should attempt to assign to God so utilitarian a place in the struggle for a better world (whether at the individual or the collective levels). The world as God has created it, and as it has been even under the dominion of a theism which has been generally accepted, at least in public, has been an extremely wretched world. It has been this even in those areas in which Christianity has held sway in public life with what is, at least according to the theory of its high-minded theologians, its sublime concept of God. And the very fact that it has been pitiful in this sense means that in principle we cannot use the idea of God in this way. Atheism lays great emphasis on this simple fact of the world's wretchedness, and even if against this we were to rejoin that this wretched world is so as a consequence of man's own guilt, still the atheist could in turn reply that this pitiful state of the world, its anguish and strife, the alienation of man from himself taking place within it, in very large measure does not derive from his own guilt, but on the contrary is itself the cause of this guilt to the extent that there really is any guilt at all. And the

atheist might go on to point out that it is precisely the Christian who is
least of all in any position to maintain that God has been able to create
the world and freedom only at the risk of man falling voluntarily into sin
so that no real problem of 'theodicy' exists at all. But even if we abstract
from the problems of principle involved in this line of argument that the
world cannot prosper without God, still the man of today at least has the
impression that wherever, and to the extent that, any improvement has
been achieved in the world and that progress has been made, this has been
achieved by man himself, and that he has done it of his own initiative
even without God.

There is a question which we intend to set aside here even though it is
no merely theoretical one, but of the highest practical importance as well;
the question, namely, of what would happen if the idea of God were to
be totally eliminated in the world, if theism were to disappear not merely
in its explicit, but in its anonymous form as well. On this question we
should certainly have to say that taking human life as a whole we certainly
cannot manage without the idea of God, at least – in order to be completely
prudent – not if we include within this idea of God those unexplicitated
and anonymous forms of this encounter with God also which do exist and
which are transcendentally necessary so long as man continues to exist at
the spiritual dimension and has not degenerated to the level of an intelligent animal. Certainly we should have to refer, in this connection, to
C. G. Jung's statement according to which all human conflicts in a man of
over thirty-five have a religious origin, whether he is aware of it or not.[10]
But, as has been said, for our present purposes we shall be abstracting
from this question, ultimately crucial though it is.

Prior to this, however, and apart from it, even if this ultimate and
fundamental question has to be answered in the affirmative, still there is
very much that is possible in the world which, it was formerly believed,
required an immediate and explicit basis in theism. There is much in
human life at the individual and social levels which in earlier times derived
its stability from the idea of God, yet which today can in fact be aimed at
as a goal, even without any recourse to an explicit theism by means of a
liberal and humanistic education, by consciously aiming to develop
psychic mechanisms and social methods of training, by means of social
pressures and conditions of interdependence, and finally by the police.
It is true that today at least not enough experiments have yet been carried
out for us to be in a position to lay down what can be achieved in the way

[10] C. G. Jung, *Die Beziehungen der Psychotherapie zur Seelsorge* (Zürich, 1948), p.
16.

of a genuine humanism and a tolerable mode of social living among men by a genuinely atheistic society in which all the surviving elements of an earlier mode of living based on theism have effectively been eliminated. Nevertheless, while not calling in question the fact that the idea of God has an ultimate significance of its own, we may perhaps be permitted to doubt whether there are any very notable differences between the average morality of an atheistic society which can already be observed, to the extent that such a phenomenon does exist, and the morality of an average theistic society, i.e. one in which the idea of God has a certain validity for the purposes of public life and remains undisputed at the public level. It is true that we can produce definitions, at the speculative and theoretical level, of the pure atheist and the absolute theist, and compare them with one another, and on the basis of this we can probably give an unambiguous preference to the theist not merely with regard to the question of truth as such, but also with regard to the practical effectiveness of his tenets in producing a humane and tolerable way of life. But this theoretical construction and comparison has only a very limited effectiveness so far as the working out of a practical apologetics for theism is concerned. For first we are unable to produce this pure atheist at the experimental level, since in fact such an individual does not yet exist today. Indeed, in view of the factor of a certain anonymous and unexplicitated transcendental theism even the avowed atheist cannot be said to be a pure atheist in this sense. And second, it is only with great difficulty that we can produce that kind of theist who shapes his whole life radically and exclusively on the basis of his theist convictions.

So far as the practical apologetics for theism are concerned, therefore, we shall have to recognize that that approach in which we invoke the idea that we cannot manage either at the individual or the social level without the idea of God has to be viewed with the utmost caution and critical realism. The actual position at present is such that at least so far as our external empirical observations are concerned, atheists die peaceably and without any particular fear, and that morality considered as an empirical and statistically calculable entity in a society does not seem, in any very clear sense, to be dependent upon our position with regard to the existence of God, whether we still verbally acknowledge this, or call it in question, or positively deny it. So far as the maintenance of liberal and humane morality in society is concerned we must not, precisely as Catholics, be too hasty and over-zealous in using the idea of God as a weapon in our argument. In fact we are upholders of the idea of the 'natural law', whatever interpretation may be placed upon this concept, so very controversial as it has once more become in the present day. Now on any showing this means that there are basic principles of moral conduct such that they have to be discovered first and foremost in the nature of man himself, and in the structures of the society and the environment in which he has to live, even though any binding force which we may attach to these human norms immanent within our own world does include a theism that is postulated at least at the implicit and non-thematic level. This in itself should cause us to observe the greatest prudence and reserve in adopting the approach to apologetics described above.

To this a further and rather different point must be added. When theism is invoked as a postulate for shaping the world in a way that makes the course of human life in it reasonably humane and tolerable, it almost inevitably arouses the suspicion in the mind of modern man of being a fictitious ideology. It is quite useful, but for that very reason incurs the suspicion of being a mere fiction. The question of whether we believe in God certainly has some importance too for human living in its fully concrete reality. But if we attempt to persuade either ourselves or another to believe in God precisely *in order that* these very real advantages ensuing from belief in God may be gained, then in the majority of cases today the psychological mechanism which we seek to set in motion in this way will fail to function in view of the fact that the world as we experience it is so terrible. Some will say that the idea of God is 'too beautiful to be true'. Others will always regard the element postulated in it (and even Kant freely invoked this in his work) as the fictitious element, and will say that a God who is postulated to exist on the grounds of human needs is and remains in all cases a projection of man himself, something which is conjured up by him to help him. They will say that this postulated element is the opium of the people, valid only so long as they cannot find the help they need elsewhere, a neurosis of humanity which has gradually to be broken down.

III

The positive message that there is a living God, and that he wills to save mankind, is in principle directed to *all* men. Certainly there are in principle no explicitly definable boundaries for Christianity and the missionary movement of the Church at which her proclamation of the living God should be brought to a halt, no boundaries beyond which live men to whom theism is from the outset and in principle of no concern. It is no less obvious, and in principle still more important, that there is no form of human living in which an encounter with God does not take place at least anonymously, non-thematically, and transcendentally (or however we may wish to express the reality referred to). For everywhere where a truth is asserted as absolute there, as a matter of transcendental necessity, albeit, perhaps, in a quite anonymous and unacknowledged manner, God is present, even in those cases in which the individual involved is unable consciously to recognize this transcendental implication or to express it in words, or when, by a culpable misuse of his own freedom, he denies or excludes this radical mystery of his own existence.[11] The more firmly a Christian theism has to stand by the two principles just mentioned, the more it must guard against the danger of drawing from them conclusions which are over-hasty and ultimately false. What we mean by this is that without being false to its own nature or adopting an attitude of cowardly defeatism, and without allowing itself to be intimidated by the atheism of today, Christian preaching can be realistic enough to take into account the possibility that *de facto* even the message of theism as such, and not merely the more complex and detailed tenets of Christianity, will remain more or less ineffective so far as a great part of the future order of society and mankind is concerned. Contrary to the tacit assumptions of scholastic theology we cannot see why any *fundamental* distinction has to be drawn in this question on theological grounds between the chances of survival for an explicit theism on the one hand and those which may be ascribed to Christianity in the full sense on the other. Formerly the necessity for such a distinction was regarded as axiomatic, even though the problem involved was not clearly recognized. The reason for this was first that it was held that as many individuals as possible must have a real chance of salavation, yet without any theism this was regarded as inconceivable (in accordance with Hebrews 11:6), and second that it was not possible to conceive of an anonymous theism, a theism which had not been objectified at the conceptual and verbal level so as to become an object of conscious thought, yet which could also be accepted in freedom and which had power to justify. Today, however, the Second Vatican Council has laid down that even the atheist has a genuine chance of salvation *so long as* he is true to the promptings of his own conscience. In asserting this the Second Vatican Council was manifestly thinking too of the kind of atheist who throughout the course of his life will never become a theist at the explicit and thematic level, yet at the same time it still remains true that

[11] For a similar thesis of the author's with regard to the possibility of an anonymous Christianity in the atheist cf. 'Atheism and Implicit Christianity', *Theological Investigations* IX (London and New York, 1972), pp. 145–164.

without any encounter with God salvation is impossible. Now in view of all this there must be a theism of the sort which I have described, a theism that is anonymous, non-thematic, and even as such capable of really existing and being accepted in freedom. I cannot enter into the nature of this theism here in any closer detail.[12]

But if this is the case then I can no longer see why the chances of Christianity surviving at the historical and social level have to be regarded as less than those of theism as such; why for instance – to put it in more concrete terms – the established theology up to now finds it easier to recognize the possibility of an inculpable failure to recognize the truth of Christianity, the Church, and the obligations which these impose than to see that the same must apply with regard to the explicit recognition of the existence of God. Of course certain differences may exist even in this case. But they are certainly not so fundamental or so great as was supposed by the former established theology right up to the point at which the Second Vatican Council began. To put the matter for the moment in an exaggeratedly hostile way, and one which perhaps goes beyond the facts, it would be perfectly possible to imagine that in some future but wholly conceivable age the opportunities of survival for a Christianity that exists in concrete form are actually greater than those to be ascribed to a theism in the abstract, one which exists apart from the concrete reality and practice of a Christianity embodied in the Church. However this may be, we can at least say this much: Just as the specifically Christian message recognizes from the outset that in the case of many individuals and social groups it will *de facto* fail to make them Christian in any explicit sense, and yet in spite of this regards it as possible that such individuals will find salvation in an 'anonymous Christianity', so too a similar situation may freely be expected, or at least taken into account as possible, for the future with regard to theism as well.

In the future, therefore, it may be presumed that atheism of the explicit kind will be extremely widespread (though of course there will be very many different shades and degrees of this) ranging from an atheism of irresponsiveness and indifference towards religion as a matter of living practice to one that is very thoroughly worked out at the theoretical level, and in fact a militant atheism (admittedly, for reasons which cannot be developed in any greater detail here, an atheism of this kind, as it exists in the concrete individual, is under certain circumstances perfectly compatible with an implicit and anonymous theism). There will be a widespread atheism of this kind in the future because the situation in which the

[12] cf. n. 11

world has become secularized cannot be reversed. Now this situation is constantly renewing its impact upon men and so generating an atheism of this kind in very many of them, not indeed with any justification at the theoretical level, but nevertheless with a certain psychological compulsion.

Without prejudice, therefore, to the fundamental universality of its message of the living God, a universality which we are bound to strive for, Christianity and the Church can reckon with this prospect of an extremely widespread and enduring atheism as a 'must' of saving history in their proclamation of this message, just as the Church always reckons with the 'must' of saving history that she and her message will always remain the sign that is contradicted, and even with the fact that this contradiction is becoming more acute. However true it may be that this 'must' relates to something that should not be the case, the fact still remains that Christianity and the Church can allow this prospect to enter into their calculations and turn it to good account by allowing it to produce a kind of reaction within them. In this sense, therefore, they can allow the methods and tactics they adopt in the preaching of theism to be influenced by this factor. In other contexts also factors of a similar kind are already taken into account, as in the methods and tactics of pastoral work. For instance these may determine how certain *finite* forces are to be applied in the pastoral field and used to determine the specific directions in which pressure is applied in pastoral work. This takes place in cases in which the pastoral effort has a smaller chance of being effective and the mode and direction of such pastoral work are ordered accordingly.

IV

In the light of all this it would be perfectly conceivable for explicit theism, both in the account that it gives of itself and in its methods, to be thought of and presented as the 'wooing' of an 'élite'. Of course such a thesis is only intended as a basis for discussion with all due reservations. It is also obvious that the term 'élite', both in respect of its content and in its applicability to our present question, is highly problematical, and never at any stage intended to refer to specific *social* groups.

An initial objection might be that objective truth can have nothing to do with an 'élitist' awareness since truth is either valid for all or else does not exist. But against this the point that we must constantly keep in the forefront of our minds is precisely *which* truth is being treated of. There are truths which from the outset relate to the totality of human existence, and the recognition of these depends upon many prior factors, and a certain vision of human nature in its totality. These are truths, moreover, which always involve an element of decision and the process of objectifying them at the conceptual level also presupposes very many intellectual conditions such as can, in effect, be achieved only with great difficulty in those situations in which they are not supported by a public opinion that is homogeneous throughout a given society. Such truths as these may very well have something to do with the kind of awareness that may be called 'élitist', and however true it may be that such truths and convictions have an objective validity of their own in virtue of which they are in principle of concern to all, still as they exist in the concrete they do have the character of being orientated towards an 'élite'. Moreover such truths and convictions do exist quite apart from, and independent of the problem of theism. The loftier perceptions in the fields of aesthetics, logic, ethics etc. are in themselves truths for all, yet *de facto* they only come to be apprehended by a minority endowed with the necessary equipment for receiving them, and in this sense 'élitist'. The theism of the future can *de facto* – though this does not mean *de jure* – have an 'élitist' character in this sense. Formerly we closed our minds to any such possibility because of our belief (this is a point which has already been emphasized) that we necessarily had to accept an element of culpability in any atheist who remained obstinate in his atheism. We have already briefly indicated that this assumption is theologically invalid.

To this the following consideration must now be added. In earlier situations in the history of human thought some idea of God was certainly present in most minds, mainly because it was supported by public opinion in society as a whole. But the moment we put the question seriously to ourselves of what part this concept of God effectively played in the lives of very many of these earlier 'theists' both inside and outside of Christendom, then surely we can justifiably ask whether precisely *this* idea of God really had so very much to do with the true, living, and inconceivable God as he really is. From this we can go on to raise the further question of whether the abandonment of an idea of God of this kind, which has been brought about by the new situation which has arisen in public thought and social life, truly has altered so very much with regard to the real chance of salvation which men of this kind have. And if in reply to this it were to be objected that even in so shockingly primitive and degenerate an idea of God some kind of very decisive reference to the true God was still always present, some notion of the true God was still always guessed at, then we must rejoin that an unexplicitated reference to God of this kind still remains constantly present even in those cases in

which it is no longer labelled with the term 'God' in the mind of the individual concerned through the influence of public opinion in society as a
whole. In the light of this, and so far as a great part of the men of the
future as they will *de facto* exist are concerned, there is no need whatever
to present true theism as that which is, both at the theoretical and the
social level, simply self-evident, that which would already have to be
explicitly present even in a human group which had only reached a very
'primitive' stage of development. In stating this principle we are of course
presupposing that rational thought, even in its highest stages of scientific
and technical development, can be perfectly compatible with a stage of
development within mankind which is only very 'primitive' to the extent
that development here consists in finding within oneself the courage
explicitly to face up to the one question which is entailed by the very
nature of man as a single whole, and by the world in general.

Even the teaching of the First Vatican Council with regard to the
possibility of recognizing the existence of God by the light of the natural
reason does not invalidate the theory of the 'élitist' character of the theism
of the future. For what is being treated of in this definition is a possibility
in principle which applies to man as such. But nothing is said here about
the possibility or impossibility of an individual man in his concrete
situation coming to recognize God by the power of his own capacities as
an individual. Even Thomas Aquinas has emphasized how very much the
individual man in the concrete is dependent, even for this knowledge,
upon his social situation. Now if it is true that in the present and future
this situation entails a greater danger than formerly of raising difficulties
or obstacles to prevent man from knowing God, then it will not be surprising if many men fail to arrive at any explicit knowledge of God with
sufficient clarity and firmness. Moreover this statement is not irreconcilable
with the declaration of the First Vatican Council.

On the basis of all that we have said, therefore, there is nothing which
makes it illegitimate for us in conducting an apologetic on behalf of theism
in the future to proclaim this theism as the specially exalted gift of the wise
who are impelled to advance to an ultimate understanding of their own
existence in a way which, other things being equal, cannot possibly be
accessible to the '*profanum vulgus*' even though no-one can in principle and
from the outset be excluded from this matured experience of existence.
And surely there is a further reason too for regarding a theism of this
kind rather as the especially exalted gift of the wise. In a world which has
become so complex that it is almost impossible to gain any comprehensive
view of it, and in which the methods employed in all science proceed

along a-theistic lines (even though this in itself is justified) it is immensely difficult to view the one and ultimate question of truth as a single whole, and to make it a subject of investigation in itself, to dare explicitly and in a spirit of adoration to come to terms with that mystery which, almost *per definitionem* withdraws itself from man into its own ineffability. I believe that an explicit theism of the future will more readily be made 'attractive' even for the many if it is considered and presented as 'élitist' in character than if, contrary to all appearances and contrary to a widespread public feeling, it is presented as a doctrine which only the stupid or malicious will reject.

If the considerations which we have just put forward are to some extent correct then, while explicit theism would not have to regard every form of atheism as 'narrow-minded', it would have to regard that form which proceeds from secularization as being this; as the attitude and perspective in terms of thought and life of those who, for reasons which are very varied but also very understandable, have not – at any rate not yet – advanced to the stage of being able to achieve an overall view of the functional interconnection between the individual elements in their existence and in the world and explicitly to objectify this at the conceptual level. Because they have not yet reached this stage they cannot yet face up to the absolute mystery which ultimately, but silently encompasses this totality of the world, within which their own activities are confined. This attitude in which the theist of the future feels atheism to be 'narrow-minded', 'uneducated' and 'primitive' actually can and may (though all possible caution and educational discretion must be brought to bear here) help to determine the form of the apologetics which theism develops against this kind of atheism. The attitude here is to some extent analogous to that which is adopted by one who is genuinely expert and very highly educated in musical matters towards one who feels that the marches of a brass band or a popular song represent the supreme point of his musical experience. This attitude, in which theism justifiably feels itself superior to this kind of atheism, should come to be accepted as obvious. The theist should no longer feel himself to be the one who is defending an old theory against a modern viewpoint, but rather as the one who humanly speaking and in the concrete conditions of human living, has advanced farther than the atheist. And if this attitude were adopted then we should perhaps more easily and more quickly overcome the shock which many theists of today feel from the fact that on the one hand they assume that it is theism that constitutes the self-evident truth which all understand and are able to recognize, while on the other it is borne in upon them as a matter of experience that many do not share this theism, are opposed to it from the outset as being unintelligible, even though at the same time they cannot be described either as stupid or as ill-willed.

v

To the extent that theism is actively opposed to this atheism that stems from the secularization process it requires something more than a mere indoctrination on the lines of the old scholastic proofs of God's existence, however correct these may have been viewed as a whole. Over and above this it requires an 'initiation' in which it attempts from the outset to appeal to man as a single totality.

In the manner in which the old proofs of God's existence were put forward they were very remarkable in character. On the one hand they were presented in a way that suggested that they were seeking to prove to the individual a truth of which he had hitherto never heard anything at all. The effect they had was as if in treating of God and the knowledge that could be gained of him they were dealing with a matter which could be brought home to man from without in the same way as, for instance, the existence of a distant land to which the hearer had never yet journeyed. These proofs did not really take into account the fact that the subject of which they were treating had been latently present all along in the hearer in a manner corresponding to his particular capacities and the resources of freedom and knowledge inherent in the human spirit. They failed to take into account the fact that under certain circumstances the truth they were proposing had actually already freely been assented to. In other words what these proofs of God's existence were seeking to achieve was to objectify in the form of a conceptual statement something of which the hearer had all along been aware at the transcendental, implicit, and non-thematic level rather than to indoctrinate him *ab initio* with a completely new truth which had never been present in him in any sense at all. On the other hand, however, these proofs of God's existence were put forward by people who had never been assailed by the slightest doubt of God's existence by anything deriving from the course of their own personal lives, or still more from the milieu in which they lived. In this respect too the situation was, and for the most part still is, similar to that which prevails in moral questions. If as a result of a certain global instinct inherent in human living, and of consistently acting upon a given moral maxim in practice, the individual is already convinced of the rightness of this maxim, then he will be very quick to receive the light of the *a posteriori* justification of this maxim at the theoretical level, even though it remains true that these proofs, viewed in their true perspective, do not amount to much more than a repetition of the thesis in different terms. When the hearer is already himself a 'practising theist' and is this in a social milieu that is homogeneously theistic in its turn, the proofs of God's existence do not constitute any particular difficulty for him. But if this is not the hearer's situation then, even if he is not, as he very well may be, the better philosopher, while he may perhaps not raise many objections against these proofs, they will nevertheless fail to make any real or effective impact upon the hearer in the concrete conditions of his life.

In order to achieve such a thing something more is needed than an indoctrination of this kind at the conceptual level. What is needed is an initiation, an 'inauguration' into an experience of God that is ultimate and basic. What is more, this is needed precisely in the case of an atheist who has been influenced by the secularization process, because precisely this kind of atheist, as informed by a positivist and pragmatic mentality, is most of all remote, at least so far as any conscious reflection upon them is concerned, from those experiences which the proofs of God's existence in the usual sense assume as obviously having been present in him all along. Of course when we speak of initiation and inauguration we are initially simply enunciating a term which in its turn raises a problem without solving it. Nevertheless if any understanding has been achieved of that reality which we have already often designated as man's transcendental reference to the mystery[13] called God, if this transcendental reference is not once more confused with the concept corresponding to it and objectifying statements about it, if we do not speak of this transcendental reference in merely abstract and formal terms, but rather point it out to man in his concrete life (for it is precisely *here*, in his own life, that he makes this experience all unnoticed and undefined, whether he wills it or not) then it is no mere empty talk to speak of the possibility of and necessity for inaugurating him into an ultimate experience of God. This is not to deny that we have spoken of this initiation only in very abstract and formal terms, because at the moment nothing more is possible here.

It is a fact that a great number of those who proclaim the message of Christian theism basically speaking take as their starting-point a sense

[13] cf. K. Rahner, 'The Concept of Mystery in Catholic Theology', *Theological Investigations* IV (London and Baltimore, 1966), pp. 36–73; *idem*, 'Science as a "Confession"?', *Theological Investigations* III (London and Baltimore, 1967), pp. 385–400; *idem*, *Worte ins Schweigen* (Innsbruck, 10th ed., 1967), and the study entitled 'Reflections on Methodology in Theology', in this volume, pp. 68–114.

which is still sustained by a (mere) general social acceptance that their theism is self-evident. Basically speaking they themselves are aware only of God as an idea indoctrinated *ab externo*. They are far from having achieved with sufficient clarity a truly ultimate religious experience of their own radical reference to the ineffable mystery which we call God. Alternatively in those cases in which, and to the extent that, such an experience is present in them, they are unable either to express it in genuine and credible terms, or to combine it in an effective and living way with their indoctrinated theism. And because of this the majority of those who uphold this Christian theism are at most in a position to teach this to others at the theoretical level, and even this is something which they do only in an extremely inadequate way in their dealings with really educated atheists. Still less do they succeed in advancing from this point to achieve a truly genuine initiation into the ultimate mystery of human existence or, to put it more precisely, to instil others with the courage to face up to this experience and accept it. In the light of this it would often be better if the preachers of the message of explicit theism had experienced in the concrete conditions of their own lives more of those temptations from which the various forms of atheism, especially that form which springs from the secularization process, emerge.

I cannot refrain from adducing one example of this inadequacy, this inability to speak of theism – which, after all, is the basis and centre of the Christian faith – in a way that really springs from the situation of modern man. I am referring here to the credal formula which has recently been published at the end of the 'Year of Faith' by Paul VI.[14] It has much to say about God which is extremely acute and profound. But a truly modern credal formula of this kind should also declare how a man of today can really arrive at belief in this God, and of this we hear nothing.

[14] *AAS* 60 (1968), pp. 433–445.

8

THE POSITION OF CHRISTOLOGY IN THE CHURCH BETWEEN EXEGESIS AND DOGMATICS

Preliminary Remarks

IN order to make the problem intelligible some preliminary approach will first be necessary. The faith of the Church, and so fundamental theology and dogmatics too, recognizes the existence of a saving history, something, therefore which takes place in the 'space-time' dimension of our existence, something which is unique and unrepeatable. In this history that which we call salvation is achieved, the turning of God to man. Moreover it takes place in such a way that this turning of his really does take place in history, and is dependent upon certain quite specific events to provide it with its proper dimension and reality. That which theologians call salvation is not a truth belonging to the realm of knowledge, always the same, eternally valid, elevated *above* history. And it is not a summons or turning of God to mankind such that it has always been given in the same way. Nor is it merely man's reaction in the dimension of history to an offering of salvation on God's part which itself always remains the same. Rather salvation itself takes place precisely *as* history, the history of God's action upon man. There is a more precise question, the question of how God the eternal, with his will to save which is ultimately the same, is related to that history in which this will to save achieves its historical manifestation. But this is a question to which we cannot give any deeper consideration here.[1] In any case the exponents of

---

[1] Admittedly in any theology of saving history this is a problem which would have to be treated of at length. For a summary cf. K. Rahner, 'Universal Salvific Will. General', *Sacramentum Mundi* 5 (London and New York, 1969), pp. 405–409.

The fact that here too different conceptions of history are possible, and so different theologies, is self-evident and needs no emphasis. A good survey of the conceptions of history which are influential in the contemporary theological sphere is to be found in W. Kasper, 'Grundlinien einer Theologie der Geschichte', *TQ* 144 (1964), pp.

fundamental theology and dogmatics assume as the basis for their specific statements that there is such a thing as saving history, that God acts in history, and that the distinctions to be drawn within this action of his are not based merely upon the different reactions of men to it. They assume rather that within God's saving action in history there can be events of such a kind that in them something is achieved once and for all, that even though this action of his is in principle posited in the dimension of space and time it nevertheless imports salvation for mankind in the future, and indeed under certain conditions (as the Christ-event shows) for the whole of humanity, even those sections of it which come before the event itself.

Now in such deeds of God in saving history the word as word of God in the mouth of man is (for reasons which we shall not be treating of within the scope of the present study) a constitutive element in the saving event itself, such that without it an event could not really belong to saving history at all.[2] From this it may be concluded that the practitioners of Catholic fundamental theology and dogmatics cannot dispense with the conviction that in the historical Jesus there was an awareness and an assertion of the significance of his own function and his person such that, in the fulness and authentication which they achieve through the Resurrection, they effectively constitute the basis and the adequate point of departure for those beliefs which are proclaimed by Christian and Catholic dogma in the christology of Jesus Christ. The exponent of Catholic fundamental theology and dogmatics, therefore, must hold firm to the fact that there was a Jesus of Nazareth who, in his own understanding

---

129–169; J. Ratzinger, 'Heilsgeschichte und Eschatologie. Zur Frage nach dem Ansatz des theologischen Denkens', *Theologie im Wandel* I (edited by the Faculty of Catholic Theology of the University of Tübingen) (Munich, 1967), pp. 68–89; F. Schupp, 'Die Geschichtsauffassung am Beginn der Tübinger Schule und in der gegenwärtigen Theologie', *ZKT* 91 (1969), pp. 150–171.

[2] It is important to emphasize this because in the Protestant sphere, for instance, there is an explicitly verbal theology which is in contrast to the various theologies orientated towards saving history. In this verbal theology the 'word character' of history and 'the reference to history' inherent in the word have a contrasting significance. cf., among others, R. Bultmann, 'Heilsgeschichte and Geschichte. Zu Oscar Cullmanns Christus und die Zeit', *TLZ* 73 (1948), 659/660.

On the problem of the connection between saving truth and the truth of history a very precisely worked out *prise de position* on the part of the official Church is to be found under Nos. 11 and 12 of the Constitution 'Dei Verbum' of the Second Vatican Council. On this cf. the detailed commentary by J. Ratzinger in *LTK* II, revised and expanded (1967), 544–557.

of himself even at the pre-Easter stage had something to do with what Christian faith believes and proclaims of Jesus Christ the risen Lord. Otherwise the life of Jesus and his death would not have constituted a saving event. The post-Easter faith would, in itself and taken in isolation, be the saving event, and in the last analysis would have no necessary connection with Jesus himself or with his death.[3]

Of course – and it is only here that we really touch upon the problem with which we have to concern ourselves – Jesus' understanding of himself, his mission, and his person were not necessarily of such a kind that there is, so to say, a verbal identity between it and what is stated about Jesus Christ in the subsequent christology of the Church. But if before Easter Jesus had been only a man who, in virtue of some kind of religious inspiration and a certain consciousness of his mission, appeared as some kind of prophet or religious genius, and if in the last analysis the message he upheld had nothing whatever to do with his own person, his reality and his death, then the post-Easter christological teaching of the New Testament, and *a fortiori* that of the later Church, would after all be precisely nothing more than a religious idea which had adventitiously been projected onto this Jesus. Nor would Easter alone be of any assistance in narrowing the gap between the pre-Easter Jesus and the post-Easter christology unless it had been the seal set upon a claim of Jesus himself rather than merely the abstract experience of that validity in the life of any individual we like to choose which endures beyond his death. Indeed it would be perfectly possible to imagine a prophet who, having suffered a prophet's fate, is thought of after his death as one whom God had delivered, and is in this sense risen from the dead. But thereby he would in fact cease to be what he formerly was, a prophet, a religious genius, a man inspired by God, who perhaps expressed certain very important truths with regard to the relationship which man bears to God. Even if he had undergone a 'resurrection', his life and his death would not themselves achieve the status of an eschatological event of salvation with a significance for all men. Certainly the apostles were able to express the ultimate truth with regard to the function and person of Jesus in saving history only in the knowledge that he is not only the crucified Lord, but the risen Lord as well. But conversely the experience of an individual having undergone some kind of abstract resurrection cannot be any substitute for a knowledge of his function and person, which must be supplied from elsewhere.

[3] The concept of 'retrospective interpretation' does not seem sufficient of itself unambiguously to elminate a misunderstanding of this kind. For the validity of such an interpretation has itself in turn first to be established in theological terms.

Of course we can say that the Resurrection of Jesus is the enthronement of this individual, in which he is accorded the status of the bringer of salvation in the absolute, and the entire christology of the Church might be developed on the basis of this. But even then the question would still remain of whence this interpretation of the Resurrection acquires its justification, and how it has emerged at all. This question becomes more urgent today in view of the fact that a contemporary exegesis and theology will not accept that the post-Easter Jesus has expressed and formulated a christology defining the significance of his own Resurrection. Moreover if the Resurrection of Jesus is not to be viewed merely as an external apologetic argument from miracles, in other words if it was itself a witness, an element in what is being borne witness to, then Catholic theology still cannot dispense with the truth that the pre-Easter Jesus recognized and stated so much about his own mission and function in saving history that this, when confronted by and combined with the experience of his definitive fate of having been delivered by God, provides the starting-point for that christology which is already present in Paul and John, and then extends further to the christological dogma of the Church. The question of precisely what understanding of himself in the pre-Easter Jesus is being referred to here is one which we shall have to spend a little futher time in investigating.

For the historian the question of what significance the pre-Easter Jesus perceived in himself with regard to his function and his person is not so simple to decide. And hence even in the New Testament itself, when we meet with the titles of glory and concepts of exaltation etc. in which the explicit post-Easter faith of the Church in Jesus Christ is expressed there, we cannot *ipso facto* assume that it is Jesus' own understanding of himself at the pre-Easter stage in his life that has been expressed in these.[4] For everything which we read about Jesus in the New Testament, and moreover even in the gospels (including the earliest of them, that of Mark), which purport to record Jesus' own words, is already an avowal of faith in Jesus Christ (if we may reduce this avowal to a single clear and simple formula).

Now the exponent of fundamental theology and dogmatics tells us that in order to enquire into the self-understanding of the pre-Easter Jesus we must discern what lies behind this avowal of faith, though at the same time this does not imply any withdrawal from the faith of the early Christian preaching to a purely neutral and secular standpoint in which we view the

---

[4] On this cf. also F. Hahn, *Christologische Hoheitstitel* (Göttingen, 2nd ed. 1964).

matter merely in the light of historical science. And the exegete too does not in principle dispute the fact that it is possible to enquire into what lies behind the avowal of faith in this sense,[5] or the fact that there are words of Jesus himself which are absolutely authentic, so that it is possible for us to some extent to isolate them with a sufficient degree of historical certainty from the whole complex of sayings attributed to Jesus in the New Testament in which he is already being interpreted by anticipation as the Christ of Easter. On the other hand, howeveer, this same exegesis makes it clear to us today that this self-understanding of the pre-Easter Jesus which we can still to some extent discern is not so immediately or obviously identical with what is asserted of him by the post-Easter community and the later dogmas of the Church, and what the New Testament itself has introduced into this self-understanding of the pre-Easter Jesus by a process of interpretation (even though objectively speaking this process of interpretation is perfectly justified). And thus the more precise question, and the one that is crucial for the exponent of fundamental theology and dogmatics, is this: whether the findings which contemporary exegesis has been able to arrive at with regard to the pre-Easter Jesus' awareness of himself and his own understanding of his task and person are still sufficient as a point of departure for the New Testament christology to be found in Paul and John, and for the Church's dogmatic teaching about Jesus Christ. This is the question with which we are concerned here, and to which – even at this stage I must assert this much in anticipation of my argument – an affirmative answer is justified.

The Historical Jesus as a Dogmatic Problem

Before we attempt to enter directly into the question which we have just posed it may perhaps be appropriate to say something further about certain more general assumptions and broader perspectives without which it is quite impossible to answer such a question at all. The *first* point that we must bear in mind is that historical certainty and the sort of certainty which we can achieve in the concrete conditions of our human existence (if we may so express it) are two different things. And the difference between them is something which we should clearly recognize and freely take into account in our faith.

We may begin by invoking a quite simple example to illustrate what we

[5] The 'Bultmann' school itself has recently discovered the historical Jesus and the significance which he has for the early Christian preaching. cf. the relevant works by E. Käsemann, G. Ebeling, H. Bornkamm, H. Braun.

mean by this. Someone has a mother. He has a quite specific and unique relationship to this woman. He accepts all the consequences that ensue from a relationship of this kind. Now if we were to ask him what real grounds he has for knowing that this individual, in relation to whom he behaves and acts as a son, really is his mother, whether he really has any certainty of this at the levels of natural science or metaphysics, or even merely of scientific history, then surely he would in the end be forced to answer: 'At this level I have no such certainty'. Certainly we can see no reasonable grounds for calling this personal conviction of his of this mother-son relationship in question. But at the same time we have never yet reflected, at the level of 'scientific exactitude' upon this conviction of his. In other words we have no scientific or absolute certainty of the genuineness of this relationship. We could if we wished make a scientific problem of this relationship involving a whole range of difficult questions.

Without having to analyse this 'case' in any greater detail at this point we can easily perceive in the light of an example of this kind that the two kinds of certainty are two different things: the attitude which prevails at the level of the individual's own existence in the concrete, and which involves this immanent and personal certainty, together with all the radical consequences ensuing from this on the one hand, and the process of scientifically reflecting upon the grounds and presuppositions for such an attitude of '*existentielle*' certainty on the other. This process of scientific reflection is important and indispensable. But it can never adequately include or replace that more ultimate and global certainty which belongs to human living in the concrete and the actual experience of this. We cannot demand this from the process of scientific reflection, because it is in principle incapable of achieving any such thing, since in any given instance the explicit content of knowledge arrived at as a result of scientific consideration is only given in an act of cognition which as such is not in its turn made the subject of reflection, and which at least in the case of those kinds of knowledge which are of 'existentielle' significance, at the level of concrete human living, inevitably plays its part in influencing the actual content of the considerations involved. This difference between the certainty of science and the certainty which belongs to the ultimate dimension in which we achieve the fulness of our own existence cannot be eliminated. The individual must learn to live with this difference. He must not use it as a weapon to destroy that other, and more ultimate certainty inherent in life itself (in our case the certainty of faith), whenever this certainty, which may be more ultimate, becomes unacceptable to him for some reason or other.

Now let us apply the insight which we have merely been able to indicate above, to our present problem. All the statements of exegesis considered as a historical science belong to the category of theoretical reflection and speculation, and of historical criticism, and here they have a legitimate place of their own. But even in this case we must not suppose for one moment that the human, global, and total conviction of Jesus Christ as the absolute bringer of salvation would not be legitimate so long as that other certainty arising from theoretically reflecting upon the historical assumptions implicit in this faith has to be qualified as a lesser certainty in terms of epistemological theory. We have in principle the right to say, 'Of course in exegesis many questions remain open. There is much that continues to belong to the sphere of mere historical probability, and subject to a discussion among the exegetes which is endlessly prolonged. But this cannot and need not represent any attack upon the believer in the absoluteness of his faith. For this faith is in fact based not merely upon the data of exegesis and the certainty belonging to these, but is also sustained by the experience of personal grace, by a certain interior self-assurance in the Christian understanding of existence which has never been consciously reflected upon to the full, by the totality of Christian living in the concrete, by the collective experience of Christendom, in a history extending over two thousand years. In accordance with the saying attributed to Peter in the sixth chapter of John (6:68 f.) this faith can always remind itself that anyone who abandons the Christian faith cannot find anywhere else to go where he will be able to discover a brighter light to illumine the meaning of existence.'

While on the one hand it is justifiable to ask, at the level of historical reflection, what data can be found with regard to the pre-Easter Jesus and what degree of certainty these have to offer, still on the other hand we must not assume in this that these data to which we can attain are the sole factors by which the absolute assent of faith in Jesus Christ is sustained. Now the converse of this is also true. It does not imply that this absolute assent of faith in Jesus Christ has nothing whatever to do with the data of history with which exegetical speculation is concerned. If someone came to us and proved to us positively and unambiguously that for instance Jesus himself either never existed at all or *certainly* understood himself merely as having some kind of religious mission to arouse his fellow men with a message which had nothing whatever to do with himself, his own person, and what he himself did, then our faith would no longer have that reality of saving history as its content, then our faith would be vain. Faith in saving history has an historical content. It cannot dispense with a content of this kind, and therefore it cannot dispense with the historical element in it either, or with the process of reflecting upon history, even though we can never adequately carry this through. At the same time, however, this faith is not born of scientific speculation alone. It would certainly be a heresy, and one which could not be tolerated within the Catholic Church, if anyone sought to maintain that faith in Jesus as the Christ is absolutely independent of the historical experience and self-interpretation of the pre-Easter Jesus. But it would also be false to suppose that the content and the certainty of faith in Jesus Christ are the mere product of historical speculation as practised in exegesis.

A *second* preliminary principle must be mentioned, which is necessary if we are to supply a reasonable answer to our basic question. It is obvious, yet still for the most part forgotten, that that utterance of God which we call his revelation requires our own capacity to hear it for it to take place at all.[6] To state the matter once and for all *in globo*: the statements which God addresses to us exist only in the statements which we receive with our minds. Basically speaking this is a truism, even if we take into account the fact that the revelation of God also takes place in the events of our own historical environment. For in order for these to be capable of being revelation events at all they must include an element of verbal interpreta-tion of the purely factual element in them, and one which is not merely applied to these events from without, but is an intrinsic and constitutive element in these events themselves, necessary for them to have the status of revelation events at all.

If therefore the statements which God addresses to us exist only in statements which we ourselves formulate in our minds, then this clearly raises the problem of how we can know that these statements which we formulate in the subjectivity of our own minds are statements of God with an objectivity of their own. We cannot enter into this problem at this point in our investigations. Here we must confine ourselves to pointing out that it is merely one instance, albeit the most radical, of a general range of problems that arises in epistemological theory, that namely of how we can apprehend the objective element in reality without standing outside the subjectivity of our own acts of cognition (something which is

---

[6] On this idea cf. K. Rahner, J. Ratzinger, *Revelation and Tradition*, Quaestiones Disputatae 17 (Freiburg, 1966); K. Rahner, 'Propheten', *LTK* VIII (2nd ed. 1963), 800–802; *idem*, 'Wort Gottes', *LTK* X (2nd ed. 1965), 1235–1238; *idem*, 'Theology in the New Testament', *Theological Investigations* V (London and Baltimore, 1966), pp. 23–41; *idem*, 'Scripture and Theology', *Theological Investigations* VI (London and Baltimore, 1969), pp. 89–97.

precisely impossible). But on the basis of this special quality which belongs universally to all subjective cognition in which the objective is apprehended, we can at any rate understand that the subjectivity inherent in knowledge, and which can never be overcome, is the mode in which the objective is presented to us and not that which causes this objective element to be veiled by the merely subjectivist factors. This is also true of faith. The objectivity of the revelation of God always exists in the subjective expression of an individual, in other words in his 'hearing', his 'faith' which, in a very extended sense of this term, also includes the attitude of listening obediently to the message of God as brought to us by the bearer of revelation. The history of revelation and the history of faith are ultimately speaking two sides of one and the same process. The very fact that the address of God takes place in the concrete only in the mind of the individual who bears it in history means that the revelation of God is a historical process, a history such that what takes place in it is not always the same. All this is at basis a self-evident datum of Catholic dogmatic teaching, which is constantly aware of a saving history and also of a history of revelation.[7]

It is only now, however, and after these preliminary considerations, that we arrive at a point which is especially important in its bearing upon our basic question. We have to recognize that even Jesus, as man and in his special character as the bearer of revelation, likewise utters the revelation of God to the extent that he himself in his human subjectivity hears and accepts what he has to say. And in all this this subjectivity of his can have, and has had, in its turn, an individual history. The nature of divine revelation then is such that its ultimately basic acts take place solely in the mind of the individual who hears it. However the process of human hearing in this sense has a collective, and even more an individual historicity of its own. And again this applies to the humanity of Jesus too, which is real and true. And in the light of all this it is not only not difficult in principle, but actually and positively necessary, to recognize that that revelation which takes place in the subjective human consciousness of

---

[7] Hence too one of the points with which the Constitution 'Dei Verbum' of the Second Vatican Council is explicitly concerned is to demonstrate the unity which exists between word and deed in the revelation event. On this cf. the commentary mentioned in n. 2, and also the projected schema worked out by myself in collaboration with J. Ratzinger: 'Le schéma du P. K. Rahner. De la révélation de Dieu et de l'homme faite en Jésus-Christ', *Vatican II: Unam Sanctam* 70 b (Paris, 1968), pp. 577–597, and also H. Waldenfelds, *Offenbarung. Das Zweite Vatikanische Konzil auf dem Hintergrund der neueren Theologie* (Munich, 1969).

Jesus and in his preaching is also a historical entity. What contemporary exegesis establishes *a posteriori* with regard to the self-understanding of the pre-Easter Jesus is, at basis, something which the dogmatic theologian has had to postulate all along *a priori* on the basis of the principles indicated above with which he has to work.[8] Of course what applies throughout the history of human thought applies in this case too: we can only reflect upon and explicitate the implications inherent in our own position when *a posteriori* the historical situation is given, and also some concrete stimulus from without impelling us to do this. But this does not alter the fact that given these conditions we can then recognize implications of this kind *precisely as such*. Thus it is not surprising that in dealing with certain implications in the basic conception of the Church's christology with regard to the historicity of revelation, and also the historicity of the human awareness of Jesus as the bearer of revelation, we only explicitate these at that stage at which exegesis, with its *a posteriori* approach, discovers this historicity.

Exegesis, therefore, establishes that Jesus expressed his own understanding of himself in terms which are far from being identical with those of the later christology of the Church, and indeed not even identical with those of the christology of the primitive community or the gospels of Paul and John. And exegesis further establishes that in expressing the significance of himself Jesus may have avoided certain terms used in the theology of his environment, indeed that he could not use them at all, even though they do subsequently reappear – albeit in altered form – in the christology of the primitive Church. Finally exegesis actually establishes that a certain historical development is to be observed in this self-understanding on Jesus' part (e.g. with regard to the fact that he came to include his own death as an integral element in this self-understanding of his). Moreover this historical development is actually such that it is wholly reconcilable with the Church's dogmatic teaching to the effect that God was immediately present to Jesus in his human subjectivity (this is what the established dogmatic theology means by saying that the 'vision of God' was present from the outset in the human soul of Jesus, though in order to reconcile this with the findings of modern exegesis we must understand this 'vision' as consisting in a 'basic content' in the human subjectivity of Jesus which was only gradually objectified, though also with complete clarity, in terms of the *a posteriori* material of the theology of his

[8] On this cf. also A. Vögtle, 'Revelation and History in the New Testament. A Contribution to Biblical Hermeneutics', *Concilium* I/3 (Dogma), 1967, pp. 20–26.

environment). Now all these theses or hypotheses of exegesis, strange though they may seem to us at first sight, turn out, on closer examination, but also in the light of the basic data of the christology of the New Testament and the Church herself, to be such as we should have expected.[9]

We may therefore explicitly draw attention to the fact that the position today regarding the relationship between historical and critical exegesis and its findings concerning the self-understanding of the pre-Easter Jesus on the one hand and the dogmatic and fundamental theology of Jesus as the Christ on the other, does not, in the last analysis represent an uneasy compromise between the two which is maintained through thick and thin in order that critical exegesis and traditional Christian faith may to some extent be able to co-exist with one another. Rather, on a deeper view, the position between the two is one that we should expect on any really genuine understanding of the faith, and from a christology which is that of the Church but at the same time one that is the outcome of a process of radical self-realization. This interpretation of the current position is not invalidated by the fact that the dogmatic theologian only recognizes the *a priori* implications of his own position at the radical level when he encounters them *a posteriori* in the findings of exegesis. In the encounter between dogmatics and exegesis, therefore, the position is, in the last analysis, far from being as critical as is sometimes assumed, though of course this position will only gradually become clearer in the course of further discussions between exegetes and dogmatic theologians. We shall have to accustom ourselves to this situation, and it is only gradually that we can do so. But when we have achieved this we shall no longer be surprised to find that Jesus of Nazareth does not explicitly put forward a christology of the kind maintained by the Church herself. We shall achieve an ever-better understanding of the fact that while the formulations of the Church's christology remain justified and indispensable, still they are not of such a kind that it is precisely *they* which, simply as they stand, constitute that which is self-evident and clear to the utmost possible extent, while that which is presented in the New Testament as christology, and

---

[9] On the question of the self-awareness of Jesus in dogmatic theology cf. chiefly K. Rahner, 'Dogmatic Reflections on the Knowledge and Selfconsciousness of Christ', *Theological Investigations* V (London and Baltimore, 1966), pp. 193–215; also H. Riedlinger, *Geschichtlichkeit und Vollendung des Wissens Jesu*, Quaestiones Disputatae 32 (Freiburg, 1966); E. Gutwenger, 'The Problem of Christ's Knowledge', *Concilium* II/1 (Dogma) (1966), pp 48–55; and from the exegetical point of view A Vögtle, 'Exegetische Erwägungen über das Wissen und Selbstbewusstsein Jesu', *Gott in Welt* I (*Festschrift für K. Rahner*), J. B. Metz, W. Kern *et al* edd. (Freiburg, 1964), pp. 608–667.

above all as the self-understanding of the pre-Easter Jesus, is merely that which is ambiguous, 'elusive', and obscure in its expression, and less developed by comparison with the firmness and lack of ambiguity in the christology of the Church. Rather we must learn to view the intrinsic convergence of the two kinds of statement in such a way that the moment we reach that point in unfolding the formulations of the Church at which they become perplexing, this brings us back once more to the formulations of the New Testament, while conversely the formulations of the Church have done nothing else than to take seriously, and really to investigate radically, the quite homely and simple and humanly assimilable statements of the pre-Easter Jesus and the statements about him in the New Testament. Exegesis and dogmatics are not two enemies seeking to engage in a life-and-death struggle against one another, and yet precisely still allowing one another to survive. We often express the matter by saying that one or other of the findings of modern exegesis are 'still sufficient' for dogmatic christology. But this precisely does not mean that the dogmatic theologian would 'properly speaking' have expected something more from the exegete. If he really takes seriously the historical nature of revelation, and therefore the history of Jesus himself, he cannot want or expect anything more at all from the exegete.

This brings us at last to the real theme, the central question, of our considerations. We have seen that with regard to the self-understanding of the pre-Easter Jesus modern critical exegesis has isolated and established this by setting aside the interpretations superimposed upon it in the post-Easter christology. Now as we have already said at the outset of this study, what we are seeking to establish as the basic thesis of these considerations of ours is that once we presuppose the experience of the Resurrection this self-understanding of the pre-Easter Jesus as isolated and established by modern exegesis provides a sufficient basis and starting-point for the dogmatic christology of the New Testament and of the Church. In other words the present-day exponents of fundamental theology and dogmatic christology have no need to feel themselves abandoned by modern exegetes. They must not have the impression that the axioms and assumptions necessary for their work have been withdrawn from them by this exegesis. Of course it cannot be the function of the systematic theologican once more to recapitulate at this point the data yielded by modern exegesis, and which represents the 'residue' (*sit venia verbo*) of Jesus' understanding of himself, once the subsequent accretions of christological interpretation have been set aside. This is something which we are assuming here, and we are seeking only, to the extent that such a thing is possible within the scope of a brief study, to justify the thesis formulated above.

For this we must take as our initial starting-point a really correct understanding of the Church's dogmatic teaching on christology. It is necessary to build a bridge to unite present-day exegesis, with its critical methods and findings, to that body of dogmatic teaching on Jesus Christ developed by the Church which must be retained as permanently valid. And the two halves of this bridge must be projected outwards from both sides at the same time – including, therefore, the side represented by systematic theology. Both departments must refuse to content themselves with any facile compromise, but rather each proceeding from its own axioms must seek to achieve a new encounter, so that a genuine and intrinsic reconciliation may be achieved between the ancient dogmatic teaching and the findings of modern exegesis. For this ancient dogmatic teaching is in fact that of the Catholic exegete too and, moreover, precisely as such.[10] But for this purpose fresh ground will also have to be broken from the side of the systematic theologian. He too will have to think out afresh those formulations of this dogmatic teaching which, though ancient and self-evident to him, still need constantly to be subjected to fresh questioning, in order to achieve a fresh apprehension of his own essential message. This implies that the dogmatic theologian must be prepared to make a fresh start on the basis of the ancient and radical statements of christology itself as these have been defined, so as to eliminate from this christology as he *de facto* conceives of it all those distortions and misunderstandings which have crept into it and which are ultimately Monophysite in character.

The very manner in which a systematic theologian recognizes, formulates, and emphasizes at a specific point within his system these ultimate principles, and chiefly that concerning the true human nature of Jesus, entails a certain danger, and one which has not yet really and permanently been eliminated. This is the danger that at some other point, or in other connections within the same christology, or perhaps because of the religious mentality it entails and the expressions appropriate to this, he may once more forget these principles and – if we may be permitted to

---

[10] The first steps in this direction have already been taken. cf. e.g. H. Vorgrimler (ed.), *Exegese und Dogmatik* (Mainz, 1962); K. Rahner, 'Biblische Theologie und Dogmatik in ihrem wechselseitigen Verhältnis', *LTK* II (1958), 449–451: *idem*, 'Biblische Theologie und Dogmatik', *Handbuch theologischer Grundbegriffe* II (1963), pp. 523–525; R. Schnackenburg, '*Konkrete* Fragen an die Dogmatik aus der heutigen exegetischen Diskussion', *Catholica* 21 (1967), pp. 12–27.

formulate it in these terms – fall back into the attitude of an average Christian, who all too often is still either partly or wholly a Monophysite, even though he knows and repeats the sound and correct formulations of the catechism. In the mind of this 'ordinary consumer', orthodox though he may be, a strange and unconscious line of thought all too often and too easily asserts itself, by which Jesus comes simply to be identified with God who, in some remarkable manner, avails himself of the 'humanity' of Jesus as a sort of livery which he wears, or an instrument, in order to render himself 'noticeable' to us here below.

In truth, however, the Christian dogma of Chalcedon lays down that without prejudice to what we call the hypostatic union, Jesus really and in very deed is a man. The word 'is' as employed by us in the formula 'Jesus is God, is the Son of God, is the Logos' suggests a further 'is', a further synthesis between the subject and the material content of the predicate as, for instance, when we say 'Fritz is a man', asserting thereby not merely that this humanity is one with the subject Fritz, but that there is a real identity between the two. In the case of Jesus, however, his humanity is precisely not identical with God in this way, and on any right understanding of the Church's dogma this is precisely not what is being maintained, but rather what is excluded. We might put to the 'ordinary consumer' Christian who intends to be orthodox the following question: 'Can Jesus tremble before the inconceivability of God? Can he, radically thrown back upon his own feeble creaturehood, adore God as the inconceivable? Can he go to meet a fate which is dark so far as he is concerned?' And then, even though this 'ordinary consumer' has himself all along been saying that Jesus is truly man, he will suddenly be brought up short and the 'yes' which he must pronounce in reply to this question will not come easily to his lips. And yet this 'yes' belongs to Catholic dogma right from the outset, and not merely to the findings of a modern exegesis. The Jesus of the Chalcedonian dogma, which was directed against Monophysitism and Monothelitism, likewise has a subjective centre of action which is human and creaturely in kind, such that in his human freedom he is in confrontation with God the inconceivable, such that in it Jesus has undergone all those experiences which we make of God not in a less radical, but on the contrary in a more radical – almost, we might say, in a more terrible – form than in our own case. And this properly speaking not in spite of, but rather because of the so-called hypostatic union. For the more radically any given individual is related to God existentially, and so too in his concrete mode of existence as a creature, the more such a creature achieves the state of self-realization; again the more radically any given individual is able to experience his own creaturely reality, the more united he must be with God.[11]

Thus we have genuinely to eliminate from the christology which we actually live this element of Monophysitism and Monothelitism (though today we should more properly call it Mono-subjectivism), not merely in the explicit verbal formulations of its tenets, but in our own ultimate and uncircumscribed understanding of our religion. Once we have achieved this we shall find it all the more easy to acquire a free and uncircumscribed understanding of what modern exegesis has worked out with regard to the pre-Easter Jesus. For when we can freely allow our interest in Jesus (to put the matter somewhat paradoxically) to be in a genuine sense concentrated more on his significance for the kingdom of God and for God himself than on his actual status as a 'person', we can recognize that in his own individual history real questions arise for him, and that he is surprised, that he achieves insights and realizations at the conceptual level about himself which are only gradually articulated and expressed, and which surprise himself. At the same time, however, we understand that these are always discovered in the process of developing an understanding of himself which is based upon that element which ultimately lies at the very roots of his existence, and which dogmatic theologians are accustomed to call the 'immediate vision of God present in the soul of Jesus'. The fact that this is the only way in which the dogmatic theologian can do justice to the data of modern exegesis is not the sole reason why he has to take into account the fact of a genuine humanity in Jesus. He *must* do this because otherwise his position would be contrary to the dogmatic teaching of Catholic theology, in other words to his own principles.

There is one point which the dogmatic theologian must again and again make clear to himself on the basis of his own principles and data. It is that however true it may be that according to these dogmatic principles Jesus constitutes a unique reality in saving history such that he must not be placed on the same level as any other prophet, religious personality or inspiring leader, still it is also true that he must be fitted organically into a basic conception of saving history as a whole, even though in fitting him

---

[11] On this axiom cf. also F. Malmberg, *Ein Leib – ein Geist* (Freiburg, 1960), pp. 315–333; K. Rahner, 'On the Theology of the Incarnation', *Theological Investigations* IV (London and Baltimore, 1966), pp. 105–120; B. Welte, 'Zur Christologie von Chalkedon' *Auf der Spur des Ewigen* (Freiburg, 1965), pp. 429–458; K. Rahner, 'Incarnation', *Sacramentum Mundi* 3 (New York and London, 1968), pp. 110–118.

in in this way we only realize his position at the supreme point of saving history viewed precisely in this way as a totality after we have achieved the *a posteriori* experience of Jesus. He does indeed constitute the supreme point of this saving history, unique and unsurpassable, but he is this precisely within this saving history itself. We are presenting the uniqueness of Jesus in a false light if we regard him merely as the Son of God, setting him in this sense over against men as though initially these had nothing to do with God, or when we view him simply as a messenger from the other world of the divine, entering a world which again has nothing to do with God.

Against this the real position is that whatever place we occupy throughout the whole history of mankind, we are children of God. God himself never ceases to dwell and to hold sway in his own divine nature at the innermost centre of this history throughout its course in virtue of an absolute, albeit a completely free and grace-given act of self-bestowal, thereby constituting the ultimate principle and the ultimate driving force of the history of this present world. Whether we always recognize this, whether we arrive at a conceptually objectified and consciously formulated statement of this basic grace-given mystery of the world and its history or not, whether we open ourselves in faith and in love to this ultimate reality of our own existence, or alternatively incur mortal guilt by closing ourselves against it (though even then we cannot banish God and his will to bestow grace from our world) – these are yet further questions, and ones which we shall not be treating of here. The process by which this ultimate and grace-given mystery of God's self-bestowal instilled into the very roots of human nature and into the very roots of history itself achieves its own due fulness – a process of self-realization achieved in knowledge and love – constitutes the *single* history of revelation and salvation, because the history of knowledge and the acceptance of this basic mystery of the world which consists in God's self-bestowal is itself the history of this self-bestowal of God as imparting revelation. God is not to be thought of as merely 'over against' the world and its history in virtue simply of being its first 'cause', untouched by the world itself and transcending it. Rather in the outward movement of his love he has inserted himself into the world as its innermost *entelecheia*, and he impels the whole of this world and its history towards that point at which God himself will be the innermost and immediately present fulfilment of our existence in the 'face-to-face' presence of eternal beatitude.

Without prejudice to the uniqueness of Jesus he must be viewed in his place in this saving history which is the history of God and the world both in one.[12] Such a view need not obscure this uniqueness of his, but it will eliminate from it that element of the exaggeratedly miraculous, the mythological, which comes to be associated with the idea of an inter-mediary whom God sends from another world constituted by his own life into a merely secular world. Let us therefore take as our starting-point a conception of saving history of the kind we have described; one in which God, in an act of gracious self-bestowal, is always at work from the heart and centre of the world itself, and which is co-extensive with the history of the world in general. Let us set clearly before our eyes the fact that a saving history of this kind, which is always the history of God's freedom and man's freedom, presses on towards a point at which this history of God's self-offering and the free acceptance of this in the world becomes irreversible, and manifests itself in the dimension of history in this irreversibility that belongs to it. If we approach the question in this way then, on the basis of this realization of its own significance which is achieved in saving history, we have obtained a view of that point at which Jesus stands, at which God accepts the world in such a way that he can no longer let it go, and at which the world, through this self-bestowal of God, obtains as its own gift that deed of creaturely freedom in which this freedom of the world definitely accepts God's offering of himself. Then we are standing at that point at which a man, from the ultimate roots of his own being, signifies the definitive address of God to the world, *and at the same time* the assent of the world to this God.[13]

Assuming that an understanding of the question has been achieved from both these perspectives, we can now apply ourselves directly to the consideration of our basic thesis. According to the findings of contemporary exegesis it can be said even today that the pre-Easter Jesus understood

---

[12] In this connection cf. especially my article, 'Christology within an Evolutionary View of the World', *Theological Investigations* V (London and Baltimore, 1966), pp. 157–192, and also the study entitled 'Christology in the Setting of Modern Man's Understanding of Himself and of his World', in this volume, pp. 215–229.

[13] On this cf. the author's article, 'History of the World and Salvation History', *Theological Investigations* V (London and Baltimore, 1966), pp. 97–114; 'Church, Churches and Religion', *Theological Investigations* X (London and New York, 1973), pp. 30–50; *idem*, 'Jesus Christ', *Sacramentum Mundi* 3 (New York and London, 1968), pp. 192–209; *idem, Ich glaube an Jesus Christus* = Theologische Meditationen 21 (Einsiedeln, 1968); in addition to these, A. Darlap, 'Fundamentale Theologie der Heilsgeschichte', *Mysterium Salutis* I (Einsiedeln, 1965), pp. 3–156; K. Berger and A. Darlap, 'History of Salvation (Salvation History)', *Sacramentum Mundi* 5 (London and New York, 1970), pp. 411–419; E. Klinger, *Formaler Vorentwurf und geschichtstheologische Einführung zu Mysterium Salutis* III/1 (Einsiedeln, 1970).

himself as the absolute eschatological event of salvation and the eschatological bringer of salvation.[14]

Of course for this statement to represent the findings of modern exegesis it is not necessary for absolutely all exegetes to subscribe to it. In any historical science, in view of the complicated nature of the facts under investigation, this is something which from the outset we should not expect. In this connection we may remind ourselves once more of that difference between the relative certainty or probability of historical knowledge, even as a presupposition of faith on the one hand, and the absolute assent of faith as such on the other. What the precise terms were in which Jesus made this self-understanding of his real in his life, and in which he actually expressed it, whether and how far he drew upon religious ideas and concepts which were already present beforehand in his environment for expressing this significance which he saw in himself – these are questions which the dogmatic theologian can freely set aside, seeing that the exegete tells him that while there are indeed many particular unsolved questions and difficulties with regard to the details of the self-understanding of the pre-Easter Jesus, still it can be stated with a sufficient degree of reliability that Jesus understood himself as something more than merely some kind of preacher with a mission to arouse men to a sense of religion such that his message merely pointed to a relationship between God and man, a relationship itself already existing independently of the message pointing to it. He understood himself, rather, as one in whose message (precisely as *his*), and in whose person that which he preached was actually made present in a new and irrevocable form as a new and unsurpassable summons of God. In this sense we say that the pre-Easter Jesus (including in this concept his actual message in itself) understood himself as the eschatological event of salvation and the eschatological bringer of salvation.

The self-understanding of Jesus in this sense is something that we must take with the utmost seriousness and realize in the full depths of its significance. We must take seriously the fact that in Jesus' understanding of himself his message constitutes that which is new, that which has not always been present. At the same time, however, despite the infinity of the possibilities open to God, and the openness of history itself to that which is new, this message constitutes also that which is ultimate and unsurpassable, as well as that which is inseparable from his own person. Once we have

[14] In this connection critical exegesis speaks of an 'implicit christology'. Cf. R. Bultmann, *Glauben und Verstehen* I (Tübingen, 1952), 204/205; also *idem*, *Theology of the New Testament* I (London, 1952,) pp. 42 ff.

realized all this, then we have arrived at a point of departure from which we can attain to the Church's dogmatic teaching on christology, provided only that this is not itself misinterpreted in a Monophysite sense. What we call the divine Sonship of Jesus of Nazareth as a metaphysical and substantial reality in fact has no further content whatever beyond what can be expressed in the affirmation: Jesus is the eschatological, i.e. the unsurpassable and abiding, Mediator of our relationship with God. This precisely can never signify a prophet, an inspiring religious leader, or a religious genius. For the message precisely of *this* kind of individual is in principle always capable of being separated from his person and his religious works. This is because the reality to which he points in this preaching exists independently of himself. Moreover, since he is a mere man, existing at one isolated point in history, the truth which he proclaims always is, or always should be, expressed with the proviso that this message will be made out of date once those further possibilities are realized which are open to God and which also exist in history. Now if on his own understanding of himself Jesus is not one of the prophets in this sense, and if it is obvious that on any Christian understanding of God he cannot be interpreted as a demi-god either, then, when the christology of the Church speaks of the unity between this event of salvation in the concrete and this Mediator of salvation in the concrete – a unity involving the duality of two natures as distinct, the divine and the human – it is simply stating in different terms this self-understanding of Jesus as the eschatological bringer of salvation. The converse of this is of course likewise true.

When, therefore, exegesis emphasizes that the pre-Easter Jesus speaks in the first instance not so much of his own person but of the advent of the kingdom of God which has become quite new and actual, then this should not surprise the dogmatic theologian in the light of his position either. For if this kingdom of God has come definitively, victoriously, and in a manner which can no longer be surpassed by any fresh events of salvation in his person and message, and if Jesus himself declares precisely *this* to be the case, then *ipso facto* he has spoken about his own person. If he has come, as we confess, '*propter nos et propter nostram salutem*', then the message he had to convey to us first and foremost was: 'Your salvation is there now as judgement and grace.' And if it is true that he possessed a genuinely human subjectivity, which achieves the truth most proper to it precisely at that point at which it looks away from itself to the inconceivable God and his love, and to mankind as brothers, and in a certain sense loses itself in both directions, then we should precisely not expect him to speak of himself in that explicitly self-reflecting manner which is employed in the dogmatic christology of the Church. We understand his true nature only when we see it as absolutely one with his function in saving history. If therefore he speaks of this function of his, *ipso facto* he has spoken of his own 'nature'. If he says that in him God has uttered his ultimate assent to the world in a way that is ever more unsurpassable and irrevocable, and that in virtue of this the kingdom of God is irrevocably present in the world (though at the same time it still constantly has to impose itself in history) then, at basis he has already spoken more clearly of himself than if he had spoken of himself in isolation, presenting us, so to say, with a mirror image of himself by a certain process of introversion after the manner of the christology developed by the Church. Certainly this latter is inevitable and good at the retrospective stage. But it is such that even then it can only really be understood by us when we make real to ourselves in our faith what he is for us, and what has taken place through him and in him in that saving history which is our own. We must understand that a dogmatic formulation, however much it is, and continues to be, binding upon us, is not something which simply has to be defined in order that everything may be 'clear'. We must recognize that in the case of any dogmatic formula, in order really to understand it and make it real to ourselves in our faith, we must think back to that in which it properly originated as well. And if we realize all this then we will no longer listen to what we are told about the self-understanding of the pre-Easter Jesus with that attitude of slight mistrust and surprise with which we ask ourselves how in that case he did not express himself 'more clearly' about his own significance. The true meaning of the dogmatic teaching of christology has already been grasped (indeed it may perhaps actually be more assimilable to us in our concrete human lives in this form) when for instance we have really understood that saying of Jesus which runs: 'Whatsoever you have done to one of the least of these my brethren, you have done it to me' (Mt. 25:40). There is no conceivable claim which could be more radical than this, that he himself is always and in all cases involved in the ultimate relationship between two individuals.

We have still to justify in fuller and more precise terms the thesis that the concept of a bringer of salvation in the absolute *ipso facto* implicitly contains the dogmatic teaching of christology, once it has been taken with the full and radical seriousness due to it, thought out and re-stated in different words. At this point, however, I am compelled to refer to expositions which I have put forward elsewhere.[15] Here therefore I may confine

[15] cf. n. 13.

myself to reiterating once more this one point which I have already made: everyone who is genuinely a Christian will concede that the message which Jesus addresses to him is unsurpassable. We must, however, recognize the immensity of the implications *ipso facto* contained in this statement, for all its apparent innocuousness. For it might be said: Every prophet, however much he may appear as a messenger of God with a momentous and stirring message to convey, must still retain an awareness of the fact that in this message of his he is forming only a single tiny drop from the boundless ocean of the eternal Godhead. Furthermore he can only utter this message precisely as the messenger of God so long as he submits himself in the most radical manner to the fact that tomorrow another messenger will come who, from the boundless fulness of God, in which all eternity and the future that still lies before us is comprised, draws some quite different message, yet one that is no less momentous and that renders the old one out of date. In other words every prophet must, in a true sense, allow for the fact that saving history remains open to further, unforeseeable and sometimes revolutionary developments beyond any to which he can point. Nevertheless in a very real sense that one brief statement which we have just taken as our starting-point, and to which every Christian subscribes, puts a definitive end to all this. Otherwise it should not be taken seriously at all. In itself and without any further addition this one brief sentence states that no single word that Jesus utters can be surpassed or invalidated in its further application to the world even by God himself. The message which Jesus utters through his person and through his words can be the unsurpassable and abiding word of God only if the reality that it constitutes (including in this the words that he utters and the fate that he endures) is God's own reality in the manner which we seek to express by the term 'hypostatic union'. Otherwise saving history would be open to further extensions into the future which would no longer stand under the law of Jesus Christ. Alternatively, if we wish to deny that this one brief sentence has the definitive finality which we have ascribed to it, we would have to subscribe to that completely distorted anthropomorphism according to which God, the infinitely wise and powerful, is thought of as breaking off the history of revelation and salvation at a certain point in a completely arbitrary manner *ab externo*, even though in itself, considered as God's own history, infinite further possibilities still remained open to it. Or again we would have to postulate that through his person and his words Jesus had, after all, only expressed what is true always and everywhere, and attainable from any point in history. And this would mean that there would in truth be no history of revelation and salvation. Even taken by itself, therefore, this brief statement which we have taken as our starting-point as a statement which, after all, every Christian can surely make his own, implicitly, but in a very true sense, contains the whole christology of the Church. Admittedly this point would require a more extensive development and justification than we can accord to it here.

Once more we may formulate our basic thesis: If Jesus understood himself to be the eschatological event of salvation in the absolute, and the Mediator of salvation in the absolute, and if this self-understanding on the part of the pre-Easter Jesus can, with sufficient certainty be recognized as present in him even by modern historical and critical exegesis, then we have found an adequate point of departure for the christology of the Church. At the same time this is not to deny, but on the contrary to imply, that in the dimension of Jesus' own conscious reflection upon himself, this self-understanding of his can in its turn have a history of its own. And this history in itself only attained its definitive fulness in his Resurrection. Only through this event did it become credible in a definitive sense for us.

If it is true, then, that a christology of the Church is possible on these premises, it is equally true that these premises for a christology of the Church are themselves unalterable. It is perfectly justifiable for an exegete to point out the historical problems which these premises entail. But if he goes beyond this, if he seeks to say, rather, that he has come to recognize with positive and unambiguous historical certainty that the realities presupposed here simply did not exist at all, then the premises of fundamental theology and dogmatic theology for the Christian faith would really be destroyed. But I believe that no exegete would claim to be able to substantiate such a position. On the contrary, even a very critical approach to exegesis, so long as it remains open to what is unique and peculiar to Jesus, will conclude that the self-understanding of Jesus presupposed here is to be affirmed.

The Resurrection

If we are to speak of the Resurrection of Jesus and the credibility attached to it, then properly speaking we should explicitly state and make clear certain principles at the level of existential ontology and anthropology upon which we shall be basing our arguments. We are accustomed to think of man to some extent in a dualistic sense, and because of this we find it difficult to grasp the fact that what is meant by the definitive state of man, his state of being redeemed and having attained to salvation, is basically speaking the same as that which we call the Resurrection of Jesus and of man in general. For basically speaking it is inconceivable either in terms of modern anthropology or biblical anthropology that there should be any absolute division between a fate which we attribute to the physical side of man and the fate which he undergoes at the spiritual level and in his personhood.[16] Now if we evaluate and understand this point correctly, then the following two statements have exactly the same meaning: first, 'This crucified one is he who has been received by God in such a way that he, together with his fate and the decision which that fate involves, has been ratified by God as having an eternal validity', and second, 'He has risen'. It is necessary for us to recognize the fact that for ourselves too we can hope for no other definitive form of deliverance than that which, on any correct understanding of Christian terminology, we call Resurrection. And if we did perceive this more clearly then we would see that right from the outset the individual may justifiably and confidently ask this question of history itself: Is there any point within this history at which I find an event which makes it possible for me confidently to assert, 'So-and-so is the one who has been accepted and saved by God, in other words the one who has risen from the dead'? We should begin by reminding ourselves of all these general perspectives and prior assumptions for our understanding if we intend seriously to enquire into what is truly meant by the Resurrection of Jesus, and why it is worthy of belief. Even here it is not a question of a miracle of God being inserted into a spiritual situation in which nothing of the kind could possibly be expected at all. It can perfectly well be the case that it is only through the *a posteriori* experience that an *a priori* perspective of hope already transcendentally present within us is brought to the stage of conscious and explicit realization. But when it is brought to this stage we recognize it as something which has been present all along, although, it may be, in a very unexplicitated way. This is the one principle which should be borne in mind from the outset and all along in seeking what the Resurrection of Jesus means.

Secondly we should achieve for ourselves a clear understanding of what

[16] For fuller details on this cf. my articles ,'Auferstehung Christi', *LTK* I (2nd ed., 1967), 1038–1041; 'Resurrection', *Sacramentum Mundi* 5 (1969), pp. 323–342; 'Dogmatic Questions on Easter', *Theological Investigations* IV (London and Baltimore, 1966), pp. 121–133; 'Experiencing Easter', *ibid.* VII (London and Freiburg, 1971), pp. 159–168; 'Encounters with the Risen Christ', *ibid.*, pp. 169–176.

really can be meant in *theological* terms by resurrection. The moment we picture to ourselves a dead man returning once more into our temporal dimension, with the biological conditions belonging to it, we have conceived of something which has nothing whatever to do with the Resurrection of Jesus, and which cannot have any kind of significance for our salvation either. In fact to say that any individual has risen from the dead must precisely be tantamount to saying: 'This man in this fate of his which seems so absolutely negative, has in a true sense, as himself, and together with his history, really attained to God.' What it does not say, however, is this: He has once more extricated himself from the process of death, and is once more there on the same plane as ourselves. This is in fact precisely not any sort of concession to the modern spirit of the time, after the manner of the demythologizers, but belongs so obviously to the very content of dogmatic teaching that this dogmatic teaching itself would otherwise have no Christian meaning whatever. Once we recognize this, then, precisely on *this* basis, and not merely on the basis of contemporary exegetical criticism, it becomes evident that the question of whether we could touch the risen individual, whether he could eat, etc., is absolutely secondary, and this not merely because it suits us of today to take this line, but because it is positively demanded by any true understanding of the ancient dogmatic teaching of the Church. One who has achieved the definitive finality of his own existence cannot be subject to the material changes we undergo. He cannot exist in a temporal dimension such as belongs to us. He cannot remain dependent upon other physical entities such as temperature, tactibility etc. In other words, even if we were to take all these stories in an extremely literal sense, we would still even then have to interpret them as meaning that in terms of the range of experience and understanding open to us the individual risen from the dead had undergone 'in himself' a process of *transposition*. It should be clear that this 'transposition' sets the risen individual 'in himself' on a different plane just as much as it attests the fact that he has been eternally and definitively saved by God. To questions such as whether if we were already even now in a glorified state we could see the marks of the wounds of the risen Lord, whether then we would still have a head and hands in the same way that we do now etc., we should in principle reply: This is something which we do not know and the reason that we do not know it is not that we adopt an attitude of critical scepticism and are no longer willing to accept very much by faith, but rather that the intrinsic meaning of the dogmatic teaching itself does not admit of answers being found to questions of this kind. Whether Christendom has or has not always recognized this fact so clearly as is entailed by the radical nature of resurrection – this too in its turn is a secondary question.

As Catholics we believe in a development of dogma, that as the awareness of our faith becomes more and more developed, we achieve a deeper understanding of the dogma itself. And under certain circumstances certain conceptual models, or perhaps even errors which have crept into our understanding at an earlier stage are gradually eliminated in this process. The ultimate goal of the process itself is not that in this way we shall gradually argue away the very substance of the dogma itself, so as to leave no room for it in our world, but rather that from its own true and innermost centre an ever better understanding may be achieved of what it truly signifies. Even Paul recognized that all realities, and so too the conceptual models we use to understand them, undergo a radical transformation that extends right to the ultimate roots of their nature. Hence we cannot, on the basis of the models we currently use to understand existence, vividly portray to ourselves what eternity is like. On any radical view this is just as impossible in the case of the soul or spirit of man as it is in the case of the physical side of his nature. Yet because we are inclined to accord a certain priority of value to the spiritual side, we find it easy to suppose that at the spiritual level we can live on throughout all eternity in the same mode as that in which we are living in the present. Yet this is quite untrue. We know nothing of the eschata beyond the fact that we are and that we receive the history of our own reality and free decision and our relationship to God as something that is permanently definitive. We have no conceptual models to explain to ourselves precisely *how* this comes to be. All we know is that we cannot conceive of man as a sort of space rocket with two stages, in which the lower stage, that which is called the 'physical side' will one day fall away so that then a 'spirit', with the special dimension of reality belonging to it, will continue on alone to enter definitively into the glory of God. We know that man is one and cannot be separated into two compartments. If we believe in a consummation then we believe in *our* consummation. The fact that in accordance with the intrinsic complexity and historical development of human nature this consummation must appear different in respect of each particular element in man – this too is, admittedly, a point that is clear. But as for any positive conceptual model showing us *how* we should represent this to ourselves – this is something which we do not and should not have, for if we did have it then quite certainly we should be misinterpreting the meaning of 'eternity'.

All this is very obvious to man when he is thinking of *his own* resurrection according to the affirmation which we make in the creed. But obviously it also applies to the case of the risen Lord. For in fact he is risen in that which we call his human nature, his human reality. If he then manifests himself to the disciples in a quite specific mode, then inevitably this has the force of a 'transposition' of that which he himself is into our conceptual world. Yet it is clear from the outset that we can never adequately separate this 'for us' aspect of the risen Lord from the 'in himself' aspect of him. I cannot work out for myself whether or not the glorified wounds of the physical side of Jesus actually exist in the 'in himself' dimension which belongs to him as risen. I do not even know whether one who has been glorified has a head. I have no positive grounds for denying it, but ultimately speaking I do not know it, and, moreover, it is a matter of indifference. All this still does not in the least alter the fact that I believe that I am not simply some transitory element in this world, but rather, that as this particular individual, the physical side of whose nature I must include in my concept of myself, I have a kind of existence which is destined to endure, for which I am answerable to God, and which will have an eternal validity in his life.[17]

If we have ever devoted any intelligent consideration to these matters, then, while of course not all those particular questions are immediately clear which we can raise with regard to the Resurrection and manifestation passages, still many of these questions will cease to appear to us of such acute and radical importance. Of course this in itself is still not enough to provide an answer to the question of precisely *how* the disciples really did experience, at the ultimate heart and centre of this Easter experience, the existence of Jesus as delivered from death, and so in some sense having an abiding and eternal validity in God. This too is a point on which not much can be said. Why is this? It is because we ourselves have precisely not undergone this experience. But even *in* an experience of this kind of one who, having been delivered, definitively possesses his own history, the true heart and centre of this experience is of course, in the very nature of the case, not something which can initially be verified by touching him with our hands etc., or laying them upon a wound in his side. It is obvious from the outset that we cannot weigh and measure the risen

---

[17] Hence, despite the very extensive 'historical' attestation of the Resurrection it would certainly be false to confine our attention solely to these accounts as such. H. Schlier rightly regards the Resurrection of Jesus as constituting a borderline problem between exegesis and dogmatic theology. cf. his 'Über die Auferstehung Jesu Christi' = *Kriterien* 10 (Einsiedeln, 1968), pp. 69–71.

Lord, cannot photograph him with our cameras, that even a team of television reporters could not make a documentary about him. He does not belong to the world of our experience. For this reason it is extremely difficult now to express in more precise terms exactly *how* the apostles made this experience. Nevertheless we can from the outset say this much: If they had been able to touch him in the same way that we touch things at the everyday level, this would in fact not have constituted the true experience of the definitive state which this man Jesus had attained to at all. For in that case the more solid the disciples would have felt such experiences to be at that time, and within the dimension of this world, the less they would have experienced that in which the essence of resurrection in fact consists: the fact that this man is he who has been definitively delivered. We must simply say: These disciples did maintain that they had undergone this experience, and these individuals actually described this experience. But in these descriptions of theirs it is clearly apparent that they were very conscious of one fact, and actually point to it with what is relatively speaking considerable exactitude, the fact namely that their experience was no mere subjective impression of some abiding validity in Jesus, such that it still maintains a permanent force for us, the fact that the point of departure in this experience was him and not their own subjectivity; that it constitutes something quite different from visionary experiences in other contexts with which these men were perfectly familiar. In the case of Paul too we find him on the one hand uncompromisingly presenting himself as a mystic gifted with visions and similar phenomena, and yet at the same time on the other being plainly conscious of, and emphasizing (even to the point of using a different terminology) the fact that the experience of the risen Lord is something quite different.

The question still remains: Is the experience which these disciples attest for us susceptible of abstract investigation and explanation in rational terms, or is any such rationalizing abstraction contrary to the experience asserted by them to have taken place on the grounds that if we do subject it to this rationalizing process even that which they do record of it in all honesty thereby ceases to have any further validity? At this point the Christian says: 'Well, I accept this experience from themselves as being unique, but at the same time as something which has really been attested. I believe with them.' If we say, with the exegetes of our own time, that the Resurrection is not an event that took place in historical fact,[18] but that

---

[18] For an orientation from the Catholic side on this question the following studies are particularly suitable: J. Kremer, *Das älteste Zeugnis von der Auferstehung Christi* = Stuttgarter Bibelstudien 17 (Stuttgart, 1966), and *idem, Die Osterbotschaft der*

the historical fact consists rather simply in the faith and the conviction of the apostles and disciples about the Resurrection, then this again is not a statement which the dogmatic theologian, on any right understanding of this statement concedes to the exegete and the historian only reluctantly and with a 'gnashing of teeth'. The situation is, rather, that here too we have something which is at basis obvious from the very nature of the case, and, moreover, from the very nature of the case as the dogmatic theologian views it from his *own* standpoint. For one to rise from the dead in such a way as to rise into the inconceivability of God obviously in the very nature of what is signified by this is not something which is intrinsically included, or should be included, in the dimension of historical experience as found in other contexts. This, however, is in no sense to exclude the fact that this experience involves *some reality* which is not identical with itself as such.

The disciples do not create the Resurrection of Jesus *by* their experience. Rather they experience (this is a witness that we must accept from them if we are willing to believe at all) the Resurrection of Jesus. The Catholic interpreter of the apostles' experience of the Resurrection says, 'What I accept from them is that they had experience of one who had risen'. He does not say, 'I postulate the experience of Jesus in virtue of the fact that I postulate an experience of faith'. And it is in this sense too that Paul understands the Resurrection. If we wish to deny this experience to the apostles and Paul, then that is a matter for our own free decision. But what we cannot say on any showing is what Bultmann and others have said in their interpretation of the Resurrection, namely that the apostles themselves would also have understood it in this sense. What the witnesses of the Resurrection intended to convey was that in the risen Lord they experienced a reality which is immediate, radical, and inseparable from the saving significance which this event bears for us. On the other hand, however, God would have had no reason to cause an individual to rise from the dead unless that individual had some significance for us. Thus we can uncompromisingly state that Jesus properly and radically became he who had risen from the dead only when he had attained precisely to *that* point towards which everything tends as its goal, and at

---

vier Evangelien (Stuttgart, 1967). On the whole cf. also the relevant studies in the volumes which have recently appeared, *Mysterium Salutis* III/1, 2 (Einsiedeln, 1969/70), and also the comprehensive discussion of the early Christian tradition of the creed in K. Lehmann, *Auferweckt am dritten Tag nach der Schrift* = Quaetiones Disputatae 38 (Freiburg, 2nd ed., 1969).

which he is present in my faith too as he who has risen from the dead. The very fact that reality quite in general is a single reality which is intended to be made present in the subject endowed with spiritual faculties – this fact in itself is enough to justify us in making the assertion we have just made. Whether we refuse to accept the apostles' witness to this experience of theirs or not – that is a matter for ourselves.

But in any case if we are honest we must not assert, as the sceptics so often do, that it is possible in the twinkling of an eye to provide a serious explanation of this experience of the apostles (which, after all, is on any showing a piece of historical data) even without according to the experience as its subject matter that reality which it is intended to have in their eyes. If anyone says they were precisely people who were religiously inclined, who could not bear to be parted from their Master, and so precisely ended by conjuring up the idea that he had risen from the dead – if anything of this kind is intended to be taken as a serious explanation of the apostles' experience, then this again belongs to the realm of uncritical rationalism. And even though nowadays this 'explanation' is usually formulated in somewhat loftier and more polite terms, it still belongs to this realm of uncritical rationalism. If anyone understands the Resurrection *aright*, if at the centre of his own existence, he yearns for his own 'resurrection' since on any true anthropology, he can only understand himself as a man who hopes for that which is described in terms of resurrection, then, in my belief, he has also achieved an *a priori* perspective such that, while it certainly does not excuse him from the *free decision* of faith in the Resurrection of Jesus, still at the same time it does justify him in believing in such a thing as the Resurrection of Jesus, i.e. in accepting the Easter experience of the disciples as a matter of his own intellectual honesty. Incidentally it may be said that the disciples were precisely not stupid or primitive men. We have only to represent their concrete situation to ourselves. There is someone who was a very nice man, put forward very remarkable ideas, and who was yet condemned and killed by the legitimate political authorities and also by the religious authorities accepted by the disciples themselves. How on this showing are the disciples, without something more than this happening to them, to arrive at the idea that it is all quite otherwise than it seems, that the reality has, after all, turned out gloriously? The Easter experience of the disciples really cannot be explained away as simply as the sceptics suppose.

But let us put the question to ourselves once more: If we are sceptics and doubters, have we any positive meaningfulness to offer for our lives and the lives of others? Anything which makes life itself more meaningful?

And if in reply to this we sought to say, 'Oh yes, all that about the Resurrection of Jesus would certainly be very beautiful, but it is too beautiful to be true', then the reply to this would be to ask, 'Why should not man prefer the darkness of his existence to consist in faith in an absolute light than to commit himself to this darkness as one who has been banished from the light'? This is all the more true in view of the fact that man as he is does not, after all, basically speaking, or in his life as he lives it in the concrete, allow himself to fall into the void of the absurd. For, in spite of everything, he is, in his existence, one who is decent, loving, faithful. In the very act of achieving the fulness of his existence he still says again and again, 'There is a light'. And basically speaking is not the attitude of Christians precisely tantamount to saying, 'Despite all that is unintelligible, dark, cruel and brutish, there is a hope justified even prior to any theoretical process of reasoning, that existence has a meaning'. Now if this meaning is such that it affects the whole man, and not merely a spiritual element within him, then it thereby asserts that man will be the risen one. But once he achieves this plane of thought, then once more it does not involve any 'hara kiri' of the intelligence when he believes that message of the apostles, on which they have staked their lives, that they have made the experience of *the* risen one as the instance of resurrection that is radically first and provides the foundation for all the rest. And it is he who justifies us in hoping for our resurrection.

9

CHRISTOLOGY IN THE SETTING OF MODERN MAN'S UNDERSTANDING OF HIMSELF AND OF HIS WORLD

CHRISTIAN revelation certainly claims to be God's word, to be addressed by God to man, a word which does not depend upon any historically conditioned perspectives of human understanding as its prior condition, a word which in its message goes beyond all such perspectives, and in which that which we call the grace of faith itself creates the true perspectives of understanding for that which God wills to utter to man as his word in the form of human words. Nevertheless it is still not the case that the perspectives of understanding which are developed in human history and subject to change have no significance for the manner in which divine revelation is communicated and comes to be understood. At the beginning of the Epistle to the Hebrews (1:1) we are told that God has spoken at various times and in many ways. And this statement serves to express and to emphasize the historicity of the revelation event itself, the fact that divine revelation has a history of its own such that neither the content nor the mode of revelation remain always the same. Now one of the factors that plays a decisive, though not an exclusive part in shaping this historicity of revelation itself is the historical situation in which revelation arises. Ultimately speaking, therefore, the divine sovereignty of revelation consists not in the fact that it presupposes no conditions already existing in history, that it has no perspectives of understanding such that they are historically conditioned and subject to variation and change, but rather in the fact that it is not, ultimately speaking, subject to these historical conditions even though it is posited in them. From the divine standpoint all these prior conditions in history are actually conditions designed to make revelation possible, which God himself as revealer creates and himself foreordains as the condition of his deed of revelation. In this sense, therefore, secular history must be thought of as a secular element in the divine revelation in which God himself is communicated. Even if as Christians we say that revelation closed with the end of the New Testament age, with Jesus Christ and the eye-witnesses to him, and with his apostles, so that no new public revelation can any more take place, even if we say that all that still remains to be done is to preserve and hand on through 'tradition' that which has definitely taken place in Jesus Christ, still this does not mean that from the apostolic age onwards this revelation is to be conceived of as an entity which has been 'frozen' into its definitive form so that all that we still have to do is to push it on through the dimension of future time and space.[1] Nor does this statement imply that that development of dogma, that further unfolding of the revelation that has been 'closed' which does undoubtedly take place is independent of the historical situation. The historical situation and the historical process in which particular perspectives of understanding are changed and altered are, on the contrary, demonstrably something more than the mere external situation for the development of dogma. Rather they are the ferment within this such that without it such development would be totally inconceivable.[2]

In the light of this it is obvious that theological work consists to a large extent in answering the question of how the perspectives of any given age give rise to fresh problems for the traditional dogmatic teaching that has been handed down, and how this teaching must be interpreted afresh (which does not mean circumvented while pretending to interpret it) in the light of such perspectives. This has been the case right from the first. But surely what is specifically new in the theological work today as contrasted with that of earlier ages consists in the fact that today the situation for theology is not merely unreflectingly lived through and allowed to exercise an influence on theology unconsciously. Instead this situation itself becomes the object of conscious reflection and can therefore be related explicitly to the theological work itself. Formerly there was no scientific awareness of the developing history of ideas in the present, and of course a fortiori no futurology either. And because of this theology was merely passively influenced by the historical situation in which its work was done and this passive influence was unconsciously

---

[1] Hence right down to the Middle Ages the inspiration of Ecumenical Councils and a revelation of the Holy Spirit have been spoken of almost as self-evident factors. On this cf. H. Bacht, 'Sind die Entscheidungen der ökumenischen Konzilien göttlich inspiriert?', *Catholica* 13 (1959), pp. 128–138. Y. Congar, *Tradition and Traditions* (London, 1966).

[2] cf. the author's articles, 'History of Dogma', *Sacramentum Mundi* 2 (New York and London, 1968), pp. 102–108, 'History of Heresies; *ibid.*, pp. 18–23; 'Theology II. History', *ibid.* 6 (New York and London, 1970), pp. 240–246.

introduced into the theology itself. Today, on the other hand, this encounter between theology and the contemporary situation must take place at an explicit and conscious level, though of course only to the extent to which the individual from his place in history is capable of achieving such a level of conscious reflection on his own situation, for the attaining of it always remains an asymptotic goal. As a pointer to this new situation in theology we may regard it as a significant fact that in the decree 'Gaudium et Spes' of the Second Vatican Council a description was included of the contemporary secular human situation certainly for the first time in a decree of the official Church carrying such authority.

With these prior assumptions, therefore, let us put to ourselves the following question: Having regard to the contemporary situation of human thought, the view which modern man takes of the world, what are the implications of this for christology? What impulses could this contemporary situation give rise to for christology in terms of fresh currents in theological speculation? This question is raised in view of the fact that for many centuries the officially authorized christology of the Church has hardly made any progress at all, at any rate not such as has been made clear in the average Church member's awareness of his faith. In answering such a question we are faced from the outset with the hard problem that it is only with great difficulty that we can describe this contemporary situation in secular thought. And this is a difficulty which we must labour under from the outset in striving to answer the question of what the implications of this situation are for christology. Hence only a few quite primitive characteristics of the contemporary situation in terms of ideas can be mentioned here, and our question will be related to these. It is in these terms, then, such as they are, that we shall be attempting to answer the question of what this situation may demand of a christology that is in keeping with the times. It is also obvious that the reply we give to this question could strictly speaking only be arrived at by working out a fresh christology, and this of course is something which cannot be accomplished here.[3] Again we cannot claim either that the order in which the characteristics we have in mind will be presented is based on any well founded system, or that the order in which they appear here will correspond to the degree of importance to be attached to each particular landmark of the contemporary situation which we shall be mentioning.

Our age is certainly characterized by a profound conviction of the

[3] On the questions with which a new christology of this kind is confronted cf. K. Rahner, 'Current Problems in Christology', *Theological Investigations* I (London

unity between spirit and matter.[4] In fact our own times are to a large extent decisively influenced by a dialectical materialism. For a large section of mankind this represents an ideology which has been constitutionally imposed, protected and propagated, and because of this, and in addition to its dominance in this sphere, it has also had a very profound effect in influencing the situation in terms of human thought in the rest of the world as well. Even if as philosophers and Christians we decisively reject this materialism, still the element of truth in this error (for unless there was such an element of truth the importance of materialism in the present age would be totally incomprehensible) can be regarded as consisting in a recognition of the unity between spirit and matter. For in the traditional 'ideology' of earlier Christian ages this unity had, after all, not been recognized with sufficient clarity.

This unity of spirit and matter in a sense which is philosophically and theologically acceptable to a Christian, cannot of course be established here *in extenso*, or in its own right. If this were possible, we should be putting forward the following thesis as its content: Spirit and matter have necessarily an intrinsic connection with one another, because both of them derive from the one infinite Spirit which is God as their Creator. All creaturely spirituality has an essential connection with matter, because ultimately speaking, although in very varied ways, creaturely spirituality is a receptive and intercommunicative spirituality (even in the case of the 'angels'), and matter in the metaphysical sense is the necessary condition for finite spiritual beings to exercise an intercommunicative influence upon one another. We must assume here the concept of an essential self-transcendence on the part of an existing creature sustained by God as its ultimate cause, and on the basis of this assumption we can freely assert that the development of biologically organized materiality is orientated in terms of an ever-increasing complexity and interiority towards spirit, until finally, under the dynamic impulse of God's creative power, and through a process of self-transcendence of this kind, it becomes spirit.[5]

---

and Baltimore, 1961), pp. 149–200, and also *idem* 'Jesus Christ', *Sacramentum Mundi* 3 (New York and London, 1968), pp. 192–209.

[4] This idea is developed more deeply in my article, 'The Unity of Spirit and Matter in the Christian Understanding of Faith', *Theological Investigations* VI (London and Baltimore, 1969), pp. 153–177.

[5] A similar line of thought, though developed from a different starting-point, is to be found in Teilhard de Chardin, *Man's Place in Nature* (London, 1966). On the author's conception cf. chiefly K. Rahner and P. Overhage, *Das Problem der*

Now assuming a unity of this kind between spirit and matter, then (quite apart from other treatises such as that of eschatology) this has a direct significance for christology. One instance of this is that on this assumption it is easier to understand why the Incarnation has a significance even for the angels, namely because these too belong as such to the cosmos which is one and material at the same time. But more than this there is a further problem (one which is already to be found even in Origen's works), which can be rendered more intelligible, the problem, namely of why the Logos becomes man without also becoming an angel. For in finding a solution to the problem entailed in this state of affairs we must not invoke any arbitrary dispensation on the part of God. Again on the basis of this unity between spirit and matter it also becomes clearer for christology why the assumption of a spirit-creaturely reality by the Logos actually constitutes a hypostatic union with matter, an Incarnation of the Logos in the true sense, which attains to and commits itself to matter itself as such – in other words the radical potentiality of the world as such – and why the total reality of the world is *ipso facto* touched to its very roots by the Incarnation of the Logos precisely in virtue of the fact that matter must be conceived of fundamentally and from the outset as one. Finally there is one further point which can be made still more unambiguously clear on the basis of this unity between spirit and matter. This is that in the *de facto* free ordering of this total reality the creative deed of God, and that too in its bearing upon the material world, was from the outset an element in that wider and more radical decision of God's will to impart himself to that which is other than himself and not divine.[6] There can be no doubt that in accordance with Augustine's phrase relating to the humanity of Jesus, *'Assumendo creatur'* the humanity of Jesus is the object of God's creative will because it is through the hypostatic union that the Logos wills to utter itself into the external world.[7]

Hominisation = Quaestiones Disputatae 12/13 (Freiburg, 1961), esp. pp. 43 ff., and also 'The Secret of Life', *Theological Investigations* VI (London and Baltimore, 1969), pp. 141–152.

[6] On this cf. the author's contributions entitled 'On the Theology of the Incarnation', *Theological Investigations* IV (London and Baltimore, 1966), pp. 105–120; also 'Incarnation', *Sacramentum Mundi* 3 (New York and London, 1968), pp. 110–118.

[7] A fuller treatment of this is to be found in F. Malmberg, *Über den Gottmenschen* = Quaestiones Disputatae 9 (Freiburg, 1969); cf. also *idem*, ' "Ipsa assumptione creatur". Ein Versuch scholastisch-theologischer Glaubensinterpretation', *Ein Leib – ein Geist* (Freiburg, 1960), pp. 315–353.

Nevertheless because of the unity between spirit and matter, and because of the ultimate unity of the world constituted by matter as such, this humanity of Jesus constitutes an element in the world as a whole, while conversely this world constitutes in a very radical sense the environment, the concomitant setting, indeed the very physicality demanded by the Logos in its act of uttering itself into the non-divine. Now if this is true then it must also be said that the whole of creation in the *de facto* order imparted to it is from the outset posited as the condition enabling God to impart himself to the non-divine by becoming the addressee and the recipient of this self-utterance of his. On this showing the entire supernatural reality constituted by grace and Incarnation (taking both of these as mutually conditioning elements in a single act of self-bestowal on God's part) no longer appears as a subsequent addition to a world that is considered merely as having been created by God. On the contrary, the creation, considered as the constitution of the non-divine 'out of nothing', is revealed as the prior setting and condition for the supreme possibility of his imparting of himself 'to the outside world' to be realized, a self-bestowal in which he does not constitute some other being, different from himself, but imparts himself, and thereby effectively manifests himself as the *agape* that bestows itself.

An essential trait in modern man's understanding of himself and of his world is the conviction that the world is not a static reality, but rather a world in process of becoming, subject to the process of evolution and history. It is not our task here to distinguish evolution and history from one another in any more precise terms, even though it is of the highest importance, in other contexts at least, to draw the lines of demarcation between the two, and even though we are in danger of denying the true nature of human history itself, if in our conception of it we make an exaggerated or over-facile use of the conceptual model of physical or biological evolution. The fact remains, however, that in this connection in his understanding of himself and his world modern man conceives of the reality involved in terms of evolution. In former times the basic conception of the world and of man was that they were created by God at the 'beginning of time', and never lost this radical reference to their own origins and basis. But this abiding reference to the transcendent and ultimate basis of all reality was unquestioningly interpreted as a state of being sustained in being, as '*conservatio*'. God creates a world and maintains it in being. And however much the phenomenon of becoming takes place within it, this process of becoming consists in the reproduction, constantly renewed, of what was already there before; or at any rate it is

a becoming which unfolds on a stage which has been firmly and immovably established once and for all, and in such a way that this firmly established sphere of the world, this stage of the theatre of the world, itself
remains unaltered. From ancient times, and from the beginning of the
Christian age right down to the theology of the baroque period, the image
of the world was such that the basic constituent of reality was not time
but space considered as a static entity, and history in the truest sense – in
other words the history of salvation and perdition – was the movement
of reality towards a specific and definitive point within this system as
spatially conceived. Of course even prior to the advent of the modern
interpretation of the world and of man these basic ideas were interwoven
again and again with perceptions and expressions of belief which ran
counter to this basic conceptual model involving a static interpretation
of the world, and which could only be made to conform to it with difficulty
and to a limited extent. But this does not alter in any respect the fact that
the activity of God was regarded primarily as consisting in the upholding
of a static world, one which, insofar as it had any 'movement', moved in
cycles, ultimately turning back upon itself, and not achieving any linear
advance of history towards a future that remained open before it. In
accordance with this God was also thought of as he who belongs to
another world, he who, as unmoved Mover, does not contribute to bringing history to its fulness by impelling it towards new and different points.

In contrast to this the man of today experiences the world as a becoming, a changing, and a history. He thinks of space rather as a function of
time,[8] history as a process of linear development which leads to ever more
complex systems, systems which are at the same time present in the
subjective awareness of those involved in them. Hence the question
naturally arises for Christian faith of how in more precise terms we should
conceive of God and his relationship to the world if we take this model of
a dynamic and evolutionary world as our premiss. In order to pave the
way for our answer to this question we must explicitly draw attention
to a further point, namely that there is much which Christian faith has
recognized all along and which in reality stands opposed to the ancient
conception of the world, even though this was long preserved in christendom, and even though the opposition involved was with difficulty

[8] We are not concerned here to produce an exact scientific description of the
relationship between space and time in the sense appropriate to physics. Such a
description is, after all, not required in the present context. On this cf. also my article,
'Theological Observations on the Concept of Time' in this volume, pp. 288–308, esp.
n. 1.

concealed. At the same time these very factors, recognized from the first by Christian faith, exhibit a positive affinity with the basic conception of the world and man which belongs to modern times. Christianity has never been merely a doctrinal system of eternal ideas, pointing on to realities with an eternal validity and prescribing a mere mystical sinking into God which involves a withdrawal from history. On the contrary Christianity is the proclamation of a saving history in which the true absolute which is significant for man is the historically concrete. At least on the religious terrain which is most proper to it Christianity has all along constituted an ideology which is evolutionary in character. The only point was that the Christian tradition represented this saving history as being played out on the fixed and static stage of the material and biological world, and as a result saving history itself was in constant danger of being conceived of in terms of this static concept of the world, and so of being under-valued as being, in the last analysis, an epiphenomenon in the world and nature of a very secondary kind, this in turn leading ultimately to it becoming incredible and so denied. Some awareness of a future new earth, an eschatological consummation of the material world as a whole, a con-summation to which man too could actively contribute, was indeed in-cluded at one point or another in the conscious faith of Christianity. But it did not emerge as a distinctive trait in its own right in any theological cosmology or cosmic eschatology. Instead it constantly remained sub-merged beneath a conception of salvation in which the individual spiritual subject was considered to be delivered from the world and its history and taken into that other world of the eternal God who is outside all history. Properly speaking, therefore, what is needed is not so much a transposi-tion of the Christian understanding of the world and man into an evolu-tionary view of the world, but rather the bold and radical carrying through to its logical conclusion of that view of the world which essentially and in principle has been present all along in Christianity, and still is present in it, as opposed to those portrayals of the world which have been superimposed upon it and are alien to it, and to which Christianity itself has formerly been exposed as a result of the influence of a Hellenistic view of the world.

Admittedly in establishing this basic point we have still not answered the real question with which we are concerned, that namely of how in more precise terms we should understand the relationship of God to the world. In answering this question we must inevitably touch upon the old meta-physical problem of the immanence and transcendence of God in relation to the world. In principle the philosophical and theological teaching of Christianity about God has always also been aware of and spoken of an immanence of God in the world, even though in doing so it has always fought against the danger of interpreting this immanence in a pantheistic sense, and making God in some way simply identical with the world as a whole. But this immanence of God in the world precisely as above and beyond the world and in this sense transcendent, was nevertheless in some respects abbreviated in the traditional theology of the seminaries, and in two respects its characteristic traits were not fully brought out: this immanence had, so to say, a static character. It was not understood (at any rate not clearly enough understood) as the immanence of the divine dynamism in the world as a becoming, but rather as the immanence of God as conserving and maintaining the abiding orders of being. Certainly over and above this teaching of the divine 'conservatio' a further teaching was presented of the divine 'concursus', God's collaboration with the activities of his creatures. But this divine collaboration was, nevertheless, merely the providing of the necessary divine assistance for the 'actus secundus' of a stable and unchangeable being to be brought to its own due fulness. It was not conceived of as the dynamism in virtue of which the world advances and develops its own nature to the point of producing essentially new and different realities.

But it is precisely this that we must straightway go on to treat of if we are to discuss with all due seriousness an evolutionary view of the world. Certainly this modern view of the world is to a large extent corrupted in its own basic conception in that it seeks to interpret the element of the new appearing in the history of the natural order and of the spirit as being constituted once more merely by the chance variations and combinations of basic elements which have been present all along. Again that view of the world which is presented as modern all too often proceeds from the basic misconception that something radically new, qualitatively different and higher, cannot be the outcome of an evolution from below (on this showing, therefore, there would never really be any such radically new element), and that what really emerges in such an evolution from below is not something genuinely new, but rather something that is quantitatively more complex. Against this, however, whether we be Christians or philosophers or natural scientists, we must genuinely and freely accept the element of becoming in the world for what it is. We must recognize the possibility of a genuine development from below into something higher, denying neither that this 'something higher' is genuinely new in time, nor that it has connections with what already exists in time. And if we do this then in the very nature of the case we cannot escape from the concept of becoming as a genuine process of self-transcendence. All creaturely being is being in process of becoming, but all becoming, if it is really worthy of the name, is the becoming of that which is qualitatively higher, and which, nevertheless, is the act of that which is lower. And it is precisely this that is signified when we speak of self-transcendence. That which is higher is not merely added on to the lower stages in the world's development, but is actually enacted and attained to through these lower stages in a process of genuine self-transcendence. What was formerly signified by the terms 'conservatio' and 'concursus' in Christian theology is nothing else than the dynamic impulse towards precisely this self-transcendence present in all being in virtue of the immanence of God.

It is not possible here to pursue any further the dialectical relationship between the immanence and transcendence of God in relation to the world. But on any showing the immanence of God in the world must be conceived of as of so radical a kind that the process of self-transcendence inherent in being in process of becoming genuinely is and remains an active process of *self*-transcendence. At the same time, however, the transcendence of God must be maintained, and that too not merely by reason of God's sovereign independence of the world, but in order to ensure that what emerges from this process of becoming is that which is genuinely new. And this too must be maintained in such a way that that which comes to be is genuinely new and not merely an explicitation of that which has been present all along. Thus we can see that the state of becoming genuinely inherent in the world of itself postulates the fact that God is simultaneously immanent and transcendent in it in a single act.

Probably the account of the immanence of God provided in the traditional theology of the seminaries is inadequate in a second respect also. We cannot here treat of the philosophical question which we already find arising again and again in the philosophy and theology of the Middle Ages, the question, namely, of what precisely constitutes the relationship between the 'esse' of God and the 'esse' of the creature, or, to express it more exactly, what the consequences are for this relationship when we consider that the creation of finite being by God does not presuppose nor, properly speaking, even create, the difference between God and the creature, but rather, from the standpoint of God, that God himself through his own being precisely *is* this difference in himself. Taking this as our starting-point, it would once more be possible to attain to an immanence of God in the world or an immanence of the world in God. And such a consideration would also have its significance in enabling us to realize those further truths with regard to the immanence of God which have to be stated on the basis of a specifically theological premiss.

But this difficult approach must be set aside here. We can achieve a still more radical understanding of the immanence of God in the world by more directly theological methods. We have already said that the creation can and should be conceived of as an element in, and prior setting for, the self-bestowal of God, that act in which he does not create something different from himself and set it over against himself, but rather communicates his own reality to the other. If and to the extent that we have understood that the created world is the subject to whom the divine self-bestowal is addressed, and is the condition and prior setting posited by this self-bestowal of God in itself, and enabling it to take place, if, in other words, the world emerges within the process of God's self-bestowal, then it naturally follows that there is an immanence of God in the world (though always, of course in a way that allows for the difference between it and that which belongs intrinsically to the world). This immanence is not merely that of the Creator in the creature, but rather that the recognition of which comes to be developed in Christian theology in dealing with the question of the indwelling of God in the spiritual creature through grace. But once this recognition is achieved, then this indwelling of God is no longer understood merely as constituting a particular phenomenon occurring here and there within the world, but rather as a fundamental relationship which God bears to the world in general. The proper *topos* for achieving an understanding of the immanence of God in the world in theology, therefore, is not a treatise on God worked out in abstract metaphysical terms, but rather the treatise on grace, admittedly taking this as teaching not that some created quality of grace is instilled by a creative act, but rather as teaching that the existence of God bears a quasi-formal relationship to the world such that the reality of God himself is imparted to it as its supreme specification.[9]

It seems to us that we have strayed far from the proper theme of our investigation. What has all that we have said to do with christology? We have attempted to perceive a more radical theological significance in the modern understanding of the world as a world of becoming that exists in a constant process of self-transcendence. The world can really be a world of becoming in the unity of spirit and matter that belongs to it, and in a linear process of history in which an ever higher degree of self-transcendence is achieved, precisely because the mystery most interior to it, and as such precisely elevated above it, is the absolute being of

[9] On the manner in which this connection between grace and history etc. is to be thought of more precisely cf. E. Klinger, *Offenbarung im Horizont der Heilsgeschichte* (Zürich, 1969).

God, whose basic act (an act which also includes God's creativity) is the self-bestowal of God upon that which is not divine. The whole history of the becoming of the world, therefore, proceeds in ever higher stages of self-transcendence towards that point at which this self-bestowal of God can be and is accepted as such. Now in this history of the world considered as the history of self-transcendence that being which appears as a subject capable of accepting such a self-bestowal on God's part is called man. The acceptance of this self-bestowal of God by man and in conformity with the nature of man (considered as a transcendental subject endowed with ultimate freedom on the one hand, and as a historical and inter-communicative being on the other, such that these two factors mutually condition one another) has, as it has *de facto* taken place, a two-fold aspect: on the one hand it takes place always and everywhere where a transcendental subject in this sense takes possession of himself in freedom. This is because this subject is always endowed with the offering of God's self-bestowal even when, in the exercise of his own subjective freedom, this self-offering of God and the acceptance of it at the level of an 'anonymous Christianity' remain quite unexplicitated and unconscious. On the other hand, however, in accordance with the historical nature of man, this acceptance of God's self-bestowal must in increasing measure achieve an historical manifestation. It must be explicitly objectified, and that too not of course merely in words, but in acts in which the real fulness of human existence and of history is achieved – precisely in that which we call saving history and revelation history. For this is nothing else than the historical event of that transcendental self-bestowal of God and the acceptance of it in the dimension of human freedom.

This brings us to a point in our argument at which christology can be fitted into a modern understanding of the world and history taken as a whole.[10] If the history of matter and spirit in the unity constituted by these two is a history of an ever renewed process of rising to self-transcendence, then the supreme, ultimate, and 'eschatological' self-transcendence is that in which the world freely opens itself to the self-bestowal of God himself as Being and Mystery in the absolute, and in which the world accepts this in the power of this self-bestowal of God itself. The acceptance of the world by God in his act of self-bestowal then, and the acceptance of God in his act of self-bestowal by the world are manifested historically in such a way that these two acceptances are seen to constitute a unity. Moreover,

[10] On what follows, therefore, cf. also K. Rahner, 'Christology within an Evolutionary View of the World', *Theological Investigations* V (London and Baltimore, 1966), pp. 157–192.

this manifestation achieves its irrevocable climax at that point at which these two acceptances become definitive and irrevocable (however much further saving history in general is prolonged). Now if we accept this, then we have precisely accepted what we call the Incarnation of the divine Logos, the Mediator of salvation in the absolute. The fact that this event, in which man attains to God in an ultimate act of self-transcendence, and in God's own self-bestowal upon man in its most radical form, has taken place precisely in Jesus of Nazareth – that is a fact that cannot, of course, be deduced in a transcendental christology which recognizes the idea of the God-man as the supreme point, and at the same time the point of intersection between the ultimate self-transcendence of the world reaching out to God and the self-bestowal of God upon the world in its most radical form (both taking place in history). On the contrary, the fact that this event has taken place in Jesus of Nazareth is ascertainable only through the historical experience of the crucified and risen Jesus, an experience which as such cannot in its turn be communicated any further. But this does nothing to alter the fact that an 'evolutionary view of the world' can conceive of the idea of the Incarnation as the asymptotic goal of a development of the world reaching out to God, provided only that such a view of the world conceives of the self-transcendence of the world in the power of God and God's own immanence in the world in sufficiently radical terms for us to realize that this process of self-transcendence only attains its end at that point at which it recognizes and accepts the self-bestowal of God as the supreme and unsurpassable apogee of the dynamic immanence of God.

Nor is a transcendental christology of this kind, within an evolutionary and dynamic conception of the world in general, invalidated by the consideration that *de facto* such a transcendental christology is only developed *a posteriori* and after the experience of the God-man has already been achieved. This sort of (ultimately mutually) conditioning relationship between *a posteriori* experience on the one hand, and the transcendental interpretation of the experience on the other, is also to be found in other contexts. In a transcendental christology of this kind, as fitted into the totality of an evolutionary view of the world, the Christ-event is not something which is enacted upon a sort of cosmic stage which is static and unaffected by what is taking place in him, but rather constitutes the point to which the becoming of the world in its history is from the outset striving to attain. An objection that might possibly be raised against a transcendental christology of this kind, and against the christo-centricity of the world and its history which it entails, is that the *de facto* history of Jesus of Nazareth, circumscribed as it is in terms of space and time, and, after all, empirically speaking, so limited, cannot in any way be adequate for what is claimed for it by this transcendental christology. To this we should first and foremost reply that the ultimate and the greatest of all conceivable histories, namely the radical commitment of the creaturely spirit in faith, hope, and love to the infinite mystery of God, always makes a modest impression, and seems to be a peripheral event within the world's course on any view which is restricted to the superficial dimension of everyday empiricism, and yet for all this constitutes the ultimately real and ultimately decisive in that which takes place in the world. It must further be said that we are not viewing the Christ-event in Jesus of Nazareth in a way that is in conformity with its true meaning and essence unless we bear in mind two factors: the First and Second Coming of the Incarnate Logos must be understood as a unity, as a single event still in process of achieving its fulness, such that in it the Life, Death and Resurrection of Jesus constitute merely the first beginning of an event which will only have achieved its fulness and definitive state when the world as a whole is illumined by, and brought face to face with, the immediacy of God, and in this sense when Jesus himself will have 'come again'. This in itself implicitly contains the second point which has to be borne in mind: Christ can only rightly be understood if in him the 'head and body' which is the Church, and ultimately the world itself, are apprehended in their unity as constituting the one and whole Christ.

The irrevocable self-bestowal of God upon the world which has taken place in Christ, and the definitive acceptance of this by the world in Jesus Christ, do not simply bring history to an end. Rather they merely confer upon it its proper sphere, within which alone it can be unfolded. Hitherto (following the secular and Marxist view of history) history has been thought of as developing in the manner of a pre-history to that point at which man liberates himself from his own self-alienation, and only so begins his own true history, in which he freely disposes of his environment and of himself. Now to this view we should have as Christians to reply that this freedom which man himself has to work out in the course of his history is conceded to him as in fact legitimate and attainable (admittedly at the 'this-worldly' level, and always in a merely asymptotic sense) precisely in virtue of the fact that he is now fulfilling this task of his in history (even here it is still always possible for him to go astray) in the dimension of that which has been irrevocably addressed to him and which has achieved its historical manifestation in Jesus Christ, namely the self-bestowal of God as the absolute future. It is in the light of this that there is real hope for the 'this-worldly' history in this sense, and it is also made free, whatever catastrophes may befall, to cling onto this hope because precisely it achieves its fulness in the dimension of God's uttering of himself to it as the absolute future. Now this self-utterance of God is present as such, and God does not merely move the world in its history as its unmoved Mover, as such unattainable to it.

10

REFLECTIONS ON THE PROBLEMS INVOLVED IN DEVISING A SHORT FORMULA OF THE FAITH

A POINT that has been under discussion for some years among Catholic theologians is whether it is not necessary today to have some brief new basic formulae in which the Christian creed can be expressed in a manner appropriate to the contemporary climate of ideas.[1] It is pointed out that the apostolic creed actually had a function of this kind, chiefly as the baptismal confession of the adult catechumen, and indeed that such quite brief formulations of the creed are already to be found in the New Testament.[2] Emphasis is laid upon the fact that, even assuming that a full and basic religious instruction has been given, a summary of this kind is still necessary today, in order to preserve what has been learnt at the catechumen stage of instruction, and in order to achieve a clear organization of the 'hierarchy of truths' without which the content of the Christian faith all too easily becomes amorphous, or alternatively the believer comes very easily in his religious practice to attach an exaggerated value to what is merely secondary. It is argued with some justice that it is necessary for the Christian layman to have at his command some

---

[1] In this connection the author may refer to an attempt which he himself has already submitted at an earlier stage, cf. 'The Need for a "Short Formula" of the Christian Faith', *Theological Investigations* IX (London and New York), pp. 117–127; in the same connection reference should also be made to the following: P. Brunner, G. Friedrich, K. Lehmann, J. Ratzinger, *Veraltetes Glaubensbekenntnis?* (Regensburg, 1968), and H. Schuster, 'Kurzformel des Glaubens und seiner Verkündigung', *Rechenschaft des Glaubens* (edited by E. Hesse and H. Erharter) (Vienna, 1969), pp. 117–135; also 'Bemühungen um eine Kurzformel des Glaubens', *Herder-Korrespondenz* 23 (1969), pp. 32–38 and the extensive bibliographical survey, 'The Creed in the Melting Pot', *Concilium* 6/1 (1970, Dogma), pp. 131–153.

[2] A penetrating discussion of these credal formulae in the New Testament is to be found in K. Lehmann, *Auferweckt am dritten Tag nach der Schrift* = Quaestiones Disputatae 38 (Freiburg, 2nd ed. 1969).

brief formulation of his faith and his creed orientated towards what is essential in it. For although there is no need for him to be a specialist theologian, he nevertheless has to take responsibility for his faith in the non-Christian environment in which he is placed. It is also significant that in the 'Year of Faith' Paul VI published a 'Confession of Faith of the People of God',[3] and even though it must be admitted that on the whole this has turned out to be too detailed, and to draw too much on the language of seminary theology for it to serve as a short formula of the kind we are thinking of, still for all this it does in its own way bear witness to the need for a short credal summary of the faith of the kind we have in mind.

The assumption underlying all these considerations is of course the idea that the Apostles' Creed, however old and honourable it may be, however important it is for it to be used at appropriate points in all the Christian Churches, and however true it may be that it will always constitute a permanent and binding norm of faith, is, nevertheless, simply incapable today of fulfilling the function of a brief formula of this kind in any adequate manner, precisely because it has too little direct contact with the contemporary intellectual situation for its claims to be attended to.[4] Chief among the factors which make this apparent is the very fact that the existence of a God transcendent above the world or, at any rate at first, the meaning of the word 'God' is, or has been able to be, taken as self-evident. Now in an age of anti-metaphysical pragmatism and world-wide atheism it is, after all, manifest that this has ceased to be possible without further justification. Hence a desire evinces itself for a new basic formula, or new basic formulae, of the faith.[5]

[3] *AAS* 60 (1968), 433–445.

[4] An attempt to interpret afresh the ancient formulae themselves is to be found in G. Rein (ed.), *Das Glaubensbekenntnis. Aspekte für ein neues Verständnis* (Stuttgart, 1967). The credal formula devised by D. Sölle in his 'Credo', *Meditationen und Gebrauchstexte* (Berlin, 1969), pp. 24–25 is intended to be taken as a programme for future discussion.

[5] The intellectual climate of the new age is in fact such as again and again to compel theology to give fresh presentations of Christianity in its 'essence'. cf. among others C. H. Ratschow, 'Wesen des Christentums', *RGG* I (3rd ed. 1957), 1721–1729; A. von Harnack, *Das Wesen des Christentums* (Leipzig, 1913); G. Ebeling, *Das Wesen des christlichen Glaubens* (Hamburg, 1964); R. Guardini, *Das Wesen des Christentums* (Würzburg, 1938); M. Schmaus, *Vom Wesen des Christentums* (Westheim b. Augsburg, 1949); G. Söhngen, *Die Einheit in der Theologie* (Munich, 1952), pp. 288–304; K. Adam, *Das Wesen des Katholizismus* (Düsseldorf, 13th ed., 1957); K. Rahner, 'Christentum', *LTK* II (2nd ed., 1958), 1100–1115; H. U. v. Balthasar, *Glaubhaft ist nur Liebe* = Christ heute 1 (Einsiedeln, 3rd ed., 1966); *idem*, 'Summa

Even if we assume that such a desire is justified, a whole series of questions do of course still remain unanswered with regard to the postulate itself, and even prior to the actual composing of one or several such new basic formulae. And these questions must be clarified. Perhaps it is only in attempting to compose the formulae themselves in the concrete that we can clarify questions of this kind. Alternatively it may be that such questions should be clarified even before we undertake the composition of such basic formulae. Whatever the connection may be between the two stages, such questions must be recognized and solved.

At least some of these questions may be indicated at this point. First we should mention the question of whether such formulations at the conceptual and doctrinal level really are so important today. For this is an age in which pride of place is given to the practical rather than the speculative reason, and in which precisely in the religious sphere men are positively allergic to speculation and theorizing. It is an age in which men commit themselves to decision and action in preference to adopting a contemplative attitude towards life. In such an age, then, may it not be that the feeling is that there is no urgent need whatever to produce doctrinal statements of this kind with regard to the nature of Christianity? And in view of this may it not perhaps be that any attempt to compose such basic formulae cannot in fact have any real success? Here we are presupposing that Christianity, in contrast to other religions, cannot dispense with a certain conceptualized statement of its beliefs as an element inherent in its own nature. Assuming this, then, to be the case, we must adhere to the opinion that even in the contemporary situation the demand for a basic formula of this kind is far from being antiquated or out of date, the more so since such a basic formula can certainly be understood precisely as representing a critique of, and a counter to, any excessive conceptualizing, over-defining, and so 'dissecting' of what is properly signified in the Christian faith.

A further question is whether we can seriously count upon being able to compose a single basic formula of this kind which will be acceptable to the whole of christendom (at least Catholic christendom), and indeed such a formula as can perhaps, like the Apostles' Creed, have the character of expressing the official teaching of the Church, and which in virtue of this

---

summarum', *Spiritus creator* (Einsiedeln, 1967), pp. 322–344; J. Ratzinger, *Einführung in das Christentum* (Munich, 8th ed., 1969), In this connection the author may draw attention to a more large-scale publication which he himself is preparing for the immediate future on the subject of 'An Introduction to the Concept of Christianity'.

fact could actually replace the Apostles' Creed in the Church's religious practice and liturgy, or whether alternatively it is from the outset no longer possible to conceive of any such single formula finding universal acceptance. I believe that this question must be answered in the negative, and in accordance with the second of these two alternatives. There will no longer be any one single and universal basic formula of the Christian faith applicable to the whole Church and, indeed, prescribed for her as authoritatively binding.[6] In this sense the Apostolic Creed will never have any successor, and is therefore destined, for certain purposes, to endure.

To show how impossible it is to produce any such new, single and universal basic formula of the faith we may begin by pointing to the fact that certain attempts which have been made to compose and officially introduce a world catechism to be enforced throughout the world have failed and have met with unanimous resistance on the part of preachers and exponents of catechetical theory; and this despite the fact that at one stage a Tridentine catechism was actually produced with this kind of official authority (although despite its advantages it never succeeded in imposing itself as a schoolbook for practical use), and despite the further fact that under Pius XII Gasparri actually attempted to compose a new world catechism of this kind. Against all such attempts it is justifiable to point out again and again that the differences between the individual peoples, cultures, and social milieux, and also those which arise from the different mentalities of the hearers, all have a bearing on the concrete situation in which the faith has to be preached. And nowadays these differences are too great for us to be able to address these hearers in all parts of the world through the medium of one and the same monotonous and uniform catechism. And if this is true then the same also applies to basic formulae of the kind we are thinking of, but in this case not merely because of the differences between the hearers themselves, but also because of the very brevity of such formulae.

Any basic formula of this kind must, precisely in spite of its brevity, as far as possible be directly intelligible to the hearer, and capable of being 'brought home to' him without much commentary. Now in view of the immense differences between the various outlooks it must be concluded that it is quite impossible that any one basic formula can be produced such that wherever it is used in the world it will be understood in the same sense and have the qualities indicated above. Already in the

---

[6] On this cf., in the present volume, 'Pluralism in Theology and the Unity of the Creed in the Church', pp. 3–23.

New Testament itself a great difference is apparent between the basic formulae which it includes. We have only to think of the differences between the attributes of glory by means of which the reality of Jesus and his saving significance for us are expressed.[7]

Certain further and different considerations must now be added to this principle which we have enunciated that in view of the differences in the situation in which the gospel has to be preached it is necessary to have precisely *different* basic formulae in the Church. The consideration put forward so far should in itself have been enough to make it necessary for basic formulae of this kind to be devised afresh already at that stage at which Christianity emerged from the Hellenistic and Roman civilizations, and also from that which belonged homogeneously to the West. Thus taken in themselves those brief formulae of the faith which were adequate for the situation in the West should not merely have been 'exported' as they stood. Probably we can only fully explain the fact that they were 'exported' in this way if we take into consideration the repellent sense of superiority characteristic of European colonialism and imperialism. Now the moment the authority of this European imperialism in the sphere of theology ceases to be accepted without question, and the moment the Western civilization, formerly homogeneous as it was, falls into an intellectual and cultural pluralism that is extremely far-reaching, it immediately becomes clear that despite the unity of the Church herself, and the fact that this Church adheres to one and the same creed, it is no longer possible for us of today to count upon having one and the same homogeneous theology. Even in theology (taking this to signify a process of systematic reflection upon the Christian faith in the light of the total situation and the self-understanding of man as a whole) there necessarily emerges today a pluralism of theologies which, while they certainly may not contradict one another, are nevertheless, as they exist in the concrete, no longer capable of being integrated into any single system of theology by individuals or particular groups. In the universal Church of today it is recognized as legitimate that there should be a pluralism of 'situations' constituted by the different theological schools of thought, such that all of them are equally justified, and that they are no longer dominated or presided over by a European outlook. And this has perforce given rise to a pluralism of theologies such that it is beyond the powers of any one theologian to master them all. Now while it is true that creed and theology are two very different entities, that they have been so all along, and that

---

[7] cf. F. Hahn, *Christologische Hoheitstitel* (Göttingen, 2nd ed., 1964).

a fortiori they will continue to be so in the future, still at the same time it is no less true that there is no such thing as a creed which is capable of being formulated in total independence of any system of theology. Even formulae of the faith bear the characteristic imprint of some specific school of theology to such an extent that even in the New Testament itself, for all its unity as the expression of revelation, it is possible to discern several different theologies. In view of the fact, therefore, that the differences between the various theologies of today are too many and too wide for us to master them all, we must not expect that any one uniform basic formula can be produced such that it carries equal authority for all members of the Church.

Perhaps the Second Vatican Council constitutes, to some extent, a sign of this fact in itself. Certainly it has been able to achieve a certain eclectic amalgamation between the traditional neo-scholastic theology of the nineteenth century and the beginning of the twentieth on the one hand, and modern movements in theology on the other, and on this basis to produce certain universally accepted statements of doctrine. And in view of the contemporary pluralism of ideas the possibility of achieving this even at the public and official level was far from self-evident. From this point of view alone it has been a remarkable phenomenon. But even the Second Vatican Council itself has not attempted to produce any new official definitions of doctrine. What prompted it to refrain from this was probably not merely the more sympathetic, undertsanding and tolerant attitude which it adopted towards 'heretics', but also the feeling that a lengthier statement of doctrine, expressed in positive terms and in a single homogeneous theological language equally intelligible to all, is something which the Council can no longer so easily be expected to produce today. Moreover, in this way the Church avoids exercising her authority to the point of exhaustion by producing definitorial decisions of doctrine, and is able to continue to restrict the exercise of her authority to negative anathemas. For even in earlier times the great majority of such official definitions of doctrine were couched in this form.

In view of this it can be said that we are justified in attempting to produce many such basic formulae. These can be different from one another not merely according to the differences between the nations, the areas of cultural and historical influence, and the world religions, all of which play their part in shaping any one specific situation, but also according to the level of social development, the degree of maturity etc. of those to whom any given basic formula of this kind is addressed.

These various basic formulae will also differ among themselves primarily in respect of that which is taken to be already recognized and accepted in any given milieu, and that which is asserted in these formulae as new and hitherto unrecognized so far as their particular milieu is concerned. For the differences between the various basic formulae must be in conformity with the differences between the various situations of the hearers themselves, and these differences of situation make themselves felt precisely in respect of what the hearer can accept as obvious in any given situation, and which can be used as a principle and point of departure for giving him an understanding of what is addressed to him as *new*. When therefore a basic formula of this kind appears more or less unintelligible in a milieu that is different from that for which it is designed, this state of affairs still does not invalidate the basic formula concerned, but on the contrary precisely justifies it.

Among the basic questions which have to be raised in connection with such basic formulae is of course to be included the special question of what is properly being expressed in a basic formula of this kind and what can be set aside. It is surely clear that any such basic formula must not be presented as a brief summary of a systematic dogmatic theology. It cannot express all at once everything which constitutes the Church's explicit awareness of the content of her faith. In none of the creeds prior to the Council of Trent was everything expressed which belongs to the Christian faith. The teaching of the 'hierarchy of truths' in the Second Vatican Council asserts, in fact, that not everything which is true must necessarily and *ipso facto* be equally important on that account, but a basic formula should contain only that which is of fundamental importance, and on the basis of which the totality of the faith can in principle and in itself be attained. We should add to this the further consideration that it is surely possible to draw a justifiable distinction between an objective hierarchy of truths and one that is conditioned by the concrete conditions of life prevailing in a given human situation. Thus in a basic formula which is intended to be only one among many the emphasis must be laid on expressing that which can truly and effectively constitute the point of access and departure for the whole content of the faith in the specific situation and the specific concrete conditions of human life actually envisaged in that particular basic formula. In view of this, then, it is clear that such basic formulae can vary very greatly even in respect of their content, and that this content should consist primarily and chiefly in that which, so far as the hearers actually involved are concerned, represents an initial point of departure, though one that holds out a prospect of success, for achieving an understanding of the Christian faith as a whole.

A further question would of course be how much to include in a basic formula of this kind purely in terms of quantity. Such a basic formula should certainly not be as long as the confession of faith of Paul VI. But even in this respect it is possible to conceive of very notable differences between the various basic formulae, ranging from a basic formula consisting of a few words, as in the Apostolic Creed, to one that consists in a few sentences, similar to that which I myself once attempted to formulate a few years ago.[8] Presumably in this respect too it is by no means necessary for the various possible basic formulae to be equivalent to one another.

We must now go on to draw attention to a further question with regard to the basic formula in general. In order for such a formula really to constitute a confession of Christian faith it must express belief in the historical Jesus as our Lord, the bringer of salvation in the absolute. And it must be related to this as a matter of historical fact. There can be such a thing as an anonymous Christianity in which grace, the forgiveness of sins, justification and salvation do take place even though the individual concerned sees no explicit relationship, so far as his conscious awareness is concerned, or as an explicit object of enquiry, between himself and the historical event of Jesus of Nazareth.[9] Again it is possible to say very much with regard to the most central reality of the Christian faith without doing this directly from the point of view of Jesus Christ. This is particularly true because in fact not even every explicit relationship to the historical Jesus is *ipso facto* that entailed in faith or, in other words, needs itself in turn to be explained in its distinctive theological character. Moreover under certain circumstances this can be achieved on the basis of quite different fundamental statements of the faith which 'quoad nos' can initially be made without any explicit reference to Jesus Christ. This applies for instance to the first article of the Apostles' Creed. Nevertheless it is obvious that even a mere *basic formula* of any explicit Christianity must explicitly contain the reference of what is expressed elsewhere to Christ or the reference of Jesus to this other truth which is expressed, and this means that it must have the structure of an affirmation of faith that is christological.

In order to express all this in a slightly more concrete form, and to illustrate what has been said up to this point, we may adduce three brief theological formulae and explain the particular intelligible content which

[8] cf. n. 1.
[9] On this cf. also the study entitled 'Anonymous Christianity and the Missionary Task of the Church', *Theological Investigations*, XII.

it is possible to arrive at in them. Why there should be precisely three such brief formulae can perhaps better be explained at the conclusion, and hence for the time being this question must remain open.

These three brief formulae attempt to achieve the utmost possible within a very brief compass. For this reason alone they are extremely 'abstract' in their formulation. They attempt briefly to express the innermost nature of that saving history in which, whether it be taken in a collective or an individual sense, Christianity consists. The abstract formulation entailed in this is obviously not of itself accessible to everyone. It is therefore evident that these brief formulae, even on their own terms, cannot claim any universally binding force. It is likewise necessary to emphasize that these brief formulae have been devised in the light of a western milieu, and in view of a European situation corresponding to this. Hence taken by themselves they cannot claim to be applicable in the same manner, for instance, to the situation in terms of culture and history of thought that prevails in Japan. In this respect they could only be understood as requiring that something similar should be attempted which would then be suitable to apply, for instance, to the situation in terms of ideas that prevails in Japan.

The first brief formula, which we can call the *theological* one, runs as follows: The incomprehensible point of reference towards which human transcendence is orientated, and which cannot, either absolutely or in the concrete conditions of human living, be attained to by speculation alone, or in merely conceptual terms, is called God. And it imparts itself to man in the concrete and historical conditions of his existence by an act of forgiving love as his true consummation. The supreme eschatological point of God's self-bestowal in history, in which this self-bestowal is revealed as irrevocably victorious, is called Jesus Christ.

Let us add a few observations by way of commentary on this first brief formula, which we have called the 'theological' one.[10] It contains three

---

[10] The following studies by the author may also serve as commentaries on this formula: *Worte ins Schweigen* (Innsbruck, 10th ed., 1967); 'The Concept of Mystery in Catholic Theology', *Theological Investigations* IV (London and Baltimore, 1966), pp. 36–73; 'Christology within an Evolutionary View of the World', *ibid.* V (London and Baltimore, 1966), pp. 157–192; 'The Church and the Parousia of Christ', *Theological Investigations* VI (London and Baltimore, 1969), pp. 295–312; 'Christology in the Setting of Modern Man's Understanding of Himself and of His World', in this volume pp. 215–229; 'Der dreifaltige Gott als transzendenter Urprsung der Heilsgeschichte', *Mysterium Salutis* II (Einsiedeln, 1967), pp. 317–401; 'Incarnation', *Sacramentum Mundi* 3 (New York and London, 1968), pp. 110–118; 'Jesus Christ', *ibid.*, pp. 192–209.

fundamental statements: a preliminary one with regard to what is meant by God. It seeks to communicate an understanding of God (in his nature and his existence) in which God is designated as the point of reference of human transcendence, and precisely in being so as the Mystery which remains incircumscribable.

In connection with this it is emphasized that this experience of God implicit in the experience of transcendence is not initially or ultimately achieved in a process of theoretical reflection, but in attaining to the ultimate fulness of knowledge and freedom in our everyday lives – in other words this experience of God is on the one hand inescapable, on the other can take place in a profoundly anonymous and preconceptual form. In this way it is intended to summon the individual to discover this experience of God which is present in any case within him by reflecting upon himself and to objectify it in conceptual terms. This first brief theological formula, therefore, must not merely say *that* God exists, so that from this it will be clear (as even Thomas Aquinas supposed) *what* he is. The brief formula is intended rather to point out also how we can arrive at an understanding of *what* is really meant by God.

The second statement in this theological brief formula declares that this God who has thus been made accessible to man's understanding is not merely man's eternally asymptotic goal, but – and it is at this point that the first unambiguously Christian statement is made – that he gives himself to man in an act of self-bestowal to be his true consummation, and that too even though it is presupposed in this that man is a sinner, so that this act of self-bestowal entails an attitude of forgiving love. This self-bestowal is stated to take place both in the concrete conditions of the individual's own existence and at the same time in the dimension of history. In this way two realities are included (and moreover in such a way that the two are seen as elements mutually conditioning one another). The first is that which (at least as offered) is in the usual theological terminology called justifying grace (the self-bestowal of God in the 'Holy Spirit' in the concrete conditions of the individual's own existence). The second, concomitant with this, is what is called saving and revelation history, which is nothing else than history as the medium in which the self-bestowal of God is achieved; the historical objectivation, therefore, continuing to unfold through history, of that self-bestowal which, at least as offered, is inserted by grace into the very roots of history to remain abidingly present there. This then is a statement of the twofold self-bestowal of God upon the world, in other words of the two 'missions' in the economy of salvation, the mission of the 'Spirit' in the concrete conditions of the individual's existence, and the mission of the 'Logos' (Son) in the dimension of history. And in this statement it will be noticed that mention has already been made of the ultimate and incircumscribable Mystery of God as abiding ('Father'). This statement, therefore, contains first an expression of the Trinity as manifested in the economy of salvation, and *ipso facto* in this the Trinity as 'immanent' too because without this the reality referred to would not constitute any real *self*-bestowal on God's part.

The third basic statement consists in the fact that this historical self-bestowal of God, of which the deed of grace in the individual's own existence is the historical objectification and the medium, achieves its supreme and eschatologically victorious point in Jesus of Nazareth. Although the need for brevity prevents us from providing any fuller exposition of this point here, this much at any rate must be said: If the historical self-bestowal of God achieves its supreme point, in which it is present not merely as directed and offered to human freedom (at the individual and collective levels) but as accepted in humanity as totally irrevocable, victorious and definitive (though this does not mean that saving history had already attained its absolute end at this point), then what is present here is precisely that which in the dogmatic theology of the Church is called the God-man, the hypostatic union (including in this the Death and Resurrection of this God-man). The third statement of this short formula thereby avows the truth that this eschatological supreme point in the historical self-bestowal of God upon the world has already taken place in the concrete in the historical person of Jesus of Nazareth. Since this eschatological event cannot be conceived of at all without including in our concept of it the fact that it has an abiding historical force in the further prolongations of saving history, an adequate starting-point for the theology of the Church is already present also in this brief formula. For in fact this can only be understood in its ultimate essence as the abiding sacrament of the saving deed performed by God in Christ for the world.

The second short formula, which we may perhaps call the *sociological* one[11] runs: Man realizes himself truly and achieves the authentic fulness of

---

[11] On this cf. especially the author's studies, 'Thoughts on the Possibility of Belief Today', *Theological Investigations* V (London and Baltimore, 1966), pp. 3–22; 'The "Commandment" of Love in Relation to the Other Commandments', *ibid.*, pp. 439–459; 'Reflections on the Unity of the Love of Neighbour and the Love of God', *Theological Investigations* IV (London and Baltimore, 1969), pp. 231–249; *Im Heute Glauben* = Theologische Meditationen 21 (Einsiedeln, 1968).

his own nature only when he turns radically away from himself and to his fellow. If he does this he apprehends (whether latently or explicitly) what is meant by saying that God provides the ambience, the assurance and the radicality of such an act of love, for it is God who, in his act of self-bestowal (at the level of both individual existence and of history) becomes the dimension within which such love is made possible. The term love as used here signifies both the love of intimate relationship and love in the social dimension. And it is the radical unity between these two elements that constitutes the foundation and nature of the Church. In this we may perhaps distinguish three assertions.

The first states that in that act of self-transcendence within his own individual existence which is achieved in the act of loving his neighbour man makes, at least implicitly, an experience of God. This first assertion, therefore, is simply a further specification of the first part of the theological brief formula. It concretizes that truth which was expressed in the first assertion of the first brief formula, namely that the achievement of the ultimate fulness of human transcendence takes place not at the level of theoretical speculation, but in the concrete practical knowledge and freedom of 'everyday' life. For this precisely signifies life as lived with and among one's fellow men. This first statement of the second brief formula is also covered from the theological point of view by the truth that love of God and love of neighbour are one, provided only that we do not reduce this truth to the platitude that we cannot please God unless we pay due heed to his commandment to love our neighbour.

The second assertion in this basic formula states that precisely through his self-bestowal God creates the possibility of achieving that relationship of love between men which is possible for us in the concrete and is the task which we have to achieve. In other words, therefore, this second assertion states that love between men (when it really achieves its proper and ultimate nature) is sustained by the supernatural infused and justifying grace of the Holy Spirit. If we have a more precise understanding of this self-bestowal of God in the sense in which it was more exactly defined in the first brief formula (in other words in the unity, the distinction and the mutual interconditioning of the self-bestowal of God in grace in the individual's own existence on the one hand, and the historical self-bestowal of God on the other, having its supreme point in the Incarnation of the divine Logos), then the statement that God has made himself the dimension in which it is possible to achieve a radical relationship of this kind between men includes also all that was said in the first brief formula and its interpretation with regard to the self-bestowal of God as constituting the essence of the Christian faith. We have only to reflect upon Mt. 25 to realize that it is certainly quite unnecessary from the outset to dispute the fact that in the radical love of neighbour as realized at the practical level the whole salvific relationship of man to God and to Christ is already implicitly present. And if anyone were to feel that what was lacking in this second statement of the sociological brief formula was an explicit statement of the reference to Jesus Christ in man and in his love of neighbour, then obviously we could reply to him explicitly: This self-bestowal of God upon man which sustains him in his love of neighbour has its supreme and eschatologically victorious point in history in Jesus Christ, and for this reason in the love of every other man Jesus Christ is loved at least anonymously.

The third assertion of this second brief formula states that a love of this kind, in which God is loved in our neighbour and our neighbour in God, has itself a dimension of intimacy at the level of personal existence, and a social dimension at the level of history which precisely corresponds to the twofold aspect of the self-bestowal of God inherent in it. Where this love achieves its supreme point, and that too in the unity of these two aspects, that which we call the Church is *de facto* present. For what is peculiar to the Church as distinct from other social groups consists precisely in the eschatologically indissoluble connection (not identity!) between truth-spirit-love on the one hand, and the historical and institutional manifestation of this bestowal of the Spirit as truth and love on the other.

A third brief formula,[12] which we can call the *futurologist* one runs as follows: Christianity consists in an attitude of open enquiry into the absolute future which wills to give itself as such in itself in an act of self-bestowal, and which in Jesus Christ has confirmed this will which it has with an eschatological irrevocability. It is the absolute future in this sense that is called God.

This briefest of all the formulae transposes the statement about the transcendentality of man in the first basic formula in that it interprets this transcendentality as a reference to the future as 'futuricity'. An absolutely

---

[12] For further elucidation reference may be made to the following studies: 'Christianity and the "New Man" ', *Theological Investigations* V (London and Baltimore, 1966), pp. 135–153; 'Marxist Utopia and the Christian Future of Man', *Theological Investigations* VI (London and Baltimore, 1969), pp. 59–68; 'A Fragmentary Aspect of a Theological Evaluation of the Concept of the Future', *Theological Investigations* VIII (London and New York, 1973), pp. 235–242; 'On the Theology of Hope', *ibid.*, pp. 242–260.

limitless transcendentality, therefore, *eo ipso* implies an enquiry into the future in the absolute, as distinct from indefinite, finite, and partial futures following one upon another. Concerning this future it is stated that it is not merely the ultimate and asymptotic goal towards which history is orientated, which, while it does indeed maintain this history in motion, will not itself be attained to as itself, but rather wills to give itself through its own act of self-bestowal. Now what is said about this self-bestowal of the absolute future which is still in process of being realized in history is what has already been said concerning the self-bestowal of God in the first brief formula, namely that this self-bestowal, which is obviously also and in all cases posited in the dimension of concrete individual existence, has a historical aspect and in this has achieved a stage of eschatological irrevocability in Jesus Christ.

There is no need to provide yet again any full exposition of the fact that in this basic principle of a divine self-bestowal upon the world which has been rendered eschatologically irrevocable in Jesus Christ that truth is already implicitly contained which is explicitly stated in the doctrine of the Trinity and in christology. Nor do we need to repeat at any length our exposition of the fact that in the experience of our orientation towards the absolute future, and that too in the mode in which this wills to bestow itself directly as itself, God is experienced, and moreover, the God of the supernatural order of grace. And this means that he is experienced as sheer mystery.

Inasmuch as Christianity consists in the adoration of the one and true God as opposed to all idols (taking these to signify the according of an absolute value to finite powers and dimensions in man) it is that attitude on man's part in which he maintains himself in openness to the absolute future and, inasmuch as this is, and continues to be, the absolute Mystery even in the consummation of this self-bestowal, Christianity consists in maintaining open the actual *question* which points to the absolute future.

These three brief formulae are certainly intended first and foremost as conceivable side by side with other possible basic formulae of the same kind, even supposing that such formulae have been conceived of at one quite specific level of conceptual abstraction. Nevertheless it is perhaps no mere theological word-play if we seek to understand these three formulae in their juxtaposition and interconnection as reflections and consequences of the Christian faith in the Trinity, or if we interpret them as the three approaches which are open to human experience, and by means of which an initial understanding can be achieved of the Trinity in its effects in the economy of salvation and, in the light of this, of the Trinity as immanent also.[13]

The first formula speaks of God in fact as the uncircumscribed point of reference of human transcendence. If we include in this conception the fact that in it the absolute and unoriginated 'principium inprincipiatum' of all conceivable reality is named, then, in a real sense the 'Father' of the Christian doctrine of the Trinity is named in expressing this incomprehensible and unoriginated point of reference of human transcendence. When in the second brief formula we say that the true scope of this is the idea of God in Jesus Christ as man making himself the dimension in which man can achieve a radical relationship with his fellow men, then in it we have named God made man, the 'Son'. The absolute future of man bestowing itself of its free and sovereign power over history which is God is, however, in a special sense the 'Spirit' of God, because it can be characterized as love, freedom, and a newness that constantly takes us by surprise.

Of course this triad of the brief formulae which we have mentioned should be conceived of still more precisely and clearly against their Trinitarian background, and it is not possible to do this here at any greater length. But at any rate we can say this much: a brief formula must on the one hand express the basic substance of the reality of the Christian faith in such a way that the most intelligible possible access to it is opened up at the level of man's experience in the concrete conditions of his existence, while on the other hand this basic substance can certainly be discovered in the idea of God turning to the world in the Trinitarian dimension of the economy of salvation. And if this is true then it is not from the outset difficult to show that there must be three basic types of such brief formulae, corresponding to the dogma of the Trinity. This does not exclude the fact that each of these basic types in turn can be very different from the others both in respect of the further distinctions which it contains and the difference of emphasis which it introduces into its content, and in respect of the due attention which it pays to the differences between these for whom a basic formula of this kind is destined.

[13] On this cf. the statement of the principles involved in the author's article, 'Remarks on the Dogmatic Treatise "De Trinitate" ', *Theological Investigations* IV, (London and Baltimore, 1966), pp. 77–102; and further the articles 'Trinity' and 'Trinity in Theology', *Sacramentum Mundi* 6 (New York and London, 1970), pp. 295–303 and 303–308.

PART THREE

Anthropology

11

THE SIN OF ADAM

THE most striking feature of the situation which exists today for an ecumenical discussion of 'the sin of Adam' is that neither on the Protestant nor on the Catholic side is there any theology on this theme which could be presented simply as *the* Protestant or *the* Catholic position. So far as the Protestant side is concerned this seems to me to be clear from the fact that here there is no general agreement as to the existence of any original sin. But on the Catholic side too the situation is not different.[1] It is true that here – at least in principle – the doctrinal definitions produced in the fifth session of the Council of Trent with regard to original sin are recognized as binding in character. But this still does not clarify the situation. In the first place since then questions have arisen bearing upon the theory of anthropological evolution, the creation of man, polygenism and monogenism. And on these the teaching authority of the Church has adopted certain definite, though provisional, positions to which due heed must be paid in any Catholic theology in dealing with the question which concerns us here also.[2] A further factor is that for the past few years even in Catholic theology attempts have been made to interpret the Catholic doctrine of original sin such that they appear all but contradictory to one another and to be opposed to the simple and literal sense of the Church's definitions. Furthermore so many questions have been raised for the Catholic doctrine of original sin in the light of the general

---

[1] An extensive account of the state of the discussion at the moment is provided by A. M. Dubarle, 'Le péché originel, recherches récentes et orientation nouvelle', *RSPT* 53 (1969), pp. 81–113. cf. also P. Schoonenberg, 'AT, NT und Erbsündenlehre', *TPQ* 117 (1969), pp. 115–124. In what follows we cannot enter any further into this point. This study reproduces a lecture which the author delivered in March, 1968 at a conference of ecumenical work at Paderborn.

[2] An account of these positions is given by J. Feiner, 'Der Ursprung des Menschen', *Mysterium Salutis* II (Einsiedeln, 1967), pp. 562–581; see also Z. Alszeghy, 'Development in the Doctrinal Formulations of the Church concerning the Theory of Evolution', *Concilium* 3 (1967) 6/13 (Church and World), pp. 14–17.

situation prevailing today in theology itself and in secular anthropology that a mere repetition of, and simple commentary upon the Catholic dogma of original sin would, taken by itself, in no sense constitute an answer. For this reason unless a certain attempt is made to answer these questions, at least on the individual's own account and on his personal responsibility, it is no longer so clear that even the official teaching of the Church on original sin can be adduced as a real and vital factor such that it is adequate to sustain a real faith. For this is never possible unless a confrontation is achieved between the content of this faith and the totality of the believer's own understanding of himself prevailing at any given time.

In this situation the only course still remaining open to the Catholic dogmatic theologian is to put forward his own understanding of the official Catholic teaching on original sin without claiming thereby that this particular understanding is obviously or unquestionably identical with that official teaching.[3] All that he will claim on behalf of his understanding of the question until the contrary is proved is that he has put forward an interpretation of the official teaching of the Church's faith with regard to the existence and nature of original sin which it is possible to hold within the Church; in other words that this personal understanding of his has been formulated in an attitude of unreserved obedience towards the teaching of the Church and that it remains as a point for discussion submitted to the Church's understanding of her faith as a whole. What we are asking, therefore, is whether in an interpretation of this kind the Church can recognize that it is her own understanding of her faith that is being reproduced. Whether the Church will react on the basis of her total understanding of her faith to this personal understanding of mine which I am submitting for her consideration, when she will do so, what form her reaction will take, and what its outcome will be – these are questions which still await an answer. For the time being it is sufficient that the dialogue to be maintained between the two sides should be a peaceable one. For the point to be decided in this dialogue is whether a personal understanding of the doctrine of original sin as put forward here is to be designated as 'Catholic'.

In a subject as extensive as this it is not possible to examine all the relevant factors, and for this reason there is much that must be put forward here in the form of a simple statement without any further arguments to justify it. And again it will not be possible here explicitly to define our

---

[3] For a better understanding of the author's personal position cf. his article, 'Original Sin', *Sacramentum Mundi* 4 (New York and London, 1969), pp. 328–334.

position with regard to other expressions of opinion on original sin which have been put forward from the Catholic side.

We shall proceed straightway to the question itself and put the question quite simply: What do we really mean when we speak of 'original sin'? We believe that this is the only way to arrive at a meaningful answer to the question of the 'sin of Adam', because the doctrine of original sin in us is the sole point at which the theological question of the 'sin of Adam' can be raised and answered – and answered moreover on grounds which we are just about to discuss. In terms of content both questions are one, a point which is already recognized and made clear in the combination of the two scholastic terms 'peccatum originale originans – peccatum originale originatum'. For us the sin of Adam is a theological datum only in virtue of the fact that *our* sinfulness, which we assert of ourselves, is a sinfulness that has been 'derived'.

I

Methodological Presuppositions

1. Our information about the 'fall of the first man' and the situation of perdition which it entails for all those descended from him has not come to us through an eye-witness account emanating precisely *from* that event in 'perdition' history. No such eye-witness account has been handed down to us either through a tradition deriving from that first man or as transmitted in the writings of the Old or New Testaments, nor has any such account been communicated to us by God as one of the parties concerned in the original event by any direct act of revelation such that it derives from no further source apart from God himself. On the contrary all protology, and so too the doctrine of original sin, is *ipso facto theology*, albeit a theology worked out in the writings of the New Testament (and the Old) themselves, and thereby guaranteed, so far as we are concerned, to be valid. In other words all protology comes to us as explicitated and deduced from a more original source, from a primary revelation. This more original starting-point, from which the doctrine of original sin is arrived at in a process of aetiological retrospection is man's awareness, as part of the basic Christian revelation, of the fact that he himself is a sinner who obtains forgiveness and salvation solely through Christ. Why and how a doctrine of original sin, and moreover one that is rightly understood, can be deduced from this – these are questions which cannot yet be raised at the present stage. Our first task must be to concentrate on

the starting-point and methods to be adopted in working out this doctrine, and to point out the formal characteristics of these.[4] This formal starting-point and these aetiological methods have this much at least to be said in their favour that *de facto* it is not until the New Testament, and in connection with the message of Christ, that a doctrine of original sin appears with the radical significance which the Church perceives in her understanding of it.[5] By contrast, in the Old Testament it has not properly speaking yet been evolved.[6] This heuristic principle is also to be recommended on the grounds that in fact *any* specific question in theology at all must enquire into the 'transcendental horizon' which it itself presupposes.[7] Thus it is only in terms of the particular 'transcendental horizon' involved here that we can understand what would otherwise be quite unintelligible, namely why original sin really applies in some sense to us ourselves, and is not reduced to the level of a mere fact of the past and one to which we can be quite indifferent. It can be stated quite in general that we understand the past and what derivation from the past means from the present and the fact that realities in the present are, of their nature, derived, and continue to be present as such. Thus we understand them by relating them as present and as experienced in this sense to their own origins in the past. It is true that the Catholic theologian cannot dispute the fact (even though this is a point that not all contemporary Catholic exegetes are still willing to admit as correct) that in Romans 5 scripture does contain a doctrine of original sin and, moreover, substantially that which (whether explicitly or implicitly) was subsequently defined by the Council of Trent.[8] But the Catholic theologian is not thereby prohibited from viewing even the

[4] On this K. Rahner, 'Grundsätzliche Überlegungen zur Anthropologie und Protologie im Rahmen der Theologie', *Mysterium Salutis* II (Einsiedeln, 1967), pp. 406–420, esp. 417 ff.

[5] For a summary on this cf. S. Lyonnet, 'Péché IV', *Supplément au Dictionnaire de la Bible* VII (Paris, 1966), 509–565.

[6] We cannot enter specifically into the contrary positions upheld on this point by H. Haag, *Biblische Schöpfungslehre und kirchliche Erbsündenlehre* (Stuttgart, 1966) and J. Scharbert, *Prolegomena eines Alttestamentlers zur Erbsündenlehre* (Freiburg, 1968). With regard to my personal controversy with Haag on his position I may refer to the number of the *Quaestiones Disputatae* referred to in n. 16.

[7] On the transcendental approach in theology cf. K. Rahner, 'Theology and Anthropology', *Theological Investigations* IX (London and New York, 1973), pp. 28–46, and *idem*, 'Transcendental Theology', *Sacramentum Mundi* 6 (New York and London, 1970), pp. 287–289. Also in the present volume the article entitled 'Reflections on Methodology in Theology', pp. 68–114.

[8] In the Council of Trent this passage is itself officially interpreted: DS 1512 and 1514.

teaching of Romans 5 as 'theology' in the sense defined, and so interpreting this teaching itself in terms of its own origins so as to establish more precisely its exact meaning and bearing. Nor is he forbidden to hold that a doctrine of original sin can be found in Romans 5 only if the passage concerned is read in the whole context of the Pauline doctrine of justification and the Pneuma. Nor yet is he bound to read into or read out of Romans 5 everything which has already been taught with regard to original sin by a traditional, but ultimately non-binding seminary theology or exegesis. For instance even to a Catholic it is a completely open question how we should interpret Romans 5:12d.[9]

2. Methodologically speaking it should probably be stated straightway at this initial stage that what is in question here is not, in the last analysis, the actual term 'original *sin*', but that an *additional* factor is a certain established ecclesiastical *terminology*, as it were of a disciplinary kind, and though this too is important and needs to be respected, it must be distinguished from the reality itself and the various ways in which it can be expressed. We have several reasons for saying this, and among them is the fact that the theology of Eastern Christianity (for this also has won an undisputed place for itself in contemporary Catholic theology, as has recently been recognized by the Second Vatican Council) for the most part avoids using the term 'sin' in this connection. But we must also bear in mind the following factors which are also vitally relevant: Even the traditional Catholic seminary theology explicitly teaches (and this is a point which has never been disputed by the teaching authority of the Church) that the terms 'sin' and 'sinfulness' as applied on the one hand to the condition which man owes to his descent from Adam, and on the other to the condition which is the outcome of his own personal decision to go against God, are used in a sense that is merely *analogous*.[10] This condition of man, therefore, in the first and second case must not be thought of as strictly one and the same, even though the same terms are used to describe it. For both conditions are induced in man by two different causes, exterior to the condition itself. Anyone who makes the opposite assumption, following an implication which might be drawn from the Church's teaching, and *then* disputes the existence of original sin, has not

[9] On this cf. also S. Lyonnet, 'Le sens de ἐφ ᾧ en Rom 5:12 et l'exégèse des Pères grecs', *Biblica* 36 (1955), pp. 436–457.
[10] cf. Patres Societatis Jesu Facultatum Theologicarum in Hispania Professores, *Sacrae Theologiae Summa* II (Madrid, 3rd ed. 1958), pp. 833 and 939–949 'Ergo ratio peccati est analogica, non univoca, cum diversa ratio voluntarietatis sit peccato personali ac originali' (*ibid.*, p. 949).

properly speaking thereby denied any dogmatic teaching of the Church. It would even be possible to imagine a situation (corresponding to an analogous instance which actually is *de facto* to be found in the linguistic usage of the Church) in which the Church actually forbade us to call the condition which we derive from Adam original *sin*, without thereby altering her own dogma. The reason for this is that all along there has been a danger of misinterpreting this word so as to suggest that it is through Adam and our descent from him that we have in the strict sense been constituted as sinners, whereas we are such and become such as a result of our own personal and inalienable decision, unique in each particular instance, to go against God.[11]

3. In presenting our interpretation of the doctrine of original sin we shall exclude the question of monogenism and polygenism,[12] i.e. we are of opinion that on a more exact interpretation of the Church's dogmatic teaching on original sin we do not have to hold that the theory of monogenism is contained in it either as a necessary premiss or as a direct doctrine. It is true that Pius XII declared in 'Humani Generis' that Catholic theologians were not free to uphold the theory of polygenism.[13] But in the first case even he did not declare that monogenism had either explicitly or implicitly the force of dogma, and secondly we may surely say that the development of Catholic theology since 'Humani Generis' has made such advances (advances that have been tolerated by the Church's *magisterium*) that the opinion that polygenism is not irreconcilable with the doctrine of original sin is no longer exposed to the danger of being censured by the authorities of the Church.[14]

When therefore we use the term 'Adam' in the course of the following arguments we mean humanity in that form in which it existed at the beginning of its own history, and from which all subsequent humanity originated, from which we are all descended. In saying this, however, we are abstracting from the question of whether this humanity in its original form consists in a single couple from the numerical point of view, or in a

[11] An interpretation of the doctrine of original sin from this point of view is to be found, for instance, in K. H. Schelkle, 'Schuld als Erbteil?' (Einsiedeln, 1969).

[12] A summarizing presentation of the problems entailed here is provided in the article 'Monogenism', *Sacramentum Mundi* 4 (London and New York, 1969), pp. 105–107.

[13] On this cf. the detailed interpretation in K. Rahner, 'Theological Reflexions on Monogenism', *Theological Investigations* I (London and Baltimore, 1961), pp. 229–296.

[14] cf. K. Rahner, 'Evolution and Original Sin', *Concilium* 3 (1967), 6/13 (Church and World), pp. 30–35.

'population' more widely extended in terms of space and time which emerged from the animal kingdom and in which the historical origins of the human race as a single entity are to be located. For the fact that we are leaving this particular question open certainly does not imply any belief that the doctrine of original sin is to be explained away in 'existentialist' terms in a doctrine which *merely* expresses something about every man, 'man as such', the Adam which we all are, without implying any further statement with regard to the fact that he has descended through a unique history from an origin that is genuine, concrete, and real.

4. In order to be able adequately to meet the claims that are made upon it a doctrine of original sin today should develop a formal philosophy and formal theology of the *beginning*,[15] because only on the basis of this can we achieve any understanding of the necessity, meaning and methods of that retrospective aetiology of which we have already spoken. Of course it is not possible to develop these here. But even so we may attempt a few indications of how it might be done as some poor substitute for this.

Man is a historical being, and it is a necessary law of his nature that he is conscious of himself as being such. Hence protology and eschatology, a statement of the fact that he has derived from the past and is orientated towards the future, necessarily belong to that understanding of himself in which he conceives of himself as given over to himself in the here and now and committed to himself in a present that belongs to him. Inasmuch as he is that being that can only exist in a state of co-existence with other men any such protology must, so far as he is concerned, always and necessarily be the protology of the beginning of *humanity*, and this because and to the extent that precisely *this* kind of beginning does not simply consist in what belongs to the past, and so at most still survives in historical records, but is rather that power which extends into his own present, controlling it and shaping it as the law governing his own emergence on the plane of existence. A further point entailed in the relationship between past and future as the powers presiding over the present is that it is in the light of the future that the past is revealed. The emergence of the future constitutes the growing revelation of the origins, even though this future is never simply the mere temporal explicitation of the past. The beginning also presides over the present in the further sense that it is that which has been withdrawn from it. For invariably we encounter ourselves as those who have already come to a free decision, and we never encounter ourselves at that original starting-point which there must once have been

[15] A more detailed analysis of this matter is to be found in A. Darlap, 'Anfang und Ende', *Sacramentum Mundi* I (Freiburg, 1967), pp. 138–145.

(if in fact it is right to make freedom responsible for itself) and which invariably we only have in that form, or lack of form, which it has acquired as a result of our freedom itself, though in this the two factors involved, that which belongs to the origins and that which we ourselves have done, can never be distinguished with complete clarity in any given case. This applies to the individual and to every community which has come to exist as a historical entity through the exercise of freedom. The beginning which has been withdrawn from our control (we might even call it the *Urgeschichte*) is constituted as now in force in virtue of that original stage which is prior to our own freedom and hidden from us, *and at the same time* in virtue of the event in which freedom was first exercised, which *per definitionem* is different in kind from the freedom which we can exercise now. For this latter kind of freedom is always exercised throughout in a situation which creaturely freedom, whether our own or another's, has already helped to shape, a situation which has rendered that which belongs to the origins withdrawn from us, so that we can no longer draw upon its nature to illumine our own acts, but are compelled, rather, to seek it in the future, pursuing protology in eschatology.

For our present modest purposes, however, the chief point in this formal theology of the beginnings is this: for an anthropology that is existential-ontological in character, and especially one that is theological, 'beginning' is from the outset not the first moment in a whole series of moments following one upon another, but rather the basis, of its very nature unique, on which the whole of history rests, a basis which, in virtue of the fact that it has been posited by God himself, and of the uniqueness of the free act which educed it from sheer ultimacy, is itself *sui generis*.

To anyone who does not recognize all this the doctrine of original sin must either appear as sheer mythology or else a rationalistic view of it will be taken in which, as *peccatum originale originans*, it will be assigned to the same level as, and regarded as the first in a whole series of, sinful acts of basically the same kind, each one of which, and so the first as well, has, as we recognize from our everyday experience, further consequences in that it leads on to other and later sinful acts. In truth, however, what we call original sin (considered as the sin 'of Adam') belongs to the initial constitution of that ultimate beginning which is withdrawn from us and never recurs, and the true nature of which is only gradually revealed in the light of the future which is Christ.

II

The Nature of Original Sin

In the light of the principles we have just mentioned, therefore, we shall attempt to provide a statement of the Catholic dogma of original sin.[16] It is claimed that in this statement this dogma will suffer no diminution, even though in the course of making it theological ideas will be used which perhaps are not universally accepted.[17] For it is inevitable that there should be some such, and it could be demonstrated that the same is true of *every* theological statement of the doctrine of original sin.

1. We shall be speaking, then, of that self-bestowal of God (who is of his nature holy) upon man in grace which *ipso facto* sanctifies him prior to any moral decision on man's own part, i.e. which sets him in the ambience of God in his holiness. Now this self-bestowal of God upon men (whether as offered or as accepted) is given by God to the whole of humanity (and to the individual man as a member of this) only in virtue of the fact that this humanity as a historical and derived reality (through 'generation', as the ancient formulations express it) draws its existence from Christ and is orientated to him. But this bestowal is not given to the individual man in virtue of the fact that he derives physically and historically from this human race, and in virtue of this derivation of his is a member of it. For the individual man his derivation from, and thereby his union with the single human race is neither the basis nor, in any direct sense, the medium of his justification and sanctification by the self-bestowal of the holy God in his Pneuma. We must repeat the terms we have used here: '*Basis and medium.*' A distinction has to be drawn between these two concepts because on a 'Scotist' conception of the relationship between supralapsarian and infralapsarian grace the will of God towards *Christ* was the basis for the sanctifying will of God towards mankind even prior to sin being committed. Now on this assumption the derivation of man from the single human race, insofar as it enters into the question at all of how grace is conferred on the individual man, enters into it at most as 'mediating' to him that grace which was 'Christian' all along, and so from the outset cannot constitute the basis for this grace. And

[16] On what follows cf. also K. H. Weger, *Theologie der Erbsünde* = Quaestiones Disputatae 44 (Freiburg, 1970), together with the excursus, 'Erbsünde und Monogenismus'.

[17] On the teaching of the Church herself cf. also P. Schoonenberg, 'Der Mensch in der Sünde', *Mysterium Salutis* II (Einsiedeln, 1967), esp. pp. 916–927.

precisely for this reason too derivation and descent must properly and explicitly be excluded as a medium. This derivation and descent do not enter into the question as the 'sacrament', the sign and the medium for grace.

2. But against this, according to the will of God and the intrinsic specification imparted to the human race by this in itself, the descent of the individual man from the single human race and its divinely ordained beginning *had* to be if not the basis, then at least the direct medium, in which that justifying holiness of man was communicated to him which is prior to his own personal existence, and therefore has the force of an existential modality. This is because this holiness was intended as a gift to, and claim upon, humanity as a whole by the Creator of mankind, who graciously willed to 'raise' it. This creation in view of grace, in which God created the spiritual order of nature, causing it to exist both in many individuals and in a single race as a prior condition for his divine self-bestowal, may have been conceived of by God (in the Scotist sense) all along from the very beginning in view of Christ as the supreme point in history and the point of eschatological irreversibility of this world as endowed with divine grace, and if this interpretation is correct, then even the supralapsarian grace of the 'original state' was a grace of *Christ*. But even supposing this to be the case, and indeed precisely on this view, descent from and union with the human race in this sense (as that which provides the origins of the individual) was capable of being, and should have been the medium in which this sanctifying grace was communicated to the individual man. Now it is not this if it remained merely at the level of a remote prior condition for this endowment with grace, though of course it would still always have been this also. To say that this descent and derivation are not the medium ('sacrament') in this sense is *contrary* to the original will of the Creator in his act of bestowing grace. The absence of that holiness which is an existential modality imparted by God's own holiness prior to the concrete conditions of individual existence, inasmuch as this was intended to be mediated through human descent but in fact is not so – this is rightly called a state of sinfulness, and it is this that is meant by original sin (peccatum originale originatum). On the basis of this principle the definitions of original sin given in the Council of Trent can be developed, although they do not have to be presented in the same way here. Likewise we shall not here be treating in any explicit way of what is traditionally expressed under the heading of concupiscence in the doctrine of original sin. This too should be accounted a legitimate approach because according to the Tridentine doctrine of

original sin concupiscence as such should not be viewed simply as that which gives original sin its proper nature as a state of sinfulness in the true sense.

3. In itself, then, the factor of human descent should have the function of providing the medium for this 'holiness' to be imparted to man. Now its failure to do this is only conceivable as the outcome of the guilt of those men who existed at the beginning of the human race and provided the origins of the rest. In this connection it makes no difference whether humanity itself is conceived of in terms of monogenism or polygenism, provided only that it is recognized as a real unity, something which is possible in any case and independently of the question of polygenism. At all events: the only possible reason for the non-existence of something which, according to God's will, should exist can be personal guilt. But since the guilty act at the moral and personal level is not that of the descendants themselves, and since obviously a personal act of this kind can neither be 'inherited by' others or 'accounted to' them, it follows that this guilt which constitutes the non-existence of that which, as we have said, should exist, is the guilt of that part of humanity from which the rest originated. This also serves to show in radical form the merely analogous character of original sin by comparison with an act of personal guilt and the state of guilt ensuing from this. This too is a point which cannot be expounded here at any length. That state of analogous guilt which is called original sin is not a projection of the personal state of guilt 'of Adam' to us, but is constituted by the absence of the holy Pneuma which, prior to any moral decision, sanctifies man interiorly when it is present, or would sanctify him if it were so, but the absence of which correspondingly, prior to any personal decision, constitutes an analogous state of guilt, seeing that this deficiency consists not merely in the fact that the holy Pneuma is not present, but implies a deficiency which is the opposite of the situation which *ought* to exist.

A few explanatory observations must be added on this point:

(a) It is necessary to postulate personal guilt at the beginning as such of the '*Urgeschichte*' in the theological sense, but in accordance with the manner in which, as we have seen, this beginning is radically withdrawn from us. Unless we postulate this we cannot conceive of a situation which ought not to be the case, a state which is contrary to the will of the Creator. But if original sin is not to be explained away in a rationalizing sense as consisting in the sum total of the personal sins committed by men in the course of history, if, in other words there is a state of sinfulness such that it is prior to the personal decision of any given individual, and such that the fact that it ought not to exist cannot simply be referred back to God (as though the very constitution of finite man as different from God were *eo ipso* and of itself to be identified with the constitution of the sinner as such by God himself), then this state of affairs which ought not to exist must be constituted by creaturely guilt at the 'beginning'.

(b) This personal guilt at the beginning of human history, regardless of how we may conceive of its subject in more precise terms, does not, however, constitute the state of guilt arising from original sin as though this were the extension and prolongation of the personal state of guilt inherent in the *peccatum originale originans* as subject. The effect of it, rather, is simply that the human descendants of this subject do not possess the state of sanctification by God's self-bestowal in Christ *precisely as descendants*.

(c) The deficiency which inhibits a state which 'ought to exist' inhibits sanctifying grace. It does this inasmuch as the state which ought to be, and to which this deficiency is opposed, is not that which, in accordance with the moral demands of God, should be brought about by the individual as such in his own capacity for free decision, and as a matter of personal duty. Rather this state which ought to be, and to which the deficiency of which we are speaking is opposed, is that which is constituted by the will of the *Creator* as such in his will to endow humanity with grace.

It is what has been expressed under the heading (b) and (c) that constitutes the merely analogous character of original sin as opposed to a personal state of guilt which is identical with the personal act, and which is directly opposed to the moral demands which God makes upon the free individual as such. The other differences entailed in the merely analogous connection between original sin and personal sin derive from these two basic factors.

(d) It follows from what has been said that the concept of original sin has nothing to do with that of a 'collective guilt'. For what is posited in the term 'collective guilt', to the extent that it is not simply the final sum total of the personal guilt of many individuals, is that the personal guilt of a particular individual or individuals is as such transmitted to others. Now whether or not such an idea is conceivable at all, it has in any case nothing to do with the idea of original sin.

(e) A further point which must not be overlooked is the following: In the concrete order of salvation in Christ (whether we interpret this in an infralapsarian or a Scotist and supralapsarian sense) 'original sin' is always to be understood as a dialectical element in counterpoint to *that* effective will of God to save men which, on account of Christ, always imparts that sanctification through Christ (at least as 'offered') which was not imparted through descent from 'Adam'. Original sin and grace, therefore, to the extent that both these realities are prior to the personal decision of man, do not, properly speaking, follow one upon another in a temporal succession, but rather both together imply a single dialectical *'situation'*[18] of man (as a being endowed with freedom) to the extent that a specification is imparted to him both by the 'beginning' (that which provides the origins of mankind) and by Christ as the 'end' and 'goal'. Thereby he is placed in a situation in which he has to decide in the concrete conditions of his personal existence which of two factors he will take as the freely chosen basis for his actions: either the factor of his descent from the beginnings of humanity, or his orientation towards the future in Christ (the first of these is that state of sin spoken of in Romans 5 : 12d, while the second is the faith which justifies).

(f) If original sin is to be interpreted and understood in the sense explained here – in other words as a datum of New Testament theology, and not merely as revelation in its most basic form (for in this form it is to be found in Romans 5 alone, if at all) – there is one point that must be recognized. This is that descent from 'Adam' was in itself intended according to the will of God as Creator to be the 'medium' of grace. Now if we are asked how we know this, then we must point to two factors:

i. It is the solidarity of mankind in salvation and saving history (which is to be conceived of as all-embracing, and which after all is a motif that runs through the whole of scripture) that constitutes the basic assumption underlying the doctrine of the universality of salvation as one and the same for all, the doctrine of the redemption of all through Christ, of the Body of Christ, the Church, and of the radical importance of love of neighbour, which is something more than the fulfilment of any one particular commandment. For after all solidarity in salvation and saving history surely implies in itself that man is intended to receive salvation in virtue of the fact that he is a member of this human race.

ii. In scripture the fact that Christ is the originator of salvation is always viewed in its application to man precisely as a *sinner*, and not merely to man as one to whom the grace of God as imparting a share in the divine nature is not due. Moreover, while this sinfulness is conceived of

[18] This concept is also used by P. Schoonenberg. cf. *ibid.*, pp. 928 ff., and *idem*, *Theologie der Sünde* (Einsiedeln, 1966).

Admittedly a question which should be raised in this connection is how the existentiality of such a situation is to be established metaphysically.

primarily as personal, still its *universality* is surely not to be conceived of as absolutely radical and ultimate unless we recognize a certain sinfulness which is prior to the personal decision of the individual as such, so that in this personal decision this prior state of sinfulness is made manifest by a process of ratification. Unless we assumed the existence of a sinfulness of this kind we would have to concede that each individual man in the history of individual freedom takes as his starting-point a situation which, after all, is, from the point of view of salvation, precisely neutral, and then we would no longer be able to conceive in any effective or real sense of how the *universality* of personal sinfulness comes to exist. Nor can it be said that this answer merely transfers the problem from the many individuals to the individual or individuals at the beginning of humanity. For what we are concerned with here is not to maintain that the sinful decision taken at the personal level at the beginning is as such extended to all others and *so* constitutes a universality of pre-personal sinfulness. This pre-personal and dialectically universal sinfulness is constituted only by the following facts and in the following way:

By reason of the sin which took place in the *Urgeschichte* at the beginning mankind as such is incapable of acting as the mediator of grace, and it is precisely in this way that a universal sinfulness comes to exist which is *sui generis* in character. The personal sin at the beginning creates a *situation* for all which should not exist, and it is as arising from, and concomitant with this situation that that reality is simply given which we call original sin, taking this term in its correct sense.

(g) From what has been said it will surely also be clear that the doctrine of original sin is ultimately contained as a simple implication in the truth that all of us as sinners have been redeemed by Christ, and must be redeemed by him. But this redemption consists not merely in some kind of liberation from guilt, but in that justifying sanctification in which God imparts his own holiness in his holy Pneuma, and that in this whole saving event the individual is always involved in virtue of the fact that he is also a member of the human race as one, a unity which Christ both presupposes and constitutes at the same time.

4. Finally we must speak explicitly once more of the 'sin of Adam', in other words of *peccatum originale originans* as distinct from original sin, *peccatum originale originatum*, which is a specification that applies to *us*. Thus by way of résumé we can state the following:

(a) That beginning of the single human race which is withdrawn from our view and control is characterized by the fact that in it a state of original freedom existed, i.e. one such that the situation in which it existed was still unspecified by any decision of human freedom (whether that of the individual himself, or that of others).

Logically speaking, this statement is self-explanatory, and moreover it does not contradict the empirical ideas which we have evolved today of 'early' man, because this situation of freedom exists independently and is capable of realization regardless of which particular category of material in this world was available to this freedom as the medium in which it could be exercised, and how far this original freedom was, or could be, consciously *reflected* upon, and inherent in a subject capable of reflecting upon himself.

(b) The subject of such a free decision at the beginning can freely be conceived of as a 'group'. For even a humanity conceived of as polygenist in origin constitutes a real unity, however varied the aspects which it displays, and as a humanity of the 'beginnings' is distinguished from a '*humanitas originata*' by the ultimacy and originality of its freedom.

(c) The decision of this group is conceivable as a decision which all the members of this group take as individuals, since in fact, after all, these would be relatively few in number. In the light of the interpretation of the role of decision at the beginning in the factor of *peccatum originale*, however, it is also perfectly possible that this decision is that of one individual, assuming here that according to God's will the *humanitas originans* was intended to mediate grace only if it had continued as a *whole* and wholly sinless through its decision. An interpretation more or less on the following lines is perfectly conceivable: If on the one hand man is inevitably personal *and* communicative at the same time, and both aspects mutually condition one another, and if further the *humanitas originans* on any showing constitutes a unity, and as such is to be distinguished from the *humanitas originata*, and if by its initial free personal decisions it specifies the existential situation of the *humanitas originata* in manifold ways, then it is perfectly conceivable that the decision of *one individual within* this unity (and one who thereby plays his part in specifying this *humanitas originans*) can actually fulfil the function of this *humanitas originans* as mediating grace.

(d) Since the 'polygenist' view of the origins of mankind has to be adopted, at any rate to the extent that at least two of its members are not derived from a single human nature, it surely has no theological relevance, but rather belongs to the realm of imagery and modes of expression, when scripture (in general) regards 'Adam', as opposed to 'Eve', as the bearer of *peccatum originale originans*. Again the Adam-Christ parallel does not compel us to take the opposite view, since the parallelism (one-all) also remains in force if the *humanitas originans* is interpreted as *one* and seen as distinct from the *humanitas originata*.

(e) This historical derivation of our state of sin, and the difference between 'imitatio' and 'propagatio' in the Catholic doctrine of original sin, must be maintained. This is possible, since humanity has a history. The individual understands himself only when he apprehends himself as deriving from a real history. The decision of the individual constantly plays its part in specifying, in the most varied ways, the situation of freedom which applies to all others. Man as such (the state of being man, humanity in process of achieving itself) first begins at the point at which freedom is exercised. Humanity is also one in its saving history. If we consider these simple principles, which contain no mythological implications, then the statement that humanity, or real membership of it, does not imply any mediation of divine grace to an individual member of this humanity because at the beginnings, and from the beginnings onwards it was a sinful humanity, is not mythological either. This statement, however, properly speaking contains everything which is stated in the doctrine of original sin, and hence too the doctrine of original sin is no mythologem. Such a mythologem would be present if this doctrine were to imply that the subjective and personal guilt of one or a few individuals as such were projected onto their descendants. But this is far from being the content of the dogma of original sin. This implies the existence of a real guilt at the beginnings, but only as the basis for a primitive deficiency of the sanctifying grace of God, and that, moreover, only *to the extent that* humanity is descended from this beginning. The existence of a real sin at the beginning, however, is no myth, however important it is for us not to portray this sin to ourselves as a concrete phenomenon. If it were a myth, then ultimately and logically speaking, the same would absolutely have to be asserted of the history of human freedom. This is a reality which we experience.

5. It must be conceded that the classic doctrine of original sin contains many further aspects besides those which have been discussed here, above all the question of the existence and loss of the so-called preternatural gifts of the original state, of freedom from concupiscence and from being delivered up to death. But this is a question which cannot be taken as a subject for theological consideration any further here.

I2

ON THE ENCYCLICAL 'HUMANAE VITAE'

O N the twenty-fifth of July 1968 Paul VI published his long-awaited encyclical, 'Humanae Vitae' on the right principles governing the procreation of new life.[1] This encyclical had been announced years before. It had been prepared for, in a manner which had not previously been usual, by the work of a commission, and its publication had been repeatedly postponed. In spite of this it provoked the greatest surprise among Catholics and in the non-Catholic world. Side by side with the measure of agreement which it received, and which certainly must not be under-estimated, it also met with worldwide contradiction. Now certainly this is partly to be explained by the simple fact that the supreme authority of a Church comprising millions of believers had pronounced on a question affecting the personal lives of countless individuals. Apart from this the subject-matter of this question is 'of interest' to many more than merely the Catholic believers. But this alone is not sufficient to explain the opposition which it provoked. This is to some extent understandable when one considers that on the question treated of in the encyclical married Catholics had already arrived at a definite opinion (regardless of which this was), and had applied this in the practice of their lives. Furthermore, among moral theologians too, at least for some considerable time, there had no longer been any unanimity of opinion on this question, and it was becoming ever clearer that the practical importance of the question itself had grown immeasurably as a result of the 'population explosion'. This opposition, especially as found even in the Catholic Church herself, is a fact, and it is with this fact that we shall chiefly be concerned in the considerations which follow.

[1] *AAS* 60 (1968), pp. 481–518.

I. Preliminary Observations

Before we go on to treat more directly of the problem itself, certain preliminary observations have to be made which are necessary for a right understanding of what follows.

A Catholic must take this encyclical seriously. Certainly we shall have to state more precisely and to define what this in fact implies in the present context. But the encyclical itself must be taken seriously. It is the pronouncement of a pope. It is certainly the outcome of mature thought and preparation. In the Catholic Church it has a notable doctrinal tradition behind it. Under these circumstances it is meaningless and contrary to the seriousness with which the question should be taken, and the respect due to the authority of the pope, if our reactions to the encyclical simply take the form of short-sighted emotionalism; if all we can do is to produce crude and distorted summaries of its contents, and to ascribe to the pope motives which are designed to render his pronouncements unworthy of belief from the outset. Anyone who from the outset maintains his own opinion as indisputable without any self-criticism, anyone who believes that a more recent idea is *a priori* and certainly more correct than an earlier one, anyone who simply argues on the basis of the undesirable practical consequences of the papal pronouncement, is thinking pragmatically and so even from his initial standpoint evading the question of truth. And anyone who does this cannot, as a Catholic, do justice to the encyclical.

Now what we shall be treating of in these considerations of ours is not that which constitutes the heart and centre of the papal encyclical. In other words we shall not be investigating the question of whether and why objectively speaking it is immoral, or alternatively need not necessarily be so, for a man deliberately, and as his own free personal act, to exclude the possibility of new life coming to be as a result of an individual married act. Here let us simply confine ourselves to noticing in this connection that on any sound view of the basic principles involved it is a crude simplication of the papal teaching to represent it as an absolute prohibition, even at the theoretical level, of any deliberate control of the birthrate, whereas in reality what the encyclical is concerned with is to reject *certain specific methods* of such birth control. In this connection, however, it must be admitted that for the normal and average reader of the encyclical it is even so not clear how the control of the birthrate which is conceded to be necessary can *de facto* effectively be achieved in the concrete conditions which prevail at the social and individual levels without applying the very methods which have been rejected.

Here, therefore, we shall not be treating directly either of the material problem in itself or of the question of truth which it involves, even though these constitute the heart and centre of the encyclical. It would be impossible to carry out such an undertaking within the limits of a single brief article. In any case we would have to treat of the basic assumptions underlying the papal position: the nature of the natural law, its 'immutability' and historical development, the competence of the teaching authority of the Church in relation to this natural law, the relationship between the natural law and revelation, what constitutes the essence of 'human nature', how we can recognize this, the relationship which the person as a free agent bears to the reality which is already there for him to act upon (the reality called 'nature'), man's capacities in relation to that 'nature' which he himself has, his powers to shape and direct himself, and how far he is subject in this to certain moral restrictions. All these prior factors, which have had an influence on the papal decision, are so difficult, and matters of such widespread controversy among contemporary Catholic theologians, and, moreover, even in the encyclical itself so fleetingly indicated, that it is impossible, within the limits of a brief article, to treat of these factors which are the premises of the papal thesis even though in themselves they do need to be discussed. The same applies to the meaning to be attached to the papal position itself, and the justification for this. For from this point of view we should have to treat of the question of whether, and on what grounds, any given individual married act in the concrete, even taken in itself as individual, and independently of married life as a whole, is subject to an unequivocal moral judgement. It must be remembered that the individual married act has a twofold importance: it is conducive to married love and at the same time it is an act from which new life may possibly be generated. In view of this we would have to treat of the question of why *every single* married act must be such that it has both these significances together. A further point which we should have to discuss relates to the fact that 'nature' itself allows us to take these two aspects apart from one another and to take either one of them as our motive for the act. Moreover even according to the encyclical itself this is a state of affairs which can deliberately be taken advantage of in regulating births. The point which we should have to discuss in this connection, therefore, would be why *man himself*, under certain specific provisos, cannot separate the two aspects in the married act in any *individual* exercise of it, so long as this continues to be accorded its proper place within the totality of a married life which remains in principle willing to propagate new life. This question becomes still more acute when we consider that after all the power freely to shape and direct himself inherent in man himself, and distinguishing him from animals, is itself in turn an intrinsic part of 'human nature', so that there can be no question of this power of self-manipulation through his own 'nature' being *in principle* conceded to man as a matter of *morality*. The only question can be, rather, whether in this specific instance the moral boundaries governing such self-manipulation are or are not overstepped. In all respects we shall surely have to say that on these questions a specific position has indeed been adopted, but this is merely stated rather than explained or proved in any effective sense. It becomes clear in the encyclical itself that the real and primary reason for adhering to this position is the need that is felt to hold firm to the traditional teaching of Pius XI and Pius XII. This fact certainly carries a not inconsiderable theological weight, the more so since in individual moral questions a certain global 'instinct' can be right even when it is incapable of being explicitated to the utmost at the level of rational theory and speculation. Yet in view of the fact that *according to the encyclical itself* what is in question here is not simply a divine revelation of a moral norm, but rather a principle of the 'natural law', it would have been desirable for the material grounds for holding the papal thesis to have been justified by more precise arguments. But, as has been said, these are all questions which cannot be treated of here.

While therefore we are setting aside that which constitutes the true essence of the question here, still in doing so we must not overlook or treat as of no importance that which is held among Catholics as a matter of common conviction even though not all of them will give their interior agreement to the papal position or apply it in practice in their lives. After all the encyclical does give expression to a conviction that is held in common by all Catholics (though by comparison with the basic outlooks and practices of non-Christians it is far from being simply a self-evident truism!), namely that sexual life is subject to moral laws which themselves derive from the very nature of the realities involved, and which are designed to ensure that human happiness can be achieved in sexual life, the conviction, moreover, that under certain circumstances it is necessary both for the individual and for society to control the birthrate. Again this is something that is also subject to moral laws stemming from the very nature of marriage itself. And a further conviction held by all Catholics and expressed in the encyclical is that hedonism and moral libertinism in sexual matters lead not to a liberation of man from oppressive taboos but ultimately to a de-humanization and to unhappiness. If we want to arrive at a correct evaluation of the encyclical, this general Christian conviction must be clearly recognized. And there are really no apparent grounds for supposing that in the present age it is superfluous to speak of this universally held Christian position or to uphold it in public in the secular sphere even though in doing so we must guard against the danger of unduly blackening the outlook of secular society today in the sphere of sexual morality. A further point is that the encyclical rightly recognizes the dangers that would be entailed if the state were allowed to act in a totalitarian way by claiming exclusive rights over the practice of birth control. Here there are dangers which must really be taken seriously even though we may hold the opinion that the state cannot simply and in every respect leave it to the individual as such to cope with the problem of the population explosion, and even though in this connection the encyclical remains too much at the level of the general, the abstract, and the imprecise. What we shall be concerned with in these considerations of ours, therefore, is the simple fact that even within the Catholic Church herself the encyclical has not met with any unanimous agreement either in theory or in practice. And surely the fact that this is so – regardless of whether we regard it as normal or as extremely regrettable – is beyond all question. The very way in which the Church's members have reacted to the encyclical up to now is in itself enough to demonstrate this point, and in this connection it makes no difference, ultimately speaking, whether this reaction is the same in all countries, or which individuals, groups and official bodies in the Church have been responsible for it. This fact in itself and as such constitutes a theological problem, and moreover this is particularly true in view of the fact that in this case the reaction in the form of opposition is far greater, far swifter, far more decided and far more vocal in the public life of the Church than has been the case on earlier occasions of doctrinal pronouncements by the popes. What then is to be said at the *theological* level with regard to this opposition which the encyclical is meeting with and will continue to meet with in the manner we have described? This is the sole question with which we shall be concerned here.

II. The Encyclical as a Reformable Statement of Doctrine

This encyclical is not a papal definition ('*ex cathedra*') of the moral norms which the Pope lays down with regard to the 'inadmissibility' of any 'artificial' prevention of the possibility of procreation in the individual married act. In itself and as it stands this is a truism. Its real significance and implications may initially be pointed out by means of an extensive quotation from the Doctrinal Letter published by the German bishops in 1967, which will then be explained in greater detail.[2]

'We are here concerned with the presence or possibility of errors in those statements of doctrine which, though promulgated by the Church, do not have the force of definitions, and which themselves in turn can vary very greatly in their degree of binding force. On this question we must begin by recognizing soberly and firmly that it is a rule of human life quite in general that it must always be lived (as conscientiously as possible) in accordance with tenets which, while on the one hand they are not recognized as absolutely certain at the theoretical level, must neverthe-less be respected as valid norms for thinking and acting (here and now), because provisionally at least they are the best that can be found. Every individual is aware of this from the experience of his own life in the concrete. Every doctor in his diagnoses, every statesman in the judge-ments he has to make from his particular situation in politics, and in the

[2] The study which follows was written immediately after the Encyclical had appeared. Since in the meantime a very intense discussion has been initiated on this subject further reference may here be made to the following works, even though, in the nature of the case, it is impossible at this point to provide any full account of our position in relation to them. cf. F. E. v. Gagern, *Geburtenregelung und Gewissensent-scheid. Die bekanntgewordenen Dokumente der päpstlichen Ehekommission* (Munich, 1967); F. Greiner, 'Nach "Humanae vitae" ', *Hochland* 60 (1967/68), pp. 681–686; F. Boekle and C. Holenstein (edd.). *Die Enzyklika in der Diskussion* (Zürich, 1968); B. Häring, *Krise um 'Humanea Vitae'* (Bergen-Enkheim, 1968); D. v. Hildebrand, *Die Enzyklika 'Humanea vitae' – ein Zeichen des Widerspruchs* (Regensburg, 1968); G. Martelet, 'Pour mieux comprendre l'encyclique "Humanae vitae" ', *NRT* 90 (1968), pp. 897–917, 1009–1063 (On this cf. A. Winter, 'Neues Licht auf "Humanae vitae"?', *StdZ* 183 (1969), pp. 206–210): *Humanae vitae oder die Freiheit des Gewissens* edited by members of the 'Humanea vitae' action group of Bochum University of the Ruhr (Olten, 1968); K. Rahner, 'Im Beichtstuhl nach der Pille fragen? Spiegel-gespräch über die Enzyklika zur Geburtenregelung', *Der Spiegel* 22 (1968), No. 39 (23.9.1968), pp. 166–176; K. Rahner, Cardinal Renard, B. Haering, *A propos de l'encyclique 'Humanae vitae'* (Paris, 1968); F. Oertel ed., *Erstes Echo auf 'Humanae vitae'. Dokumentation wichtiger Stellungnahmen zur umstrittenen Enzyklika über die Geburtenkontrolle* (Essen, 1968); 'Schreiben der deutschen Bischöfe zu "Humanae vitae" ', *Herder Korrespondenz* 22 (1968), pp. 484–487; 'Stellungnahmen zur Enzyk-lika "Humanae vitae" vom 25. Juli 1968', *Diakonia* 3 (1968), pp. 300–312; W. Wickler, 'Das Missverständnis der Natur des ehelichen Aktes in der Moraltheologie', *Stimmen der Zeit* 182 (1968), pp. 289–303; A. Antweiler, *Ehe und Geburtenrege-lung* (Munich, 1969); A. Auer, 'Nach dem Erscheinen der Enzyklika "Humanae vitae" ', *TQ* 149 (1969), pp. 75–85; F. Boeckle, *Freiheit und Bindung* (Kevelaer, 1969); A. Günthor, *Kommentar zur Enzyklika 'Humanae vitae'* (Freiburg, 1969); E. Hamel, 'Conferentiae episcopales et encyclica "Humanae vitae" ', *Periodica* 58 (1969), pp. 243–349; J. Noonan, *Empfängnisverhütung* (Mainz, 1969).

decisions which have to be taken on the basis of these judgements, is aware of this fact. The Church too, in her doctrine and practice, cannot always or in every case allow herself to be confronted with the dilemma either of arriving at a doctrinal decision of an ultimately binding nature, or simply remaining silent and leaving everything to the individual, allowing him to hold any opinion he likes. In order to guard the true and ultimate substance of the faith she must, even at the risk of including some error of detail, provide explicit directions in matters of doctrine such that these have a definite degree of binding force even though, if they do not constitute any definition of the faith, they do have a certain provisional character even to the point of possibly including some error. Otherwise she cannot possibly proclaim her faith, interpret it, or apply it to the fresh situation which arises in the individual's life in such a way that it shall be an effective force in determining the course of life to be pursued. In such a case the position in which the individual Christian stands in relation to the Church is first and foremost an analogous one in the sense that as an individual he recognizes that he is bound to accept the decision of the specialist even though he knows that this is not infallible.

'In any case there can be no place in catechetics for an opinion opposed to the provisional pronouncements of the Church in matters of doctrine, even though it is right, under certain circumstances, to instruct the faithful as to the nature of, and the limited degree of weight to be attached to provisional doctrinal decisions of this kind. This is a point on which we have already spoken. Anyone who believes that he can retain his own private opinion, and that he is already even now in possession of that better insight which the Church will achieve in the future must take stock of himself in an attitude of sober self-criticism, and ask himself before God and his own conscience whether he has the necessary breadth and depths of specialized theological knowledge to be able to deviate from the current teaching of the official Church in his private theory and practice. Such a case is in principle conceivable. But subjective presumptuousness and over-hasty opinionatedness will have to answer before the judgement of God.

'It pertains to the right attitude of a Catholic towards his faith seriously to strive to attach its due and positive value even to a provisional doctrinal pronouncement of the Church, and to make it his own. The position here is similar to that in the secular sphere, for here too far-reaching decisions have to be taken on the basis of fallible insights arrived at as conscientiously as possible by others. So too in the sphere of the Church, no-one need feel ashamed or diminished in his human dignity when he commits himself in his own mind to the Church's doctrine, even in those instances in which it cannot from the outset be accounted as definitive. It is possible that in specific instances the development of doctrine in the Church advances too slowly. But even in arriving at a judgement of this kind it is necessary to be prudent and reserved. For in a Church composed of individuals subject to the conditions of history, time is needed to achieve such developments in doctrine, since they cannot proceed more swiftly than the necessity of preserving the substance of the faith without loss allows.

'We do not need to fear that in adopting the attitude we have described towards the Church and her pronouncements we shall be refusing to meet the claims of our own times. Often enough the serious questions which are raised by our own times, and which we have to answer on the basis of our faith, make it necessary for us to re-think the truths of our faith anew. In this it is perfectly possible for fresh shifts of emphasis to be introduced. But this is not to call the faith itself in question. It contributes, rather, to a deeper apprehension of the truths of divine revelation and of the Church's doctrine. For we are firmly convinced, and we see that experience confirms us in this, that we have no need either to deny any truth for the sake of the Catholic faith, nor to deny the Catholic faith for the sake of any truth, provided only that we understand this faith in the spirit of the Church, and seek always to achieve a still deeper apprehension of it.'[3]

The first point to be made is that the papal encyclical clearly falls under the heading of the kind of doctrinal pronouncements of the Church which the bishops refer to in their doctrinal letter, namely doctrinal pronouncements which are authentic but non-definitorial in character, and so at least in principle susceptible of revision. At no point in the encyclical is any formulation to be found which could give rise to the impression that it is an *ex cathedra* definition that is being treated of. In this respect, indeed, it is possible to say that the formulations are actually more cautiously worded than, for instance, Pius XI's pronouncements in '*Casti Connubii*'. Now it is clear in the very nature of the case, besides being explicitly stated as a norm in canon law, that an official statement of doctrine constitutes an *ex cathedra* decision only if this force is *explicitly* attached to it (even though this can be done in very different ways). In accordance with the

---

[3] *Schreiben der deutschen Bischöfe an alle die von der Kirche mit der Glaubensver-kündigung beaufratgt sind* (Treves, 2nd ed., 1968), pp. 12–14.

norms laid down in the Doctrinal Letter of the German bishops which we have cited, therefore, the following distinctions, both formal and material, can be adduced with regard to the *binding force* of the encyclical.

A doctrinal statement by the Pope in which no definition is presented is in principle a teaching that can be revised. Of course it cannot straightway be concluded from this that such a document has no importance for the instruction, understanding and formation of conscience of an individual Catholic. On the contrary, so long as the Catholic Christian does not radically reject the official teaching authority of the Church (and thereby ceases to be a Catholic) this document is in principle and from the outset a declaration which should cause him to maintain a critical attitude with regard to himself and his personal understanding in such a way that he must also seriously take into account the fact that a decision of this sort has been arrived at by the Church's authorities under the guidance of the Spirit and with the utmost conscientiousness. For this reason it must be considered right, even when it contradicts one's own subjective opinion, which is not in any true sense protected from error from the outset. A Catholic who has no understanding of what is signified by a 'presumption' of this kind must incur the reproach that he is in love with his own subjective opinion in a way that is childish and emotional, and that he is not bringing to bear that attitude of self-criticism which we must bring to bear with regard to our own opinions, however deeply rooted they may be, even though these appear to represent the voice of our own 'conscience'. Such a Catholic as this is so enclosed within an attitude of retarded individualism that he fails to understand the extent to which any 'ideological' convictions, or convictions affecting mankind as a whole, invariably have some connection with an 'institution'. And again he is enormously under-estimating the fact that as a Catholic a man must have grounds which are really proved and tested to the last detail, and have really been reflected upon in a spirit of self-criticism in order to be able conscientiously to disassociate himself from an official declaration of doctrine on the part of the Church. What still remains to be said over and above this with regard to the importance of taking an official declaration of doctrine positively and seriously will be set forth at a later stage.

This is one aspect of the attitude which a Catholic ought to have towards an official declaration of doctrine on the part of his Church. The other aspect, however, can be formulated as follows. A non-definitorial declaration of this kind really is in principle susceptible of revision, and the Catholic or the theologian has in principle the right, indeed the duty, to take cognizance of this fact. To say that an official declaration of doctrine can in principle be revised does not of course *ipso facto* imply the presumption that one who recognizes this fact is convinced that the specific official doctrinal declaration involved is actually *de facto* false, inadequate, or in need of revision. One the contrary it is the opposite presumption and approach that is intended, but then only and precisely as a *presumption* which in a specific instance may later have to yield to the superior conviction, conscientiously arrived at in the theory and practice of an individual, that the opposite position to that adopted in the official teaching is correct. Whether in the particular case with which we are concerned in the *concrete* (even abstracting from any ultimate decision on the question of truth with regard to the papal declaration) there are *de facto* grounds which make it morally justifiable to disagree with this declaration – this is a point which we shall have to discuss later. First let us simply draw attention to the fact that (even if we abstract from all the 'classic' instances of papal declarations of doctrine which have subsequently been revised, such as those of Vigilius, Honorius, many statements contained in the Bull 'Exsurge Domine' of Leo X, and in several of the papal pronouncements with regard to the moral justification of usury etc.) there actually have been in very recent times papal declarations of doctrine to which the same weight has been attached as to this encyclical, yet which have not merely been susceptible of revisious 'in theory', but which have, whether tacitly or explicitly, actually been revised. We may for instance recall the doctrinal pronouncements of Gregory XVI and Pius IX with regard to a liberal and democratic social order which would certainly not be formulated in this way by any pope today. We may recall many of the pronouncements in the field of exegesis and biblical theology put forward against Modernism at the beginning of this century, and which today are almost totally out of date. From this alone it can be concluded that the Catholic has the right and the duty to take into account the fact that an official pronouncement by the Church on doctrinal matters so long as it does not imply any definition, is susceptible of revision. These examples also show, if we realize their full significance in the concrete, that to 'allow for' the possibility of such revision is not in principle only permissible once such a revision actually has taken place quite in general in the Church. For in that case such revision would never have been undertaken at all, and at the same time it cannot be assumed that in practice such revisions only come to be made in the first place as a result of the pronouncements concerned actually having been contradicted by individuals who, from the point of view of conscience, were un-Catholic in their thinking and acting.

However in view of the formal authority of this Encyclical, as also with regard to the fact that it is in principle capable of being revised, something further must be said more from the point of view of its actual *content*. For even in respect of the basic norms expressed in it this actual content in itself is not so clear-cut in its message as might appear at first sight. And this also has its significance for the question of its formal authority. What we mean by this can only be indicated quite briefly here. For even if, in all simplicity, we assume the correctness of the norm laid down by the Pope, it is still always possible to raise the question of *what*, in more precise terms, this signifies. After all it is conceivable, in principle at least, that what is being formulated here is an 'ideal norm' such that it is not *ipso facto* clear that it can effectively be 'realized' in all its moral obligations in every situation in human life, or by every individual and every social group. For instance even at the time of the Old Testament patriarchs monogamy was a moral norm which derived in the most basic sense from the nature of man and of marriage itself. Yet in the concrete situation in terms of human living and at the stage of development of human 'nature' of that time, neither the individual nor the social group concerned was capable of putting it into practice to a sufficient extent for an obligation to monogamy actually to be imposed in the concrete circumstances prevailing at that time and in that area. Could it not be conceivable that something similar is the case with regard to the basic norm of the encyclical? It is not *ipso facto* against such a parallel to say that the norm in the encyclical has been explicitly formulated and promulgated in a manner which is quite different from the other case. For even in other cases too we recognize a certain 'delayed action' in the developing recognition of moral norms as this emerges among specific peoples, civilizations and human groups and comes to be apprehended as morally binding in practice. And we can still see the effects of this 'delayed action' with regard to a moral norm which was actually proclaimed during the age of Christianity. Here we have only been able to indicate the fact that the recognition of moral principles has a historical development of its own. But in the light of this it is conceivable, at least in principle, that even in the case of a moral norm that has been officially proclaimed and is 'ex hypothesi' correct, it may only be at some subsequent point within a given age or a given society taken as a whole that its content really comes effectively to be understood in such a way that it has the force of a moral obligation in actual concrete fact. In that case the force which such a norm carries already in the present concrete circumstances consists in the obligation to strive for that degree of apprehension on the part of the individual and the society in which this norm can be recognized as binding in content as a matter of direct concrete practice. In all ages Catholic moral theology has recognized the idea of 'invincible error' as valid with regard to moral norms of a more detailed kind. It is true that it has applied this idea almost exclusively to the conscience of the individual as such. But it is perfectly conceivable, as is also apparent from the moral history of mankind, that it can also be applied to the collective moral awareness of an age or of larger social groups. From this point of view it can at least be said that it is not absurd from the outset to ask whether the moral norm of the encyclical may not perhaps have been proclaimed as an 'ideal norm' which, while it does indeed carry a direct and practical binding force already in the here and now for many individuals who differ very greatly among themselves and in the way in which their consciences have been formed, still does not carry the same immediate moral obligation for a wide range of people at the existing stage of their moral development.

This *question* can at least be *raised* as such with regard to this moral norm which has been laid down by the Pope. Indeed the moment we assume that it is materially correct it actually must be raised because on the one hand we have to be realistic enough to allow for a large measure of rejection of this norm even within the Church, while on the other there are many cases in which it is rejected in practice, and in which even so this practical refusal to observe it should not be qualified as subjectively speaking grave sin. Thus in fact the theological question does arise of what is implied by a discrepancy of this kind between an officially proclaimed norm on the one hand, and the 'ex supposito' largely inculpable failure to accept it on the other. This is a question that really does impose itself. And precisely on the assumption that the papal norm is objectively correct, the solution to it can, after all, surely be found only in the direction we have just indicated. But in that case this has a further significance also for the question of the formal binding force of this norm. On our hypothesis this would be, in a certain sense, that degree of binding force to be attached to a norm which defines a goal to be aimed at in the moral development of the Church and of society, but which, in the actual circumstances prevailing, is far from having yet been attained to, even though it is intended to be attained to. The case here is similar to that of loving God with one's *whole* heart. This too implies a radical obligation, yet at the same time does not say that this total love is already attainable in the 'here and now'.

III. Deviant Decisions of Conscience

We now come to the grounds which make it permissible for us to allow for the fact that subjectively speaking the individual Christian may believe himself justified in conscience in deviating from the papal teaching. Whatever approach we adopt to this question, our first task must be to define the precise limits of the 'state of the question'. For the purposes of our present investigation what we are concerned to achieve, therefore (and this is in accordance with the limits which we have defined for our considerations as a whole) is not to present arguments which, in our opinion, objectively demonstrate that the papal norm is incorrect or at least incapable of proof. Our sole aim here is to make clear that apart from the abstract possibility of an inculpably erroneous conscience there are grounds for holding that in this particular concrete instance even a Catholic conscience can, by a psychological process that we can understand, arrive at the (subjective) conviction that it is not bound by the papal norm.

(a) The first point to which we must draw attention in this connection is that we are arriving at too facile a judgement on the situation in which a subjective conscience is placed if we assume that this conscience is simply being subjected to a conflict between a harsh norm proclaimed by the Church and an easier course of action which has only moral laxity, superficiality, and hedonism to commend it. On the contrary not a few cases arise in which such a conscience finds itself caught up in what is (at least to all appearances) a conflict between moral *duties* on *both* sides. This is surely a point which does not need to be clarified at any greater length here.

(b) A further point to which attention must be drawn is that in this question, as a factor in the concrete situation of human living we must not over-emphasize the formal authority of the official teaching body with regard to its effectiveness. For in fact even from the point of view of sheer formal logic the matter appears to be very simple: the Catholic Christian in principle acknowledges the Church's teaching authority in moral questions also. It still continues to be authoritative for him even in the case in which he fails to perceive – at any rate with sufficient clarity – the material justification for this particular official decision in matters of doctrine. In other words – for this is how we might express the simple conclusion that appears to follow from this – even according to the dictates of his own conscience he has to adhere to this concrete norm. In reality, however, the matter is not so simple. First we must simply recognize the fact that despite the formal logic of the position which has been indicated above a formal authority can be over-strained from the psychological point of view, and that too not merely in the individual case, but also in collective situations. Man in his concrete behaviour is in fact not made up merely of logic. For instance a case that is perfectly conceivable and actually arises again and again is that of a Catholic doctor who in principle and theory recognizes the Catholic doctrine that any direct termination of pregnancy is forbidden. Yet in the concrete instance in which it is a question of saving a mother who already has many children he is psychologically in no position to realize the moral force at the psychological level of a norm to which he adheres at the conceptual level to such an extent that he either observes this norm in the concrete individual case, or alternatively disobeys it and incurs subjective guilt in doing so. A somewhat similar situation is perfectly conceivable even at the 'collective' level in the case with which we are here concerned, and may apply to wide areas of the Church even when we assume the objective correctness of the papal norm.

(c) A further point which must in all sober realism be emphasized is that in the case with which we are here concerned the individual and collective consciences of Catholic Christians neither have nor can assume any absolute certainty with regard to the objective correctness of the papal norm.

(d) Once this situation is taken duly into account the arguments *against* the papal norm acquire, both theoretically and practically speaking a far greater effectiveness, at least at the subjective level, than we could ascribe to them if – as in the case of a dogma – we could assume the absolute correctness of the papal teaching (regardless of whether we clearly saw the reason for it, or how we coped with the arguments against it).

(e) It must further be emphasized that in a question of the natural law it is far from being a matter of indifference whether we realize the *intrinsic* basis in reality for a norm of the *natural law* or not. In a case in which we completely failed to achieve this degree of understanding we would have to say that to observe a norm of this kind would indeed be an act of moral obedience *to the authority of the Church*, but it would no longer be an act in which the *intrinsic morality of what is actually prescribed in itself* would be attained to *subjectively*. Now this is certainly not a matter of indifference.

(f) In addition to this the actual situation in which the individual stands is such that while he may recognize this authority formally and in principle, still in the concrete individual case it is all too often made effectively present to him as nothing more than a moral demand for a given line of conduct in practice, so long as it does not succeed in effectively enabling him to understand how its demand is justified from the real nature of the case.

From this point of view alone we must be realistic enough to allow for the fact that in the case with which we are concerned, even though formally speaking we may acknowledge the teaching authority of the Church, and assume that the papal norm is correct, still there will be very many Catholics who neither recognize nor acknowledge in any effective sense that this norm has any binding force upon their own consciences.

So far all that we have been saying has been expressed in very formal terms. Now, however, we have reached a point at which it must be said quite decisively that there certainly are notable *arguments against* this papal norm. We cannot estimate the force of these arguments by asking ourselves whether they supply an objective and unambiguous proof of the contrary position to that upheld in the papal norm, but rather, from the standpoint of whether they are capable psychologically, albeit on the basis of objectively real considerations, of *de facto* causing the mind and conscience of an individual Catholic to hold the opinion that the papal norm is incorrect and, moreover, in such a way that he can foresee such a state of affairs emerging not merely in this or that individual case (a possibility which will certainly not be contested by any moral theologian) but in larger groups as well within the Church. If this is indeed the case, then here too we must not overlook a fact that a state of mind of this sort in such a group will have the effect of confirming the conviction of the individual.

Now such arguments are certainly to be found. In this connection only a few indications are possible here.

(a) First the line of argument against such positions adopted in the encyclical is surely too brief to be very effective so far as its power to convince at the *de facto* psychological level is concerned. It hardly goes beyond the actual statement of the thesis. It fails to show why the natural constitution of an *individual*, with his particular human powers, *ipso facto* and of itself alone lays a moral demand upon the individual concerned. To say the least the impression it arouses is as though man's capacity deliberately and consciously to shape and direct himself is power added on purely *ab externo* to a closed and 'static' nature, and not that which constitutes human 'nature' precisely as human. It therefore fails to demonstrate in any enlightening way the fact that man (admittedly with all the necessary provisos) precisely does *not* remain any longer *within* his own 'nature' when he deliberately induces a state of affairs which 'nature' itself also in fact produces again and again through the factor of the 'safe period'. All this is not said in order to deprive the line of argument adopted by the Pope of its own intrinsic force, but simply in order to make it clear that *de facto* in the case of many individuals it will turn out to be psychologically ineffective.

(b) An additional point is that a notable majority both of the theologians and of the bishops who were included in the Papal Commission set up to study this question declared themselves *against* laying down this norm, which has been published in the encyclical. In the light of this fact it is difficult to hold out any hope that a notable majority of Catholics will regard the line of argument adopted in the papal encyclical as carrying conviction. It has already been pointed out that any attempt to counter this position by having recourse to the formal papal authority alone will not help in a way that is psychologically effective.

(c) Finally in this respect the following factor has to be borne in mind: the papal encyclical recognizes that when there are serious grounds to justify it the safe period may be used to control fertility. In view of this we shall surely feel able to go on to say that even assuming the correctness of the papal norm we can still defend the position that it is morally permissible to make sure that these safe periods really are safe; that the woman concerned does not become fertile even during them as a result of factors which are biologically abnormal (and therefore 'unnatural'), in other words through ovulation taking place at a time when it is not expected. According to this line of argument it would be morally permissible to ensure the regularity of the 'safe period' by means of a 'pill' (it makes no difference whether one has already been found which is suitable for this purpose or not). The argument here would be that this would simply be a way of 'supporting' and regularizing 'nature', but not altering it. Now assuming for the moment that such a course of action is permissible, then the only difference in practice between the sort of 'birth control' which is in conformity with the papal norm and the sort that corresponds to the point of view opposed to this is that the papal norm would regard the use of the pill as unlawful during a period of about three days within the menstrual cycle (it would be lawful, therefore, for all the rest of the days) because in these three days a normal ovulation takes place and should not be prevented by the 'pill'. Of course to the moral theologian who accepts the papal norm this difference is vital to a degree. But in spite of this we are compelled to doubt whether this difference can be effectively apprehended and accorded its true value by the average human conscience.

If such refinements are introduced into the case, then the difference between the papal and the 'modern' position will no longer be understood by the average conscience, and will be felt to be so much hair-splitting. The *effect* is the same even though the means by which man seeks to achieve it are different: in the one case through his 'knowlege', in the other through his biological 'techniques'. In both cases it is *intended*. The sole difference, so far as the conscience of the average man is concerned is that something which he is permitted to do for all the rest of the time is unlawful for the specific period of the three days. It must be reiterated that what we are treating of here is a line of argument not about the true nature of the case in itself, but about the insights demanded of the average man in the process of forming his conscience. From this point of view, therefore, we must expect that in practice the papal norm will not be accepted.

IV. The De Facto Situation Among Catholics Since the Encyclical

From all that has been said up to now we must surely be realistic enough to draw the conclusion that so far as the outlook and living practice of the majority of Catholics is concerned the situation after the encyclical will be no different from what it was before. The number of protests which have already been raised even within the Church are in themselves enough to demonstrate this point. Moreover all the considerations which we have put forward so far in any case make it probable. The majority of Catholics will regard the norm presented in the encyclical as *de facto* not merely '*doctrina reformabilis*' but actually as '*doctrina reformanda*'. They will apply to the case in question those principles which have been stated in the doctrinal letter of the German bishops with regard to the possibility of deviating from that teaching of the official Church which, though authentic, has not been defined. In this situation a point that is crucial for any theological judgement upon it is that (though certainly not in all cases, still in very many) the 'bona fides' of the individuals concerned, the fact that at least in their subjective consciences they are inculpable, even when they do deviate from the official norm in this way, cannot be contested. Furthermore we cannot regard such a state of 'bona fides' in the concrete as a mere isolated case arising here and there. Rather it is a state that applies to large groups within the Church and to the Church's public life.

It cannot be proved by any *a priori* line of theological argument that such a situation is impossible in a case such as this, in which the teaching of the Church that is in question is indeed authentic, but nevertheless objectively speaking capable of revision. Teaching of this kind is *of its very nature* exposed to such a situation, even though it is still far from being the case that it must therefore arise in all cases wherever such teaching is proclaimed as authentic yet capable of reform. Certainly a situation of this kind actually has arisen often in the past, albeit not with such a full glare of publicity as in the present instance. For instance we can certainly state that with regard to many official doctrinal pronouncements in the field of biblical theology put forward at the beginning of the present century the great majority of exegetes had already abandoned these officially pre-scribed positions even before the teaching authorities themselves pru-dently withdrew from them. In the case of an authentic pronouncement of the teaching authorities such a situation is possible, and on all human estimation has *de facto* arisen in the case with which we are here con-cerned.

The importance to be attached to a doctrinal pronouncement of this kind, and the authority of the Church herself in her official doctrinal pronouncements, are not helped by covering over this situation or attempting to suppress any public awareness of it in the Church. Both within and without the Church so much will be said and written, and so many opinions will be put forward concerning this situation, opinions which cannot be suppressed and will not allow themselves to be suppressed by such expedients, that it could only do damage to the authority of the Church if those who in principle acknowledge their allegiance to the Church's authority were to attempt to remain silent. What we are con-cerned with here (and this is in conformity with the limited field of enquiry which we have defined for these considerations of ours) is in fact not whether this situation is, in every respect to be approved of, but rather what ought to be *done*, assuming that it already *exists*.

In such a situation the task of the bishops will be no easy one, the more so (though this is not the only reason) in view of the fact that in recent years they have more or less clearly adopted a public attitude which is either directly or indirectly at variance with the norm enunciated in the encyclical. A bishop need not, and certainly should not, take as his start-ing-point the conviction that it is absolutely certain that the positions unequivocally opposed to the papal norm are correct. And he cannot assume this to be the case. It is certainly impossible to maintain any such position so long as we view the question in a spirit of self-criticism and guard against any short-sighted emotionalism. But so long as he does not proceed from a conviction of this kind any bishop, regardless of which position he personally is inclined to adopt in view of the objective realities involved, can honourably and in all subjective honesty point out to the faithful over whom he presides the weight and importance to be attached to a papal pronouncement of this kind. He can exhort the faithful and the priests to be self-critical and so to take seriously a norm of this kind, laid down as it is by the supreme authority of the Church. He can put the question to the conscience of the individual believer whether he can have, or actually has, a sufficient conviction, supported by serious arguments, to make it lawful for him in conscience, either in theory or in practice, to deviate from the papal norm, or whether alternatively he is falling prey to an unconscious allergy against any teaching authority in the Church which is very widespread today, and so reacting merely emotionally without reflecting that in the gospel too claims can be put forward which at first seem to demand too much of man, driven as he is by his own impulses, and so appear to him incapable of fulfilment.

But a bishop need not and should not act either as though the papal pronouncement were absolute and incapable of revision, or as though any deviation from it necessarily implied a radical denial of the teaching authority of the Church such as would objectively separate the Catholics concerned from the Church. We have a right confidently to expect that on this question the bishops will proceed in conformity with the general norms which the German bishops themselves have formulated for such cases. Certainly a bishop will have to do his best to ensure that in the pulpit and in other contexts his priests will treat of questions of sexual morality in such a way that they continue clearly to maintain a genuine and positive attitude towards the teaching authority of the Church. But in a society in which there is still only very little that can be achieved at the merely discrete level, '*in camera caritatis*', it is impossible to avoid a situation in which the basic principles of the doctrinal letter of the German bishops, even as applied to the specific case, will be set forth *in public*, and in which it will be explicitly asserted that it is quite conceivable for a Catholic in 'bona fide' to deviate from the papal norm. It seems to be impossible for a bishop to have recourse to the disciplinary measures available to the Church's *magisterium* against a priest merely on the grounds that he is applying these principles to the case with which we are concerned, now that *those same* principles have been proclaimed by the bishops themselves in a presentation that is discrete, credible, and respectful in its attitude towards the teaching authority of the Church. To take such a course would be to deprive those same principles of their due weight, and to discredit the honesty of the bishops themselves in proclaiming them. For principles are there to be applied to concrete cases.

What we have already said in itself carries certain implications with regard to the attitude which priests should adopt in the pulpit and in the confessional. Even today one who is charged with proclaiming the gospel message has a very high and important task in upholding a Christian morality of sex. It has already been pointed out at an earlier stage that even today there is a great body of doctrine, held in common by all Catholics on this question, which the priest must boldly and unashamedly uphold. He has to point out again and again that marriage is something more than a mere egoism shared by two individuals, more than the legitimization of mere instincts, that it consists in a genuine and personal monogamy in which each partner strives to achieve the eternal salvation of the other, and that it is a love that entails a lifelong faithfulness. He has to point out that it is subject to the law and the grace of the gospel, that in principle it must be permanently open to the procreation of children, that the norms of birth-control are essentially ethical in character, and as such affect the whole man, etc. Again and again in the course of pastoral discussions in preparation for marriage, and in counselling married people (both in the confessional and outside it) the priest has to strive to instil an understanding of the Christian conception of marriage in the believers. He neither need be, nor should allow himself to be, manoeuvred into a situation in which it appears as though the sole question which arises in the ethics of marriage today is that concerned with the arguments *for* or *against* the 'pill'. Even today it is in principle perfectly conceivable that he will encounter individuals who, if it is left to their own judgement, will reject the 'pill'. In view of the 'authenticity' of the papal pronouncement he has certainly no right, in relation to such consciences, to seek to 'teach them better'. It would be still more reprehensible (although unhappily it does already occur in practice) if a priest in the confessional were to deprive people of their confidence when they had the joyful will and the Christian courage to increase the number of their children. On the other hand, however, he can also allow for the fact that there is a genuine state of 'bona fides' in many believers such that they do not incur guilt by deviating from the papal norm. If *in general* he acts in support of an understanding and a genuine respect for the papal norm (with the due provisos which the actual realities themselves require) he will in practice in the majority of cases in the confessional be able to refrain from making any attempt to 'upset' the 'bona fides' which is firmly present, or which may be assumed, in the penitent. For in accordance with what has been said so far, in the majority of cases he will not merely not succeed in this, but also in making such an attempt in the current situation he will fail to abide by the traditional rules, which lay down that a 'bona fides' of this kind must not be 'destroyed', but rather left untroubled. For today in effect any attempt of this kind would not as such be productive of any good, even in the sphere of public morality. In accordance with this the only cases in which the priest in the confessional will still have a 'duty to enquire' as to the use or non-use of the pill will be those in which he is forced to presume from positive signs that the penitent is keeping silent about his use of the pill, and that this is *contrary* to his subjectively 'better' conscience.

The theologians who have to present Catholic morality as from the professor's chair find themselves in a particularly difficult situation today with regard to this matter. First we are surely justified in saying that even in this official position of theirs they have the right and the duty to say everything which we have said up to now in the form of general considerations and the consequences to be drawn from these for the course of action to be followed by the bishops and the priests. But certain explicit questions still remain to be treated of which have been omitted in the above treatment. In 'Humani Generis' Pius XII had already declared that even if a papal pronouncement in matters of doctrine does not have the force of an *ex cathedra* definition, it is no longer open to free discussion among the theologians. It is true that this pronouncement has not been repeated in 'Lumen Gentium', the Constitution on the Church of the Second Vatican Council, even though it was at first included in a projected schema of this Dogmatic Constitution. But even in this Constitution it is laid down that a doctrinal statement of this kind has to be upheld by the theologians with a 'religious obedience' (No. 25). This certainly raises a special difficulty for moral theologians in their teaching, the more so since it is certainly reasonable to draw a distinction here according to whether, in the given case, it is a personal opinion that is being treated of, which remains at the private level and is held as a matter of personal theory and practice by someone who in doing so observes a '*silentium obsequiosum*', or whether it is an opinion which is upheld with a certain degree of publicity within the Church.

Over and above what has already been said at the beginning of this section we must surely adopt the following position on this question: in the concrete conditions prevailing today in the Church and in public life in the world, the respect which the moral theologian has to pay in his teaching to an authentic but not defined pronouncement of the Church's *magisterium* can no longer imply that the moral theologian concerned must either defend a doctrinal pronouncement of this kind through thick and thin as absolutely the only opinion which is certain and admissible for all ages, or else he must simply be silent. In conformity with what has been said up to now he cannot in honesty adopt the first position, and if he adopted the second he would both be failing in his task as a moral theologian and at the same time doing no service to the Church, to the moral standards of the faithful, and to the Church's teaching authority. Hence the moral theologian will on the one hand have to do his utmost to make the arguments supporting the papal doctrine intelligible to his hearers – in other words he will have to uphold the formal authority of the Church's official teachers (within the limits here laid down), and present the objective arguments supporting the papal position – on the other hand, however, he will not have to be silent concerning the difficulties against this papal teaching, neither those which actually exist as a matter of objective fact, nor those which may be very effective at the subjective level, for the very reason that this would have the effect of making his presentation unworthy of belief in the estimation of his hearers. Over and above this he will seek to help his hearers genuinely to form their own consciences even if he is unable to ensure that all of them will form them in the same sense. It can be said that in the concrete individual case this line of action on the part of the moral theologian is sufficient to ensure that he is adequately taking into account those principles to which we have just referred. It must be remembered that even according to the traditional interpretation these principles as stated by Pius XII and the Second Vatican Council do not in principle exclude the possibility of a theologian dissenting from an authentic statement of teaching of this kind, and that today it would be utopian to suppose that such dissent must always and in every case remain locked up in the private conscience of the theologian concerned. These factors alone are enough to ensure the validity of the approach which we have described. Moreover even in former times the theologian was not forced to keep his dissenting opinions to himself in this way. For otherwise the revisions which *de facto* have been arrived at – whether explicitly or tacitly – of other such official pronouncements of the Church would never have been made at all. Something which is necessary for a theological development, which *de facto* has existed all along, and is ultimately recognized by the Church's *magisterium* as well, cannot in principle or from the outset be contrary to morality.

So far as the adherents of the Christian faith, and above all Catholic married people are concerned, all that is essential has strictly speaking already been said, and, moreover, is already contained in the written statement of doctrine published by the German bishops. If, after maturely searching his conscience, a Catholic Christian believes that in all prudence and self-criticism he has been forced to arrive at a point of view which deviates from the papal norm, and if he follows this in the practice of his married life, then, so long as he observes those principles which have already repeatedly been mentioned as of general application to all Christians, such a Catholic need not fear that he has incurred any subjective guilt or regard himself as in a state of formal disobedience to the Church's authority. If he really succeeds in sincerely forming his conscience in this way, then such a Catholic has in principle no obligation to subject the judgement of his conscience which he has arrived at in this way to fresh questioning each time he receives the sacrament of penance. Admittedly in the contemporary situation the Catholic has one further duty to perform over and above those we have mentioned: his love for, and faithfulness to the Church must be such that he does not allow himself to be led astray by the scornful criticism of the Church and her sacrament, and the sometimes unbridled insults to which they are subjected, and which he can hear and read everywhere today where the 'question of the pill' is discussed. He must actually have acquired all the necessary information for understanding the true situation in this question. He must know how to distinguish between reformable and definitorial statements of doctrine on the part of his Church. Furthermore he must achieve a clear understanding of the fact that a teaching authority of the Church cannot in every case be forced into the dilemma either of having to speak with its supreme and infallible authority, or else simply keeping silent. Finally he must recognize that the examples of an alleged fallibility in the Church's teaching authority in the current controversy have been adduced by journalists who are either wholly or partially uneducated in theological matters. And all these examples involve decisions which were either not *ex cathedra* at all or which have nothing whatever to do with pronouncements of the Church's teaching authority (as, for instance, alterations in the Church's marriage laws, on the question of cremation etc.). Now if a believing Catholic does inform himself to this extent, then, even in the atmosphere of tension which now prevails, and which is in part artificially stimulated, he will be able to remain calm and composed and to preserve an attitude of trust towards the Church.

V. The Significance of the Current Situation as Constituting a Representative Example

What a Catholic or a theologian is experiencing today in our question is not really anything abolutely novel. For developments of doctrine and situations in which doctrinal developments such as the present one were still possible, even though the subsequent history could not be predicted with any clarity, have obviously existed again and again in the course of the Church's history. The new element in all this is simply the fact that such developments and situations arise and advance, or alternatively change, more rapidly nowadays, and so make a sharper and more urgent impression on the awareness of the individual within the brief span of his single lifetime; and further that this question affects the concrete life of an incalculably greater number of individuals, and affects it more directly than other dogmatic questions. Whatever the situation may have been over the last hundred years from the psychological point of view in the awareness of the average Catholic with regard to his attitude towards the Church, it is not true to suggest that the Catholic Church either has understood herself in the past, or understands herself now as a Church in which everything that is important is already clear from the outset, and already possessed as a matter of absolute certainty; or as a Church in which every fresh discovery of truth takes place solely and exclusively through the pronouncements of her supreme official teachers. The teaching authority in the Catholic Church, and above all in those cases in which it does not produce any definitorial pronouncement (and in many cases it is quite incapable of doing so) is an important and essential element for the discovery of truth and the development of doctrine in the Church. But it is not the sort of official body which acts in isolation and in every respect in total independence of other real elements in the Church, and so presides over this discovery of truth or development of doctrine in a totalitarian manner. Even the *ex cathedra* decisions of the popes or Councils have properly speaking always arisen, in some sense or other, as a final seal of approval accorded to a development which has been sustained by factors quite different from the official teaching body itself or the formal authority attached to this. The authority of the official teachers in the Church and the respect due to this do not require, therefore, that we who are in the Church shall act as though all theological views upheld in the Church consist simply in an obedient repetition of some declaration on the part of these official teachers. On any true understanding there is, even in the Catholic Church, an open 'system' in which the most varied factors (the 'instinct' of the faithful fresh, insights on the part of individual Christians and theologians, fresh situations that arise in a particular age, the new questions to which these give rise and much else besides) work together to throw fresh light upon the Church's own awareness of her faith, and to produce a development of doctrine.

And in all this this open 'system' considered as a whole, in which the official teaching authority has its proper and necessary place, is not taken over and directed in any exclusive or totalitarian sense by this official teaching body in itself.

These are factors in the Church's understanding of her own nature which are properly speaking self-evident. Today we are experiencing them in a particular concrete instance in a way that is perhaps painful but that should not, on any ultimate view, have been unexpected to us. In such a situation the question arises of what attitude the individual Christian in the Catholic Church ought to adopt in his own conscience. For deciding this question there are indeed numerous principles, of which we have mentioned only a few in the present discussion. But in this particular concrete case, as also in the important decisions which he has to take in other areas of his life, these principles do not relieve the individual Christian of the responsibility of arriving at a sincere decision in his own personal life, or of his responsibility before God as an individual. The two factors of free responsibility even in the process of arriving at the truth on the one hand, and of paying due heed to the teaching authority of the Church on the other are united and combined in the process of arriving at this decision. And to unite the two factors in this way is a task that arises ever anew, one which cannot be achieved *solely* by speculating on abstract principles. According to the teaching of the Church herself there are certain cases in which the individual's own subjective conscience with regard to truth is blameless, either when it fails to lead him to the Church and her defined doctrine or even when it leads him out of her. The question with which we are here concerned, however is certainly not, objectively speaking, a case in which anything of this kind necessarily must take place.

13

THEOLOGICAL OBSERVATIONS ON THE
CONCEPT OF TIME

IN the considerations which I propose to put forward here I shall not
be taking as my starting-point the problems of modern physics,
non-Euclidian geometry, the fundamentals of the theory of aggre-
gates, or the natural philosophy developed on the basis of all this, because
this cannot justly be demanded of theology as a scientific discipline.
Nevertheless this is regrettable. For in Catholic theology, which in this
respect differs from several tendencies in Protestant theology, the opinion
cannot *a priori* be upheld that, quite apart from the methodological
differences between his discipline and that of the natural scientist, the
actual area of subject-matter which he has to investigate is so different
from that field of reality with which the natural scientist has to deal that
from the outset there are no points of contact between them, and therefore
no possibilities of conflict either. Nevertheless this restriction, regrettable
though it may be, is rendered increasingly inevitable by the fact that the
pluralism which exists among the contemporary sciences is too great for
any *one* mind any longer to achieve an overall synthesis. At the same time
this contemporary situation itself in turn creates problems which did not
exist before, and so demand a completely new approach. These too, as far
as possible, have to be solved. We may further justify the fact that we are
not, in any primary sense, taking as our starting-point for the considerations presented here the sort of problems that are raised by the natural
sciences[1] on the grounds that according to its own demonstrable under-

[1] Hence we cannot here enter any more closely into the problems of space and time
entailed in the scientific theorizing of the natural scientists. Thus a bibliography may
be sufficient on this point: See M. Schlick, *Raum und Zeit in der gegenwartigen Physik*
(Berlin, 4th ed., 1922); H. Reichenbach, *Die Philosophie der Raum-Zeit-Lehre*
(Berlin, 1928); A. Wenzl, 'Das Paradoxon der Relativierung der Zeit in der Relativi-
tätstheorie', *Forschung und Fortschritt* (1958); G. Frey, 'Der Zeitbegriff in den Natur-
wissenschaften', *Studium generale* 14 (1961); P. Mittelstaedt, *Philosophische Probleme
der modernen Physik* (Mannheim, 1963); *Die Problematik von Raum und Zeit* =

standing of itself theology is a science which is concerned with the interpretation of human existence, a field which is existentially and onto-logically prior to man's interpretation of himself at the level of the natural sciences. For this reason theology can and should pursue its own tasks without having to wait for the findings of the natural sciences as the necessary prior condition enabling it to achieve what is proper to itself.[2] Precisely in virtue of the account which his science gives of its own nature the theologian must, after all, enter into dialogue with the natural scientist, and at the same time in doing so retain the right to state his findings without having first studied the findings of natural science, and before the natural scientist himself has pronounced upon these. He can then leave it to the dialogue itself to achieve the further developments necessary, developments which in fact have not already been anticipated by what the theologian himself asserts in the sphere of his own interpre-tation of his faith and his theology.

The Christian believer and his theology are in the highest degree con-cerned with the concept of time. Whatever may be meant by this in more precise terms, Christian dogma recognizes the creation of the world as having a temporal 'beginning', and rejects the doctrine of a 'world that has already existed from eternity' as a heresy.[3] It recognizes a *history* of salvation and perdition which is unique and linear in its advance, and rejects the 'eternal return of all things'. This Christian dogma recognizes certain absolutely unique events occurring at particular points in space and time in saving history, and looks for the end of all history. It ascribes to the human existence of the individual a personal history developed in a freedom which does not give the subject concerned the power to go back over his course at will, or the possibility of limitless revisions, but consists rather in the forging of that which is definitive, that in which time as a process will be raised to its definitive outcome, that which is called the

---

Naturwissenschaft und Theologie 6 (Freiburg, 1964); R. W. Meyer, ed., *Das Zeit-problem im 20. Jahrhundert* (Bern, 1964); W. Büchel, *Philosophische Probleme der Physik* (Freiburg, 1965); H. Weyl, *Philosophie der Mathematik und Naturwissen-schaft* (Munich, 1966); C. F. von Weizsäcker, *Die Tragweite der Wissenschaft* I (Stuttgart, 2nd ed., 1966); H. Sachsse, *Naturerkenntnis und Wirklichkeit* (Brauns-chweig, 1967); A. Koyré, *Von der geschlossenen Welt zum endlichen Universum* (Frankfurt, 1969).

[2] On this cf. K. Rahner, 'Science as a "Confession"?', *Theological Investigations* III (London and Baltimore, 1967), pp. 385–400.

[3] A brief and precise explanation of this point is to be found in W. Kern, 'Zur theologischen Auslegung des Schöpfungsglaubens', *Mysterium Salutis* II (Einsiedeln, 1967), pp. 464–546, esp. 519–529 (bibliog.).

'eternity' of man in salvation or perdition.[4] The doctrine of the faith includes the concept of the 'fulness of time', the biblical concept of the *kairos*, the possibility, appointed and given once and for all, for man of his freedom to achieve definitive salvation. It includes the concept of the '$\dot{\epsilon}\phi$ $\ddot{\alpha}\pi\alpha\xi$',[5] i.e. the event which, taking place at a particular point in time, remains as an unsurpassable existential modality for all times. Faith is aware of the flux of time as an enslaving power over man, from which he is liberated by the grace of God in Christ. And it recognizes saving time, in which that can take place which endures blessedly in force for ever.

There is the theological concept of hope, which is act *and* expectation both in one, reaching out into a time that lies open before man, and which he can never seize upon or bring under his control by his own autonomous planning. Theology considers the concept of divine providence through which God is not merely the sole Lord of time and history, but also guarantees that time shall be shaped and directed in a way that is ultimately meaningful for history, and does not allow this to be fragmented and so to sink into a formless succession of particles of time following one upon the other. In the doctrine of the Incarnation of the divine Logos Christian dogma apprehends the tremendous fact that time becomes, in a true sense, predicated of God who is 'in himself' immutable, God who assumes and undergoes a personal history of his own in time, and 'in the world' itself. In the concept of the development of revelation and dogma as history an encounter is achieved between truth and time, and it becomes clear that time is not merely a specification of physical and material reality, but also one that applies to the spirit as such. Among the insights of the Church's dogmatic teaching is included the truth that the ultimate essence and outcome of the history of *nature* and of the world itself are specified by the history of man's achievement of salvation or perdition in freedom. And from this the further truth emerges that the time inherent in material reality is not, in the last analysis, the power which dominates human history, but on the contrary remains one particular and subordinate element in the time that belongs to personal freedom. Ultimately speaking, therefore, it is the former of these that must be specified by the latter and not *vice versa*. The New Testament uses a whole range of concepts which include both purely temporal aspects and at the same time

[4] cf. K. Rahner, 'The Comfort of Time', *Theological Investigations* III (London and Baltimore, 1967), pp. 141–157; *idem*, 'Immanent and Transcendent Consummation of the World', *Theological Investigations* X (London and New York, 1973), pp. 260–273.

[5] cf. A. Winter, "$A\pi\alpha\xi$ $\dot{\epsilon}\phi\acute{\alpha}\pi\alpha\xi$ im Hebräerbrief (Dissertation, Rome, 1960).

a theological content and weight: αἰών, αἰώνιος, ἡμέρα, ὥρα, καιρός (ἔσχατος), τα τέλη, σήμερον, ἐνεστῶτα-μέλλοντα θάνατος, ἐφάπαξ, νῦν, παραυτίκα, παραυτά, ἐρνέσθαι, φθορά, ἐκθές, ἀνάμνησις, etc. Thereby it provides an immediate basis for a theology of time. Theology reflects (or should do so!) upon the concept of *that* 'simultaneity' in virtue of which the believer achieves immediate contact with the saving event of the 'past' in 'anamnesis'. Theology recognizes the sacraments as events of grace having the character of 'anamnesis' and at the same time anticipating the future. It is clear, therefore, that the dogmatic teaching of Christianity must concern itself particularly with the concept of time.

Now this conclusion contrasts strangely with the fact that there is hardly any 'theology of time' in the established theology of the seminaries, and therefore (as dependent upon this) in the average Catholic's conscious awareness of his faith. Of course some controversies have arisen in the history of dogma and theology which do relate to time. This applies for instance to the struggle against Gnosticism and against an Origenist doctrine of *apokatastasis*, and also the controversy of the Mediaeval schoolmen 'de aeternitate mundi', i.e. in more precise terms with regard to the possibility or impossibility of establishing the finitude of the temporal world by philosophical argument. But any systematically worked out doctrine of the nature of time has never been arrived at in the established theology of the Church. The statements about time which this contains have remained scattered throughout the particular theological treatises, ranging from the treatise on creation to that on eschatology. What is true with regard to any formal theology of history is also true with regard to a theology of time. It does not yet really exist, and even though here and there time is inevitably spoken of in the treatises which exist on particular topics, still even here the question is not for the most part entered into very deeply in this established theology. It assumes as self-evident a popular understanding of time, and when it does reflect upon it more precisely it does so with the aid of a Greek understanding of time which derives its primary orientation from the model of κίνησις, in other words, in the last analysis, from the idea of changes of place. In the light of this we can understand that from the ancient conception of the world right down to the most recent times the idea of saving history has been worked out according to the model of changes of place. 'Heaven' does not *come to be* in time, but history is basically speaking presented as a movement (or return) taking place in a sphere within which certain specific and qualitatively different points can be discerned, each with a theological relevance of its own. This failure to reflect upon the real nature of time is also shown, for instance, by the fact that the actual word 'time' (tempus) only arises as a specific topic in the official doctrinal documents of the Church in contexts in which the beginning of the world through creation is being spoken of.

In arriving at this conclusion we do not of course intend to dispute the fact that a far more profound and radical Christian understanding of time evinces itself in many theologians ranging from Irenaeus and Augustine[6] to Pascal and Kirkegaard,[7] or that the understanding of time commonly accepted among Christians, even though insufficiently reflected upon, has still had a considerable influence upon that conception of time which is characteristic of modern philosophy.

This omission, strange and surprising though it is, has reasons of its own which are readily understandable. Everyone imagines that he knows what time is as constituted by past, present and future, and in a certain sense is justified in this even though for the most part he is overlooking the principle that that which has been 'known all along' is, and must continue to be, that which constantly calls for fresh questioning. And hence theology too seems able to manage with this awareness of time which is prior to any ontological speculation upon it. For the message of faith is intended to be intelligible to all. And even when theology draws upon, or attempts to draw upon, the specialist concepts of philosophy it does not in its turn produce any official doctrinal interpretations of these, but uses them on its own account and at its own risk in its proper field, and in so doing often fails to achieve any unanimity in the use of such concepts.

Hence it is perhaps appropriate to show by means of a few examples – more are not possible – how theology must, in order to cope with its own problems, concern itself with achieving a deeper understanding of the concept of time, and how in the course of its own enquiry it encounters problems which require it to take into account certain relevant factors which fall outside its own boundaries. From these few modest preliminary

---

[6] On this cf. U. Duchrow, 'Der sogenannte psychologische Zeitbegriff Augustins im Verhältnis zur physikalischen und geschichtlichen Zeit', *ZTK* 63 (1966), pp. 267–288.

[7] The central discussion of this concept of time, which is also particularly important for the considerations on simultaneity already mentioned above, is to be found in S. Kierkegaard, *Philosophische Brocken* (Vol. 10 of the German edition) (Düsseldorf, 1952), esp. pp. 7–107; in this connection cf. also *idem, Der Augenblick* (Jena, 2nd ed., 1909); *idem, Abschliessende unwissenschaftliche Nachschrift* (Vol 16 of the German edition) (Düsseldorf, 1957/58); *idem, Einübung im Christentum* (Vol 26 of the German edition) (Düsseldorf, 1951).

soundings we shall pass on somewhat arbitrarily and abruptly, because nothing else is possible here.[8]

I

The dogmatic teaching of the Church lays down that the world is not 'eternal', but has been created in time and with time, and that it has a 'beginning'. Here we must dispense with any more detailed investigation of the 'theological qualification' attached to this statement, though it is consistently qualified, at least in the manuals of Catholic dogma, as *'de fide divina et catholica definita'* (Reference being made here to D 428, 501–503; 1783). Let us simply notice in passing that nowadays a small question mark is here and there appended to this qualification.[9] Insofar as any dispute arises in the established theology with regard to this statement, it is at most concerned with the question of whether it constitutes merely a statement of revelation or also has the force of a statement of the findings of 'natural' philosophy. Here we may adduce Thomas as an example of the first position, and Bonaventure as an example of the second. Possibly it may be asked in more precise terms here whether with regard to this point of controversy still further distinctions are offered to show precisely *which* finite and created reality is being treated of in each particular case. But even if we set aside this controversial point, we must still ask whether the actual *meaning* of the dogma itself is unambiguously clear. Certainly no further explanation of a binding character has been put forward by the official Church as the outcome of any conscious investigation of the actual dogma itself. But can it be said that its meaning is clear? What does it mean to say that the world has a 'beginning', that real time is 'finite' in respect of its extension back into the past, and therefore that the world is not 'eternal', not existing from all eternity? Theology itself in fact explains that we should not interpret this statement as though we could, by tracing

[8] The considerations put forward here are not of themselves to be thought of as constituting a systematic plan for a theology of time of this kind. In such a theology we should probably also have to take into consideration and develop more strongly our own evaluation of the way in which the concept of time has been discussed among philosophers ever since the introduction of the Kantian antinomies. But, as the title of this study shows, it is the prior conditions for, and also the insoluble difficulties encountered by, such a theology of time that we are seeking to make apparent here. For such a theology must have an awareness of these if it is to pursue its proper task in an intelligent way. In general reference may be made to the article, 'Zeit, Zeitlichkeit' I–V, *LTK* X (2nd ed. Freiburg, 1965) 1324–1334 (Bibliog.).

[9] cf. W. Kern, *op. cit.*, p. 524.

the course of time backwards, arrive at some point at which the world no longer existed, as though space and time in the material sense were still present, though empty, so that only God still existed. Established theology itself states the world as a whole cannot be conceived of in such a way that it would be reasonable to ask whether it could have existed either 'earlier' or 'later', because, as applied to the material world, there is not and cannot be in the concrete any 'earlier' or 'later' at all. And such a question derives merely from the illusion of the 'transcendental phantasy' which fails to understand that the world actually *has* time as the specification of itself, but as a whole does not in turn exist *in* time.

But what is finite time as material, seeing that it cannot in its turn be expressed in time, because otherwise it would once more have its place in a material time? Can the *finitude* of the totality of time be real in any other way than in virtue of the fact that it is conceived of as (and actually is) a part of a wider extent of time which is just as real as itself, something which, *ex supposito*, cannot be the case?

We might begin by imagining to ourselves what it would be like for us to set up a clock beside the world and proceeding at the same rate as it such that it would always be co-existent with the world (whether this always exists or not), and then say: now since the time which this clock tells is finite, so too the time of the world is finite. But this clock would either be a part of the world as such or not. In the first case, as a particular element of the world it could not tell us anything *more* about the temporality of the world as a whole than any other individual element in the world, namely that it itself exhibits a finite number of changes. But the idea that because of its continuous co-existence with the world the world itself too exhibits only a finite number of processes, and so has a finite time – this is an idea which we could not assume, but would rather have to have proved. But how?

In the second case the clock would be a world in itself. But in that case it would first have to be proved that two absolutely disparate worlds, having no real connection with one another, are conceivable at all, and, even assuming this, that the two absolutely disparate times belonging to them could, nevertheless, serve as measures of one another, and that a non-finite time could not be continuously co-existent with an absolutely disparate finite time.[10] But how are we to prove this without constantly

[10] For if it were possible, e.g. for a non-finite time permanently to co-exist with a finite one in such a way that one of the two time-series involved was unknown to us, then we still could not say whether that other was finite or infinite, and it would be of no avail to attempt to represent it to ourselves in terms of the one that we did know.

assuming what appears to be the case from the transcendental phantasy, namely that time is a unique and homogeneous medium, constantly present for all and for each, of the realities which must from the outset exist in it in order to exist at all? Are we to say that the statement, 'The world has a beginning' means 'If we count up the total number of states, real yet distinguishable from one another, in which the world and the elements belonging to it have existed up to now, we shall arrive at a finite sum total'? But a computation of this kind presupposes on the one hand that the individual states themselves, as constituting a numerical series, are subject to time and have a temporal extension (otherwise they could not constitute time), and on the other that they must not be thought of in turn as materially continuous with one another, but rather as temporal 'atoms' of the states or conditions through which the world passes such that they cannot materially speaking be broken down into any smaller units.[11] But is this assumption conceivable, and not rather a contradiction in itself? Why, for example, could not as much 'take place' in those particles of time considered as a specification of such computable states as in the totality of the time that is measured? Why is it assumed in this clarification of the meaning of the dogma that there is an absolute flow of time proceeding at a regular rate such that nothing can have any place in the units of it except precisely these states, any one of which, so it is alleged, is materially different from the rest. To put it in other terms, if the statement that material time is finite is to have any meaning, does it not presuppose (at least in principle, even though it may not be something that we ourselves can realize) that time is measureable, that the units of time can be calculated, and in that case does not the question necessarily impose itself of how any such measurability, even if it is only a measurability in principle, is to be conceived of? Is the computability of the events related, at least in principle, to actual occurrences such that these are ultimately accessible at all to the empirical methods of the natural sciences, or is the sort of finitude that is signified here one which is, so far as these empiricial methods are concerned, capable of being divided *ad infinitum* into ever further elements, whether hypothetical or actually

---

The only assured assumption here, albeit one that we should have to prove, is that an infinite time-series can never be represented in terms of a finite one.

[11] For the idea of a primary unit of extension and a primary unit of time, the so-called time atom cf. e.g. P. Jordan, *Das Bild der modernen Physik* (Berlin, 1957), pp. 147 ff. On what follows cf. also what is said about the model proposed by K. E. v. Baer in H.-D. Bastian, *Theologie der Frage* (Munich, 1969), pp. 52 ff.

observed, so that in principle such an enumeration never comes to an end and hence cannot of itself tell us anything with regard to the finitude or infinity of what *it precisely* is able to enumerate.[12] But in that case what does the finitude of that which is in principle incapable of being calculated or measured signify? Does it still have anything to do with time, or is it simply concomitant with the fact that everything belonging to the world without exception is dependent upon God? In other words is the finitude of the time that belongs to the world not after all merely another term for that reality which, in other contexts or on other approaches, is called contingency? To express the question in yet another way: time is experienced as a mutual relationship of the constituents of the world to one another precisely so long as we are considering the intrinsic temporality of the individual, and not time as an external factor, the 'space-time' dimension and the measure of time as a starting-point for every understanding of time.[13] Does it have any essential meaning to transpose this relationship from the constituents of the world as a totality to the totality itself, and, as is or seems to be the practice in dogmatic teaching, to express finite time as applicable to the world as a whole?

It seems that material time, that is time as constituted by a temporal interval between two entities, can only exist if between the two lies a temporal process of development in virtue of which they are both connected, and at the same time held apart from one another. How are we to apply time as thus conceived of to the world as such and in its totality? On this showing, then, is the dogmatic teaching saying anything more than precisely that the world consists of realities which have a temporal relationship *between one another*? But who has ever seriously disputed this? And is this all which the dogmatic teaching is intended to express? Before we go any further in enquiring into the meaning of the dogmatic teaching we must pause to introduce a certain methodological consideration.

In principle it neither can nor should be disputed that a *de fide* pronouncement can contain implications which only become clear in a confrontation with those secular findings and hypotheses which are arrived

---

[12] On the problem of the continuum referred to here cf. H. Weyl, *op. cit.*, pp. 47–90.

[13] For a more searching philosophical discussion of the distinctions in the concept of time indicated here reference may be made to the basic studies in H. Bergson, *Essai sur les données immédiates de la conscience* (Paris, 1889); E. Husserl, *Vorlesungen zur Phänomenologie des inneren Zeibewusstseins* (Halle, 1928); M. Heidegger, *Sein und Zeit* (Halle, 1927).

at, and objections which are raised, at a later stage, so that then it becomes necessary to maintain the pronouncements against the difficulties that arise in this way. Certainly, therefore, we must be cautious in invoking a certain hermeneutic consideration which is often too hastily applied today, namely the suggestion that at the time when a given dogmatic statement was formulated such and such factors had not yet been realized, had not been conceived of, and could not be taken into account. In other words the dogmatic pronouncement concerned could not have expressed anything about them.[14]

But in the concrete instance with which we are concerned we must, after all, surely lay down the following principle: the dogmatic statement concerning the temporal nature of the world must always, and from the outset, be read and understood in the context in which it is enunciated, in the context of a *veritas salutaris* – in other words of a saving statement ('evangelium') addressed to men and of an appeal to their free decision ('law') to accept 'irrevocably' the definitive salvation in a definitive exercise of freedom. Only so long as the statement regarding the temporal nature of the world is consistently and strictly read in this context do we escape the following dilemma: either the statement concerned is intended to be one which merely describes a 'phenomenon' of popular experience, but which nevertheless neither can be nor in fact is an object of revelation (the temporality of worldly things as a phenomenon is in fact something different from the temporality of the world) *or* it is intended to be a statement the meaning of which can only be clarified and authenticated by means of the resources of contemporary natural science with its still unresolved problems, something which, in terms of theological method, would, nevertheless, be impossible to carry out. Thus it appears that the considerations put forward so far with regard to the meaning of the dogmatic pronouncement on the temporal finitude of the world, in virtue of the insoluble difficulties[15] into which they have led us, can justifiably be undertstood as a demand to consider this general context within which the dogmatic statement itself is to be read, and in the light of which its dogmatically binding meaning is to be determined.

[14] cf. K. Rahner and K. Lehmann, 'Kerygma und Dogma', *Mysterium Salutis* I (Einsiedeln, 1965), pp. 622–707, esp. 686–703; P. Schoonenberg (ed.), *Die Interpretation des Dogmas* (Düsseldorf, 1969).

[15] On the insoluble problems which arise in connection with the concept of time cf. the first antinomy of the pure reason in I. Kant, *Critique of Pure Reason* (London, 1929).

II

In the light of all this we are now in a position to fix a starting-point (and at the same time to anticipate the conclusion) to state the following: the dogmatic pronouncement regarding the created nature of the world in and with time (= the dogmas of the Fourth Lateran and the First Vatican Councils) is intended to express the following: Man is an element in the world in virtue of the unity of spirit and matter[16] in him, and the factors entailed by this, the resurrection of the flesh and the consummation of the world in the 'new heaven and the new earth'.[17] Now because of this, and in spite of the limitations it implies, the world must be such that man can be that which he is: a being endowed with a freedom to be exercised in time and history which attains to the definitive finality of God in the definitive finality of its own free decision.

In what follows this statement will be developed in two parts: (a) It tells us something about a qualified temporality inherent in man which can be experienced and verified directly from the way in which he lives; (b) secondly it introduces a (discreet) extrapolation of this temporal factor, applying it to the world as a whole.

(a) With regard to the first part of this statement it is of course impossible here to develop at any length either a theological anthropology in general or a theology of history and freedom in particular. Here too we must exclude from the outset the question of whether there is a kind of time which is already in force and being directed irreversibly forward as a necessity of nature even at the sub-human level – especially in organic things (or in virtue of the law of entropy which prevails throughout the cosmos as a whole), in other words whether even independently of man there is a process of change which unfolds in a linear development and can only unfold in this way.[18] For so long as we do not ascribe any false individuality to the various types of organism and, in accordance with this, are cautious in the value we attach to death in their case, it would perhaps be conceivable to interpret the history of living things as a series of expansions and contractions (on the analogy of a pulsating world),[19]

[16] cf. K. Rahner, 'The Unity of Spirit and Matter in the Christian Understanding of Faith', *Theological Investigations* VI (London and Baltimore, 1969), pp. 153–177.
[17] cf. K. Rahner, 'The Theological Problems Entailed in the Idea of the "New Earth" ', *Theological Investigations* VIII (London and New York, 1973), pp. 260–273.
[18] We may compare, e.g. the main principles of thermo-dynamics.
[19] cf. W. Büchel, 'Das pulsierende Universum', *StdZ* 177 (1966), pp. 119–126.

and so to doubt whether the history of living things follows a linear course and to ask ourselves whether the real 'death' in organic matter does not consist in the formation of a new germ or seed, in other words a return to the point of departure. On this view that which we regard as death in this sphere would be only a relatively secondary episode in the transformation of matter.

It will not even be said that this theory (which, by a process of extrapolation, we would then go on to apply to the world as a whole) is the sole possible starting-point for achieving an understanding of the statement regarding the temporal creation of the world. Certainly in terms of theology it would be possible to formulate another and different starting-point.[20] We could for instance take the theology of saving history, the covenant, the Incarnation etc. in this sense. Here, however, we prefer to take as our starting-point the theory we have formulated above, because on the one hand it has the advantage of being closer to the experience of the individual, and on the other the alternative theories which we might use as a starting-point (which are in any case connected with ours, and among themselves) probably do not yield any more help for achieving an understanding of what is meant by the statement that the creation took place in time and had a beginning than that which we can achieve on our theory. Finally it may be observed that by adopting this theory as our starting-point we can bypass the problem of biblical hermeneutics, how in more precise terms we should interpret the 'not yet' sayings of scripture as such (Gen 1:1; 2:4; Ps 90:2; 102:26; Prov 8:22–30; Mt 13:35; 25:34; Lk 11:50; Jn 17:5, 24; Eph 1:4; Heb 4:3), the problem, in other words, of how far we can interpret them as making an objective statement about the finite time of the world by pointing to an empty void in space and time 'prior to' the existence of the world, or how far they present a conceptual pattern for expressing the radical dependence of the world upon God regardless of whether or not it did actually exist 'all along'.

In any case however man experiences himself as a historical being endowed with responsibility and freedom in such a way that he exists in a time the very meaning of which involves a clear and irreversible forward orientation, and which cannot be conceived of as capable of being reversed in the opposite direction without thereby denying the very nature of man as deciding what his final and definitive state is to be. At least through his first free act and through his death man experiences this history of the exercise of his own freedom in time as finite, with definite limits in the past

<hr>

[20] cf. W. Kern, *op. cit.*

and the future, and this has the effect of ruling out, so far as the personal history of the individual as such is concerned, any 'pre-existence' or any indeterminate prolongation of his life into the future. Here, in a theological consideration, there is no need to examine any more closely the question of how far these data of a theological anthropology are already given or could be discovered even independently of the supernatural order of grace in which man is called to receive God's self-bestowal, and independently also of the divine revelation in which this summons is interpreted. The one point upon which there can be no doubt is that these data belong intrinsically to man's understanding of himself at the Christian and theological level, and that is sufficient here, where we are concerned with the theological interpretation of a dogmatic statement (i.e. that concerning the temporal nature of the world). This man who experiences time as irreversible in this sense, with a beginning and end, within the history of his own freedom is aware of himself as a real element of the world *and at the same time*, in a manner unique in each particular case, as the totality of the world. In this awareness of his there is a dialectical unity in which the two elements involved are mutually interconnected. In his physical side he experiences himself as a partial element of the world and of the history of nature, and in the radical unity of his nature as constituted by spirit and matter he cannot conceive that his history as a free being, considered as something that takes place in the material world as subject to time, is something enacted, as it were, on a static stage, and something that is brought to an end once the historical person himself and the effects of this history of his make their exit from this world. On a Christian view the history of nature can, in the last analysis, be understood only as an element in the history of the free spirit in its dialogue with God who bestows himself in grace, and hence the material time of the world is to be conceived of as an element in the material time of this history of the free spirit.

All this still does not do much to throw light upon the intrinsic nature of this time that belongs to the world, because in fact, while we should have a right understanding of the real distinction between spirit and matter, the distinction itself cannot be eliminated. But surely what has been achieved here is a general orientation for our understanding of the time factor in the world, which in principle must never be overlooked: this temporal factor must never be interpreted in such a way as to leave no room in it for the time that is intrinsic to the personal spirit with its beginning and end. As has been said, what we are demanding here is not so self-explanatory when we consider that materiality is an element that is intrinsic to the concrete subject of this history of freedom, and is in part affected by it. And this materiality is also an element in the material world which cannot be isolated from the world. A further point is that the subject of freedom considered as a historical process in this sense cannot be interpreted as a *mere* constitutive element in the world. As '*anima quodammodo omnia*' it has a real-onto-logical relationship to the world as a totality, and could not be considered to have achieved its due fulness so long as the fulness of this relationship itself had not yet been achieved, as would be the case if the world itself were conceived of as still in a state of openness and becoming in a time that ran onwards into the indefinite future.

(b) Taking these as our prior assumptions, in the second part of our statement we shall now go on to say that the world and its modes of existence must be conceived of in such a way that they are *capable* of being the sphere within which precisely *this* history of the free person in time can take place, and at the same time an intrinsic element in that history. This is a cautious and almost negative assertion: the world does not have to be such that, while still remaining an intrinsic element in this history, it so to say cuts off its temporal span at the beginning and end of it. The positive element in what we are saying about the mode of existence proper to the world, to the extent that it is a real element which is different in relation to the spirit as such, is precisely *whether* it is possible to make some positive statement about something which is, initially, still completely open. *In the last analysis*, moreover, this question can actually remain open because what we are concerned with is the *veritas salutaris* of man in his freedom as a finite historical being, and properly speaking nothing else than this, provided only that we recognize that this truth in itself already involves some statement about the world to which man belongs, while recognizing also that it is only with difficulty that we can arrive at any clear reflection upon these implications contained in the *veritas salutaris*. But if despite this fact the attempt is to be made, and we are to try to apply the positive content in this negative statement, then we may perhaps say the following: any positive statement about an 'everlasting' world with a limitless range of specifications, is inconceivable from the outset if the statement in question relates to the world precisely *as* the environment in which a finite mode of freedom exists, and the concomitant conditions of this. For this is not the sort of world with which a finite freedom can be involved. It must be admitted that even when we have said this, it still remains obscure what is meant in positive terms by a negation of this sort ('a world with many, but not limitless, specifications'). But it must be observed that at any rate in the case of an existing world which constitutes the material of finite freedom by the limited number of specifications to which it is open, we do not *have* to suppose that this world is the product of an infinite number of temporal states following one upon another in a limitless series in time. Hence it is at least superfluous to postulate an endless series of this kind. On this basis a finitude of this present world can be asserted and maintained as at any rate a more intelligible interpretation of the content of the dogma regarding the temporal finitude of the world. Moreover the significance of this can be understood in its implications for the religious fulfilment of human living even though it may not be quite clear to us what finitude and infinity are intended to signify when these two concepts are related solely to the totality of the material time inherent in the world as a single whole.

To express the point in different terms: we can and must positively assert that the time of the world is finite (even when it is not clear what this implies or does not imply) if, and to the extent that, we regard the time belonging to the world as the material for the finite freedom of man as related to the totality of the world. For in that case to postulate an infinitude of the world's time would imply that it was of such a kind that in principle it could not be the material of man's finite freedom in this sense. Now even if we accept that the world's time does in fact constitute one element in the time which creaturely freedom involves in this way, we might still raise the further question of precisely *how* this world's time is constituted 'in itself' and taken in isolation,[21] that is conceiving of it in abstraction from this connection which it has with man's finite freedom. But surely the reason why it is so difficult to make any statement on this point is that despite all the objectivity we may achieve in our knowledge of the physical world, and despite the fact that we are able to measure the time belonging to this, even this time is in real fact only experienced within the experience of the concrete individual as rational and spiritual, and as a being endowed with freedom even in the act of formulating his theory about the time of the world. In such an act the individual is indeed concerning himself with a quality inherent in objective experience. But at the same time this same quality is inherent also in the subjective fact of the individual himself even though at the same time it does go beyond this. Now in these circumstances it is in principle never possible to isolate this quality completely from the subjective aspects, because the very act of reflecting upon it is itself in turn subject to the same conditions and the

[21] cf. I. Kant, *op. cit.*

quality being reflected upon is inherent in this act itself. It is this, in fact, that gives rise to all the representations of the transcendental phantasy, representations which we can recognize negatively as such, but which we cannot positively eliminate. What the term 'representation' here is intended to stand for is not that which is false, but rather that kind of reality which has both an objective and a subjective side. Now while it does not fall within the purview of the natural sciences to offer a critique of transcendental 'representation' in this sense, still transcendental 'representation' is a factor with which they have to work. And in view of this it can surely be said that whereas in investigating any given temporal element the natural sciences must always seek for that which came before it, the same does not apply to theology (or metaphysics). For these disciplines must assert that time is finite in the sense we have defined. And yet this does not imply any contradiction between the two different approaches. For time is not *ipso facto* constituted as infinite merely by the fact that any number of material temporal elements which we can discover is in principle capable of continuous further increase. And this in itself is sufficient to justify the statement we have just made.[22]

III

To the problems which we have presented up to this point, and which derive solely from the dogmatic teaching that the world was created in time, certain further considerations must be appended, which are intended to broaden the subject of investigation a little further.

(a) For the theologian it is the time that belongs to saving history that is primary.[23] The time of saving history means the history of personal freedom as engaged in dialogue with the God of grace in his act of self-bestowal at both the individual and the collective levels. When we say

[22] Without analysing any further here what, on this showing, is the meaning of time as such (on this cf. also what follows) reference may simply be made to the fact that the methods used in the natural sciences are consistently formulated in such a way as to lead to an understanding of the functional connections between individual facts, But the dimension in which these facts are manifested taken as a totality cannot itself in turn be an object of investigation by these same methods of natural science. And since the space-time world considered as a totality is not an object which is empirically discoverable natural science cannot say anything either with regard to the possible infinitude of this totality.

[23] A bibliography on this point has been compiled by W. Kern, *op. cit.*, n. 40; cf. also the article, 'Zeit III, IV', *LTK* X (2nd ed., Freiburg, 1965), 1329-1334.

that *this* time is primary we mean that it provides a standard of measurement in the light of which, so far as the theologian is concerned, all other time has to be considered, and that too in such a way that the 'content' of this kind of time also specifies the modality of time as such. Now this statement has constituted the heuristic norm in the considerations we have offered up to this point, and we have been compelled to adopt it by reason of the insoluble difficulties which we encounter in the question of what in more precise terms the dogmatic statement that the creation took place in time really means. Of course it would be possible to adduce further considerations in support of this statement. We might, for example, advert to the question of *how*, on this showing, we could conceive of the revelation of this dogma in the concrete. And in the course of answering this question we might show that it can be understood as an implication of God's self-bestowal precisely as conceived of in terms of salvation and revelation (and that it cannot be understood in any other sense). For in this self-bestowal of God salvation and revelation, and man's own ultimate understanding of himself, are achieved all in one.

(b) Any extrapolations in which we transfer our conceptions of this kind of time (i.e. the time belonging to saving history) and the special qualities belonging to it to the time in which material events purely as such run their course, can only be undertaken with the greatest caution and with a limited degree of success. This latter point is of course something that we experience and recognize in our everyday lives and work in the field of natural science. But what we establish in this is temporal development and temporal processes as distinct from one another, time as it appears to be and not as it is of its essence. What time is 'in itself' is no more directly ascertainable in this experience than the existence of an existing thing is *ipso facto* ascertainable in its essence in virtue of the fact that we constantly have to do with existing things. In the same way too we do not, ontologically speaking, *ipso facto* know what matter is in its essence merely in virtue of the fact that we constantly have to do with material things. But strange though it may appear at first sight, we can draw upon our experience of the spirit (as being in possession of itself) so as to state in negative terms what matter is, namely precisely that kind of being which is not given over to itself (and this negative character is inherent not merely in our knowledge but in matter itself as a specification of this), and in just the same way the only way in which we can determine what physical time is as such is in negative terms and from our knowledge of that time which belongs to the free operation of the spirit. And this negative character, considered as a negative inherent in the time of material being, is precisely that negativity which prevents this time as such from being raised in itself to any definitive and final state and being brought to an end in this. In the light of this we are here once more justified in principle in approaching the matter with the same caution which we have adopted in dealing with the question of whether we ought to postulate a finite and calculable series of states extending backwards into the past beyond physical time (whether considered from the standpoint of physics, philosophy or dogmatic theology), or whether there is no necessity for this. Just as matter as such is not endowed with self-awareness and freedom, and so not 'in confrontation with' itself so as to be capable of achieving it own definitive consummation, so in the same way physical time is in itself 'negative' in the sense of being incapable of any definitive consummation. Considered as 'potentiality' in this sense it is probably unlimited in either direction, past or present. As such then it does not begin or end at any specific points. The only sense in which any beginning or end can be ascribed to it is in virtue of the fact that it constitutes an element in the time inherent in the history of personal freedom, and to that extent must have a beginning and ending of this kind within this. And surely this phrase 'to that extent' marks the limits beyond which we cannot go.

(c) It must clearly be recognized that exactly the same relationship prevails between a secular and theological understanding of time as between nature in itself and nature as *de facto* endowed with grace, and between a philosophical and secular self-understanding on the one hand, and revelation and theology on the other. Manifestly time is not a modality which is present in a univocal sense everywhere where anything takes place, but rather a modality[24] which admits of intrinsic variations, and hence is analogously applied to the various realities of which it is predicated.[25] And this in itself is tantamount to saying that in principle, even though for the most part this fact is overlooked, all the problems entailed in correctly defining the relationship between nature and being that has been raised to a supernatural level must necessarily lead us back to the problem of time.

[24] cf. the article mentioned in n. 23, especially 1328 f.

[25] There is no need here for any further extensive metaphysical speculation or for entering into the Heideggerian understanding of time as set forth in *Sein und Zeit*; for it is also apparent that this is recognized in the theory of relativity, where time is no longer conceived of as an independent dimension. For here the world is understood as a four-dimensional space-time continuum, in which time is dependent upon the changes and developments of the continuum as a whole.

It is no purely abstract or formal interest that prompts us, for example, to raise the question of whether even in a *'status naturae purae'* the free person would have been impelled towards an absolute and total decision determining his own final destiny by the same impetus which is inherent in every free act to the extent that it involves a decision regarding the self-offering of God in grace.[26] This instance too serves once again to show how cautious the theologian must be if he seeks to make any statement about natural time as such. For him the concept of *natura pura*, though peripheral, is a necessary one, yet one which as such can never be applied purely as a positive datum in its own right, because we can never go beyond the limits of an experience raised to a supernatural level. And just as this is true, so in the same way and in the same measure merely secular and natural time (even as this is applicable to personal freedom at the purely natural level) is likewise a peripheral concept. The opinion that man experienced it purely in itself could be an instance of that culpable blindness in which, even in the present order of grace, an attempt is made to understand 'nature' purely as it is in itself. That is one side to the question. On the other hand the following position is of course valid: it must be remembered that grace presupposes nature as the condition distinct from itself which nevertheless makes it possible for it to be itself and to maintain the distinction between itself and nature (even though, so far as our conscious understanding is concerned, it is not possible materially speaking to follow through this distinction completely to the end). And the case is exactly similar when we come to speak of a 'supernatural understanding of time', if we may so express it, and in doing so envisage *that* time which is achieved in free dialogue with God in his self-bestowal, and only in this. Here too we are presupposing a secular understanding of time and secular time itself as the condition, distinct from supernatural time, which makes it possible of achievement. Just as grace wills the world to be worldly, and as such to increase, and positively establishes it in its own autonomy, so too the 'time of grace', as a unique kind of time that belongs to God's self-bestowal and derives its own ultimate quality from God's eternity positively wills the existence of a time of this world, i.e. a time that is open to decision, to hope, to the unforeseen, as the sphere for *that* activity which fashions the possible from the utopian and so time itself.

(d) Perhaps it may be appropriate in this series of improvised theological remarks on time to say something also with regard to the 'eternity' of

---

[26] For more precise details on this cf. K. Rahner, 'Erbsünde und Monogenismus' in K. H. Weger, *Theologie der Erbsünde:* Quaestiones Disputatae 44 (Freiburg, 1970).

THEOLOGICAL OBSERVATIONS ON CONCEPT OF TIME 307

God.[27] In using this term, the established theology conceives initially of an existence extending without cessation in either direction, backwards and forwards alike, and it then goes on to improve this idea by invoking the Platonist ἔστι μόνον (as distinct from ἦν, ἔστι καὶ ἔσται), or by the saying added by Boethius: *tota simul* and the *nunc stans*. It conceives of eternity, therefore, as the non-temporally-extended possession of existence. It is therefore initially understood precisely according to the model of '*duratio*'. '*In cognitionem aeternitatis oportet nos venire per tempus*', says Thomas. And of course in a certain sense all this is obvious and inevitable. But it might perhaps be said: We can best arrive at an understanding of the eternity of God (albeit still always treating of this '*per modum negationis et eminentiae*' if we envisage *that* factor in *our own* (not simply physical!) time which is experienced in it, and perhaps is only experienced there precisely as it in fact is. For what we are treating of here is the event of God's *free* bestowal of *himself*, in which, namely he wills the final consummation of a love that is freely given, and which is prompted by no further reason beyond itself, and does not depend upon any empty possibility prior to itself. It is, after all, in this that man experiences his own 'eternity' as something more than simply a further prolongation of an entity, so that it has an indeterminate extension. And *this* is the point of departure for understanding the eternity of God *per modum negationis et eminentiae*.

(e) A brief word on the sort of time which belongs to God himself. Here we have the same theological problem as arises in connection with the 'immutability' of God. The very fact that the problem arises at the same point enables us immediately to understand this. With regard to the immutability, and therefore the non-temporal nature of God, however, Christian theology must not make the question simpler than it in fact is in view of the fact that the Logos became true man, and therefore entered into time. Christian theology must hold firm to the 'immutability 'and 'eternal' timelessness of God 'in themselves'. At the same time, however, it will have to say that God *himself*, in the otherness of the world, undergoes history, change, and so too time; the time of the world is his own

---

[27] On this and on the section which follows cf. K. Rahner, 'Theos in the New Testament', *Theological Investigations* I (London and Baltimore, 1961), pp. 79–148; *idem*, 'Gott', *LTK* IV (2nd ed., 1960), 1080–1087; *idem*, 'Gotteslehre', *ibid.*, 1119–1124; *idem*, 'Observations on the Doctrine of God in Catholic Dogmatics', *Theological Investigations* VIII (London and New York, 1971), pp. 127–145. M. Löhrer, 'Dogmatische Bemerkungen zur Frage der Eigenschaften und Verhaltensweisen Gottes', *Mysterium Salutis* II (Einsiedeln, 1967), pp. 291–315.

history. As the eternal he does not merely establish time by creating it, but freely assumes it as a specification of his own self. *Assumendo tempus creat tempus*, as we might say, adapting in this a saying of Augustine's. He thereby causes his own eternity to be the true content of time. He creates his own time in order to impart to it his own eternity as the radical effectiveness of his own love. Temporal becoming is not merely the distinguishing characteristic of that which is different from God, but that which, precisely as different from God in this way, and permanently maintaining itself as different, can become, and has become the distinguishing seal of God himself. Ultimately speaking this is possible because the difference between creaturely time and the eternity of God removes time from eternity but not, properly speaking, eternity from time. For if God himself causes the difference he sets that which he has established apart from himself, but not himself apart from that which he has established. Being different from eternity is a predicate of a time that has been established. Eternity as predicated of the God who establishes time implies, however, in the fullest sense, the temporal as an element in itself. And hence, in assuming it as his own time, he can be both he who establishes it and he who assumes what he has established.

(f) It is because time – from the viewpoint of God and man alike – is first and last the modality of the loving freedom exercised in God's act of self-bestowal, that there is the sort of time that is *kairos*, a unique and privileged time, a 'once and for all now' and an 'only now and not at any other time', a fulness of the times etc. It is because time is ultimately constituted by God's act of self-bestowal on that which is other to himself, in other words because ultimately speaking this is one act and takes place once and for all, that it is precisely not the case that everything is possible at any time, or that time is the empty sphere in which anything and everything can be fitted in and moved from point to point. Time rather is the modality of this one event, such that it is only in the achievement of this that it itself comes to be. The neutral homogeneity of physical time is, insofar as it exists at all, merely the condition making it possible for the freedom of love to manifest itself as free love in the gift of God and its acceptance. For God is the love that is unconditioned, and this physical time constitutes a temporal sphere within which this free love can take place 'here and now' even though it might also have taken place 'there and then'.

14

THEOLOGICAL CONSIDERATIONS
CONCERNING THE MOMENT OF DEATH

IT is evident that Christian theology recognizes dying and death as
one of the basic themes of its own message, and has to proclaim the
message of the death of Christ, the death that takes place at the beginning of saving history, the death of man, the first and second deaths, the
life of God that overcomes death, and the celebration of the death of
Christ in the Church's cult. But even abstracting from this, we must
recognize that a new situation has arisen in contemporary thought which
has a bearing on this question. It is a situation of radical pluralism among
the sciences, one in which the problems, methods, and findings in each
particular science are so wide-ranging and so different among themselves
that no-one who is not a specialist in the particular science concerned
can any longer achieve an overall view of it. In this situation, then, as it
exists today, it is quite essential that there should be discussion and dialogue among the sciences themselves, including philosophy and theology,
on this question also. They must conduct such a dialogue if the life of the
individual and the scientist is not to be reduced to hopelessness, and in
fact if the individual science is not itself to suffer as a result of being
isolated from the other sciences. The current question of the limits of
a doctor's duty to preserve life as it arises in the study of medicine is
certainly a question of this kind, which needs to be treated of at the inter-
disciplinary level. There can be no doubt that this question is of concern
not only to the doctor, not only to the jurist, but to the theologian and
moralist as well. For the care which needs to be taken in preserving life,
and the limits to be attached to this, refer not merely to a procedure carried
out solely in the biological sphere as such, but have a significance for man
as a whole. Now this is of concern to the theologian also, hence he cannot
pass over this question as though it were irrelevant.

Now it can be said with perfect justice that on a question of this kind
it is only at the end that the theologian can be given a hearing, because in

finding the answer to this question so many biological, medical, and even juridical factors have first to be taken into account, factors in which the theologian is in no sense competent, and which he simply has to take cognizance of as the findings of other sciences. But we can also say that these *a posteriori* sciences themselves in turn have *a priori* perspectives and premisses of their own, albeit for the most part unconscious, and also that they have need of principles of this kind in order that from the findings of these departmental sciences norms can be arrived at applicable to human activity as such and considered as a single whole. The philosopher, and the theologian inasmuch as he works as a philosopher, giving the philosophical interpretation of existence a still more radical dimension, may number himself among those who are competent to deal with these prior assumptions, and in view of this it is surely justifiable once more for the theologian to open the discussion. Admittedly in doing so he must be aware that in the question which is here being treated of it is only when his general considerations have been supplemented by contributions from the other sciences and their findings that they can become concrete norms for human action.

From the standpoint from which the theologian views this question of the limits of the doctor's duty to maintain life, the question of precisely *when* the death of the patient has supervened and how it can be recognized surely takes pride of place even though there may be other questions too which need to be considered from the point of view of morals and theology. Here, however, we shall not be entering into these other questions. For as a matter of principle and in the abstract we can certainly say this much: the doctor can relinquish his efforts only when the individual is dead, and not before. And this remains true even though in hopeless cases where death is inevitable but has not yet supervened, many further questions do arise as to the circumstances in which, and the degree of intensity with which the doctor must still continue to strive to prolong such lives as these, or alternatively at what point he can relinquish this struggle while still doing everything possible for the individual concerned in the way of ordinary care. But abstracting from these cases, and the special problems they raise in the concrete, the axiom we have just mentioned, namely that the doctor should only relinquish his efforts when the patient is dead, seems to be a truism which is self-evident and does not help the doctor in arriving at a moral judgement about his work. But the matter is not so simple as this. For today the question of when someone dies in his human nature is much more difficult to answer than in former times. For the sake of clarity attention must first be drawn to the fact that dying and death (as 'death that has been died') are not simply one and the same, and yet so far as our ultimate understanding is concerned it is only from a knowledge of what death is that we can say what dying is as distinct from illness in general. But this death of which we speak is both the most familiar of everyday occurrences and at the same time that which is dark and mysterious to us. Hence the inevitable and bewildering embarrassment always arises at this point that we have to speak of dying and not of death, and yet at the same time it is impossible to do this without constantly speaking of death at the same time.

Medicine, and above all medical ethics, are faced with a new situation today because of the possibility of transplanting organs, for these are actually transplanted 'alive' from a dead person (and also precisely because of the question of when a doctor should give up positively striving to prolong a human life in a case in which any personal and spiritual life of the individual as human has ceased, or is no longer present, and in which it cannot be restored by any efforts on the part of the doctor). In this situation the problem of the borderline cases arises with quite fresh acuteness, the problem namely of when that human life for which the doctor must positively strive with the application of all his medical skill is still present, and when it is no longer so; in other words when human life as such has ceased, when the process of dying in the human being as such has been terminated by death even though, perhaps, specific organs or combinations of cells still 'survive' and can be maintained 'alive', i.e. capable of functioning either within or without the human organism.

This simple observation alone makes it much more difficult than formerly for the theologian to say when the death of the human being has taken place. Indeed it is not even certain from the outset that the question of where precisely the borderline lies between human life and death can be answered in the same way by biology, medicine, and above all by specifically medical ethics on the one hand and by theology on the other in such a way that these answers can be made formally and materially to coincide. It is of course immediately obvious that in dealing with the question of when in a specific case death has taken place and when it has not yet done so the theologian cannot dispense with the factor of experience at the quite primitive level, any more than he can dispense with the judgement of the biologist and the doctor. Hence in arriving at a concrete judgement in any particular case he is constantly dependent upon these sciences and the developments in them, even though strictly speaking the essentially theological statement of what constitutes human death in general and as such is unaffected by these developments in the sciences we have mentioned.

But conversely the question with which medical ethics is faced of when a human being as human is dead is intrinsically connected with the question of what a human being as such is. And this means that it is a question which the doctor can only answer if he is prepared to go beyond the limits of his own science and to allow philosophical and theological anthropology to have some say in the matter. At the same time this is not to assert either, in any unequivocal sense, that medical ethics can *simply take over* the philosophical and theological concept of when a human life as such does or does not exist. It cannot take over this concept in such a way as to be able to assert that the doctor's duty to strive to maintain a human life ceases *ipso facto* at that point at which, from a philosophical and theological point of view, such a life appears no longer to be present.

It would even be possible for a case to arise, and that too for the most varied reasons which will not be discussed here, in which the theologian and philosopher might perhaps accept the biologist's view that life in the strictly biological sense was still present even though they themselves believed that they could no longer recognize any specifically *human* life still remaining. And even in such a case it might very well be that it would be the doctor's duty either positively to extinguish the life that still remained nor to neglect any normal care on its behalf. In such a case in fact he might still have to presume that human life was present, and so that he was obliged to do his utmost to preserve it.

Nowadays in fact the theologian must presumably say that both with regard to the emergence of life at the level of the strictly human, and with regard to the termination of such life there is a question which he cannot answer with any certainty, the question namely of whether the fact that life of this kind manifests itself at the level of human biology *ipso facto* means that it is certainly, and in all cases, human life in the sense that has a theological relevance and entails moral demands upon man himself, and above all upon the doctor. Certainly the theologian will hold firm to the proposition that specifically *human* life, which as such is under the protection of certain moral principles, can be present and, in the case of life deriving from *human* generation must actually be presumed to be present, even in those cases in which no really conscious personal activity is any longer present, or at least can no longer be established. But when he considers specific borderline cases of embryonic development which have miscarried from the first, when he regards the survival of tissues which in some conditions no longer have anything to do with human life in the theological sense, when he bears in mind that in a heart transplantation, which is, at least in principle, morally legitimate, on the one hand the death of the organ donor as such is presumed to have taken place, while at the same time (from the biological standpoint) it is also presumed that the heart continues to be alive, then the present-day theologian will hardly be any longer in a position to assume, as he formerly did, that the axiom applies uniformly to all cases that any life deriving biologically from man is always and invariably human life in the theological sense as well. A further point is that if we take this axiom as our starting-point then it becomes difficult to assign any place to that 'life' which must be ascribed to the sperm and egg-cells even before they have become united. And yet a further relevant factor is that today we are surely once more in a position in which we can give no completely clear answer to the question of the precise point in time at which the fertilized human ovum begins to have a soul.

These then are all problems which the theologian has to bear in mind. Moreover in order to proceed with his theological considerations at all he has to be in a position to assume that from the biological aspect it is at least in principle possible (which does not mean *ipso facto* that this possibility is made actual) that life is present at the spiritual and personal level. In view of all this then he will surely have to recognize that in those cases in which the biological substrate for life at *this* level, i.e. (in non-sicentific terms) the human brain, is no longer present or has ceased to retain any life, biological life at the specifically *human* level is not present either, or that it has ceased to be present.

In terms of the principles which provide him with his own starting-point, therefore, the theologian will defend the position that human life as human has been terminated at that point at which the death of the brain has supervened, even though he has to leave it to the biologist and medical scientist to work out the precise criteria for deciding when this takes place. And this means that the theologian will recognize that the process of human dying precisely as human has come to an end also, even though other organs and tissues may 'be alive' or 'continue to survive' in a biological sense either within the organism as a whole or outside it. I have already said that even when we have defined in anthropological and theological terms the borderline between human and non-human life, or human and non-human death, this still cannot be accounted *ipso facto* and of itself a sufficient and assured basis for medical ethics in treating of the question of when a doctor can relinquish his efforts to preserve the life entrusted to him with his medical skill, and the further question of what means he should use, whether normal or exceptional ones, in carrying out this task of his. It is perfectly possible, as we have already said, that a doctor's idea of the life that is entrusted to him as a doctor may not coincide with the theological and anthropological concept of human life. Indeed it may not even be desirable that the two ideas should be made to coincide. But this problem, together with its deontological implications, cannot be treated of any further here.

We have established, then, that both as conceived of in itself and in its implications for medical ethics the life which the doctor strives to preserve from dying is not simply to be identified with that specifically human life which is of immediate concern to the theologian, and which he takes as axiomatic in his researches. At the same time, however, the two concepts of life here, the medical and the theological ones, are intrinsically interconnected. For in the last analysis the obligations which arise from, and the value to be attached to the work of the doctor derive from the fact that it is man as such, and not merely some kind of biological organism, that is the object of his concern. Hence, while maintaining the provisos which we have already indicated so far as medical ethics are concerned, we should still say not only that the struggle waged by the doctor against death derives its ultimate value and its moral necessity from the fact that it is the life of man as such – in other words the life of a person with a spiritual mode of existence that is being treated of, but also that precisely because of this this struggle and the moral obligation to maintain it also have intrinsic limits of their own. Even if, for want of time and the necessary competence in the field, we cannot here embark upon an investigation of the difficult cases involved (although this might perhaps be of great interest primarily for the doctor in his work in the concrete), still we may conclude that the point at which the doctor may willingly concede victory in his struggle against death is determined by the specifically human factor involved in living and dying.

What we mean is this: as a medical scientist, a biologist, and one who is governed by the obligations of medical ethics in the most direct sense, the doctor will certainly be seeking only to prolong life and the struggle against death with all the means at his disposal. And from this point of view he can only feel death as a terrible defeat which is so much the contrary of what he wills that he feels it almost shameful to be forced to concede victory to it. Even so, however, the patient with whom he has to deal as a man and a doctor is a human being, one whose life is specifically human, i.e. this life constitutes a personal history which of its own intrinsic nature seeks its own consummation. The intrinsic nature of this history is such that it is never for one moment intended to be prolonged indefinitely into an indeterminate future. Rather it has a definite shape such that of itself it demands to be rounded off and to achieve a consummation which goes far beyond any mere state of further prolongation.

Of course prior to the moment of death itself it is never possible as a matter of empirical human experience to state unambiguously the precise point at which a given life achieves its intrinsic consummation in death even though, from the theological point of view, it must be stated that it is possible for a specifically human history of this sort already to have achieved its intrinsic consummation even before the possibilities of prolonging life at the biological level have been exhausted. To that extent the doctor must certainly continue to strive right to the very last to prolong life in his sense of the term. But what does this phrase 'right to the very last' imply? From the viewpoint which we have just achieved we shall, after all, be in a position to begin by stating the following: When a doctor has done all that is in his power and still a dying man has finally died, then precisely as a man the doctor is not simply one who has suffered a catastrophic and meaningless defeat, but rather one who can willingly suffer the sick person to die, one therefore who has not failed to fulfil his task but on the contrary has effectively completed it. For in fact he has provided his fellow man with that span of life in the biological sense within which his specifically human life considered as the history of a free person has in fact been able to achieve its consummation. He has provided him with a span of biological life in this sense which was never for one moment intended to, or sought to be extended into the unforeseeable future. And this remains true even though it is at most only very approximately that we can state *prior* to death (in all cases except the sort of death that results from sheer old age) precisely how far this span is meant to be extended in order to be able to constitute the sphere for a personal history of this kind advancing towards a consummation which it demands intrinsically and of its very nature.

In the light of these considerations we may after all suppose, without entering into individual cases or being superfluous, that a doctor who is struggling to avert death is justified in adopting two rather different attitudes towards the life which he is attempting to save. There is the kind of life which at least to all appearances offers no real basis for a truly personal kind of living, and his attitude to this will be rather different from his attitude to a life which will still be lived at the fully personal level, or which can at least be restored to provide once more a possible basis for such personal living. Certainly, even before death, the doctor may feel more willing to let the former kind of life be terminated than the latter.

Perhaps this may serve as some guide for drawing a certain distinction within the general attitude which the doctor ought to take towards the death of an individual, a distinction which is all too often forced upon the doctor in the difficult situations in which he often has to exercise his medical skill. For all too often he is quite unable to escape from the responsibility of having to choose *which* of several sick or dying individuals he should concentrate upon, devoting his utmost efforts and resources as a doctor to saving him before the rest.

More than all the rest of us doctors find themselves again and again having to stand beside the death-bed engaged in the struggle against death. Their will is to save life, and when death has proved too much for them their task is ended. All that we can still ask of them is at most whether what is lying there really is a dead man. It might appear that their concern is with life alone, and that they have nothing to do with death. But as men, when faced with the dying in this way, they must inevitably be reminded of the approach of their own fate. They may suppress, but cannot avoid, the question of what really happens at this moment when a man dies, when as human he becomes subject to death, or better: they cannot avoid asking what happens in their own death, in 'my particular death' which is slowly and inexorably advancing upon us. And the more human a doctor is (for it is only as human that he brings his medical activity and his medical ethos to their due fulness), the more the specific-ally human question of what death is becomes a question for the doctor himself, the question that the doctor asks as he gazes after the man to whom he has devoted his care. For there the doctor must see the anticipa-tion of his own death, he who lives as a helper in the midst of men, none of whom can escape the destiny of having to die. The man in the doctor can perhaps attempt to suppress this question. He can attempt to answer it in an epicurean sense, by saying that there is no such question, since it is no question for us so long as we are alive, and no question for the dead man seeing that he is no longer there. The man in the doctor can, perhaps, respond to this question with a helpless shrug of his shoulders. He can endure his own helplessness in humility and with a secret trust in the fact that a question that is faced up to, not suppressed and not run away from, conceals within its depths its own answer, even though we may not have raised it from these depths of our own existence to the surface level of our conscious awareness and so expressed it in words. At least the question ought to be present in this sense in the mind of every sincere man. In this sense at least it can and must be endured by every man. In this sense at least there can be no escaping from this question in all its inexorability. It still arises even when we resolve that it should not arise at all, or that it is unanswerable. It is clear even though we do not commit ourselves to answering it that to try to answer it on the basis of biology alone would *ipso facto* and from the outset be a failure to recognize the question itself.

For the point of the question is the death of *man*, man who is alive not merely at the level of the material and the biological, but on the plane of self-awareness, personhood, freedom, responsibility, love and faithfulness; man whose mode of existence is such that it is charged with the responsibility of his self-awareness and his freedom. The question of what constitutes the consummation of a personal history at this level is still not answered even when on the one hand we have established that biological life comes to an end, and on the other hand are not prepared on these grounds alone to find an optimistic and over-facile answer to the question by adopting a conceptual image of man as consisting of two parts, each existing independently of the other. On this conception, then, prior to the biological death the two parts would have been adventitiously combined while after it the 'immortal soul' would continue on ultimately and alone in an indefinite prolongation of its existence. Even if we do not produce an over-facile answer of this kind to the question of human death, it still remains true that in any case it is not *ipso facto* answered once we have established the termination of life at the biological level. Such an answer would be nothing else than an illegitimate overstepping of the limits of a materialist biology which is quite incapable of including within its purview man at the specifically human level, and hence too is incapable of stating in any adequate way what constitutes the consummation of the personal history of a man as such. The question is there. This question has to be endured, and this question cannot be answered solely in biological terms. Hence too it goes beyond the competence of a doctor to answer it simply as an exponent of medicial science.

But how to answer it? As I have already indicated above, even a theologian who in all modesty and diffidence hazards an answer to this question can take cognizance of the fact that a man, through no fault of his own, stands at one specific point in his own personal history as a human individual endowed with spiritual faculties at which he is not yet in a position personally to realize the answer to the ultimate questions of life, even though in the absolute such an answer does exist. Instead of realizing the answer straightway at this point then, he is compelled to hold out, in an attitude of questioning openness, and hope in silence and patience for a future light to come to him. Hence the theologian too can, in all patience, freely credit the honest seeker with an attitude of perseverance and hope, as in the concrete conditions of his personal existence he endures the question of what the true nature of death really is.

At the same time, however, the Christian and the theologian may offer to the individual concerned that interpretation of the nature and meaning of death which pertains to the faith. He can do this by asking him whether this answer does not strike a chord in him, appealing to a secret and, as it were, anonymous awareness at the depths of his being with regard to human existence in general and, as a part of this, the ultimate meaning of death. As his mind moves, then, somewhere between this silent and basic understanding of existence on the one hand and the word of God on the other, can he not discover that courage, that spirit of freedom and happiness, which will enable him to make his own this understanding of death which faith supplies, to join with all those who, with their gaze fixed wholly upon the crucified one, upon Jesus Christ, freely commit themselves to death as the gateway to God and eternal life? The message of Christianity does not in fact contain any rationalist 'explanation' of death. We can only really understand what is stated to be the teaching of Christianity with regard to death when we read it in the context of what the faith declares with regard to God. Now this statement about God represents *precisely* the ultimate that can be said before falling into silence. It is a statement about the inconceivable mystery that we call God, and that is beyond our apprehension, that never at any stage constitutes a fixed landmark such as we can assign to a specific place in the calculations we apply to our own lives. Yet at the same time it is equally a statement which promises this same God of mystery as the fulfilment of these lives of ours through forgiveness and the imparting of his own divine nature to us. In terms of the message of Christianity, therefore, the word 'death' does not stand for a phenomenon of this world which can be used and manipulated in combination with all the other factors which we recognize and understand so that it has a specific place in the total system of co-ordinates which we build up for ourselves from our human apprehensions. Rather the death of man is the moment at which the whole of his history as a free being, now consummated and completed, is brought into immediate confrontation with the mystery of God, encountering this either as its consummate blessing or as judgement. And hence death is as incomprehensible as God himself. It affects man as one and whole. For we of today find it even less possible than those of former times to reduce man either to spirit or to matter. Nor can we conceive of him as a union of both these principles *in such a way that* the destruction of this unity entails no further difficulty either in reality or in our own minds. The death of man consists in the immediate confrontation of man, together with the whole of his history as a free person now consummated and complete, with the absolute mystery, with God.

We may call this confrontation the continuing life of the immortal soul in order to express the fact that man and his personal history are something more even in the inception of this, and *a fortiori* at its end, than a mere biological process in space and time such that it fades away at either end of the span allotted to it into the anonymity of the merely physical. This same confrontation of man's existence as consummated and complete with God can also be called the 'resurrection of the flesh' in order to express the fact that it is the one whole man who is brought before God, though this is not to say that the physical side of his consummation before God consists in a return to the sort of 'bios' which belongs to the dimension of space and time with the incessant process of change extending indefinitely into the future which is characteristic of this. Whichever formulation we adopt, the truth we are pointing to is always the fact that death brings man into the presence of God, God who does not permit the personal history of man as rounded off and completed to fall into nothingness, God to whom man has to answer as to how he has used his freedom, whether he has used it to love his neighbour and God himself, for he cannot escape from being called to account in this way by taking refuge in a mere cessation of existence from which he could no longer be recalled. Now if death is that which brings man as one and whole face to face with God in this way, then it is not surprising that once a man has undergone death, neither the death itself nor its effects are discoverable within the sphere of that which we can ascertain empirically, the sphere in which we lead our earthly lives as subject to space and time, for obviously we can never encounter God as one particular element within this sphere.

Death, then, is the consummation of a man's history as a free person, that in which this history breaks through into the absolute future which is its goal, and in which God as the ultimate, original, and infinite all, by whom all reality is upheld, is encountered either as judgement or as man's blessed consummation. Now if this is true then death is that towards which the will of the free person tends at its deepest and most ultimate, because this free person must seek the end of that which merely prolongs itself in time in order to achieve his consummation. It is only on the surface of our awareness that we actually see death. But at the very roots of our existence we hunger for the end of that which is unconsummated in order that consummation may be achieved. If anyone were to tell us that the state we had lived in up to now would simply continue on into eternity, in that self-same moment we would have to recognize ourselves as damned. For in that case each successive transitory moment of our lives would be divested of its own special value, a value which consists in the fact that these moments in our temporal existence provide the possibility for us to take a decision that is irrevocable. For it is the exercise of our freedom in these particular moments that gives birth to that which will remain and endure.

Inherent in the history of any man as personal and human, then, there is an ultimate and deepest tendency of the will to achieve its consummation in death. And in the light of this the doctor who stands at the death bed is placed in a situation that is unique. As a doctor he is bound to preserve life at the biological level and the tendency inherent in this to 'prolong itself'. Yet as man he is no less bound by the ultimate will to achieve the end, the consummation, that will which says 'no' to the fate to which Ahasuerus was condemned, the fate of not being allowed to die. This tension is inherent in the very life of a doctor, and it must be maintained and endured without any short-sighted surrender to one side or the other. It is a tension that underlies many of the concrete questions which a doctor has to face as part of his responsibility as a doctor when he stands at the bed of a dying man.

A doctor should take effective cognizance of the fact that what constitutes the normal circumstances of his everyday life, namely having to do with death, is also a central factor in the Christian faith, that faith which is either his own or at least constitutes a factor in the situation of human living and ideas in which he lives, whether he is a Christian or not. For while Christianity does indeed avow its certainty of eternal life it certainly does not look askance at any kind of life, or at the attempts that are made to cause it to flourish happily, to maintain it as vigorously as possible, and to defend it to the utmost from the dangers that threaten it. But this Christianity consists precisely in a professed belief in the Cross, in other words, as we might say, a belief in the Death of him whom we Christians call our Lord.

In the case of one man, the first of all, we are bold enough to believe that he was not merely made subject to death, not merely swallowed up by the absurdity of existence. Rather he himself died. He made death his own act. He himself assumes that which is beyond all human conception and control, and himself enacts what has to be suffered. This first one, whom we seek to follow in death, is Jesus. He died as we shall die: in that darkness into which he uttered that groan of his, 'My God, my God why hast thou forsaken me?'. In his death everything which makes death terrible took place, and that which death entails was truly suffered: the agony of the body, the brutal injustice which was an additional element in his case, the hatred of his enemies and their mocking self-assurance, the failure of his life-work, the betrayal of his friends, and over and above all that is terrible in death precisely that sense of futility which death entails wherever it is died amid the mourning of the dying man's fellows who cannot help him, the struggle for breath and all the pain from which no-one returns, and all the sense of being powerless to do any more in which he ceases to be heroic.

LIST OF SOURCES

PLURALISM IN THEOLOGY AND THE UNITY OF THE CREED IN
THE CHURCH

Lecture given on the 26 April 1969 at the invitation of the *Hogeschool
für Theologie en Pastoraat in Heerlen*/Holland.
Published in *Concilium* 5 (1969), pp. 462–471.

ON THE THEOLOGY OF THE ECUMENICAL DISCUSSION

Delivered as a lecture to the Theological Faculties of Copenhagen
(21 March 1968), Lund (24 March 1968), Oslo (27 March 1968), Uppsala
(29 March 1968), Helsinki (1 April 1968), Abu Turku (3 April 1968).
Published in the *Festschrift zum 65 Geburtstag von Bischof Hermann
Volk: Martyria – Leiturgia – Diakonia* (edited by O. Semmelroth,
R. Huabst, and K. Rahner (Mainz, 1968), pp. 163–199; 'Om den økumen-
iske samtales teologi', *Lumen* 12 (1969), pp. 1–39.

REFLECTIONS ON METHODOLOGY IN THEOLOGY

A series of lectures delivered between the 18 and 22 August 1969
at an International Symposium of Theologians at Montreal. Hitherto
unpublished.

THE NEW CLAIMS WHICH PASTORAL THEOLOGY MAKES UPON
THEOLOGY AS A WHOLE

First published in *Gregorianum* 50 (Rome, 1969), pp. 617–638.

THE FUTURE OF THEOLOGY

Delivered as a broadcast on the 17 December 1968 on the Bavarian
Radio in the series entitled *Abschied von Trient*; published in J. Bielmeier,
ed., *Abschied von Trient. Theologie am Ende des kirchlichen Mittelalters*
(Regensburg, 1969), pp. 121–130.

THE EXPERIENCE OF GOD TODAY

Given as a lecture in the context of discussions on the 'Theological Academy' at Cologne (16 October 1969), Essen (17 October 1969), Koblenz (22 October 1969), Frankfurt (23 October 1969) and Berlin (31 October 1969).

Published in *Theologische Akademie* VII, edited by O. Semmelroth and K. Rahner (Frankfurt, 1970).

THEOLOGICAL CONSIDERATIONS ON SECULARIZATION AND ATHEISM

A lecture at the Conference of the Secretariat for Non-Believers at Vienna on 10 September 1968, to the Theological Faculty of the University of Budapest on 19 September 1969, and at Prague on 2 April 1969 to the Professors of Theology of the CSSR.

Published in *Bollettino di Informazione* (Secretariatus pro non-credentibus) III/4 (Rome, 1968), pp. 18–20.

THE POSITION OF CHRISTOLOGY IN THE CHURCH BETWEEN EXEGESIS AND DOGMATICS

Lecture given to the Theological Academy of Berlin in the context of a Week-end Conference 4–5 May 1968.

CHRISTOLOGY IN THE SETTING OF MODERN MAN'S UNDERSTANDING OF HIMSELF AND OF HIS WORLD

Unpublished hitherto.

REFLECTIONS ON THE PROBLEMS INVOLVED IN DEVISING A SHORT FORMULA OF THE FAITH

First published in *Diakonia/Der Seelsorger* 1 (1970), pp. 4–30

THE SIN OF ADAM

A lecture given at the twenty-eighth Conference of the Ecumenical Study Group of Protestant and Catholic Theologians from 13 to 17 March 1968 at Paderborn.

ON THE ENCYCLICAL 'HUMANAE VITAE'

First published in *Stimmen der Zeit* 182 (1968), pp. 193–210. It also appeared (sometimes only in excerpts) in the following publications: F. Oertel ed., *Erstes Echo auf Humanae Vitae* (Essen, 1968), pp. 25–29; F. Böckle, C. Holstein edd., *Die Enzyklika in der Diskussion. Eine orientierende Dokumentation zu Humanae vitae* (Einsiedeln, 1968), pp. 57–63; *Die Welt* (Hamburg) No. 198 (1968) (of 25 August 1968), p. 8; 'Zur Enzyklika "Humanae vitae"', *Ehe in Gewissensfreiheit*, edited by Albert Görres (Mainz, 1969), pp. 51–71.

Translations appeared in the following languages: Italian, B. Häring and K. Rahner, *Riflessioni sull'enciclica "Humanae vitae"* (Rome, 2nd ed., 1968) Portuguese, 'Regulaçao dos nascimentos e obediência ao Magistério da Igreja', *Mariam* (Porto) 2 (1968), pp. 10–12, 93–97; English, 'Rahner on the Encyclical "Humanae Vitae"', *The National Catholic Reporter* (Kansas City) 4 (1968), No. 46 (18 September 1968), pp. 6–7; 'On the Encyclical "Humanae vitae"', *Catholic Mind* LXVI (New York, 1968), pp. 28–45; French, 'A propos de l'encyclique "Humanae vitae"' = *Foi vivante* 38 (Brussels, 1968); 'A propos de l'encyclique "Humanae vitae"' (in collaboration with Cardinal Renard and B. Häring) = *Le point* (Paris, 1969), pp. 11–54; Spanish, *Reflexiones en torno a la Humanae vitae* (Madrid, 1968); Dutch, 'Naar aanleiding van de encyckliek "Humanae vitae"', *Streven* (Amsterdam) 22 (1968), pp. 1, 5–23.

THEOLOGICAL OBSERVATIONS ON THE CONCEPT OF TIME

Given as a lecture at the Conference of the *Görres-Gesellschaft* on the theme, 'Modes of Temporality' from 15 to 20 September 1967 at Feldafing.

THEOLOGICAL CONSIDERATIONS ON THE MOMENT OF DEATH

Lectures given at the twenty-second Congress of Austrian Doctors of the 'Van-Swieten' Society on 11 November 1968 at Vienna, and on the occasion of the tenth anniversary of the Society of the Promoters of the Westphalian Wilhelms-University in Munster on 29 November 1968 at Munster.

Previous publications (of excerpts): *Jahresschrift 1968 der Gesellschaft zur Förderung der Westfälischen Wilhelms-Universität in Münster* (edited by the Society) (Munster, 1968), pp. 67–70; *Arzt und Christ* 15 (Salzburg, 1969), pp. 24–32.

In the above list of sources not all the publications in German have been recorded. Radio broadcasts are adduced only if the article concerned was specially written for such broadcasts. Only the publication in which they initially appeared is adduced, whether this was in German or in a foreign language.

INDEX OF PERSONS

Kösters, R. 26 n.
Koyré, A. 289 n.
Kremer, J. 211 n.
Kruse, H. 39 n.
Küng, H. 60 n.

Lakner, F. 127 n.
Lautner, G. 121 n.
Lehmann, K. 171 n., 212 n., 230 n., 297 n.
Leo X 272
Lohfink, N. 129 n.
Löhrer, M. 40 n., 307 n.
Lotz, J. B. 127 n.
Lyonnet, S. 250 n., 251 n.

Malmberg, F. 199 n., 219 n.
Martelet, G. 268 n.
Matthes, J. 47 n.
Metz, J. B. 26 n., 38 n., 115 n., 117 n., 120 n., 168 n., 195 n.
Meyer, R. W. 289 n.
Mittelstaedt, P. 288 n.
Möller, Ch. 115 n.

Neill, S. 26 n.
Neuhäusler, E. 26 n., 117 n.
Noonan, J. 268 n.

Oertel, F. 268 n.
Origen, 86, 219, 291
Overhage, P. 218 n.

Pascal, 292
Paul VI 52, 184, 231, 237, 263
Pius IX 105, 272
Pius XI 266, 270
Pius XII 69, 233, 266, 283 f.
Plato, 307

Ratschow, C. H. 231 n.
Ratzinger, J. 186 n., 192 n., 193 n., 230 n., 232 n.
Reichenbach, H. 288 n.
Rein, G. 231 n.
Riedlinger, H. 195 n.
Rouse, R. 26 n.

Sachsse, H. 289 n.
Scharbert, J. 250 n.
Schelkle, H. 252 n.
Schillebeeckx, 115 n., 168 n.
Schleiermacher, 118 n.
Schlette, 168 n.
Schlick, M. 288 n.
Schlier, H. 210 n.
Schmaus, M. 231 n.
Schnackenburg, R. 197 n.
Schoonenberg, P. 247 n., 255 n., 259 n., 297 n.
Schurr, V. 117 n.
Schuster, H. 116 n., 117 n., 230 n.
Seibel, W. 26 n.
Seitz, M. 121 n.
Söhngen, G. 231 n.
Sölle, D. 230 n.
Stakemeier, E. 26
van Straelen, 39 n.

Tavard, G. 26 n.
Teilhard de Chardin, 218 n.
Thils, G. 26 n.
Tödt, H. E. 131 n.

Vanneste, A. 168 n.
Vigilius, 272
Visser't Hooft, W. A. 26 n.
Vögtle, A. 194 n., 195 n.
Volk, H. 26 n.
Vorgrimler, H. 117 n., 197 n.

Wacker, P. 26 n.
Waldenfelds, H. 193 n.
Weber, L. M. 117 n.
Weger, K. H. 255 n.
Weissgerber, H. 25 n.
von Weizsäcker, C. F. 289 n.
Welte, B. 96, 199 n.
Wenzl, A. 288 n.
Weyl, H. 289 n., 296 n.
Wickler, W. 268 n.
Winter, A. 268 n., 290 n.
Wittgenstein, 102

INDEX OF SUBJECTS